INSIDE THE

HOLLYWOOD

FAN MAGAZINE

INSIDE THE

HOLLYWOOD FAN MAGAZINE

A HISTORY OF STAR MAKERS, FABRICATORS, AND GOSSIP MONGERS

Anthony Slide

UNIVERSITY PRESS OF MISSISSIPPI

JACKSON

www.upress.state.ms.us

Designed by Peter D. Halverson

The University Press of Mississippi is a member of the Association of
American University Presses.

Copyright © 2010 by University Press of Mississippi
All rights reserved
Manufactured in the United States of America

Unless otherwise indicated, illustrations are from
the Anthony Slide Collection.

First printing 2010
∞
Library of Congress Cataloging-in-Publication Data

Slide, Anthony.
Inside the Hollywood fan magazine : a history of star makers,
fabricators, and gossip mongers / Anthony Slide.
p. cm.
Includes bibliographical references and index.
ISBN 978-1-60473-413-3 (cloth : alk. paper) 1. Fan magazines. I. Title.
PN4836.S55 2010
791.4302'80922—dc22   2009030392

British Library Cataloging-in-Publication Data available

This book is dedicated to the memory of Ruth Waterbury,
and that of all fan magazine writers,
without whom there would be no film history

CONTENTS

Acknowledgments   IX

Introduction   3

CHAPTER 1.   The Birth of the Fan Magazine   11

CHAPTER 2.   The Pioneering Writers   33

CHAPTER 3.   James R. Quirk and *Photoplay*   47

CHAPTER 4.   The Studio Mouthpiece   73

CHAPTER 5.   The Fan Magazine as a Literary Outlet   93

CHAPTER 6.   New Writers, New Publishers, New Horizons   103

CHAPTER 7.   The Golden Age of the Fan Magazine   122

CHAPTER 8.   Gossip, Scandal, and Innuendo   144

CHAPTER 9.   The 1950s and the Influence of Television   170

CHAPTER 10.   The 1960s   184

CHAPTER 11.   Ms. Rona   207

CHAPTER 12.   The *People* Generation   218

CHAPTER 13.   The End of the Line and a New Beginning   226

APPENDIX 1.   U.S. Fan Magazines   233

APPENDIX 2.   Selected U.K. Fan Magazines   247

APPENDIX 3.   Fan Club Journals   248

Notes   250

Bibliography   260

Index   267

ACKNOWLEDGMENTS

I had the good fortune many years ago to interview two major fan magazine writers, Adele Whiteley Fletcher and Ruth Waterbury, and the latter became a good friend. After routinely telephoning her from a gas station at Sunset Boulevard and Laurel Canyon, Ruth would drive down from the top of the canyon—I had no car—and pick me up. I recall how flattered I was when she told me that years earlier she had provided this same service, from the same gas station, for Clark Gable. I had the impression that serving as his chauffeur was not the only service she provided to the actor. "He was a man. Believe me," she once told me.

I also met Adela Rogers St. Johns, although I cannot acknowledge that she had anything worthwhile to say, emphasizing, as she seemed to do so often, that one should never allow facts to get in the way of a good story. Bonnie Churchill discussed her and her sister Reba's career from the 1950s onward with me. Others who spoke with me of their work in the world of fan magazines are Army Archerd, Patrick O'Connor, David Ragan, Bill Royce, Micki Siegel, Bob Thomas, and Lawrence B. Thomas. I am honored that the charming and erudite Rona Barrett took the time to talk with me at such length; she also read a draft of chapter 11 and corrected a few factual errors. For sharing memories of her mother, Constance Palmer, I am grateful to Constance Van Wyck. William Schallert spoke with me about his parents, Elza and Edwin. For personal commentary on how the fan magazines documented their careers, I am grateful to Mary Carlisle, Samantha Eggar, Barbara Hale, Marsha Hunt, and Diana Serra Cary ("Baby Peggy").

As always, I must thank the staff of the Margaret Herrick Library of the Academy of Motion Picture Arts and Sciences and the Literature Department of the Los Angeles Central Library. At the former, I would like to acknowledge the incredible help of periodicals librarian Lea Whittington, along with Sandra Archer, Stacey Behlmer, Kristine Krueger, Jenny Romero, and Lucia Schultz. This and other of my books have benefited immeasurably from the help and support of Helene Mochedlover and her staff at the Los Angeles Central Library. In the course of my working on the book, Helene retired after forty-one years of service. I would like to take this opportunity to thank her again for all that she has done for me. I must also give special thanks to two remarkable and incredibly helpful individuals at the University of Southern California: Ned Comstock of the Cinema-Television Library and Dacie Taub of the Southern California Regional History Collection.

My own collection of fan magazines is now housed in the Popular Culture Library at Bowling Green University in Ohio; for help there I would like to thank Erik Honneffer and Bob McLaird. Nancy Hart at the Minneapolis Central Library provided me with documentation on Fawcett Publications. At the Museum of Modern Art, Ron Magliozzi gave me information on its *Photoplay* collection. Sadly, the museum's stills library, including the photo archives of *Photoplay* (which would have undoubtedly been invaluable in providing illustrative material for this volume) continues to remain inaccessible to all. It is amazing that this situation is allowed to continue without protest from the academic film community.

Other individuals who kindly assisted me include Ernest Cunningham, James Curtis, Bill Doyle, Robert Gitt, Patricia King Hanson, Mike Hawks at Larry Edmunds Bookstore, Marty Kearns, Antonia Lant, Leonard Maltin, James Robert Parish, Sue Slutzky, André Soares, David Stenn, Irme Summers, Kevin Thomas, and Willie Wilkerson.

This book was initially commissioned by Leila Salisbury when she was at the University Press of Kentucky. When she moved to the University Press of Mississippi, she remained faithful to the project—and for that I am eternally grateful. Without Leila, there would be no book. Once the manuscript had been delivered, Lisa DiDonato Brousseau accomplished the copyediting with style and efficiency.

INSIDE THE

HOLLYWOOD

FAN MAGAZINE

INTRODUCTION

The fan magazine is such a seemingly worthless object, and yet it is of interest and value to both the film scholar and the sociologist. On the surface, the fan magazine had its place in the history of popular entertainment simply as a publicity tool, a relatively pointless exercise in self-promotion by the film industry. One week it would eagerly be read by millions of American moviegoers and the next week consigned to the trash. The fan magazine was a transient publication offering dubious information on the equally transient world of the Hollywood movie star. Its rise paralleled that of the star system, and as the contractual studio stars began to disappear in the 1950s and 1960s, so did the fan magazine cease to have a prominent place with America's general readership. For instance, the lesser of the major periodicals *Silver Screen* sold 441,000 copies per month in 1933, dropping to a mere 151,000 three decades later.

While the heyday of the fan magazines was the 1920s and 1930s, as a phenomenon they lasted far longer. In the late 1940s, one might find as many as twenty fan magazines for sale at the local newsstand, ranging from the biggest and best, *Modern Screen*, *Photoplay*, and *Silver Screen*, to such smaller publications as *Movie Show*, *Screen Album*, and *Screenland*. Between 1931 and 1946 sales of fan magazines rose dramatically, and in the 1940s and 1950s it was not unusual for the best known of the fan magazines to boast sales in excess of one million copies and a readership of three times that number.

The importance of the fan magazine in American society as an arbiter of (not always good) taste, a source of knowledge, and a gateway to the fabled land of Hollywood and its people cannot be denied. As one contemporary observer, Carl F. Cotter, wrote, "These fans, who spent their five cents (for *Hollywood*) to a quarter (for *Photoplay*) on their cinematic scriptures, literally govern their lives by them. Not only do they pattern their hair styles, their

3

clothes, their cookery, and their behavior after those of their favorite actors and actresses as interpreted by the sob-sisters; most of them also base their most profound thinking on the words of the same authorities."[1]

The reach of the fan magazine extended far beyond America's shores, as similar periodicals, sometimes with the same American name, began publication throughout the Western world. In her hiding place in Amsterdam during the Nazi occupation of the city, Anne Frank pasted photographs of Deanna Durbin and others, clipped from the fan magazines, on her bedroom wall. The fan magazine might not eclipse the tragedy of real life, but it could offer at the least a temporary shield against it. The fan magazine was as much an escape from reality as was Hollywood itself.

After a handful of early years in which the emphasis was on publishing the synopses of current film releases in short-story form, the standard format of the fan magazine was established in the mid 1910s and remained little changed through the 1940s. There were news stories, articles, and lavish photo spreads on the established stars, the up-and-coming new arrivals on the scene, and the major films in production, as well as reviews, which at least through the first two decades of fan magazine history were surprisingly intelligent and thoughtful. The emphasis was on glamour, and the magazines were generally directed at a female readership. "There isn't a woman alive who wouldn't like to be some other woman. That's why pictures are now setting styles in clothing, in hair dress, in dancing—in fact, in everything that affects womanhood," commented *Daily Variety*.[2] In small towns across America, there could be found the many equivalents of Carole Lombard, Claudette Colbert, Joan Crawford, and even Garbo—or at least women who believed they were such.

As late as the 1950s, the Associated Press noted that male stars did not sell magazines.[3] As *Daily Variety* explained it, the female readers were attracted to male villains and male heroes. They wanted to be grabbed around the neck by Jack La Rue as much as they wished to be held in the arms of Clark Gable or Franchot Tone. But they did not care to read about character actors, and even Will Rogers got little attention until his untimely death. What the readership needed were stories of female players.[4] Time and again, the readers were asked questions such as "Is Alice Faye Still Afraid of Love?" or told of "Merry Moments with Marlene Dietrich and Her Daughter, Maria." If a male star was featured, the emphasis would more than likely be on the feminine aspects of his life, such as "Robert Taylor's Mother Chooses the Perfect Wife." It would always be "Jean Harlow's Fine Romance with William Powell," never the other way around.

Not only the stories themselves, but also the advertising for Lux and Palmolive and feminine hygiene products and the like were distinctly aimed at the distaff side. In the 1920s, female stars promoted their own products, such as Colleen Moore's Face Powder and Katherine MacDonald's waterproof Lash Cosmetic, or recommended obscure brand names, such as the $1.98 Hollywood Brassiere worn by Vera Reynolds or Betty Lou's Powder Puffs used by Sue Carol. As Gordon Kahn wrote in 1947, "This produce was no more designed for men than was the sidesaddle. It was intimately for women, as whisperingly and cozily intimate as the verbena-scented contents of her special drawer."[5]

Most of the fan magazine writers were women, of whom the most famous was Adela Rogers St. Johns, whose fame lasted far beyond the heyday of the fan magazine. Gladys Hall was the "Grand Old Dame of the Fannies," who turned out an average of six fan magazine articles a month.

Male readers had to be careful in their approach to the fan magazines. Gordon Kahn wrote of a gentleman who contacted the editor of *Motion Picture* asking, "What has Peter Lawford got that I haven't?" The reply was "A contract." "Under dryers in thousands of beauty shops the ladies chuckled over the way this upstart was given his dozens."[6] The male readership might have little interest in the latest Hollywood fashions so often featured, but it could enjoy the sight of a surprising number of female stars in semi-nude poses. Photographers such as Alfred Cheney Johnston provided "art photographs" of New York showgirls from the Ziegfeld Follies for the fan magazines,[7] and at least one publication of the 1920s, *Movie Weekly*, featured a centerfold (albeit a fully clothed one). By the 1960s and 1970s, beefcake was acceptable, but male nudity was always frowned upon. Publications like *Movie Weekly* might also titillate their male readership with articles in which female stars wrote of their sexual experiences, but these never quite lived up to the promise of the title. It was an amicable arrangement for an integrated audience. Betty Blythe wrote about "My First Love in the Paris Latin Quarter," while Constance Binney extolled "The Joy of the Ready-to-Wear."

The fan magazine documented social change in American life and society. As inhibitions disappeared and women became liberated in the 1920s, the magazines showed the new stylish attire, emphasizing the breasts and legs, and long tresses and curls disappeared as bobbed hair became the norm. Along with most Americans, the fan magazines had no time for prohibition, and alcohol was routinely featured in their stories. Through essays on the moviegoing experience in other countries, the fan magazine introduced the average American to a foreign lifestyle. During World War I, Harry Carr told *Photoplay* readers of the reality of life in London.[8] In the early 1920s, Janet Flanner, who was later to become *The New Yorker*'s famed Paris correspondent "Genet," wrote in *Filmplay Journal* of her visits to the movie theaters of Greece, France, and Turkey. This initiation of Americans was enhanced by a steady stream of articles on non-American movie stars in Hollywood, which dated back to the mid 1910s and Betty Nansen from Denmark and made a major impact with *Photoplay*'s extended autobiography of Polish-born, German screen star Pola Negri, which ran from February through April 1924.

What is surprising about the fan magazine is that it neither recognized nor acquiesced to the low social or economic status of the reader. In its early years the film industry recognized that its audience was primarily immigrant and adapted its storylines accordingly. The fan magazine was never tempted to lower itself in the same manner. There might be columns in which the often naïve questions of fans were answered, but generally the emphasis in the articles and most especially in the reviews was on quality writing. *Photoplay* began its monthly column of film reviews, "The Shadow Stage," with the scholarly Julian Johnson, who was followed by Randolph Bartlett and New York drama critic Burns Mantle. Even the lesser publication *Screenland* could boast in 1922 of H. L. Mencken as a film reviewer—with much that was negative to say about the current crop of releases.

Even in the earliest years, the writing in the fan magazines was erudite and often bordering on the heavy-handed. The storyline of a ten-minute short fictional film would be adapted to the printed word, running as long as five or six pages in length and taking far longer than ten minutes to read. The style was often closer to Charles Dickens or Marie Corelli than to the type of writing that audiences whose second language was English would be drawn. As early as 1916, one writer noted "that the majority of the readers are girls and women," and then continued, "but the publications are taken in the homes and eagerly devoured by the rest of the family. It has long been thought that motion-picture audiences only comprised the poorer classes, but how the habit has spread to folks in comfortable circumstances. These publications reach the largest city as well as the smallest rural community."[9]

The movies presented the star to the viewer, but the fan magazine could reach beyond the visual image and examine and reveal the "real" personality— his or her life, loves, and most intimate of thoughts. To most Americans, rich and poor, what the fan magazines had to say was as important as what the movies had to offer on screen. *Photoplay* perfectly captured that collective need to know what was happening in Hollywood:
Ten million breakfasts halted—
Ten million grapefruit waited—
Ten million voices whispered—
Ten million breaths were bated.
The mightiest words of tongue or pen
Were "Clara Bow's engaged again!"[10]

A fascinating cast of characters was associated with the fan magazines, with many every bit as entertaining and outrageous as the Hollywood stars themselves. J. Stuart Blackton and Eugene V. Brewster founded the first fan magazine, *The Motion Picture Story Magazine*, in February 1911. Blackton was a colorful Hollywood producer, who had married several times and had a love for what money could buy, while Brewster built up a small empire of fan magazines and then lost them all as he attempted to make his untalented wife, Corliss Palmer, a movie star. Later major figures associated with the fan magazines were physical fitness guru Bernarr Macfadden and *Photoplay*'s James R. Quirk. The latter was an eccentric and outspoken Hollywood commentator who married movie star May Allison. These men were equally obsessed with extramarital sexual conquests, and the world of fan magazine publishing was even more sex-oriented than Hollywood was criticized as being. The publishers enjoyed sex lives of which even Errol Flynn or Clark Gable might be envious.

Contemporaneous with the demise of *Photoplay* in March 1980, a former Beverly Hills high school teacher named Chuck Laufer dominated the fan magazine scene with *Tiger Beat*, *Rona Barrett's Hollywood*, *Rona Barrett's Daytimers*, and *Rona Barrett's Gossip* (later *Rona Looks at Gossip*), all aimed at the audience with which its publisher had begun his career and demonstrative of an understanding of a newer entertainment medium, television.

Fan magazine writers were often equally eccentric. Fritzi Remont doubled as a "graphologist" and offered character readings and vocational guidance. Myrtle Gebhart became obsessed with astrology. Herbert Howe had a penchant for Hispanic leading men, writing ardent pieces, almost bordering on love letters, about Antonio Moreno and becoming the lover of Ramon Novarro. Metro-Goldwyn-Mayer (MGM) publicist Katherine Albert was obviously very fond of studio leading man William Haines, happy to pretend that he was heterosexual and to fantasize of a romantic relationship with him. Certainly, her publicity for the leading man extended far beyond the studio, encompassing several articles in the fan magazines.

The publishers and writers might all be grist for a modern gossip mill but not for the fan magazines with which they were associated. Certainly, there was gossip in the pages of the fan magazines, but they never lowered themselves to the level of yellow journalism practiced by many contemporary American newspapers. One might argue that most of the interviews published in the fan magazines are lacking in substance, too heavily concerned with what the star is wearing or the surrounding décor, but one can never accuse the writers of a lack of intelligence. If anything, they often provided intellectual commentary to the statements of a star who had none.

Just as the entire Hollywood community needed the fan magazines as a collective mouthpiece, so did the fan magazines rely upon the film industry for their survival. Without the publicity photographs and access to the stars and to the filmmaking process, the fan magazines would have nothing on offer. At the same time, it did not take long for Hollywood to realize that the fan magazine was a valuable publicity tool. Fan magazines were never totally under the control of the studio heads, but they did provide a constant and reliable outlet for publicity stories. The writers of many of the fan magazine articles were also in the employ of either the stars or the studios to which those stars were under contract. The relationship was never spelled out to the reader, but it was an open secret within the industry, and the trade papers of the time would often identify a fan magazine writer as a publicist and vice versa.

Here was an incestuous relationship built on trust and mutual necessity. One fed upon the other, but which was the predator and which was the prey was open to question. Even at the height of the first Hollywood scandals of the 1920s—the Roscoe "Fatty" Arbuckle trials, the unsolved murder of director William Desmond Taylor, and the drug-induced death of matinee idol Wallace Reid—the fan magazines offered restrained commentary. The excessive reporting appearing in the daily press was not mirrored in the fan magazines. Indeed, one fan magazine, *Screenland*, was able to persuade the popular novelist

Gouverneur Morris to write a defense of Arbuckle, accused in the rape and murder of a starlet. By the 1930s, the Hollywood studios were giving the fan magazines and their writers unlimited access to stars and films in production, but subject to conditions and restraints of which the readers were unaware.

The fan magazines could well have been supplanted in the 1930s by the daily newspapers, which were beginning to provide more and more coverage on Hollywood, but the studios remained faithful to their old and trusted friends. The producers were also able to retain stricter control over the fan magazine writers in that each was required to obtain approval of his or her credentials from the industry-controlled Motion Picture Producers and Distributors of America (better known as the Hays Office). By the mid 1930s, virtually all fan magazines were submitting stories for studio approval prior to publication. When one fan magazine writer queried if the studio was to be considered as part of Culver City (its physical location) or Hollywood, it required a decree from publicity head Howard Strickling that the fan magazines might describe MGM as being in Culver City.[11] MGM maintained a list of what could not be mentioned in print, including, for example, that Norma Shearer and Robert Montgomery were both parents, a revelation that might hurt their romantic image. Children and marriage were generally off-limits to the fan magazine writers. As far as the Hollywood studios were concerned, pregnancy and sex were activities with which Hollywood stars were remarkably uninvolved. As a result of this studio control, some critics argue that the fan magazines acquired a sameness that made it difficult for a reader to differentiate one from another.

Powerful gossip columnists were what the newspapers had that the fan magazines did not and what the studios feared the most. Gossip columns in the fan magazines usually consisted of a compilation of commentary from a variety of sources or a collection of innocuous news items. For example, "Cal York" was the name of *Photoplay*'s gossip columnist, but there was no such person—the "Cal" was short for California and the "York" for New York, indicative of the two editorial offices providing the column's stories. There was no "Cal York" writing for the newspapers, but there was Louella Parsons and, by the late 1930s, there was also Hedda Hopper. The power of these two women is legendary, and they were untouchable by the studios. Not surprisingly, the two were welcome contributors to the fan magazines, despite Hedda Hopper being almost incapable of writing a sentence without outside help. Conveniently, Parsons had a substantial writing staff, comprised primarily of well-known fan magazine writers. What Parsons and Hopper wrote for the fan magazines could never be topical, however, because of a printing schedule up to two months in advance of publication. Thus, their contributions were often in the form of a feature article, and, if a gossip column, limited to reports on events unidentified as to date or time.

At the height of his power in the 1930s, gossip columnist Walter Winchell claimed an audience of fifty million Americans through his newspaper column and his weekly radio broadcasts. Just like Louella Parsons with her column in more than a thousand newspapers, Winchell didn't need the fan magazines—their circulation and readership was small in comparison—although he did write on a regular basis for *The New Movie Magazine* in the 1930s.

If the fan magazines retained some element of independence from the Hollywood studios it was because their editorial offices were seldom based on the West Coast. Most fan magazines were published in New York or Chicago. The latter was an obvious choice because, with its railroad connections across the United States, it could serve as a central distribution point. Wilford H. Fawcett is best known as the creator of *Captain Billy's Whizz Bang* and the *Smokehouse Monthly*, but he also originated the fan magazine *Screen Secrets*. It was published out of his hometown of Minneapolis, and Fawcett's successor, Captain Roscoe Fawcett, continued publication of the company's later fan magazines, *Hollywood*, *Motion Picture*, and *Screen Book*, from the same Midwestern headquarters before relocating to Hollywood for two years and then to Greenwich, Connecticut, and New York.

It is this hometown philosophy that makes fan magazines so very much an American institution. Fan magazines may be found around the world, but they are distinctly American. Just as the motion picture is an American-created art form, similarly the fan magazine is a uniquely American literary form, without precedence in the history of literature and very much a cultural symbol of its time.

Despite its popularity and its enduring life, the fan magazine has been the subject of little serious or historical consideration. There are two major essays on the subject, Clifton Fadiman's "The Narcissi," published in 1937, and Carl F. Cotter's "The Forty Hacks of the Fan Mags," published in 1939. In his highly entertaining and often overlooked *The Fifty Year Decline and Fall of Hollywood*, published in 1961, Ezra Goodman provided a personal and caustic twenty-six page commentary on the subject.[12]

A handful of book-length anthologies from the fan magazines exist, reprinting pieces, primarily from *Photoplay*, many of which are of not of any major value. Fan magazines *are* important research tools, particularly through the 1930s, but it is important to examine and analyze the articles in part rather than in whole. An article may contain a couple of lines or a paragraph of primary value—rather like a sound bite in modern politics—but the pieces in their entirety consist of much that is, frankly, ridiculous or relevant only as illustration of the social mores or foibles of the day.

In the mid 1940s it was suggested that movies are made to match the tastes, morals, prejudices, and mental limitations of a lady identified as Aunt Emma. It was for her niece, Judy, that five and a half million fan magazines were printed each month.[13] Films are no longer produced to the standards of Aunt Emma. In fact, they are primarily made these days to appeal to her teenage nephew, Bill. At the same time, there are no fan magazines, in the old-fashioned sense, and the readers who seek out and/or acquire them at libraries or on e-bay are a relatively small handful of film students and scholars and an equally small but ardent group of film buffs.

Until now, there has been no book-length study—in large part because there are few complete runs of even the most famous of fan magazines available for study. For many years, *Photoplay* has been available on microfilm, and it is generally the standard source among film students and film scholars. While it would be difficult to deny that *Photoplay* is the best of the very large bunch, it is not the only fan magazine worthy of serious attention. *The New Movie Magazine* is every bit as definitive in stature, and arguments might be made for a more serious examination of the contents of *Modern Screen*, *Picture Play*, or *Screen Secrets*.

Because of their ephemeral quality, not to mention the low regard in which they were held, fan magazines have not withstood the test of time well. Public libraries seldom if ever subscribed, and many of those that did discarded an old issue once the new one arrived. An examination of the microfilms available of a handful of fan magazines is a depressing experience in that individual pages are often missing, along with some complete issues. The first six months of *Photoplay* is not included in the microfilm edition, suggesting that none of those issues have survived in hard copy. Because of the popularity of most of the fan magazines among film buffs, or more precisely the covers of such periodicals, individual issues are often offered for sale at prices way above the budgets of all libraries. I have seen some fan magazines priced as high as seventy-five dollars each.

In their heyday, fan magazines were generally published on good-quality paper; one obvious exception is *Movie Weekly*. Where the fan magazines have suffered is in the popularity of their full-color covers. These are often missing, but to the student and scholar, it is happily the interior pages that matter, and these are generally intact.

This book provides a definitive history of the fan magazine from its pioneering days, through the golden years, to its decline into sleaze and titillation in the 1960s and later. It examines not only the corporate history, content, and writers and editors of fan magazines, but also the manner in which the fan magazines presented their view of what was happening within the film industry and beyond. Because they survived nearly the entire twentieth century, the fan magazines record the history of an industry in a unique, sometimes accurate, and always entertaining style.

CHAPTER 1

THE BIRTH OF THE FAN MAGAZINE

A fan magazine was fundamentally a film- and entertainment-related periodical aimed at a general fan, an average member of the moviegoing public who more often than not was female. (Throughout I refer to "the fan magazine" in the singular, because it was very much a magazine genre in its own right.) The common object of devotion of both the magazines and their readers was the motion picture. While film buffs might be the primary purchasers of old fan magazines today, they were not originally targeted as the primary audience. Thus, such illustrious film-buff publications as *Films in Review*, *Film Fan Monthly*, and *Screen Facts*, published from the 1950s onward, cannot be classified as fan magazines. Neither can the so-called fanzines *American Classic Screen* and *Hollywood Studio Magazine*. This, despite there being nothing more fanatical than the ardent film buff.

The origins of the fan magazine lie in the popular general magazines promoting consumer culture and social issues that began publication in the 1880s and 1890s and presented a non-elitist view of society—contrary to that found in such earlier "quality" periodicals as *Harper's Monthly*, *Century*, and *The Atlantic Monthly*. These new publications, from which the first fan magazines borrowed their graphics and their style, included *Munsey's* (founded in 1886 by Frank Munsey), *McClure's* (founded in 1893 by S. S. McClure), and *Cosmopolitan* (founded in 1886 and taken over by William Randolph Hearst in 1905), followed in the early years of the twentieth century by the *Saturday Evening Post* and *Ladies' Home Journal*.

Appearing at the close of the Victorian era, these new popular magazines were intended for mass consumption, with a readership not limited to the intellectually and financially superior. Their circulation was wide and substantial: by 1895 *Munsey's* boasted a circulation in excess of 500,000. Obviously, there was money to be made from these popular periodicals, and it was only a matter

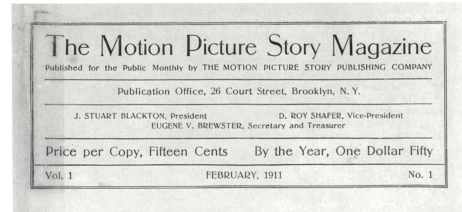

The Motion Picture Story Magazine

Published for the Public Monthly by THE MOTION PICTURE STORY PUBLISHING COMPANY

Publication Office, 26 Court Street, Brooklyn, N. Y.

J. STUART BLACKTON, President   D. ROY SHAFER, Vice-President
EUGENE V. BREWSTER, Secretary and Treasurer

Price per Copy, Fifteen Cents   By the Year, One Dollar Fifty

Vol. 1	FEBRUARY, 1911	No. 1

"Dost thou love pictures? We will fetch thee straight—
Adonis painted by a running brook;
And Cytherea all in sedges hid;
Which seem to move and wanton with her breath,
Even as the waving sedges play with the wind."
                                        —*Taming of the Shrew.*

EDITORIAL

—

PROEM

THE MOTION PICTURE STORY MAGAZINE presents its compliments to its readers and hopes for a more intimate acquaintance.

This publication is so absolutely unique amongst the hundreds of monthly magazines, its Editors feel assured that the novelty will of itself attract an attention that the publication will hold.

Irrespective of its merits as a play, the dramatized novel is assured the patronage of the supporters of the book.

THE MOTION PICTURE STORY MAGAZINE, thru the courtesy of the leading manufacturers of moving pictures, both here and abroad, is able to announce the monthly presentation of at least a dozen short stories lavishly illustrated with photographs from life of those actors engaged in the presentation of the photoplay upon which the story is based, and which will be produced within the current month at all of the leading photoplay-houses thruout the country. These stories will be among the most notable of the seventy or eighty stories to be presented each month, and will represent the very best of a varied product.

Unlike the dramatized novel, which frequently makes radical departure from the published book, these stories adhere closely to the original tale,

5

The first page of the first issue of the first fan magazine, February 1911.

of time before an ambitious entrepreneur or two would decide to publish a popular magazine aimed at the audience for what was rapidly becoming the preeminent entertainment of the time, the motion picture.

Did the film industry welcome or really want the fan magazine? At first, probably not. They were much too dangerous in the potential promotion of actors and actresses as "stars," planting the notion in the minds of the players that they might have some relevance to the success of a film and, thus, be worthy of a higher salary. Fan magazines generated fan mail, and fan mail was conclusive proof of the worth of an actor or actress. Selling the producers on the value of publicity would take time. Posters outside of theaters could be justified easily. They seldom mentioned a player, limiting themselves to the film title and the company responsible. Posters were, therefore, good publicity. Fan magazines were potentially bad for the industry.

Thus, the fan magazines were latecomers in terms of an industry interest in disseminating information on its films and their makers. A number of trade publications were extant several years prior to publication of the first fan magazine. *Views and Film Index* (later *The Film Index*) was the earliest such trade periodical, first published on April 25, 1906. *The Moving Picture World* began publication on March 9, 1907, and its closest rival, *Motion Picture News*, was first published under the title of *Moving Picture News* in May 1908. *Variety*, dubbed the "Bible of Show Business," dates back to December 16, 1905; it made its first reference to films on December 23 of that same year, and began reviewing motion pictures on a regular basis on January 19, 1907. Other early entertainment trade periodicals, such as *The Billboard*, *The New York Clipper*, *The New York Dramatic Mirror*, and *The New York Morning Telegram*, began regular coverage of the film industry around the same time. None of these publications, of course, was promoted for public consumption.

Intended to be read only by exhibitors, house organs from several producers predate fan magazines. For a short time in the mid 1910s, one major studio, Universal, converted its house organ, *The Universal Weekly*, into a semi-fan magazine, *The Moving Picture Weekly*. (In all probability, Universal also quietly published the fan magazine *Moving Picture Stories*. Beginning on January 3, 1913, it was almost entirely devoted to Universal product and reprinted pieces from *The Universal Weekly*, sometime under different bylines.)

The origin of the expression "fan" is difficult to determine. The *Oxford English Dictionary* documents the use of the word back as far as 1682, when it was written as "fann" or "phan." "Fan," as a shortening of "fanatic," is of American origin and was first used to describe an enthusiast of baseball; it can be dated back to 1889 and was in common usage by the early 1900s. In May 1911, *The Motion Picture Story Magazine* suggested that a new term for a motion picture enthusiast might be "Picture Fan."[1] In its issue of November 13, 1915, the British publication *Film Flashes* made reference to a "picture fan" coming out of one theater and immediately crossing the road to another. "Fan" had become a recognized part of the film lexicon by January 13, 1917, when poet-critic Vachel Lindsay first used it in *The New Republic*.

J. Stuart Blackton, co-founder of the Vitagraph Company of America and co-founder of the world's first fan magazine.

The earliest of the fan magazines was *Motion Picture Story Magazine*, first published on a monthly basis in February 1911. It was founded by a major figure in the early history of the motion picture, J. Stuart Blackton, in collaboration with Eugene V. Brewster, a Princeton graduate who had been named "Boy Orator" of the 1892 Grover Cleveland presidential campaign. Blackton's background was very different. Born in Sheffield, England, in 1875 to working-class parents, he immigrated to the United States and in the 1890s cofounded the Vitagraph Company of America, the most prominent producer and distributor during the early years of the motion picture. Blackton died on August 31, 1941, long after losing control of the Vitagraph Company and his periodical.[2]

If the two men had anything in common, it was their interest in women. Both were married numerous times, and both enjoyed extramarital relationships. Brewster more than Blackton realized that a fan magazine might have uses beyond the obvious. Through the Fame and Fortune contests, he was able to provide himself with a steady supply of available young ladies, inviting contestants out for long weekends at his Long Island estate.

First organized in 1919 as a joint venture between *Motion Picture Magazine* and *Motion Picture Classic*, these Fame and Fortune contests produced two major stars, Mary Astor and Clara Bow. One of the contestants in the 1919 contest was Glenda Farrell from Oklahoma, who became a successful leading lady at Warner Bros. in the 1930s. Judges included Mary Pickford, producer Thomas H. Ince, directors Cecil B. DeMille and Maurice Tourneur, illustrators Howard Chandler Christy and James Montgomery Flagg, as well as Blackton and Brewster. Aside from the last two, it is doubtful any of the filmmaking fraternity contributed anything to the decision-making process. Brewster employee Adele Whitely Fletcher recalled,

> I must say he [Brewster] had something to do in the final choice, but in the end you had to investigate these people. You couldn't let anyone win; you didn't know who they were. Clara Bow's background was horrendous. Her father used to come into the office. He was practically illiterate, and he used to smoke the most foul-smelling cigars, which were always down to nothing when he came in. He was determined that a, nothing was going to happen to his little rosebud, and b, that she was going to get all that was coming to her. Well, if you had any sensitivity at all, you were horrified at taking this girl, who was obviously going to win, because she photographed like a dream, and throw her to the wolves. I never tried harder in my life to prepare Clara Bow for what was ahead of her. We were going to do a fashion sitting, and I asked the head of *Classic* if she would bring Clara into New York and get her some underclothes. I met them at the old Waldorf on Fifth Avenue for lunch, and I can still see that vulnerable, ambitious and driven, and in a way sensitive, little figure sitting there.[3]

The Fame and Fortune contests were also open to men, but the organizers were never too enthusiastic about their chances. "Many masculine contestants have appeared," reported *Motion Picture Magazine* in 1919, "but, we regret to report, their average hasn't nearly approached the so-called weaker sex. It is up to the men to make a better showing."[4]

The contestant who made the biggest impact on Eugene V. Brewster was Corliss Palmer, a winner of the Georgia Peach beauty contest, who was summoned to his New York office in September 1920. Despite claiming that she looked on Brewster as a father or older brother, Palmer was named by his second wife, Eleanor V. V. Cator, whom he had married in 1916, as co-respondent in a 1926 divorce action. If Palmer did have a sexual relationship with Brewster in the early 1920s, she was unquestionably underage, although she was presumably born earlier than July 25, 1909, the date of birth that appears

His fame and fortune gone, Eugene V. Brewster plays backgammon with his wife, Corliss Palmer, at their modest Hollywood home in March 1931. Courtesy of University of Southern California, Regional History Collection.

on her death certificate. She was "beautiful but dumb," and there was "nothing but trouble behind that face," opined the second Mrs. Brewster. Brewster and Palmer married in October 1926, and he heavily promoted her as a movie star (always in grade B pictures) throughout the remainder of the silent era.

Between 1921 and 1923, *Motion Picture Magazine* published twenty-three articles on Corliss Palmer, while its sister publication, *Motion Picture Classic*, published one. There were pieces on her hands, the perfume she used, her figure, her eyes, and, of course, her stars (astrologically speaking). Brewster created Corliss Palmer Productions, Inc., in 1921, but all of the lady's feature films were produced in the mid through late 1920s.

The decline of Eugene V. Brewster's fortune can be directly linked to his marriage to Corliss Palmer. Complex litigation in the year of their marriage led to the sale of his magazine properties. Brewster's second wife sued Palmer for alienation of affection and received a $200,000 award. In August 1931, he filed a voluntary bankruptcy petition, listing liabilities of $17,396. (Curiously, some ten days later, J. Stuart Blackton filed a similar petition.) Brewster's half million dollar country estate in Morristown, New Jersey, was gone, and the couple was now living in a one-bedroom cottage on Selma Avenue in Hollywood. Following his separation from Corliss Palmer, Brewster was briefly engaged to a twenty-five-year-old opera singer, Dorothy McCormick, who financed a couple of books that he published. Brewster married his fourth and last wife, Liane Hill, in 1935. He died on January 1, 1939.[5]

Corliss Palmer in the 1920s.

It has been suggested that Eugene V. Brewster already had some experience in the field of fan magazines as the publisher of a five-cent magazine of fiction, although I have been unable to find any contemporary proof of this. His embracing the motion picture had little to do with the subject matter but more with the notion that in their adaptation movies provided a free source for publishers of fiction. Further, the producers of such films were more than willing to provide a publisher with illustrations at no cost.

Brewster's headquarters were located in Brooklyn, New York. Adele Whitely Fletcher recalled, "Mr. Brewster, who was a frightful character, would have lunch served every day in the basement. It was a Brownstone house in the Black section of Brooklyn. The wife of the superintendent of the building would serve lunch every day, and the steam of the food would put you off. So Fred[erick James Smith] and I would always plead we had something to do at noon, and we would walk down Duffield Street to a very nice restaurant and have lunch there."[6]

In its early years, *Motion Picture Story Magazine* bore little resemblance to the fan magazine as it is generally accepted. In terms of graphics, style, and content, the periodical was very obviously modeled after the popular periodicals of the day. The emphasis was on story adaptations of current one- and two-reel motion pictures. It was not until 1917 that short stories based on the films were relegated to a lesser position and no longer dominated the magazine, but there were often still as many as three to an issue. As an editorial in the first issue explained, "Unlike the dramatized novel, which frequently makes radical departure from the published book, these stories adhere closely to the original tale, and the reader will find no disappointment in the pictured drama thru the violence done to preconceived impressions of the various personages."[7] The major problem facing the magazine, of course, was to ensure that its story adaptations appeared simultaneous with the release of the motion pictures involved. The readership might be willing to read of films prior to their release but not months later.

Based on its content, there was little real indication of the purpose of *Motion Picture Story Magazine*. Aside from the story adaptations, the periodical featured a piece by J. Stuart Blackton on early flyers, titled "Birds and Birdsmen," and unrelated to motion pictures. A two-page article by Stanley Crawford looked at "Stage Favorites in the Film," and there were essays on Abraham Lincoln and Molière. There was also a half-page article, complete with a photograph, on screen actress Clara Williams, giving her the distinction of being the first film player to be featured in a fan magazine. It was not until December 1911 that *Motion Picture Story Magazine* published its first "star interview," a half page devoted to Florence A. Lawrence of the Lubin Company.

As to the readership, it was obvious that the thrust—as in the years to come—was toward the female members of the audience. The first two advertisements in the magazine were for the Monarch Typewriter Company and the Smith Premiere Typewriter Co., suggesting that not only was the readership assumed to be women, but also stenographers or at least office workers. With 127 pages and selling at fifteen cents a copy, *Motion Picture Story Magazine* was able to compete with the more general periodicals available on the newsstands and, unlike the latter, it was also available at most theaters. With most theater tickets in major cities selling for twenty-five cents, the price of the magazine posed no great financial hardship to the average moviegoer. As the years progressed, the fan magazines raised, lowered, and again raised their cover price, but it was always lower than the average cost of a ticket to the movies.

It has been proposed that the film-specific fan magazine is the first of its type to be directed at a predominately female audience. Other specialist periodicals, such as *Popular Science* and *Scientific American*, both of which date back to the 1800s, were aimed at a specifically male audience. One problem with this conjecture, however, is that while the so-called male-oriented periodicals were for hobbyists, the fan magazines were for the moviegoing public as a whole. Going to the movies is not a hobby, nor is reading about the films and their stars necessarily a feminine trait. It is more a matter of the publishers of fan magazines determining that the audience is likely to be more female than male, which influenced not only the content but perhaps even the price.

In 1947, Gordon Kahn visited his local newsstand and purchased nineteen fan magazines. The newsstand owner told Kahn that it was not unusual for a customer to purchase every issue on offer, but the customer was always female. Kahn asked, "When men buy these magazines, which ones do they prefer?" The owner pointed to several, and Kahn asked, "Why? More pictures, eh? Cutouts and pin-ups?"

"Nothing like it," came the reply. "It's because they cost a quarter apiece. Most of the others are fifteen. Men like to buy things they can pay for with one coin."[8]

By the late 1940s the fan magazines were an established commodity with an established content. Not so with the second issue of *Motion Picture Story Magazine*, dated March 1911, which had a little more emphasis on screen personalities, with brief biographies of the stars. Thomas Edison was featured on the cover with the statement "Published for the Public." Again, the articles were of a general nature, rather than film-oriented, but the magazine included two film-related poems and an overblown editorial taking a very lofty position on the motion picture. What is puzzling is the reprinting of several pieces from the first issue, which perhaps suggests that the February 1911 issue was a prototype rather than a mass-marketed edition.

Based on contemporary reports, the most popular content of *Motion Picture Story Magazine* was "The Answer Man" column. Here, questions from moviegoers were answered in depth by an individual with a positively encyclopedic knowledge of the subject—an individual who was, apparently, a lone female, at least in the early years. The periodical was always coy in identifying her, but her name was Elizabeth M. Heinemann.

Throughout the early years, *Motion Picture Story Magazine* adopted a serious tone, emphasizing the educational aspects of the movies—the August 1911 issue had essays on "Religious Possibilities of the Motion Picture" and "Children and the Movies"—and assuming a more highly educated readership than might be found in the actual audiences at the theaters, which catered primarily to the immigrant classes. Few at the nickelodeons could have appreciated George F. Dwyer's pompous poem, from September 1911, titled "Lines on a Criticism of a Moving Picture of 'Beethoven and the Origin on the Moonlight Sonata.'" Perhaps more appealing is a curious left-wing editorial in the March 1913 issue questioning the high price of coal, milk, beef, and eggs, and commenting, "It would be interesting to know who gets all the profits from these rises in prices." Profiting from the production, distribution, and exhibition of motion pictures was not an issue.

It was not until December 1919 when the magazine again took a political stance, this time in response to the Russian revolution, simultaneous with the production of a cycle of anti-Bolshevik films. The fan magazine editorialized that the motion picture was "the leveler," and that "Thru their medium the rich man and the poor man are learning to understand one another, thru their enlightening influence the growing tendency to that faulty creed of Bolshevism can be stamped out."[9]

Motion Picture Story Magazine began in 1911 with a circulation of 50,000, rose in 1912 to 110,000, and by 1914 was at 250,000. To encourage subscribers, the magazine offered free of charge *Comic Siftings from the Motion Picture Story Magazine*, containing 200 drawings, sketches, and engravings, and published in a limited edition of 1000 copies in February 1914.

To prove both to advertisers and to producers just how much readership and power was represented by *Motion Picture Story Magazine*, the periodical began a series of popularity contests in which readers were encouraged to vote for their favorite player. The first boasted a grand total of seven million votes being cast, with Romaine Fielding of the Lubin Company announced in October 1913 as the winner with 1,311,018 votes. The closest female player was Alice Joyce of Kalem with 462,380 votes. The following year, a Great Artist Contest was organized, with Earle Williams announced the winner in October 1914 with 487,295 votes and Clara Kimball Young winning the first prize for ladies with 442,340. Curiously, both winners were members of the stock company of J. Stuart Blackton's Vitagraph Company of America. Yet another contest, this time for Great Cast, was organized in 1915. Even stranger than the previous year's verdict was the overall achievement of Vitagraph's Mary Maurice, who specialized in maternal roles and received 2,277,500 votes against Charlie Chaplin's 1,934,550 votes. Chaplin was voted Greatest Male Comedian, with Mabel Normand Greatest Female Comedian. Other winners were Earle Williams (Leading Man), Mary Pickford (Leading Woman), W. Christie Miller (Old Gentleman), Romaine Fielding (Character Man), and Norma Talmadge (Character Woman).[10]

These personality contests were obviously precursors to the Fame and Fortune contests. The former helped prove the power and circulation of the fan magazine, while the latter provided the readership with the vain notion that they might compete with their favorite stars for a leading role on screen. In an effort to promote screenwriting for the masses, the magazine also cooperated with the *New York Evening Sun* in a 1914 scenario contest with prizes amounting to $1350.

In March 1914, the magazine's name was changed to *Motion Picture Magazine*, by which the periodical was known until its demise. There was no major change in format—the cover price was still fifteen cents—but there was an increase in advertising and, most importantly, films from all early producers were routinely featured in its pages. Because J. Stuart Blackton's Vitagraph Company of America was a member of the Motion Picture Patents Company, a monopolistic organization controlling the various patents held by Thomas Edison and others, at its beginning *Motion Picture Story Magazine* featured only films from the members of the group. The first reference in the minutes of the General Film Company, distributor of films from the Motion Picture Patents Company, to a popular film magazine occurred on November 10, 1910: "Mr. Blackton stated that he investigated the cost and the probable advantages of a motion picture magazine and that as a result of this investigation he was assured that a magazine of this kind would be a great benefit to the trade and that it could be operated at a fair profit by conducting same along the lines of other weekly, bi-weekly, or monthly magazines; the story features of the magazine being based on licensed motion pictures. Messrs. Blackton and [Frank] Marion were appointed a committee to further consider the suggestion and report." As a result of that further report, the General Film Company arranged for the incorporation of a publishing company with an authorized capital stock of $100,000. How Eugene V. Brewster became involved is unknown, but, presumably, he provided the publishing knowhow that Blackton and his group lacked.

Motion Picture Story Magazine was intended only as a publicity arm for the "licensed" companies, with the exception of the Selig and Essanay Companies, neither of which agreed to support the project with the required $200 a month. No productions from the so-called independent filmmakers, such as Carl Laemmle's IMP Company, were acknowledged. However, by 1913 there were occasional story adaptations of films produced by IMP and by another independent, Solax.

Even while the short one- and two-reel films of early cinema were being made increasingly redundant by feature films of five reels and longer, *Motion Picture Magazine* continued to concentrate on the former. As late as 1915, with feature film production dominating the industry, the magazine was highlighting stories from early American Biograph shorts then being reissued. One of the first feature films to be acknowledged by the periodical was Vitagraph's five-reel production of *The Juggernaut*, told in story form in the April 1915 issue. Another feature film from Blackton's company, *The Battle Cry of the Peace*, was highlighted not in one but in three issues—October, November, and December 1915—of *Motion Picture Magazine*.

As with the emphasis on shorts over features, so did *Motion Picture Magazine* concentrate on performers rather than producers, directors, and others behind the camera. It was not until 1915 that producer Thomas H. Ince was invited to write on his craft (May) and D. W. Griffith was interviewed (August).

Articles and story adaptations in *Motion Picture Story Magazine* were sometimes written by trade paper journalists, such Louis Reeves Harrison from *The Moving Picture World* and Epes Winthrop Sargent from *Variety*. Rex Beach contributed a story adaptation, "The Vengeance of Durand; or, the Two Portraits" in February 1913, although an article by him in May 1915 on how he came to write for the motion pictures was "as told to" Henry Albert Phillips. The first two staff members at the magazine were Elizabeth M. Heinemann and Lillian Conlon, although both were primarily involved with the business side of the publication. Edwin M. La Roche was the first assistant editor. Most employees remained with Brewster for many years. For instance, Duncan A. Dobie Jr. joined the editorial department in 1914, became advertising manager two years later, general manager in 1925, and publisher in the 1930s.

Norbert Lusk, who was to become a familiar fan magazine writer, had his first piece on "Preferences and Prejudices" of the film actors published in October 1914. Gladys Hall, who is generally considered the doyenne of fan magazine writers, made her first appearance with a poem in the February 1912 issue of *Motion Picture Story Magazine*. In June 1914, she began writing a monthly column, "Public Opinions of Popular Plays and Players." Another pioneering woman fan magazine writer, Hazel Simpson Naylor, who contributed a similar feature, joined Hall in August 1915. A very minor actress associated with the Vitagraph Company, Rose Tapley, contributed a column as "The Answer Lady" in 1916, beginning with the February issue.

Under the heading of "Photoplay Reviews," and without fanfare, *Motion Picture Magazine* began publishing reviews of current releases in July 1916. Each review was no more than a dozen lines, with the first being of *The Good Bad Man*, starring Douglas Fairbanks, which was "worth seeing." The first reviews were not signed, but by 1917 the initials of the critics were given, including H. S. N. (Hazel Simpson Naylor), R. B. C. (probably Roberta Courtlandt), and N. D. G. (Nina Dorothy Gregory). Surprisingly, and perhaps indicative of a majority readership in the New York area, *Motion Picture Magazine* also began a "Guide to the Theaters: Plays That Are Worth While" simultaneous with publication of film reviews. The reviewer was Gladys Hall, who went by the name of "Junius," and criticism was limited to plays in the New York theater district.

Rather like the United States, *Motion Picture Magazine* was neutral at the outbreak of World War I in Europe. In February 1916 it had no problem in publishing an article by John Allen Everetts, U.S. cinematographer with the German Armies in the East, who wrote of "How I Got to Przemysl and Filmed the Bombardment" (at this time it was claimed that over 7600 newsstands sold out of the issue within two weeks of its coming on sale). With America's entry into the conflict, however, *Motion Picture Magazine* did adopt a patriotic stance. The October 1917 issue featured photographs of stars working in their gardens, growing vegetables for the war effort: "I couldn't enlist in the army or navy, so I went in for gardening," explained Norma Talmadge.[11] The following month, there was a photograph of Mary Pickford presenting the company color of the Lasky Home Guard (named for Paramount producer Jesse L. Lasky), represented by leading man Wallace Reid.[12]

A major change to *Motion Picture Magazine* came with the March 1918 issue, when the self-billed "Oldest, Largest and Best Movie Magazine in the World" adopted a new format of 8½ inches by 11½ inches, a size that was

J. STUART BLACKTON
PRESIDENT

EUGENE V. BREWSTER
EDITOR & SEC.-TREAS.

TELEPHONE 6085 MAIN

MOTION PICTURE
MAGAZINE AND CLASSIC

175 DUFFIELD STREET
BROOKLYN, N.Y.

GUY L. HARRINGTON
SALES MANAGER

FRANK GRISWOLD BARRY
ADVERTISING MANAGER

November fourteenth.

Mrs. Harry Solter
Westwood N.J.

My dear Miss Lawrence,

    So many of our readers continue to inquire "What
has become of Florence Lawrence?" that we are contemplating writing an
article about you. I wonder if you would be so kind as to help me by send
-ing me the necbessary information. For instance tell me the name of
the last picture you acted in, the company and the date. Why you stopped
playing, a few interesting anecdotes that have happened in your life since
then and whether you intend to return to the screen, if so, why; and if
not, why not. Your comparison upon private life and public life
would also be very interesting. If possible will you also, if possible
send some snap-shots of yourself and home and husband, or at least a
recent photograph of yourself.

                      immediate
    Thanking you for your attention to this matter as we
wish to get it in print as soon as possible, I am,

      Very sincerely yours,

                 Hazel Simpson Naylor

In the late 1910s, Hazel Simpson Naylor writes to Florence Lawrence, generally recognized as the screen's first star, asking for information in connection with a planned feature article. Courtesy of Academy of Motion Picture Arts and Science.

to become standard for all film magazines. The change in format indicated a break with the popular, general magazines of the early twentieth century. The format size was coupled with an increase in cover price from fifteen to twenty cents. The new format was promoted with nothing more than a half-page announcement in the previous issue, and the change did not coincide with a change in volume number.[13] A glamorous portrait by Leo Sielke Jr. of Norma Talmadge adorned the cover. There were still two short stories based on recent film releases, but the new issue featured a major review section, "Across the Silversheet: A Department of the Photodrama Review," written by Hazel Simpson Naylor. Adele Whitely Fletcher, whose first contribution to the magazine was a piece on "The Divine Edith" (Vitagraph actress Edith Storey) in May 1918, took over the department in 1920, when Naylor apparently moved to Los Angeles. In addition, in acknowledgement of the readership's desire to learn more of the private lives of their heroes and heroines, Fritzi Remont began an exclusive, Los Angeles–based gossip column.

Good Things A-Coming for 1918
And the People Who Will Contribute Them

EDWIN M. LA ROCHE

DOROTHY DONNELL

EUGENE V. BREWSTER, MANAGING
EDITOR

LILLIAN MONTANYE

GLADYS HALL

contribute for the year 1918, it is no more than right that our readers should at least have a glimpse of some of our famous writers and artists. Space forbids our giving a biography or even a sketch of each contributor, but their work speaks for itself. First comes the managing editor, Mr. Brewster. It was he who first designed and

MANY of the readers of the MOTION PICTURE MAGAZINE have expressed a natural curiosity to know more about the writers and artists who have entertained them so admirably in past years, and we have concluded that, since the same talented people will continue to

editorial, but both are writers as well as executives, being regular contributors, under various *noms de plume*. It must be admitted right here that several of our writers do not always use their own names, notably our famous Answer Man, and our readers will doubtless enjoy scanning these photos in search of our famous

started the MAGAZINE, in co-operation with President J. Stuart Blackton, and his has been the guiding hand in selecting his staff and shaping the policy of the MAGAZINE from the very beginning. Elizabeth M. Heinemann was his first employee, and Lillian Conlon the second, altho these two have more to do with the business and administration part of the organization than with the

120

In the December 1917 issue, *Motion Picture Magazine* introduced readers to its staff.

In the months ahead, the modern fan magazine as we know it began to take shape. In August 1918, there were "peek-a-boo" photographs of Bryant Washburn, Douglas Fairbanks, and Jack Pickford in their respective bathtubs. The beefcake image was born. Gladys Hall contributed a short story based on Theda Bara's *Salome*, illustrated by photographs of the actress displaying considerable flesh. Actress Madame Olga Petrova contributed poetry and began a

MARTHA GROVES MC KELVIE

ROBERTA COURTLAND

HENRY ALBERT PHILLIPS

FRITZI REMONT

ROBERT J. SHORES

HAZEL SIMPSON NAYLOR

H. H. VAN LOAN

E. M. HEINEMANN

GUY L. HARRINGTON

FRANK G. BARRY

LILLIAN CONLON

GEORGE EDWARDS

LEO SIELKE, JR.

old philosopher. Whether his picture is here or not we shall not say, because he is very modest and wishes to conceal his identity a while longer. Edwin M. La Roche is Mr. Brewster's first assistant editor and right-hand man. His work is well known to all our readers, but much of his writing is not always credited to him. The same may be said of Dorothy Donnell, Gladys Hall, and Robert J. Shores, because, you see, we have the Greenroom

Jottings, the Movie Gossip-Shop, Limericks, puzzles, photoplay reviews, verses, and various other departments, with no accredited authors. It takes a lot of people to make up a magazine. We might confess right here that Lillian Montanye and Lillian May are one and the same, that Roberta Courtland and Pearl Gaddis wear the same bonnets, and that Mr. La Roche and Peter Wade always

Speaking of artists, we would like to have included pictures of Argens, Meins, Watkins, and lots of other artists, particularly one of Frank Merritt, who is responsible for many of our most artistic designs, but there is not room for all, nor for many of our regular scribes. We, of course, found a place for Leo Sielke, Jr., whose wonderful cover paintings and other designs are known everywhere.

We are naturally very proud of our staff from top to bottom—nay, there is no sleep in the same berth. Guy L. Harrington is, and always has been, the sales manager, as you all know, and Frank G. Barry is the advertising manager, while Mr. Edwards is one of our numerous artists.

bottom, because we are all one big, happy family and all on a level—and we believe that no other magazine can excel it in efficiency. These talented people will continue to entertain you, dear readers, for another year, and they will try their best to beat their record of past years. Most of these writers have been with us for over six years, and they certainly should be authorities by this time—and they certainly are. This magazine was the first in the field, and we are tempted to quote the hackneyed phrase, "We lead, others follow." We confidently promise great things to our readers for the year 1918, for we know that your magazine will be a veritable treasure-house of good things. And please dont forget that our staff promises a lot of pleasant surprises as well.

long association with the fan magazines, and stars Harold Lockwood and Constance Talmadge signed their names to individual articles. For the first time, there was advertising from a major studio, Paramount, shortly to be followed by similar promotion from Selznick, Goldwyn, and others.

The thrust of the magazine continued to be directed at a female readership, and cofounder J. Stuart Blackton continued to have a presence, despite his name no longer appearing on the masthead in an editorial capacity. His then-wife, Paula, received considerable promotion for her extremely minor films in the 1918–1920 period. Female writers dominated, including Barbara Beach, Jean Calhoun, Aline Carter, Maude Cheatham, Doris Delvigne, Myrtle Gebhart, Gladys Hall, Dorothy Herzog, Lillian May, Sue Roberts, and Harriette Underhill, while Corliss Palmer began a series of "beauty talks" in April 1921. Novelist Mary Roberts Rinehart contributed an editorial on "The New Cinema Year" in the February 1921 issue. In 1922, Adele Whitley Fletcher took over as editor, with Frederick James Smith as managing editor, and that same year, Fletcher and Gladys Hall began the popular "We Interview" series with Alla Nazimova as the first subject.

Motion Picture Magazine may have dropped the *Story* from its title, but it never completely divorced itself from story adaptations, whose appeal perhaps

Nita Naldi on the cover of the August 1923 issue of *Picture-Play*. The artwork is by legendary illustrator Henry Clive, who was also responsible for many Paramount posters of the 1920s. Courtesy of Sue Slutzky.

was to readers anxious to know what films might eventually arrive at the local theaters, readers wanting to be "in the know" as to what Hollywood had on offer. At least one early fan magazine, *Moving Picture Stories*, first published on January 3, 1913, made no secret as to its content. In later years, there was *Screen Star Stories*, which lasted only a few months in 1934 before merging with *Movie Classic*, with the latter adding story adaptations to its formula.

As late as the 1940s, there were still three prominent fan magazines whose content basically consisted of story adaptations: *Screen Romances*, *Screen Stories*, and *Movie Story*. The first, as its title suggests, was selective as to the genre of films it adapted for the printed page. Edited first by May Ninomíya and later by Evelyn Van Horne, *Screen Romances* carried the occasional feature article but never fundamentally shied away from its true purpose. In 1942, Fawcett began publication of *Movie Story Year Book*, which promised "The Year's Best Films in Story Form" and was published throughout the decade.

Dating back to 1929, *Screen Stories* remained extant into the 1960s and 1970s, although in later decades it included three or four feature stories as well as gossip columns (one by Mike Connolly) and other news-related items. As well as story adaptations of "first-run films," *Screen Stories* also included a "movie classic," obviously lifted from its archives. Thus, in January 1963 readers could get the storylines of *In Search of the Castaways* and *Taras Bulba*, along with the story of *The Petrified Forest* from 1936. However, the story was taken in whole from a 1936 issue of *Screen Stories*, and the fan magazine could not be bothered to add in the date of the film's original release—or, for that matter, explanation of its relevance.

In his June 14, 1944, "Trade Views" column in *The Hollywood Reporter*, W. R. "Billy" Wilkerson, the trade journal's editor and publisher, criticized these publications, claiming that "synopses" of the films, often poorly written, would hurt the box office for such productions. As far as he was concerned, these fan magazines were "little more than parasites living off the picture business and doing it no good at all." There was an immediate rejoinder from the publisher of *Screen Romances*. He pointed out that the so-called synopses were, in reality, short stories, little different than the condensations offered by *Reader's Digest*. Because only a limited number of grade A pictures were provided each month to his publication, it was often necessary to highlight three or four B films in each issue. Such promotion could, in fact, help promote a minor production:

> There was one instance, some years ago, when the studio was anxious to get as much publicity as possible for the film *The Great McGinty* [directed by Preston Sturges]. *Screen Romances* was near closing time. But, being an obliging soul, the editor said she would read the script and, if it proved to be a good story, she would substitute it for another "B" film. She read the script, was enchanted by it, told the publicity representative she would gladly use it.
>
> You may remember that *The Great McGinty* was a "sleeper." We have no statistics, but it would be interesting to know how many more tickets were sold than might have been had our readers not been given the opportunity to share the editor's enthusiasm.[14]

Photoplay, discussed in chapter 3, was *Motion Picture Magazine*'s most prominent early competitor, ultimately becoming the better known fan magazine, but there were others. Most notable is *Picture-Play Weekly*, which began publication on April 10, 1915, in a size and format very similar to that of *Motion Picture Magazine* and with a cover price of fifteen cents. *Picture-Play* was owned by Street & Smith, a magazine publisher founded in 1855 by Francis S. Smith and Francis S. Street. The initial format of the first movie fan magazines, with the emphasis on story adaptations, must have appealed

PICTURE-PLAY MAGAZINE

OCT. 1926

25 Cents
STREET & SMITH
PUBLICATION

MARY BRIAN

David Parga

EMIL JANNINGS - GRETA GARBO - ALICE JOYCE
THE SCHILDKRAUTS AND VICTOR VARCONI

Mary Brian is featured on the cover of the October 1926 issue of *Picture-Play*. Courtesy of Sue Slutzky.

to a company specializing in weekly and monthly periodicals featuring short stories, such as *Best Detective Magazine*, *Far West Stories*, *Love Story Magazine*, *Sport Story Magazine*, and *Wild West Weekly*. There was no opening editorial and no introduction in the first issue of *Picture-Play Weekly*, and the issue began with a piece by Francis X. Bushman, who was obviously a favorite of the editorial staff and was later, in late 1915 and early 1916, to contribute a column, "The Public Pulse," in which he printed letters from readers along with his commentary.

Story adaptations predominated, but *Picture-Play Weekly* also featured opening articles supposedly authored by popular players of the day, whose faces would also grace the magazine's covers. With its December 1915 issue,

OCTOBER   35¢

SHADOWLAND

EXPRESSING THE ARTS

A BREWSTER PUBLICATION

From October 1922, a
typical *Shadowland* cover,
featuring a stunning visual
image but no movie star.
Courtesy of Sue Slutzky.

it expanded from 34 pages to 128 (and often more than double that number),
lowered its cover price to ten cents, and became a semi-monthly, changing
its name to *Picture-Play Magazine*. On March 10, 1916, *Picture-Play Magazine* became a monthly publication. The similarity to *Motion Picture Magazine*
was now complete in every way. In fact, the only substantive change to the
magazine came with the May 1927 issue, when the hyphen was mysteriously
and without explanation dropped from the title. The price at this time was
twenty-five cents, and the slogan on the cover read "Once a Reader Always a
Reader." *Picture Play* ceased publication in 1941, when it merged with *Charm*
magazine.

Mary Pickford and Douglas Fairbanks are featured on the September 1924 cover of *Motion Picture*. The artwork is by Vargas, who was to achieve lasting fame for his work in *Playboy*. Courtesy of Sue Slutzky.

In September 1915, *Motion Picture Magazine* introduced a sister publication, *Motion Picture Supplement*. It was published on the fifteenth of each month, while *Motion Picture Magazine* appeared on the first. The price was fifteen cents. Gertrude McCoy was featured on the cover of the first issue, and Edith Storey on the cover of the December 1915 issue, which was retitled *Motion Picture Classic*. The latter was to continue as a companion to *Motion Picture Magazine* through August 1931, when the name was changed to *Movie Classic*. At this time, the cover star was Jean Harlow, and the editor Laurence Reid.

Another sister publication was *Shadowland: Expressing the Arts*, which began publication in September 1919, with a cover price of twenty-five cents. *Shadowland* was a hybrid publication, concentrating as much on allied arts as on the cinema and with a strong emphasis on quality writing, enhanced by photographs showing a fair amount of breasts and buttocks. Albert Vargas contributed a poster, "Behind the Scenes," in September 1922. The "nude" photographs were not always of women. There were many images of semi-clad, fey-looking young men from the ballet, and in August 1921 Hubert Stowitts was shown completely nude, his genitals hidden by a raised leg. Color plates painted from photographs were featured, as were interviews by Madame Olga Petrova, and reviews of the newest of New York stage productions. There were no film reviews. Slightly larger in format than *Motion Picture Magazine*, at 8½ inches by 12 inches, *Shadowland* was also more expensive, raising its cover price from twenty-five to thirty-five and finally fifty cents.

Shadowland was very much a sophisticated publication, almost too good to be described as a fan magazine. Indeed, it billed itself as "The Handsomest Magazine in the Whole World." It is no exaggeration to identify its covers as works of art. Caricatures by Wynn Holcomb are reminiscent of what Al Hirschfeld was to offer years later in the *New York Times*. Among its contributors were novelist Louis Bromfield, Willard Huntington Wright (better known as S. S. Van Dine), and Frank Harris, who first contributed in September 1922 with a piece on Anatole France. In February 1921, books were reviewed by Heywood Broun. Anna Pavlova wrote on "The Dance" in January 1921. Prior to her illustrious career at *The New Yorker*, Janet Flanner contributed an interview with Zona Gale in May 1921. There were one-act plays by Dorothy Donnell (October and December 1920) and Ferenc Molnar (April 1922).

The periodical was too good to last, and in November 1923 *Shadowland* merged with *Motion Picture Classic*. The final issue of the previous month had included literary criticism, fiction, poetry, and essays on architecture, drama, music, dancing, arts and crafts, and photography. The last issue was edited by F. M. Osborne, and serving as managing editor was the incredible Adele Whitely Fletcher, who had joined Eugene V. Brewster's staff in February 1920 as editor of *Motion Picture Magazine*. Adele Whitely Fletcher was a familiar name to fan magazine readers, one of a group of dedicated women and a handful of men whose contribution to the genre's success, not only in its formative years but in the decades to follow, was both paramount and prolific.

Writers from fan magazines and other publications gather for the wedding breakfast of Edmund Lowe and Lilyan Tashman, September 1925. From left to right, top row: Harrison Carroll (*Los Angeles Times*), Alice Tildersely (Brewster Publications), Dorothy Spenceley (*Photoplay*), Wheeler Reid (*Hollywood Life*), Mrs. Wheeler Reid, Helen Carlisle, Lucille Carlisle, Dave Epstein, Edmund Lowe, Lilyan Tashman, Elza Schallert, and the caterer; middle row: Jim Mitchell (*Los Angeles Examiner*), Mrs. Harrison Carroll, "Doc" Willis (*Screenland* and *Los Angeles Daily News*), Grace Kingsley (*Los Angeles Times*), Jimmie Starr (*Los Angeles Record*), and Leonard Boyd (*Los Angeles Examiner*); bottom Row: Mona Gardner (*Los Angeles Times*), Dorothy Manners (*Picture-Play*), Jack Townley (*Hollywood News*), Bebe Daniels, and Whitney Williams (*Los Angeles Times*). Courtesy of Academy of Motion Picture Arts and Sciences.

CHAPTER 2

THE PIONEERING WRITERS

What is perhaps most remarkable about fan magazine writers is their longevity and their ability to embrace each new breed of movie star, decade after decade. It is almost as if the subjects of the articles changed but the writers and the stories remained pretty much constant. In fact, perhaps there was a standard template used by fan magazine writers. In 1939, Carl F. Cotter wrote of the contemporary fan magazine writer Sonia Lee, who "is probably the most energetic of them all, dictating stories by the hour over an Ediphone. It is reported that she wrote her first fan story some seven years ago; each story since has been a copy of that one, with names changed and paragraphs transposed."[1]

The fan magazine writers believed quite sincerely in much that they wrote, and much that they wrote was closer to truth than fiction (with some reservations). If they lied it was as to the approachability of the stars (they were not approachable) and that the stars were all good people (many of them were bastards). The real Gary Cooper or the real Alice Faye might not be quite as "real" as the fan magazine writers claimed, but there was more than an element of truth in what they wrote. It would be difficult to parody a fan magazine article, because it was beyond parody, beyond imitation except by those with the faith of the fan magazine writer.

If what was written was not strictly true, it was at least more honest than many of the advertisements from reputable companies that appeared in the pages of the fan magazines. Who do you believe more—the star who claims in a full-page advertisement that she uses Lux each day and whose bathroom resembles a studio set, or the fan magazine writer describing the star's living quarters, fashion tastes, or secret sorrows? The dividing line between a fan magazine editorial and a paid advertisement was decidedly blurred. One example, concerning Lux toilet soap, occurred in the October and November 1930 issues of *Photoplay*, in which regular contributor Katherine Albert

Adele Whitley Fletcher.

interviewed Bebe Daniels and Alice White as to the need for a smooth skin in front of the camera. In two-page spreads that appear as much as fan magazine copy as advertising matter, the interview revealed that nine out of ten screen stars use Lux. Those readers who did spot the small print at the bottom of each page revealing the truth of the copy were advised that "Every advertisement in *Photoplay Magazine* is guaranteed."

As one critic in the 1930s noted, the fan magazine writers "honestly and passionately" believe that the intersection of Hollywood Boulevard and Vine Street is the center of the universe—not the center of this poor world, but of the universe.[2] And, equally, that "many girls lacking great beauty but possessing lovely skin have passed on the road to fame the woman with perfect features."

Many of the fan magazine writers likely had an inflated notion not only of their importance but also their glamour. Many of the female scribes chose to publish their photographs, a mistake in that they were often sadly lacking in beauty, but no less so than their male counterparts, who were less photographed. At the same time, fan magazine writers were never allowed by their writing colleagues from newspapers and general periodicals to forget that they were at the bottom of the heap in the world of contemporary letters. Because what the fan magazine writers wrote was light, frothy, and generally insubstantial, they were and would remain underrated as journalists and reporters.

Adele Whitely Fletcher was as energetic, but certainly more talented that Carl F. Cotter's representative fan magazine writer Sonia Lee. She began her career in 1916 as secretary to Sam Spedon, the director of publicity at the Vitagraph Studios in Brooklyn. Like most of her early contemporaries, Fletcher had little more than a high school education. Few of the first batch of female fan magazine writers ever attended college or university, a situation that mirrored society at the time.

At Spedon's behest, Fletcher began contributing publicity pieces on fashion and other female interests for the fan magazines. One of the earliest pieces that she recalled writing was "Talks to Girls," which appeared under the name of Vitagraph leading lady Anita Stewart. From Vitagraph, Fletcher moved on to Brewster Publications, also located in Brooklyn, eventually becoming its editorial director. From February 1920 through the summer of 1924 she edited *Motion Picture Magazine*, and in June 1924 she accepted an offer from Bernarr Macfadden to edit *Movie Weekly*. From 1931 through 1972, Fletcher wrote almost 300 articles and film reviews for *Motion Picture Magazine* and at least thirty-seven articles for *Modern Screen*, covering everyone from Nancy Carroll and Lupe Velez to Art Linkletter and Burt Reynolds. One of her later series for *Modern Screen* was titled "The Tales Their Houses Tell." "Things come out that you'd never get in an interview," Fletcher explained to me in 1973. "If you get an idea like that, then you can't fail. However dull the person is you get something from them—and God knows today they're pretty dull, and deliberately antagonistic and difficult."[3]

Fletcher was editor of *Photoplay* from 1948 through early 1952, as well as women's feature editor of *The American Weekly* from May 1952 through 1962, ghosting all the articles appearing under Elsa Maxwell's name. In the mid 1920s, Adele Whitely Fletcher gave Joan Crawford her name: "I was the editor of *Movie Weekly*, and there was a Winter Garden showgirl, Lucille LeSeur. Harry Rapf of Metro was very interested in her, and he offered a $500 prize for a name. He had very prestigious judges—oh my—but when it came time to judge, they were all very busy, and some of them were not available, and they said to me, go ahead, any name you choose is all right with us. And Joan hated the name at first—hated it."[4]

Adele Whitely Fletcher continued to work into the 1970s, contributing a monthly feature on marriage counseling, with Dr. Rebecca Liswood, for *Ladies Circle*. Fletcher also found time to author four books, *How to Give Successful Dinner Parties* (1963), *How to Decorate with Accessories* (1963), *The 6 Way Diet* (1967), and *How to Stretch Your Dollar* (1968), and coauthored chanteuse Hildegarde's autobiography, *Over 50—So What!* (1963). She died in Long Island, New York, on June 24, 1979, at the age of eighty-one.

One name dominates the fan magazine field, and that is Gladys Hall. Not only was she good, she was incredibly prolific. She wrote for numerous popular and fan magazines,[5] and among the pseudonyms that she used are Janet Reid (her mother's maiden name), Faith Service (perhaps after her novelist-cousin Faith Baldwin), and Gladys Ball.

Gladys Hall (far left) with Kay Mulvey, Dorothy Ramsey, and Ida Koverman at a 1938 "Hen Party" for Hedda Hopper. Courtesy of Academy of Motion Picture Arts and Sciences.

By 1923, Gladys Hall had published more signed articles on motion pictures and more interviews with movie stars than any other magazine writer. In addition, she had written novelettes, short stories, and hundreds of poems and had four one-act plays produced by the Threshold Players.[6] The only occasion on which she was bested by another writer was in the February 1934 issue of *Motion Picture*, in which Hall had only two stories, "The Hollywood Follies of 1933" and "Secrets of the Stars—Norma Shearer," while Dorothy Donnell Cahoun had four, "How Can Doug [Fairbanks Sr.] Stay Away from Hollywood?," "Did Lee Tracy 'Insult' Mexico—Or Did That Report Insult Him?," "A Sweep of the Fan—and Sally Rand Comes Back," and "The Stars Want Your Advice."

Born in New York City in 1891, Gladys Hall married portrait photographer Russell Earp Ball on February 1, 1912, and subsequently embarked on a successful writing career. Her name first appears on a fan magazine as associate editor of *Motion Picture Story Magazine* in December 1913. Beginning in 1922, she wrote a syndicated column, "The Diary of a Professional Movie Fan," for the Metropolitan Newspaper Service.

Arguably, Gladys Hall was at her busiest writing for *Shadowland* between 1920 and 1922. As early as February 1920, she contributed a poem, "The Hours," followed in September 1920 by another poem, "Fragment." Hall cowrote a couple of one-act plays with Dorothy Donnell, "Damnably Clever" (October 1920) and "Ask Ouija" (December 1920), as well as a solo effort, "Advance Stuff" (June 1921). Hall profiled a large number of figures from all fields of entertainment: Leo Ditrichstein (June 1920), Laurette Taylor (November 1920), Leo Carrillo (December 1920, and before he entered films), Norman Trevor (December 1920), George Arliss (January 1921), Alice Delysia (February 1921), Jacob Ben-Ami (February 1921), Fred Stone (March 1921), Effie Shannon (March 1921), Miss Mitzi (April 1921), Lionel Atwill (May 1921), Pauline Lord (June 1921), Louise Closser Hale (June 1921), Kedarnath Das Gupta (July 1921), Joseph Hergesheimer (August 1921), Marie Doro (March 1922), Sidney Blackmer (April 1922), E. H. Sothern (May 1922), Roland Young (August 1922), and poet Harry Kemp (September 1922).

With her husband, Gladys Hall moved to Los Angeles in 1927. Hall's husband quickly established himself as a noted Hollywood portrait photographer. The following year, she was a founding member of the Hollywood Women's Press Club, an informal luncheon group whose membership included a venerable listing of fan magazine writers: Katherine Albert, Ruth Biery, Regina Crewe, Dorothy Donnell, Maude Latham, Dorothy Manners, Louella Parsons, and Rosalind Shaffer. (As evidence of which sex dominated writing on the Hollywood scene, it should be noted that there was no Hollywood Men's Press Club. Perhaps the reality is that most men simply do not have the patience to deal with the stars, the publicists, the studios, and the ever-present editors.)

Gladys Hall was a disciplined writer, rising at 8:00 each morning and sitting at her typewriter by 9:30. (Hall never learned to type, using a peck system, and was unable to change her own typewriter ribbon.) She lunched at least three times a week with a star. According to one Hollywood commentator, Hall specialized in luncheon appointments, "her appetite for news being no less voracious than her hunger. She's acknowledged as the best interview-eater in the business."[7]

Like virtually all of her contemporaries, Hall was close to a number of stars. In 1929, as a gag, she escorted to various studio casting offices Gloria Swanson, in blonde wig and heavy makeup, posing as Rosalie Grey of Poughkeepsie. When Mary Pickford decided to divorce Douglas Fairbanks, the star gave the exclusive story to Hall.[8] It was Hall who had assured the readers of *Movie Classic* in October 1931 that "Mary and Doug Will Never Be Divorced." In return for their friendship, Gladys Hall would never attack an actor or actress in print. As she explained, "People don't want their movie stars torn down. Even if there WAS anything to say against them, it's not what the public wants. The public wants to believe in Santa Claus and in the movie stars."[9]

When Hall's husband died in 1942, she returned to New York and continued her career from there for the rest of her working life. Gladys Hall died in Huntington, New York, on September 18, 1977.

Hall's attitude was mirrored by that of fellow writer Myrtle Gebhart, of whom it was reported in 1930 that "She has been accused of writing goo [because she] can see only the good in people."[10] As the writer explained, "I find it good form to mingle just enough novelty with my articles to make them take well, and still maintain a certain amount of individualty."[11] One of her employers noted Gebhart's articles "are all right as bright, breezy, intimate, informal pen pictures."[12]

Myrtle Gebhart was almost as prolific as Hall, but there was one major difference. While Hall regarded the stars as her fan base, for Gebhart it was her readership. Myrtle Gebhart was a fan magazine writer who collected her own fans, hosting tea parties for them at her bungalow court apartment on Fountain Avenue in Hollywood. While Gladys Hall shunned self-publicity, Gebhart wallowed in it, showing off her petite, four feet ten inches and 105–pound figure in countless fan magazine photographs. With blue eyes, a pug nose, and red hair, she might have fancied herself as a potential movie star, but if she had the necessary ego, she did not have adequate good looks.

Born in Texas on July 7, 1901, Gebhart proved that one might take the girl out of the South, but one could never take the South out of the girl. While writing on African-American actor Stepin Fetchit in 1929, she noted, "Being a Dixie daughter, at first I rather resented the negro actor. Down in Cotton Land, there is never any question of 'place.'"[13] However, she did at least choose to write about a player of color, something that few of her contemporaries, with the honorable exception of Herbert Howe, would have done.

From Texas Gebhart moved briefly to Chicago, where she wrote just as briefly for the *Chicago Herald-Tribune* before coming to Hollywood in the early 1920s, with the vain hope of becoming a screenwriter. Her earliest pieces were accepted by Charles Gatchell, editor of *Picture-Play*, in 1922, and the first star she interviewed was Thomas Meighan, although the article was not published in that fan magazine. As of June 1924, she was a staff writer for *Picture-Play*; a feature writer for the *Los Angeles Times*; Hollywood correspondent to the *Boston Post*; and a contributor to *Motion Picture Magazine*, *Movie Weekly*, *Photoplay*, *Screenland* (for which she wrote film reviews), *Sunset*, and *Business Woman*, and she handled publicity for Bruce Guerin. By the late 1920s, Gebhart had also added *Extension Magazine* to her portfolio. She once boasted to a friend that she had conducted five interviews in a row at MGM in one day. Her monthly income in the mid 1920s was in excess of $500, more than many lesser players and character actors under studio contract would receive. Among the pseudonyms she is known to have used are Caroline Bell,

Myrtle Gebhart visits Ricardo Cortez on location for *The Pony Express* (1925).

John Addison Elliott, Doris Irving, Barbara Little, Martha Marsden, Betty Morris, Helen Ogden, and A. Sharpe Spurr (the last obviously used when writing about Westerns).[14] Gebhart also edited *WASP Whisperings*, the publication of the Women's Association of Screen Publicists, and ghostwrote Dorothy Reid's "Memoirs of Wallace Reid," published in *Picture-Play*.

In 1929, Gebhart became obsessed with astrology, and that predilection appears to have affected her enthusiasm for writing and, thus, her earning capacity. The woman who once earned $500 a month was down to little more than $2000 a year in the 1940s and less than $1500 by 1952. She had earned $25 a week for a daily column of 400 to 500 words in *The Boston Post*, but by September 1953 she was earning only $12.50 a week, and the newspaper published her for the last time on October 4, 1956. On April 20, 1953, writing to California Bank requesting a loan, she explained the reasons for her current financial circumstances: "The mags now want only pieces about the stars' love affairs and such, frivolous stuff, 90% of which is untrue. Being a trained factual feature writer and reporter, I can't write such." Myrtle Gebhart died in Los Angeles on September 16, 1958.

Women film critics were not unknown. For example, *Motion Picture Magazine* relied on at least four women: Roberta Courtlandt, Adele Whitely Fletcher, Nina Dorothy Gregory, and Hazel Simpson Naylor. There were others active in the silent era, including Mary Boyle at *Photoplay* and Delight Evans at *Screenland*. Even the trade papers had a small coterie of female critics, such as Lillian W. Brennan at *Film Daily* and Mary Jane Warren at *Motion Pictures Today*.

However, the most prominent of female critics of the silent era did not work out of Hollywood but New York, reviewing films and interviewing movie celebrities for the *New York Tribune* from 1916 onward. Her name was Harriette Underhill, and she was born in 1883 in Troy, New York, to parents interested primarily in horse breeding but also in the theater. She began her career at the *Tribune* in 1908, as a reporter of horse and dog shows and as a celebrity interviewer. The first movie she claimed to have seen was the Charles Ray vehicle *The Coward* in 1915. Underhill was so impressed that she asked her editor to be allowed to be the newspaper's film critic. Her reviews were always sensible, sincere, and honest.

Underhill's contributions to the fan magazines are generally limited to *Photoplay* and *Motion Picture Magazine* and more often than not to lesser-known celebrities such as June Elvidge (*Photoplay*, January 1918), Olive Tell (*Photoplay*, February 1918), Tom Moore (*Motion Picture Magazine*, February 1920), and Gladys Leslie (*Motion Picture Magazine*, June 1921). She did get the opportunity to profile the Duke of Windsor in the December 1924 issue of *Photoplay*, and, as evidence of her critical skills, she wrote the review section, "The Shadow Stage," in the April and May 1918 issues of *Photoplay*.

Harriette Underhill ceased to be the *Tribune*'s main critic in 1924, when Richard Watts Jr. was appointed, but she did continue to write a Sunday column. She died on May 18, 1928, from bronchitis. As evidence of her popularity with the Hollywood community, only weeks before her death the celebrities visiting at her bedside included Ramon Novarro, King Vidor and his wife Eleanor Boardman, and Goldwyn's new star Lily Damita, about whom Underhill wrote her last article, published two days after her death.

A popular couple associated with the fan magazines was Frederick James Smith and Agnes Smith. Prior to the latter's becoming editor of *Motion Picture Magazine* in January 1926, she had worked at *Photoplay*, *Picture-Play* (as a critic), and the *New York Morning Telegraph*. Agnes Smith wrote twenty-four articles for *Photoplay* between 1919 and 1928. When Louella Parsons put together her first staff in 1918, Agnes Smith was hired as a writer, along with Frances Agnew, and Parsons considered the two to be the best working for her. (Agnew does not appear to have written for the fan magazines, but she did author an early volume on *Motion Picture Acting*, published by the Reliance Newspaper Syndicate in 1913.) Smith was the sister of writer Sally Benson, whose 1942 novel was the basis for *Meet Me in St. Louis* and who was also a respected screenwriter.

Frederick James Smith edited *Motion Picture Classic* and *Shadowland*, was one of the first editors of *The Dramatic Mirror* (handling its vaudeville news in 1914), and was managing editor of *Photoplay* and *Screenland* before taking on the duties of managing editor of all Brewster publications in January 1926. In the early 1920s Smith was New York film correspondent for the *Los Angeles Times*, and as "Beverly Hills" he wrote the film reviews for *Liberty Magazine* in the 1930s. Generally, Smith combined his duties as editor of various fan

Laurence Reid (far right) with Joan Curtis and Greer Garson. Courtesy of Academy of Motion Picture Arts and Sciences.

magazines with that of film reviewer. As late as July 20, 1940, he was writing for *Liberty* about Ann Sheridan.

Excluding his work for *Liberty*, there are in excess of 350 fan magazine articles and film reviews credited to Smith. Some of his earliest pieces are on Mary Pickford (*Motion Picture Classic*, September 1917), Mrs. Sidney Drew (*Motion Picture Magazine*, September 1917), and director Herbert Brenon (*Picture-Play*, February 1918). In all, he wrote at least thirty-seven pieces for *Motion Picture Classic* and an incredible 294 for *Photoplay* between September 1917 and April 1937, including "The Shadow Stage" film review column from February to August 1923 and in June 1927. His last articles were for *Silver Screen* in 1940 and 1941.

According to *Los Angeles Times* writer Harry Carr, in 1918 Smith was "a shy, diffident boy."[15] Of another fan magazine writer, Hazel Simpson Naylor, Carr wrote at the same time that she was "a sweet, attractive little girl of about 22. She is a Smith College graduate; comes from a very fine Buffalo family and is a lot smarter than Smith." Frederick James Smith died, at the age of fifty-three, while making a telephone call from New York's Algonquin Hotel on August 5, 1941.

Laurence Reid began his career as a film reviewer for the *New York Evening Mail* in 1914, later moving in a similar capacity to the *New York Review*, the *Dramatic Mirror*, and one of the two most prominent trade papers, *Motion Picture News*. After six years with the last, in July 1925 Reid was appointed

Edwin and Elza Schallert.
Courtesy of William Schallert.

editor of *Movie Weekly* as well as a member of the editorial board of two other Brewster publications, *Motion Picture Magazine* and *Motion Picture Classic*. He met his wife, Mary Boyle, while working at *Photoplay*. She was an occasional contributor to the magazine, writing, for example, on actor Johnny Hines in August 1925. Reid's later career included stints at Fawcett Publications (for twenty-five years) and Ideal Publications (for five years).

Throughout its entire existence, Reid was closely associated with *Movie Classic*, the successor to *Motion Picture Classic*. Billed as "The Newsreel of the Newsstands," *Movie Classic* began publication in September 1931. Reid was listed as editor, with Stanley V. Gibson as publisher, although the first issue contains no editorial page and no reason for its being. It was heavy on gossip, with Marquis Busby writing a column, "Our Hollywood Neighbors: Goings-on among the Players" and the pseudonymous Cholly Hollywood appropriately contributing a column titled "Anonymously Yours." Reid not only edited, but also served as film reviewer and wrote yet another gossip column, "Between Ourselves." A further gossip column, "Looking Them Over: Gossip from the West Coast" by Dorothy Manners was added in 1932. In May 1936, Hedda Hopper made an appearance with a gossip column titled "Hollywood Highlights," which did not last out the year and was replaced by another column authored by The Boulevardier.

Sensationalism and the personal lives of the stars was the emphasis in *Movie Classic*, with pieces such as "William Powell Weds Carole Lombard" by Joan Standish and "Rex Lease Parts from Bride" by Nancy Prior (both in the first issue), " [King] Vidor-[Eleanor] Boardman Marriage Ends—Disappointed at

Not Having Son" by Ruth Wingate (September 1932) and "Actors [Douglass Montgomery and Jack La Rue] Narrowly Miss Death at Hands of Fiend" by Hal Hall (November 1934). By 1935, much of the gossip was replaced by fluff, but the content remained constant.

With Reid still in command, Dorothy Calhoun took over as Hollywood editor in 1933, James E. Reid as editor in 1935, and Eric Ergenbright as editor in 1936. *Movie Classic* was absorbed by *Motion Picture Magazine* in March 1937, but Reid continued as editor.

In 1953 Laurence Reid retired to the East Coast (he had been born in Warsaw, New York) and died, at the age of eighty-nine, on September 20, 1976. Reid was never a great critic—his reviews were often simplistic—but he did have an innate sense of what was good or bad in filmmaking.

Quite rightly, Edwin Schallert (1890–1968) is best known as the music and drama editor of the *Los Angeles Times* from 1919 until his retirement in February 1958. (He had joined the newspaper in 1912 as a financial editor.) Unlike the majority of his contemporaries, who had barely graduated from high school, Schallert had received a college education. He was an intellectual who lectured at Stanford University in the 1920s and wrote occasional articles on astronomy.

While working for the *Times*, Schallert was a frequent contributor to the fan magazines; for example, in August 1921, he wrote on Gladys Walton for *Motion Picture Magazine*. With his wife, Elza Baumgarten, Schallert contributed a monthly column, "Hollywood High Lights," to *Picture-Play* magazine. Subtitled "Reeling off Recent Events That Have Transpired in the World of the Studios," the column was surprisingly fact-filled and a treasure trove for the historian willing to browse through the pages of a nonindexed periodical. For example, in May 1925 readers learned that Colleen Moore was confined to bed with a dislocated vertebra as a result of an accident while on location for *The Desert Flower*; Mildred Harris was badly burned in a fire at the Harold Lloyd studio; Jack Holt had a bruised nose; Helen Ferguson sprained her shoulder after a fight on location for a Hoot Gibson film; Marie Prevost had the flu; Pauline Garon underwent a throat operation; Erich von Stroheim had a sprained ankle; and ingénue Lucille Ricksen had been forced to give up film work "because of a lingering illness and is sad and broken in spirit." Can so much illness and so many accidents have been covered in such detail elsewhere?

As Schallert recalled for Associated Press correspondent Bob Thomas, "I would do it [cover the studios] by streetcar. The town was a lot smaller then, and there was an intimate friendly atmosphere that is lacking today. You were on personal terms with all the stars, and it was unheard of for a publicity man to be present at an interview."[16]

When the couple was married in 1921, Elza was working as a publicist for Sid Grauman and another legendary theater owner, Thomas L. Tally. The latter was noted for the advertising of the musical accompaniment for his film presentations, "Come and see Tally's Giant Organ," and for refusing to raise his admission prices above ten cents, because ten cents was all that movies were worth. Elza's income was $100 a week, while that of her new husband was just $40. His fan magazine work was necessary for the extra income that it brought in.

Schallert's actor son, William, remembered that his father had little of a home life, going to bed at 2:30 a.m. and rising every morning at 10:00 a.m. His parents were "very busy people," rarely at home on the weekends. They were both fluent in German, and in the 1930s Elza interviewed many German refugees in Hollywood. As William Schallert pointed out, it was his mother rather than his father who should be acknowledged as the fan magazine writer, with her career extending beyond *Picture Play* to *Photoplay* and *Modern Screen*. She also hosted a radio show on the NBC Blue Network in the 1930s.[17]

Edwin Schallert was prolific, and, because of the *Times* connection, he had considerable power. It is little surprise that in 1957 he was awarded a Golden Globe by the Hollywood Foreign Press Association. Assisting him at the newspaper were Philip K. Scheuer, who joined the staff in 1927 and became Schallert's successor, and John Scott, who joined in 1929. In later years, Schallert became a heavy drinker, and it was never known if he would actually deliver a review on time. He would start out by seeing the first half of the film at, say, Grauman's Chinese Theatre in Hollywood in the morning, have a few drinks, then, if his luck held out, view the remainder of the film at a downtown Los Angeles theater, and still be in time to hand in the review. However, Schallert was not completely unreliable. Knowing his propensity for alcohol, he would always tell assistants Scheuer and Scott to "Hold yourselves in readiness."[18]

The most famous woman associated with *Photoplay*, which she joined in 1919, was Adela Rogers St. Johns, although it is wrong to label her as simply a fan magazine writer. She was as much a star as those whose lives and careers she covered, and with her supposed intimate relationships with so many, she was dubbed the "Mother Confessor of Hollywood." Adela Rogers St. Johns was, in a way, the Barbara Walters of her day, knowing how to drag out every last ounce of tears and emotion from her interview subjects, but she was far more aggressive than her modern-day counterpart. Her boss at *Photoplay*, James R. Quirk, pointed out that "Adela knows more about Hollywood and the motion picture colony than any person in the world."[19] Unfortunately, in later years, she boasted only a selective memory, conveniently believing more in Hollywood fantasy than reality.

Born in Los Angeles on May 20, 1894, the only daughter of famed trial lawyer Earl Rogers, Adela began her career in 1912 as a cub reporter on the *San Francisco Examiner*. By 1930, she was billed as "The World's Greatest Girl Reporter," covering choice crime assignments, including the Lindbergh baby kidnapping, for Hearst's *Los Angeles Examiner*. More than anything, it was as a reporter that Adela Rogers St. Johns left her mark, although she published her first short story, "The Black Cat," in 1918, her first novel, *The Sky Rocket*, in 1923, and continued to author books, including a biography of her father, *Final Verdict* (1962); an autobiography, *The Honeycomb* (1969); and *Love, Laughter and Tears: My Hollywood Story* (1978).

Adela Rogers St. Johns with Clark Gable (1939). Courtesy of University of Southern California, Regional History Collection.

For *Photoplay*, Adela Rogers St. Johns not only provided stories on the stars, but also wrote fictional pieces, which one academic categorized as "light exposés of the sillier sides of stardom [that] amplify our understanding of the film industry during this period."[20] It was actually Ray Long, editor of *Cosmopolitan*, who in 1922 had suggested that she expand her career by writing fiction for his publication. While not exactly feminist but with strong female characters, these pieces, which are lengthy enough to be defined as novellas, demonstrate the manner in which Rogers St. Johns used her fan magazine connection to advance her career as a multifaceted writer. The most prominent of these *Photoplay* novellas are "The Love Dodger" (April–July 1924) and "The Port of Missing Girls" (March–August 1927).

As John Paris Singer pointed out, Adela Rogers St. Johns was a defender of Hollywood and its lifestyle, and thus her fiction often comes across as "false and phony." He continued, "She attempted to provide a portrait of Hollywood life that balanced its vices and virtues. Writing primarily for women's magazines, St. Johns set herself the task of evoking for readers the aura of transgression that surrounded Hollywood stardom while at the same time assuring them than the film industry posed no essential threat to the dominant social and sexual ideologies."[21]

Fellow *Photoplay* writer Herbert Howe interviewed Rogers St. Johns for the magazine in 1923. It is difficult to determine how much of what he had to say is fanciful and how much accurate. He did, however, point out in regard to her fiction, "It is a throwback to the French school of de Maupassant, yet as pungently American as O. Henry. She doesn't know she has style. It's her own unstudied expression, which happens to be in vibration with Hollywood. An evocation of Hollywood."[22]

More than any other fan magazine writer, Adela Rogers St. Johns had a major role in the Hollywood film industry. She wrote several silent screenplays, including *The Red Kimona* [sic] (1925) and *The Patent Leather Kid* (1927), and her first novel was the basis for a 1926 film, also titled *The Sky Rocket*, one of seven works adapted for the screen in the 1920s. She was portrayed on screen by Norma Shearer in *A Free Soul*, a 1931 adaptation of Rogers St. Johns' 1927 novel of the same name dealing, in fictional fashion, with her relationship with her father. Among her other screen credits are *What Price Hollywood?* (1932), for which she received an Academy Award nomination for best original story. After her retirement from newspaper work in 1948, Rogers St. Johns worked briefly as a story advisor to Louis B. Mayer.

The writer was married three times. The first, when she was nineteen, to copy editor William Ivan (Ike) St. Johns, whose surname she retained; the couple divorced in 1927. In 1928, she married Stanford football star Dick Hyland, divorcing him in 1934. A third marriage to airline executive F. Patrick O'Toole ended in divorce in 1942. Rogers St. Johns, who gained a reputation for her feisty personality in later years, died in Arroyo Grande, near San Luis Obispo, California, on August 10, 1988.

While the fame of Adela Rogers St. Johns has extended beyond her death, she is not the premiere name associated with the history of *Photoplay*. That honor belongs to James R. Quirk, who created the "modern" *Photoplay* and is very much the father of the fan magazines.

CHAPTER 3

JAMES R. QUIRK AND *PHOTOPLAY*

Photoplay is the most famous of all fan magazines, a publication that began in the pioneering days of the motion picture and survived through the demise of the star system, the rise of independent filmmaking, and into an era when the public got its entertainment news from the pages of *People* and similar magazines. Ultimately, it is the yardstick by which all other fan magazines are judged, thanks in large part to its growth and fame under the editorial guidance of James R. Quirk.

As Quirk noted in a March 1931 editorial, "Almost every department and new idea introduced by *Photoplay* has been speedily copied by others. The Shadow Stage, our reviews of pictures, has been imitated in form and appearance almost shamelessly. It has come to a point where, until you get into the text, you can hardly tell one magazine from another. In the trade it is called 'the *Photoplay* formula.'"

Just as James R. Quirk was not the founder of *Photoplay*, neither was the title the invention of the periodical. The word "photoplay" was first coined in 1910, when the Essanay Company announced a contest to discover a new one-word name as a substitute for "moving picture show." In October of that year, the three judges, George Kleine, Fred C. Aiken, and Aaron Jones, awarded the $100 prize to a Sacramento, California, exhibitor named Edgar Strakosch, who had come up with the name "photoplay."

Photoplay was first published in August 1911. No copies of that first issue or of the next five issues appear to have survived. The earliest copy of *Photoplay* to be found in any library or archives is the issue for February 1912, identified as volume 2, number 1. Because volume 2 consists of six issues, one may assume that the first volume also consisted of six issues, and, therefore, *Photoplay* first saw the light of day in August 1911. That first issue, published in Chicago, was described by Richard Griffith as "a sort of theatre program,"[1] and

47

James R. Quirk with his wife May Allison on a visit to Los Angeles. Courtesy of University of Southern California, Regional History Collection.

in 1925 Quirk made reference to *Photoplay*'s beginning as "a picture theater program."[2] Unlike *Motion Picture Story Magazine*, which cost fifteen cents, until November 1912 *Photoplay* sold for ten cents.

Subtitled "Motion Picture Stories," indicative of the periodical's primary ingredient, the February 1912 edition of *Photoplay* was published by the Photoplay Magazine Publishing Company of Chicago. The contents were similar to those of *Motion Picture Story Magazine*, with the emphasis on story adaptations from films produced by the independent companies, as opposed to those belonging to the Motion Picture Patents group. No staff was listed until April 1912, when N. Gladstone Caward was identified as editor; a month later his name appeared as Neil G. Caward, with Frank A. Lear identified as president and general manager. Staff changed routinely. In July 1912, Edwin J. Ryan was managing editor and a month later the New York manager. In September 1912, A. H. McLaughlin was publisher and Ryan advertising manager. In July 1913, J. E. H. Bradley was listed as president, C. W. Griffin as secretary-treasurer, and Kenneth G. Cloud as manager. The copyright was in Cloud's name. A. W. Thomas was editor in December 1913, and in November 1914 August Cary was editor.

The contents remained constant with story adaptations predominating, along with an occasional article, a poor one-page "Answer to Inquiries," which was no competition to *Motion Picture Story Magazine*'s "The Answer Man" column, and a popular players contest. In October 1913, a department titled "Jest Jokes" was added, offering readers the opportunity to share their favorite jokes and providing the periodical with a free source of material. From ten cents a copy, the cover price went up to fifteen cents in November 1912. No issues were published between March and June 1913, suggesting that the magazine was in dire financial straits.

When it did resume publication in July 1913, the reported circulation was 26,000, and the implication was almost that this was a new periodical: "This issue of *Photoplay* starts a new era in motion picture publicity, for with its appearance the great photoplay industry has a POPULAR magazine." The actual contents of the issue suggest neither a new era nor a magazine with a popular approach. The story adaptations that predominate all relate to minor independent productions. There is the first part of a supposed autobiography from an unidentified screenwriter and a piece supposedly written by actor J. Warren Kerrigan. The New Rochelle–based Thanhouser Company was best represented with an article on the home life of Little Marie Eline, "The Thanhouser Kid," and a piece credited to "The Thanhouser Kidlet."

The relationship between the magazine and the independent producers was evidenced by a full-page advertisement in the October 23, 1913, issue of *The Universal Weekly*. *Photoplay* promised "snappy stories from Universal films," an interview with Universal's King Baggot, and a report on the company's trip to Bear Valley. Exhibitors could purchase copies of the magazine at ten cents each for resale at fifteen cents.

The contributors familiar to fan magazine readers were not in the frame until March 1914, when regular Mabel Condon had a story adaptation under her name, and in June 1914 she contributed an interview with Universal actress Ethel Grandin. One surprising author in November 1913 was B. P. Schulberg, a legendary executive figure in later years at Paramount, who contributed the story adaptation of a Famous Players–Lasky feature film, *His Neighbor's Wife*, which must have been released under a different title. Schulberg also wrote the story adaptation for *Caprice*, a Mary Pickford vehicle, in January 1914.

James R. Quirk's name first appeared on the magazine's contents page in January 1915, when he was listed as vice president, with Edwin M. Colvin as president and Robert M. Eastman as secretary-treasurer. These last two were executives with the W. F. Hall Printing Company, which had acquired the magazine as a result of unpaid printing bills. Despite extravagant claims as to Quirk's transformation of *Photoplay*, there was little change between the December 1914 and January 1915 issues of the magazine. The former, published by the Cloud Publishing Company with Augusta Cary as editor, featured nine story adaptations (including one identified as a novelette) along with nine articles. Richard Willis interviewed the Gish sisters, Cary interviewed Blanche Sweet, and the featured piece was part 2 of actress Florence Lawrence's "Growing Up with the Movies," written in collaboration with Monte M. Katterjohn. It is as good an issue as *Motion Picture Story Magazine* might offer at this time. As one contemporary critic reported in 1914, prior to Quirk's involvement with *Photoplay*: "Handsome in appearance and replete with features and departments, 'The Photoplay Magazine' has increased its vogue and influence steadily, until now it is issued with clock-like regularity and has found its way to the thousands of news-stands. Moreover, gradually the distinctly 'western' character, which at the outset the publication assumed, has given way to a more national one, and now the magazine is quite as popular in the East as in the West."[3]

The first issue associated with James R. Quirk featured nine story adaptations (one a novelette and one a serial), along with four interviews and ten "special features." Mabel Condon offered the first of her long-running interview series "Hot Chocolate and Reminiscences at Nine of the Morning." The Florence Lawrence life story continued.

Quirk's first secretary at *Photoplay* in Chicago was Hazel E. Flynn (1899–1964), who had earlier worked as an extra at the Chicago-based Essanay Company and then in the studio's scenario department. While she did not become a fan magazine writer, Flynn was hired as the motion picture critic, editor, and columnist at the *Chicago Evening American*, sometimes using the pseudonym of Rob Reel, and from the 1940s onward was motion picture and drama editor of the *Hollywood Citizen News*.

The son of Irish-American parents, James R. Quirk was born in Boston on September 4, 1884, and educated at Harvard and Boston University Law School. He began his career as a reporter at the *Boston Advertiser*, worked briefly for former Boston mayor John F. Fitzgerald on a political paper called the *New Republic* (not to be confused with the later periodical of the same name), and then moved to Washington, D.C., and the *Washington Times*. In 1912, Quirk moved to Chicago to edit *Popular Mechanics*, later opening an advertising agency in the city with his first wife, Elizabeth North. It was his achievement in transforming *Popular Mechanics* into a successful periodical that led to Quirk's hiring at *Photoplay*.

With Quirk's appearance, *Photoplay* did not so much change as establish its prominence with a reliable table of contents, good writing (by fan magazine standards), and improved circulation. One early introduction, unique to fan magazines at this time, was a gossip column titled "Plays and Players" and conducted by Cal York, which first appeared in the April 1916 issue. (Occasionally in 1918 and 1919 "Cal York" became "Cal Yorke," but this was presumably

Julian Johnson.

nothing more than a typo.) The changes did not take place overnight, and an argument may certainly be made that *Photoplay* did not become the fan magazine with which most film buffs and scholars are familiar until 1920. It had changed its cover size to the standard format for later fan magazines—8½ inches by 11½ inches—with the October 1917 issue, seven months prior to *Motion Picture Magazine* making the same change in format. (In 1937, *Photoplay* took the unusual step of enlarging its size again to that of *Vogue*, *Harper's Bazaar*, and the new *Life* magazine. If thanks to nothing other than its size, *Photoplay* could then describe itself as "The Aristocrat of Motion Picture Magazines.")

While Quirk gets, and deserves, credit for what *Photoplay* became, his name did not appear on the publication as editor in the 1910s; he was always listed as vice president and general manager. A statement in the June 1917 issue credited Quirk as business manager and listed the magazine's owners as Edwin M. Colvin, Robert M. Eastman, James R. Quirk, and Wilbert Shallenberg. Quirk did appear in *Photoplay* as a contributor with an August 1915 interview with Mabel Normand. Long before he became a legendary Hollywood producer,

Arthur Hornblow Jr. contributed an interview with Norma Talmadge to that same issue of *Photoplay*. Quirk's name may be missing from the pages of *Photoplay*, but he was there under a variety of pseudonyms, most notably Frances Denton and Jean North, the names of his daughters. Also writing under pseudonyms was the editor most associated with the new *Photoplay*, and presumably hired by Quirk, Julian Johnson.

Born in Chicago on November 26, 1885, Johnson attended the University of Southern California, and in 1907 was appointed drama editor at the *Los Angeles Times*. In 1910, he began a long-term relationship with vaudeville and nightclub entertainer Texas Guinan, who was to symbolize the prohibition era with her welcoming phrase of "Hello sucker!" Johnson directed Guinan in a 1914 vaudeville sketch, "A Musical Mix-Up," remained with her until 1920, and is often erroneously described as her husband. Johnson was presumably responsible for *Photoplay* publishing a poem by Guinan in its April 1915 issue. Julian Johnson became editor of *Photoplay* with the December 1915 issue. His name first appeared in the magazine in April 1915, interviewing Anita Stewart. In June 1915, he began an ongoing series of "Impressions" of various players, and in November 1915 he began his biography of Mary Pickford, which concluded in February 1916.

As important as his work as editor was Johnson's contribution to *Photoplay* as its film critic with "The Shadow Stage" department, which appeared simultaneously with his appointment as editor. So important was "The Shadow Stage" considered by the magazine that it was always subtitled "Reg. U.S. Patent Office." Johnson introduced a standard of film criticism virtually unknown to both fan and popular magazines. His reviews were serious, intelligent, and, as far as can be ascertained, free of bias. The first films reviewed by Johnson were *Old Heidelberg* and *The Coward*, both of which were praised. Johnson disappeared as editor in September 1917, replaced by Frederick James Smith, as eastern managing editor and Alfred A. Cohn as western managing editor. He continued with "The Shadow Stage" until November 1917, when it was taken over by Randolph Bartlett and Kitty Kelly (not the later biographer). Randolph Bartlett's name appeared as sole critic of "The Shadow Stage" in March 1918. In the June 1918 issue, Johnson contributed a laudatory review of D. W. Griffith's *Hearts of the World*, providing a story adaptation of the film in the following issue, and in October 1918 he returned both as editor of *Photoplay* and as writer of "The Shadow Stage."

Julian Johnson retired as editor in December 1919 and as writer of "The Shadow Stage" in February 1920. He contributed occasional pieces to *Photoplay* in the 1920s, including an appreciation of Emil Jannings in February 1926. Johnson went on to a distinguished career in Hollywood, providing the titles for many major motion pictures of the 1920s, including *Manhandled* (1924), *The Sorrows of Satan* (1928), *The Beggars of Life* (1928), *The Docks of New York* (1928), and the first Academy Award winner for Best Picture, *Wings* (1927). From 1932 until his retirement in 1957, Johnson was story editor at Twentieth Century–Fox. He died in Los Angeles on November 12, 1965.

Burns Mantle (at right) with Gene McHugh and Hedda Hopper at a *New York Daily News* party on April 22, 1947.

In March 1920, Julian Johnson was replaced by an equally prestigious critic, Burns Mantle. Born in Watertown, New York, on December 23, 1873, Mantle was one of the leading theater critics of his day—hailed in later years as the "Dean of New York Drama Critics"—who began his career as drama critic of the *Denver Times* in 1898. He worked for the *Chicago Tribune* from 1907 to 1908, the *New York Evening News* from 1911 to 1922, and the *New York Daily News* from 1922 until his retirement in 1943. He contributed considerably to theater scholarship with his editing of the "Best Plays" series from 1899 through 1945.

Critic and scholar Edward Wagenknecht once commented to me that Burns Mantle's problem was that he could not understand the difference between a play and a film. I am not sure that I necessarily agree and that it is all that important. A good critic is a good critic, and Burns Mantle certainly was that. He continued in the same sophisticated and intelligent style of his predecessor but for a relatively brief period, filing his last reviews in *Photoplay* in October 1921.

Meanwhile, James R. Quirk had adopted the title of publisher of *Photoplay* with the March 1919 issue, and with the January 1920 issue his name appeared on the masthead of the contents page as editor. The golden age of *Photoplay* had begun. It was an era in which Quirk exercised considerable power, using his monthly editorials, which at times bordered on the pretentious, to chastise the industry when necessary, fight censorship, urge the public to patronize what he determined to be "good" motion pictures, and praise or denigrate the leading figures in the industry. Much as Arthur Ungar and W. R. "Billy" Wilkinson, the founding editors (and in the latter's case also the publisher) of the trade papers *Daily Variety* and *The Hollywood Reporter*, became the dominant moral personalities within the industry in the 1930s and later, so did James R. Quirk hold a similar position both within the industry and, more importantly, among America's moviegoers. He was a social commentator on the Hollywood scene, which he primarily viewed at a distance from his New York editorial office, to where *Photoplay* had moved shortly after World War I. (The magazine continued to be printed out of Chicago.) Quirk's commentary proved that the fan magazines were not conservative in attitude. At the same time, there was nothing reactionary in what he wrote. Rather, Quirk was that rare breed, a true independent.

In the 1920s, the editorial page was headed "Speaking of Pictures" and was generally more than one page in length, often touching upon a variety of subjects. In the late 1920s, the editorial column became "Close-Ups and Long-Shots," with the hyphens disappearing without explanation in the 1930s. One might well argue that in his way, Quirk was as important within the film industry as was Will Hays with the 1922 formation of the Motion Picture Producers and Distributors of America (MPPDA) and the later enforcement of the Production Code. Both men loved Hollywood, and both sought to encourage it to adopt a strong moral and ethical code.

Quirk responded to Hays' appointment as head of the MPPDA with "An Open Letter," in which he praised the former postmaster general: "The time has come to act, and I believe that you are capable of organizing the many factors of influence in America—producers, actors, directors, exhibitors, press and public—to join hands and work with you for a new ideal in motion pictures."[4]

In 1949, Hays said of Quirk, "He was an independent force, full of Celtic idealism, and he truckled to no one, no matter how important, but he was always on the side of the true, the good, and the beautiful, and his instincts were deeply affirmative and unfailingly courageous. Jim Quirk loved the film medium and wanted to see it put its best foot forward. . . . He tried to protect Hollywood and raise its sights, not exploit the weaknesses of its personalities as did other journalists."[5]

Quirk and Hays did not always see eye to eye. In September 1926, Quirk was outraged when Hays announced that the showing of alcohol on screen was disrespectful of the prohibition laws and should be outlawed. "The prohibition law is the law of the land," fumed Quirk. "Yet our newspapers, our novels and our magazines discuss it with impunity."

Hays job was not only to clean up the film industry, but also fight against the threat of federal censorship, and *Photoplay* boasted a similar viewpoint. In March 1921, Quirk compared the reform movement on a state and federal level with the Puritanism in England that led to the founding of America. Reform might lead to censorship. And, "After any reign of fanaticism in

America—quickly after—would come a social revolution approximating, for the time at least, Anarchy and Bolshevism." To Quirk, writing in May 1918, "Censorship boards, in the main, are composed of short-haired women and long-haired men—sterile types. . . . Away with these censors, these 'Don't' men. The world needs elbow room for the creators."

When local censorship boards advocated an end to film screenings on Sundays, Quirk asked that they consider "The Lonely Girl," sent to the city to find work. "It may be idle to speculate on the number of girls that blessed refuge, the photoplay, has saved from actual harm," he wrote in August 1919.

In April 1922, Quirk argued that the screen must grow up and not present a view of life distorted to fit the childish mind: "*Photoplay* believes the morals of the young should be guarded. But censorship or suppression is not the right road." Quirk saw the motion picture as art, but not the art of the modernists: "The moving picture art is not the art of the cubist, the futurist, the synchromist, the vorticist or any other what-d'ye-call-it-ist," he wrote in April 1918. "It does not base its reputation upon obscurity of meaning. It is an art which uses simple language and direct statement like the old masters of painting, like Mozart and Haydn, like Michael Angelo [*sic*]. It is an art of the people, for the people."

Quirk returned to his theme in June 1918, arguing that the motion picture was the fifth estate, "because the vast, mute, unlettered masses, demanding a voice, found it in the Moving Picture—a silent voice, speaking the language of common men."[6] Maintaining again that the motion picture was essentially an art of the people, Quirk wrote in March 1920, "To paraphrase the immortal summary of Abraham Lincoln, the Motion Picture has come to us that art of the people, by the people, for the people shall not perish from the earth."

While Quirk was always loyal to and defensive of the film industry, he could also be caustic. In February 1929, he published a photograph of MGM studio head Louis B. Mayer and arrogant film director Cecil B. DeMille. The caption quite brilliantly captured the character of these two individuals, surrounded by their yes men: "Cecil B. DeMille goes to work for Louis B. Mayer. 'Yes, Mr. DeMille.' 'Yes, Mr. Mayer.'"

Quirk was opposed to the entire notion of sound films. In May 1921, he commented that "The 'talking picture' will be made practical, but it will never supersede the motion picture without sound. It will lack the subtlety and suggestion of vision—that vision which, deprived of voice to ears of flesh, intones undisturbed the symphonies of the soul." In March 1924, he joked, "Talking pictures are perfected, says Lee De Forest, the inventor. So is castor oil." However, by August 1928, Quirk had to admit that "they will change the map of the entire motion picture business within two years."

When Henry Ford denounced the film industry as something "run and degraded by the Jews," there was an immediate response from *Photoplay*, with a special editorial in June 1921, which, unfortunately, contains some anti-Semitism of its own:

Now *Photoplay Magazine* holds no family brief for Israel. It wishes to publicly resent Mr. Ford's accusation because it is an insult to contemporary intelligence, for any form of condemnation which denounces a whole people is contemptible, archaic, and a menace to civilization. . . .

The business end of the pictures is by no means exclusively Hebraic—but, there are in it many Jews; and the Jew from time immemorial has been given to trade and barter and finance. . . .

The Jew, racially, is not adept as a creative artist. His record as an interpreter is much better, but his record as a patron of the arts is best of all. Dramatically and musically, the Jew has been the man behind the artist—frequently to his own profit, but sometimes quite the reverse—for more than a hundred years.

Photoplay was not alone in its repudiation of the opinions of Henry Ford. A small, and obscure, little magazine titled *Film Truth* published an editorial in its April 1921 issue titled "Must Henry Ford Be an Ass?—Always." It read in part, "*Film Truth* is not anti-Jewish, or pro-Jewish. In fact there is not a member of that race connected with the publication. But in this case it is anti-Ford, and that means it is for Justice, Right and decent speaking and thinking."

Some legendary filmmakers were praised, while others were ridiculed. Reviewing Erich von Stroheim's *Foolish Wives* in March 1922, Quirk described it as "an insult to every American . . . an insult to American ideals and womanhood." In January 1925, he admitted that he had misjudged the director. Yes, he was an egotist, but Quirk had high hopes for *Greed*: "Rex Ingram, in whose judgment I place confidence, tells me it is the greatest translation of life to the screen ever produced." A month later, Quirk announced after seeing *Greed* that he was never again going to be influenced by Irish blarney, as represented by Ingram. However, he had to admit that von Stroheim "is an entertaining little cuss, . . . and if he could get rid of that little mental twist that inspires him to show dead cats instead of morning glories opening to the sun, there wouldn't be a director who could surpass him."

In that same editorial, Quirk reported on the fulsome praise lavished by Charlie Chaplin, Mary Pickford, and Douglas Fairbanks on Josef von Sternberg's first film, *The Salvation Hunters*. In October 1925, Quirk told his readers that Chaplin had admitted that his recommendation was "just a little joke." Now that Quirk had seen von Sternberg's next film, *The Exquisite Sinner*, Quirk was glad to hear it: "it was one of the dullest things ever made."

Quirk's attitude toward foreign-made films was mixed. He liked *The Cabinet of Dr. Caligari*, *The Last Laugh*, *Variety*, and *Metropolis*, but he did not care for *Potemkin* and the little art theaters throughout the United States at which such films were screened. In November 1927, he wrote, "One of the 'gems' shown at a little art theater in New York was called *Streets of Sorrow*. If *Streets of Sorrow* is art then the Gypsy's Fortune Telling Dream Book is a masterpiece of literature." *The End of St. Petersburg* was dismissed in August 1928 as "just a mess of symbolic rot and disconnected shots."

With Burns Mantle's departure from "The Shadow Stage," Quirk became not only *Photoplay*'s editor and publisher but also its film critic (although some of the brief reviews of lesser films were written by others, as Quirk freely admitted). From February through August 1923, Frederick James Smith hosted "The Shadow Stage," but for much of the 1920s the film reviews represented Quirk's tastes and opinions as much as did the editorial columns. In a May 1924 editorial, Quirk responded to questions as to the approach he took when reviewing films for *Photoplay*: "The aim of this magazine is to 'report' pictures to our readers from the viewpoint of the average intelligent patron of motion picture theaters. The first thing the average man or woman wants to know about a picture is whether or not it is worth seeing. Is it good entertainment? Is it a good story? Is it well told (well cast, produced and directed)? Is it clean? Is it a picture the children should not see? That's what *Photoplay* tries to tell you."

In February 1925, Quirk explained that a complement of six writers divided the viewing of the new films among themselves. If there was doubt as to the merit of a specific title, then all six writers might view the same film. "It is our opinion," he wrote, "that anybody who tries to get a dollar and a half for a fifty-cent picture is trying to pick your pocket, and we don't intend to stand by and see anybody do that when you are friendly enough to go up to a newsstand and pay twenty-five cents for this publication." (In the mid 1930s, the reviewing staff was limited to editor Ruth Waterbury and one colleague.)

On the whole, Quirk was a fair critic whose opinions have stood the test of time. In a typical column, for August 1922, he praised two "specialist" productions, Robert Flaherty's *Nanook of the North* and Alla Nazimova's *Salome*. Of the former's director, Quirk wrote, "He has given to civilization a gift and a lesson—and every family should profit by them." *Salome* was "bizarre stuff." Of course, Quirk was not always prescient in terms of spotting potential classics of the cinema. In December 1927, he described *Sunrise* as "The sort of picture that fools high-brows into hollering 'Art!' Swell trick photography and fancy effects, but, boiled down, no story interest and only stilted, mannered acting." This despite praising William Fox in a September 1926 editorial for bringing *Sunrise* director F. W. Murnau to Hollywood, and writing of him, "I have spent many hours with Murnau. He is human. He knows life. He is a master technician. He is an artist with a rare sense of humor and a refreshing lack of that arrogance and conceit that has reduced many of our promising young directors to mediocrity in a business that requires as much artistic co-operation as the creation of a great cathedral." In Quirk's defense, one should note that his was not the only negative response to *Sunrise*. The European journal, *Close Up*, which was obsessed with the art of the film, was equally scornful of Murnau's work, saving much of its ridicule for leading lady Janet Gaynor.

In May 1931, Quirk paid tribute to Murnau at his death, writing, "Farewell, Murnau. Well done. Your friends, the art, and the motion picture public of the world will miss you. A gallant soldier in war, an outstanding genius in peace, Germany should be proud of you as a warrior, as an artist, and as the noble gentleman that you were."

The one player for whom Quirk had a deep-rooted and indefensible dislike was Lillian Gish. Louise Brooks documented *Photoplay*'s denigration of the actress, linking it to the large salary she was being paid by MGM and which the studio regretted having agreed to.[7] Certainly, Quirk and MGM studio boss Louis B. Mayer were friendly. Perhaps Quirk was persuaded to attack Gish in an attempt to dissuade audiences from attending her films and thus persuading the actress to cancel her contract. It is all supposition, and it may simply be that Quirk, as he had written, was not impressed by Gish's performances once she had left her mentor D. W. Griffith, and her later work did seem mechanical.

"She has always played the frail girl caught in the cruel maelstrom of life, battling helplessly for her honor or her happiness," wrote Quirk in a September 1925 editorial. "While she may not be the intellectual personality some writers are so fond of seeing in her because of her serenity, she has a soundness of business judgment which has enabled her to capitalize her screen personality with one of the largest salaries." He concluded, in reference to Gish's often being compared to a great Italian actress who had died the previous year, "Wouldn't it be interesting to see Lillian Gish play a Barbara La Marr role, for Duse was a versatile actress, if there ever was one?"

In March 1926, Quirk took the unusual step of contributing an article under his own name to the magazine in which he described Gish as "The Enigma of the Screen."[8] "The most baffling question of the hour is, What of her future?" Again, he compared Gish to Duse and found her wanting. Quirk used the article to praise Gish's costar in *La Boheme*, John Gilbert, claiming that the actress hurt her leading man's performance with her insistence on over-rehearsal. It was not the first time *Photoplay* had praised John Gilbert. In an editorial in October 1925, discussing *The Merry Widow*, Quirk wrote, "Not since Rudolph Valentino flashed across the screen in *The Four Horsemen* has there been such a performance of a glowingly romantic role as Gilbert gives in *The Merry Widow*."[9]

In March 1930, it was Quirk who broke the news that John Gilbert's voice was not adequate to the talkies' demands, although conspiracy theorists might argue that he was again doing the bidding of Louis B. Mayer, who wished to get out of MGM's contract with the star. Quirk quoted reporter Ruth Waterbury, who had just returned from a day in the research laboratories of the American Telephone and Telegraph Company. "I asked those scientific fellows the direct question: 'Is there anything than can possibly be done to adapt John's voice to the talking picture?' and they have me a very definite 'No.' That is just one of the weird little tricks of fate the talking pictures have played the Hollywood world. The camera was very kind to Jack. The microphone played him false. Jack's natural voice is extremely pleasant. To the ear it is well pitched and as fascinating as a Rudy Vallee song. But it just will not reproduce in its natural quality."

If there is one thing in the 1920s that stands out above all others in terms of Quirk's legacy, it is his sponsorship of the series on the history of the motion picture, "The Romantic History of the Motion Picture," by Terry Ramsaye,

Terry Ramsaye (at left) with John W. Hicks, Jr., Paramount vice president in charge of foreign production, and John C. Graham, managing director of Paramount Film Service Ltd., London, at Adolph Zukor's silver jubilee dinner.

published in thirty-six parts from 1922 through 1925. In book form as *A Million and One Nights* (1926), this is the first classic history of the motion picture and one that has never ceased to serve as a guide. The original work was commissioned by Quirk in 1920 as a twelve-part series, and the editor-publisher stood by Ramsaye as the series grew in strength and size. As Ramsaye recalled,

> It was of a piece with Jim's outlook on the Industry to believe that a sincere telling of its whole story, shorn of myth and the chatter of falsehood, which was deeply coloring all its traditions, would be a contribution to that Industry.
>
> There is a tribute to Jim's professional integrity in the fact that he was willing to wait through almost two years of research before a chapter went into type, and that he most generously supported a continuously widening field of inquiry, here and abroad, for three years . . .
>
> About the time I sent him Chapter 18, going into the second year, I was fishing a delectable pool in the Canadian wilds where Lake Nipigon starts down the wilderness stairs to Lake Superior. A courier du bois, a glum Cree Indian, paddled forty miles upriver from the railway to deliver me a telegram from New York: "What year in your story will we get to Mary Pickford? Jim."[10]

A reporter with the *Chicago Tribune*, Ramsaye had first contributed to *Photoplay* in April 1915, under the name of Terrence Eugene Ramsaye. The piece was an interview with Ida Damon, the winner of the $10,000 prize offered for solution of the Thanhouser serial, *The Million-Dollar Mystery*. It is curious just how much Thanhouser appears to dominate the content of the early years of *Photoplay*. Ramsaye also contributed a short story, "Another of *Photoplay*'s

Fiction Contest Stories," in May 1921. I suppose there is no reason why a journalist should not be permitted to enter a short-story contest, but it does seem a little odd. Aside from "The Romantic History of the Motion Picture" serial, Ramsaye further contributed a series on visits to the homes of famous film magnates, beginning with Paramount's Adolph Zukor in May 1927 and concluding with Bank of America's A. H. Giannini in February 1928.

Of course, there was much more to *Photoplay* in the 1920s than James Quirk, Terry Ramsaye, and "The Shadow Stage." One important innovation was the introduction of the *Photoplay* Medal of Honor (later known as the *Photoplay* Gold Medal), presented annually to the producer of the best film of the year. The readers of the magazine were invited to determine the winner by a mail-in voting process, and the first honoree in 1920 was *Humoresque*, produced by William Randolph Hearst, directed by Frank Borzage, and based on the short story by Fannie Hurst. Executed by Tiffany and supposedly of solid gold, the medal was 2½ inches in diameter and weighed 123½ pennyweight.[11] To what extent the readership decided on the winning film is open to question. The readers pretty much followed Quirk's opinion—for example, he editorialized in May 1923 that *The Covered Wagon* would be "the best American film drama in years," and it was the *Photoplay* Gold Medal winner—but, then, presumably Quirk knew what his readers wanted and they knew to trust him.

Several major so-called autobiographies were published in *Photoplay* in the 1920s, most notably those of Tom Mix, Pola Negri, and Rudolph Valentino. Elinor Glyn provided a "photobiography" of Gloria Swanson in May 1921, and earlier that same year, Norma Talmadge had contributed a couple of pieces under the guise of the magazine's "fashion editor."[12] There were basically three major contributors to *Photoplay* of the 1920s, Adela Rogers St. Johns, Carolyn Van Wyck, and Herbert Howe, who not only wrote celebrity articles but contributed the "Close-Ups and Long-Shots" column beginning in February 1923, before it became the title of Quirk's editorial page. In the late 1920s, Katherine Albert became a regular contributor, often with more than one article per issue.

Herbert Howe wrote a series of strange fictional pieces for *Photoplay* in the mid through late 1920s. One of the most curious, from July 1925, presented "Inside Life Stories of *Photoplay* Staff Writers," with biographies of Quirk, Agnes Smith, and Harriette Underhill. It is difficult to believe the writing ever passed for humorous in that the essays are plain silly. Quirk steals a Gideon Bible, sells it, and starts *Photoplay*. Agnes Smith is married numerous times and pledged to several religions, and because of her record is offered the position of office caretaker at *Photoplay*. Harriette Underhill is deceived by a city fellow visiting her father's farm and her wrong is righted when Quirk tells her she may write for *Photoplay*. The idea was to present lives that are even more discolored than the colorful lives of the movie folks—but it just didn't work.

On November 15, 1926, James R. Quirk married his second wife, May Allison, in Santa Barbara. Witnesses at the ceremony were Adela Rogers St. Johns and Ivan St. Johns. Allison was a Hollywood actress whose career was pretty

The February 1923 issue of *Photoplay*. Courtesy of Sue Slutzky.

much over by this time; she was best known for a series of films in which she had appeared opposite Harold Lockwood in 1915 through 1917 for American-Mutual and Metro. The couple took up residence in New York at the Buckingham Hotel, very close to *Photoplay*'s offices at 221 West 57th Street. May Allison was certainly familiar to *Photoplay* readers: she had been featured in the magazine some thirteen times since January 1916 and would continue to appear, a further three times, in the pages of *Photoplay* through September 1927. Interestingly, Quirk wrote of "The Chief Essentials of Beauty" in March 1922, but made no mention of May Allison or of any other actress.

Ruth Waterbury made her debut as a writer at *Photoplay* with a December 1922 piece on the breakup of the marriage between Rudolph Valentino and Natacha Rambova, and she became a staff writer later in the 1920s. She recalled the Quirk-Allison marriage: "She was very pretty. I don't think she had anything else but prettiness. He was married and he had the ugliest children who were no-neck monsters. He wasn't a physically attractive man. He was short and fat, and a very fat face. I think that's what drove him to May Allison."[13] In order to marry Allison, Quirk, a Catholic, had divorced his first wife, Betty North. "It became a war between the two ladies—the three ladies including the church. I think he never recovered from it. I think his guilt was so deep," commented Waterbury.

There was an addition to the masthead of *Photoplay* in 1930, with Leonard Hall's named as managing editor. His appointment may well have been necessary in view of Quirk's hectic schedule. In 1926, he had acquired a controlling interest in the magazine.[14] Aside from *Photoplay*, as president of the Magus Publishing Company, Quirk had acquired *McClure's* magazine from William Randolph Hearst in 1928, merging it with *Smart Set* the following year. *Smart Set* ceased publication in 1933, by which time it was back under Hearst's banner.

In April 1931, Cal York's column appeared as usual. Buried deep within it, so deep in fact that one wonders how many readers actually bothered to browse that far, appeared the following item:

> You haven't forgotten yet, have you, how Hollywood used to thrill over the story of Ricardo Cortez and Alma Rubens?
>
> And the surprise that came when Alma, after her cure [from drug addiction], divorced Ricardo.
>
> Now, here's another facet of the picture. While Alma lay on her deathbed a few weeks ago, Ricardo was working at First National studios, utterly unaware of how dangerously ill his one-time wife was. And not until he read in the papers, the following day, that she had died, did he have an inkling that she had been ill.
>
> After it is all over and all is said and done, perhaps there was nothing in Alma Rubens' life as pitiful and tragic as her funeral. I had known Alma for many years and I attended her funeral because I felt I wanted to pay my respects. I quickly turned away.
>
> Her mother, in order to give everybody a chance, had put a notice in the paper that the funeral would be public, at the little church in Forest Lawn. And while there were at least a thousand sightseers on the outside stretching at the ropes, they came only to see the stars that might be present at the funeral and they did not want to come inside the church, nor did they come. They were looking only for picture people and not interested at all in Alma Rubens. There were no picture people there.
>
> On the inside of the church there was a mere handful of thirty-five people, and the nearest approach to a picture person was Ricardo Cortez' brother.
>
> To me it was one of the most pathetic things I ever heard of.

May Allison.

On the surface, the piece is quite innocuous, troubling perhaps only because Cal York writes of being at the funeral and then ends by claiming to have heard of it. One individual who was not impressed by the gossip item was Alma Rubens' mother, Theresa, who filed a million dollar lawsuit against *Photoplay* for its "cruel and vicious description of conditions at the funeral," at which, as it turned out, stars were present, including Ricardo Cortez himself.

James R. Quirk traveled to Los Angeles, arriving on June 1, 1932, to fight the lawsuit in court. On the witness stand on June 21, he admitted that he wrote the item in question, and three days later he insisted he had no ill feeling against Mrs. Rubens. A few days later, Quirk became ill, and he died on August 1, 1932, at Hollywood Hospital of pneumonia, complicated with a heart disease. His funeral service was arranged by Will Hays.

Quirk left his share in *Photoplay* not to May Allison, but to his first wife and his daughters. As his successor at *Photoplay*, they and Quirk's fellow publishers chose Kathryn Dougherty (Kay-Dee as she was known), whose involvement with the periodical dated back to 1914 not in any editorial capacity but as treasurer of the company—in reality little more than a glorified bookkeeper. Dougherty's first duty at *Photoplay* was to write an obituary of Quirk, which appeared in the October 1932 issue (her first byline in the magazine), noting that "the spirit that made him so great an editor and publisher still marches on with his staff."[15]

There were many other remarks that Dougherty might have made about James R. Quirk, not the least of which being that she was his mistress. The relationship between the two probably went back to the 1910s, but, as Ruth Waterbury recalled, Quirk and Dougherty only met when he was on his way from New York, where he was based, to Los Angeles. "I think he wished he'd never begun it."

Quirk very much followed in the tradition of Eugene V. Brewster as far as his relationships with women were concerned. Ruth Waterbury recalled, "He and Ray Long, who was editor of *Cosmopolitan* got a pair of girls and went out with them.[16] One night one of them wanted the blonde and the next night he wanted the brunette. Ray Long was married, of course, and had children, but he also had a girl, Mildred Temple. So Jim said to me one day, 'You'd better order a shot of Mildred Temple. I'll run it in the next issue.' So I got the shot of Mildred Temple, who was a very pretty woman. So, when we were going over the proofs of the next issue, he said, 'Who the Hell's that?' Mildred Temple. A head shot. He said, 'Silly thing, you've got the wrong end of her photographed.' That was Mr. Q., and you had to be prepared for a lot of things like that."

Both Waterbury and Adele Whitely Fletcher had fond memories of Quirk. To Fletcher, he was "a real, rip-snorting, Irish whiskey–drinking Irishman. You could always tell if he liked the ideas that you came in with, because if he did, he'd bring this bottle out of the lower drawer and you could have a snort with him before you left."[17] Ruth Waterbury remembered:

> He was very interested in film. He was a very bright man, but he would do impossible things. One day, he came in and said, "What are you doing?" I said, "I'm thinking." He said, "Think at home." I got married at the fast age of eighteen, and, of course, I was fixated about my career. My poor, young husband. Jim would call in the middle of the night and say, "Snip—he called me Snip—if we did this on page thirty-four instead of page thirty-five. . . . Would you mind coming up here?" Your husband doesn't know why you're piling out at three o'clock in the morning to do something that he forgot about all that while.
>
> I invented, I truly invented the phrase "Going Hollywood" [apparently first used in the February 1929 issue of *Photoplay*]. This was entirely Jim's fault. He had actually invented the phrase, and he had sent the covers through to Chicago with this cover line. And he didn't know what it meant. He got me up at four o'clock in the morning, and said, "I don't know what I meant. It sounds good, but what the Hell does it mean?" On the way [to the office] I saw the morning papers on the newsstand, and there was a headline, "Dolores Del Rio and Husband Separate." I said, "That's what it is." I wrote the story, and we phoned it to

Chicago at six o'clock in the morning. This was the way Jim was. You had to be able to adjust to that crazy temperament.

He was a very amazing man. He was a very colorful man. He was a kind man, witty, and so sophisticated. But he was forever firing people. He did have an impulse to fire people. I can't tell you the number of days I would come into that office in the morning [and] everyone would have been let go: the telephone girls, the file clerks, everybody. And there we'd be, and there'd be nobody to answer the phones, there'd be nobody to do anything. And he'd say, "Snip, I didn't mean to do it." And I'd say, "Jim, there you've done it again. Now will you quit!"

Ruth Waterbury had already departed *Photoplay*, to edit *Silver Screen*, prior to Quirk's death. With Dougherty's appointment, there were further departures. Katherine Albert resigned, along with May Allison's sister, Maude Latham, who had been *Photoplay*'s western editor. There must have been an eventual rapprochement between Dougherty and Allison, because the latter embarked on a new career in 1933, writing a series of celebrity interviews for *Photoplay* under the name of May Allison Quirk. The first was with Ramon Novarro (April), followed by Alice White (May), "Queer Premonitions of the Stars" (June), Miriam Hopkins (July), and Ernst Lubistch (August). Later, May Allison remarried, for a fourth time, to Cleveland industrialist Carl Norton Osborne and retired from the scene. She died in Ohio on March 27, 1989, at the age of ninety-eight.

The reality was that *Photoplay* changed little, if at all, with Quirk's death. The articles were pretty much of the same quality, with some new writers, including Ruth Biery, Sara Hamilton, Mildred Mastin, James Fiddler, Elza Schallert, and Kirtley Baskette, appearing in the 1930s. Carolin Van Wyck was *Photoplay*'s beauty editor, with her monthly "The Hollywood Beauty Shop" column. The editorials were now written by Dougherty, twenty-one in all, and there was a change of format in April 1934, with the one-page "Close-Ups and Long-Shots" containing fewer, but longer, paragraphs and Kathryn Dougherty's photograph appearing for the first time at the head of the column. While she was as scrupulous as Quirk in acknowledging the passing of some of the great names of the cinema's past, including Lew Cody, Marie Dressler, and Lou Tellegen, she could also be more than a little insensitive, as in October 1935, when she wrote in regard to the Italian invasion of Ethiopia: "I think the Ethiopians in Addis Ababa must have learned something about Western civilization from motion pictures. . . . Undoubtedly many of Ethiopia's manpower have seen the military maneuvers of the Italian or other armies in the newsreels, and have watched bombing planes in action. . . . To that extent, at least, the terrors of modern battle are familiar to the Ethiopians."

In February 1935, Dougherty was identified as publisher of *Photoplay* and Ray Long named as editor. Dougherty continued to write the "Close-Ups and Long-Shots" columns, and in June she was renamed editor. She was back as publisher in August 1935, with Ruth Waterbury as editor, but Dougherty continued with the editorial columns until December 1935, when she was completely gone from the magazine, and Waterbury was writing the columns as part of her editorial duties.

Ruth Waterbury's *Silver Screen* was a ten-cent fan magazine, while *Photoplay* cost twenty-five cents. In an effort to fight the competition, *Photoplay's* publisher decided to introduce its own ten-cent periodical, *Shadoplay*. *The Hollywood Reporter* (January 11, 1933) announced the new magazine, explaining that *Photoplay* "hopes to fight the cheap books with a better cheap one." Frederick James Smith was identified as editor, but when the first issue, dated March 1933, reached the newsstands, his name was absent, with only Kathryn Dougherty receiving credit as publisher, William T. Walsh identified as managing editor, and Ivan St. Johns as Pacific Coast editor.

While *Shadoplay* was printed on good paper and has much the same look as *Photoplay*, it was far more lightweight. "*Shadoplay's* Guide to Pictures" featured only one short paragraph on each new film, consisting generally of a one-sentence synopsis and a one-sentence praise of the stars. The writers were relatively obscure, and there was much innocuous gossip along the lines of "Hot news from Boston. Six hundred people refused to vacate the Egyptian Theater during a fire, because Mae West was on the screen. Just didn't notice the slight additional heat, eh?"[18] There were a large number of fashion and grooming pieces, usually by Diane Whitney, and promotion of an unusual tie-in between *Photoplay* and a company selling Hollywood Fashions, "faithful reproductions" of Hollywood hats and female clothing. A full listing of stores offering these fashions appeared in the June 1934 issue.

There was an obvious implication that *Shadoplay* carried the articles that *Photoplay* rejected, and certainly it lacked name writers. On March 7, 1934, *The Hollywood Reporter* complained that it was "the 'spillover' magazine for *Photoplay*, for it comes out of the little end of the horn with annoying regularity."

Ruth Waterbury's appointment as editor in August 1935 coincided with the acquisition of *Photoplay* by Macfadden Publications. She was to continue with the magazine through December 1940, and, to a large extent, she kept alive the Quirk tradition of quality articles, reviews, and editorials. To suggest that the Quirk era ended with Dougherty's departure is wrong; if anything, Ruth Waterbury's arrival denoted a return to Quirk's standards. Waterbury had been taught by Quirk, and she knew what she was doing.

As she recalled in 1972, "I went into journalism because of my father. I was an only child, and I was the only child of very mature parents. My mother was punishing me for something, and my father said, 'Why are you punishing her. She is a natural-born liar, and when she grows up, she'll have to be a writer.'" Like Adela Rogers St. Johns, Waterbury's father was a lawyer, but Waterbury saw little similarity between herself and *Photoplay's* best-known contributor, pointing out that she was definitely an Easterner, unlike the Western-born Rogers.

Waterbury would never pretend to be a great writer, noting, "I have some sort of trashy appeal in my writing. I don't know what it is. I'm not a stylish

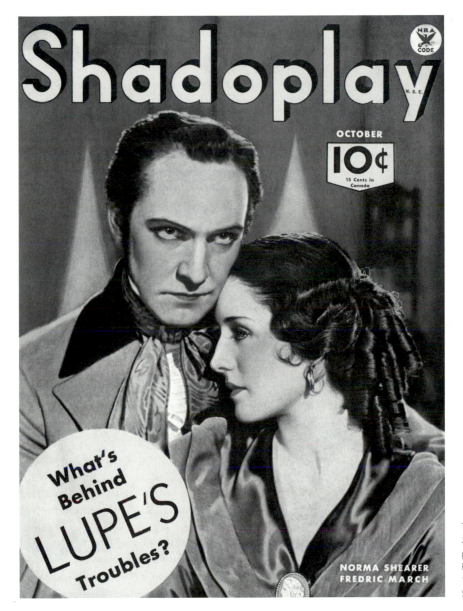

The October 1934 issue of *Shadoplay*, with the cover promoting Norma Shearer and Fredric March in *Barretts of Wimpole Street*. Courtesy of Sue Slutzky.

writer, but I have a public. I like to write. I say the people who enjoy singing, who enjoy writing, are not very good at it, and I guess that is my estimate of me. I'm very delighted when I get an assignment that's interesting. I guess I'm just a half-baked Pollyanna, but that's the way it is."[19]

At *Photoplay*, Waterbury had been able to select her own assignments, but "you had to be very adjustable with Jim." Her mentoring by Quirk was put to good use when she created *Silver Screen* in 1930, and when she returned, as editor, to *Photoplay*. As scholar Lori Landay noted, Waterbury had a watchful eye, viewing the motion picture as both a fan magazine writer and a woman.

Ruth Waterbury with Rosalind Russell on the set of *The Women* (1939).

In July 1938, she pointed out to the female stars of the screwball comedies that the tactics they used to attract men were not easily transferable to the real world.[20]

In the 1950s, Ruth Waterbury went on to work as a roving reporter for Louella Parsons, of whom she always spoke fondly. She was president of the Hollywood Women's Press Club from 1940 to 1944 and in 1948. On October 21, 1941, she introduced for the first time the Golden Apple Awards, presented to the most cooperative actor or actress in motion pictures. The first winners were Bob Hope and Bette Davis and the first losers were Fred Astaire and Ginger Rogers. Waterbury wrote two books, *Elizabeth Taylor* (1964; reprinted in 1982 as *Elizabeth Taylor: Her Life, Her Loves, Her Future*) and *Richard Burton* (1965). She died in Los Angeles on March 23, 1982, at either eighty-five or eighty-nine years of age.

In January 1941, *Photoplay* merged with *Movie Mirror*, another Macfadden publication. It adopted the latter's volume and issue numbering system, and reduced its cover price from twenty-five cents to *Movie Mirror*'s ten cents. An editorial in the first combined issue announced the addition of a new color portrait section, utilizing Kodachrome photographs from the studios, along with specially photographed portraits, both candid and formal, by Hyman Fink, who was under exclusive contract.

The signing of Fink and the use of Kodachrome photographs reflected a change not only in the illustrative content of fan magazines such as *Movie Mirror*, but also in terms of their cover art. From the earliest days of the fan magazines, the covers had always been in color or at least tinted in some fashion. A black-and-white cover was unthinkable if for no other reason than it would not sell the magazine to the casual reader at the newsstand. Within a relatively short period of time—by the late 1910s and early 1920s—the fan magazines had developed an impressive use of cover art. The illustrations were perfect reflections of the stars depicted, bringing out all the high points and none of the lows of an actress's features. Among the major illustrators represented were Henry Clive and Penrhyn Stanlaws. Obviously, the stars did not sit for these paintings, but rather the artists worked from studio portrait photographs. In time, and particularly with the introduction of Kodachrome, it must have become obvious to the fan magazines that rather than pay illustrators to copy photographs, it was easier and cheaper simply to use the photographs themselves.

George Hurrell is perhaps the most celebrated of all glamour photographers from Hollywood's golden age. Generally associated with black-and-white images, he was at one time a frequent contributor of "natural color photographs" for *Photoplay* covers. In March and April 1936, he had provided photographs of Shirley Temple and Joan Crawford to the magazine, and in the second half of 1937 Hurrell was preeminent with natural color photographs of Shirley Temple (June), Jeanette MacDonald (July), Claudette Colbert (August), Myrna Loy (September), Joan Crawford (October), and Loretta Young (December).

Immediately prior to Hurrell's takeover of *Photoplay* covers, Ruth Waterbury had achieved something of a coup in terms of signing of an illustrator. "Did you notice the new type of cover *Photoplay* has this month?" she asked readers in her July 1936 editorial. "I'm very proud of having secured so distinguished an artist as James Montgomery Flagg to draw these sketches from life for us monthly." Claudette Colbert was the first, followed by Bette Davis (August), Katharine Hepburn (September), Norma Shearer (October), Carole Lombard (November), Shirley Temple (December), and finally Ginger Rogers (January 1937).

If there was a lowering in standards at *Photoplay* following its merger with *Movie Mirror*, it was not immediately apparent. Ruth Waterbury was still writing the "Close Ups and Long Shots" column and contributed a piece on Jane Withers, and there were articles by such familiar names as Adele Whitely Fletcher, Sara Hamilton, and Hedda Hopper. Ernest V. Heyn (who had taken over as executive editor of *Movie Mirror* from Ruth Waterbury a couple of years earlier) was the new editor, succeeded by Helen Gilmore (who had been associate editor) from 1942 through 1947, and who came up with the novel idea of appointing Biddy Banton, wife of the legendary designer Travis Banton, as the "West Coast Associate of *Photoplay* Fashions." In January 1948, Adele Whitely Fletcher was named editor. She stayed with *Photoplay* until August 1952.

One of the most important things that Fletcher did, and of which she was justly proud, was the revival of the *Photoplay* Gold Medal Awards. In 1945, "They were brought out of hiding on a very grand scale," she told me.[21] Dr.

The July 1935 issue of *Movie Mirror*.

George Gallup of the American Institute of Public Opinion and its subsidiary, Audience Research, Inc., was hired to poll the public thrice annually. *Going My Way* was named America's favorite film of 1944.[22] As of the following year, awards were also given for the most popular actor and actress. From a mere banquet, the awards expanded to a segment on the *Tonight Show* with Johnny Carson in 1964, and in 1977 they became a ninety-minute television special on NBC, hosted by Angie Dickinson and Elliott Gould.

"I think when I edited *Photoplay*," commented Adele Whitely Fletcher, "it was a young woman's magazine. We had fashion. We had Claudette Colbert doing an advice column. We had personalities. We had millions in circulation."[23]

Following Adele Whitley Fletcher, there were nine further editors, as *Photoplay* gradually lost its prominence and the last vestiges of a quality publication. Between 1978 and 1979, it lost half a million readers. By early 1980, it had a circulation of only 300,000, of which one-third was in newsstand sales. At the end of its life, West Coast editor Richard Cuskelly was also writing the Cal York column.

On April 15, 1980, *Photoplay* published its last issue, its pink and scarlet cover featuring not the stars of the motion picture that it had helped to make famous, but Charlene Tilton and Victoria Principal from the television nighttime soap opera *Dallas*. Peter J. Callahan, president of Macfadden, which he had acquired five years earlier, said that the decision to cease publication was made "very reluctantly. . . . We were using our resources to finance losses in *Photoplay* and from an economic point of view, it didn't make sense." The fulltime *Photoplay* staff of six moved over to *Us* magazine, which Callahan had purchased from the *New York Times* earlier that same month.

Very obviously, *Us* was replacing *Photoplay*, with its more general coverage of all aspects of what may be termed American popular culture. As Callahan explained, "The day of the traditional movie magazines is over. You can't compete at the back of the supermarket with the *National Inquirer* and the *Star* at the checkout counters."

Callahan did consider producing *Photoplay* on a quarterly basis as a quality periodical selling for $2.00 an issue. "I'm not going to sell it to schlock pulp publishers. The title has a lot of value. I just don't want that title, with all its history and perspective, to go that route."[24] In reality, the title was pretty much all that Callahan had, in that *Photoplay*'s back issues from the so-called "golden age" were all in the public domain. The demise of the U.S. edition of the magazine did not affect the British publication of *Photoplay*, which had started in 1952 and continued in April 1981 as *Photoplay: Movies and Video*.

The Quirk legacy continued in the field of fan magazines, with nephew Lawrence J. Quirk editing *Hollywood Screen Parade* and *Screen Stars* in the 1960s. He also put out an outspoken little journal titled *Quirk's Reviews*, beginning in August 1972, which promised and delivered "Penetrating, Independent-Spirited Critiques of Films Present and Past" and proudly carried a comment attributed to James R. Quirk: "A publication that doesn't make its readers mad has no vitality." Typed on a manual typewriter and printed in offset form, *Quirk's Reviews* certainly did that, expanding its coverage from eight to sixteen pages through the years and boasting a circulation of 1000. Quirk also presented awards to deserving individuals, including this writer, who was the recipient of the twenty-fourth such award on October 10, 1984, "for his exceptional contributions to film history and authorship."

In the early years of its existence, several other fan magazines used the name *Photoplay*, some in an obvious effort to confuse their readership as to their true identity. The best of the bunch, with reasonably sophisticated articles, was *Photo-Play Journal* (May 1916 to February 1921), edited by Delbert Essex Davenport, who also contributed articles and served as its film critic using the name of Bert Essex. Billed as "A magazine with a heart, a soul and character," *Photo-Play Journal* featured the first professional writings on cinema by scholar Edward Wagenknecht,[25] and included an advice column, "For You and Me," by stage and screen star Madame Olga Petrova, who also contributed to *Photoplay* in 1922. Others were *The Photo Drama Magazine* (first published in 1921), *Photo-Play Review* (published in 1915 out of Philadelphia), *Photo-Play World* (published in 1917–1920, also out of Philadelphia), *Photoplay Vogue* (first published in 1915), *Photoplay Weekly Mirror* ("an illustrated magazine" published in 1916–1917), and *Photoplayers Weekly* (published in 1914–1917 out of Los Angeles). *The Photo Playwright*, published from April through December 1912 on a monthly basis, was intended to provide movie fans with information as to how to become scenario writers rather than provide them with news of their favorite stars.

CHAPTER 4

THE STUDIO MOUTHPIECE

"I would read things I didn't remember anything about," insisted Paramount leading lady of the 1930s Mary Carlisle. "I never remember sitting down and giving an interview to a fan magazine. Stories were made up for publicity purposes." Carlisle's response typifies the memory of most players relative to their fan magazine coverage. And yet, it is difficult to believe, for example, that she did not recall posing for a two-page photo spread on "A Day in the Life of an Extra Girl" for the November 1932 issue of *The New Movie Magazine*.

In reality, by the late 1920s and the 1930s contract players, both stars and featured performers, were interviewed by fan magazines under the supervision of studio publicists and were subject to rigorous rules and boundaries. The fan magazines and their writers published and wrote what the studios determined they should publish and write. The fan magazines and the studios fed off each other, and both had a healthy appetite.

Most stars accepted working with fan magazines as part of their contract. When Marsha Hunt was signed as a leading lady at Paramount in 1935, it marked her screen debut:

> I had an unusual amount of fan magazine promotion, simply because I was brand new and Paramount put me so quickly to work. I had to appear in court for approval of my contract because I was still a minor, and within two weeks of that I was cast in my first movie. I remember I never had a day off but what there was an interview or a sitting in the still department, taking promotional pictures.
>
> Fan magazines were a major tool for the film industry of connecting the public with their product and personalizing the casts of the movies, getting the actors known as people, as celebrities, as glamorous, larger-than-life figures. I thought it was just part of being an actor in films, and I saw the purpose it served. They

73

were kind of "honeyed." It was all exaggerated, and we were all made to be infinitely more attractive, more romantic, prettier, handsomer, and brighter and more gifted than we were. But that was what sold tickets. They didn't have any truck with scandal. It was a very wholesome world they drew for us.

I showed Barbara Hale an article on her and her new husband, Bill Williams, titled "Pretty as a Bride" and published in the October 1946 issue of *Screen Romances*. The actress immediately acknowledged that the piece, in which she visits the office of editor Evelyn Van Horne and discusses beauty tips, was all true. Hale was keen to point out that the fan magazines generally published the truth—albeit innocuous truth about her children and her home life. "Sometimes, they put the comma in the wrong place. You said the same thing but when they printed it, there was a different meaning."[1]

In earlier years, there was certainly less control by producers, and many writers had a free hand. Diana Cary, who was child star of the 1920s "Baby Peggy," provided a fascinating firsthand account of the relationship between a player and the scribes recording her work,

> The writers came after me, not the other way 'round. Adela Rogers St. Johns . . . wrote two articles on me—both of them sheer fiction, all the birth dates and birth places wrong, my discovery story her own version, my great love for dolls, including dolls of me (which I sold but never played with!), and the rest pure make-believe. When I was three, Willis Goldbeck interviewed me for *Motion Picture Classic* (1922), "Seen But Not Heard." He may have consulted Century [her producer] as to phone number and where to find me, but I doubt if it was set up by the studio.
>
> When I was taken over by [producer] Sol Lesser, he organized a publicity blitz. The ubiquitous Gladys Hall, apparently in New York in October of 1923, interviewed me and my family there for an "in depth" story. I have also seen two or three others in the major magazines by writers who were not limited to fan magazines, but who free-lanced in other more high-brow magazines. With Lesser I suspect he contacted all of these writers himself as he was a very aggressive publicist.
>
> However, when I returned to Hollywood at thirteen in 1932, not only was I being marketed as an "ingénue" of 18, but the entire market had changed. We were advised to hire a "publicity agent," a brand new parasite. We did and she actually placed an article in seventeen of the twenty-three fan magazines then in existence. By then I believe the mags had a few reliable staff writers working their beat, and of course the front office of every major [studio] was fully geared to plant stories, not necessarily waiting for free lancers to do the leg work for them. I was handicapped by my young age—I couldn't do the nightclub circuit and be seen dancing and drinking with another "hot" young property. Throughout the 1930s I remained a merely curious artifact to be dug up occasionally by news archeologists from the rubble of Hollywood's "Stone Age," otherwise known as Silent Films.[2]

Diana Cary when she was known as "Baby Peggy."

If, as has been suggested, the fan magazines were as synthetic as the world portrayed by the movies, then the fault lay equally with the Hollywood studios that marketed their vision of the "real" world in their films and created a picture of the "real" life of the stars in the fan magazines.[3] Life, as represented by the fan magazines, was truly imitating art, as represented by the Hollywood motion pictures. The interrelationship between the movie producers and the fan magazines was obvious from the beginning. Fan magazine writers often spent their time working as studio publicists or press agents, alternating careers, with little regard for the dividing line between the one and the other.

The prominent studio head J. Stuart Blackton was cofounder of *Motion Picture Story Magazine,* and just as his company, Vitagraph, was a member of the Motion Picture Patents group of producers, so did his magazine emphasize the releases of that organization. Competitor *Photoplay* was unquestionably created initially with the backing of the nonmembers of the Motion Picture Patents group, the independents, providing publicity for their releases.

There was obviously a relationship between *Picture-Play Weekly* and the Essanay Company in that the magazine routinely featured story adaptations of the Charlie Chaplin–Essanay comedies during 1915. The completely unknown and perhaps pseudonymous writer B. Quade must have worked hard to flesh out the stories of the ten-minute Chaplin comedy shorts, with their minimal plots written by the comedian, to come up with the ten or more pages of text needed by the magazine. So successful was the Essanay/*Picture-Play* combination that the latter was able to publish, in October 1915, *The Chaplin Story Book*, selling for ten cents and containing all of the story adaptations of the Essanay comedies, along with "The Life" of the comedian.

While Frederick James Smith was critical of D. W. Griffith's work in print in the 1910s, he did not acknowledge that he was also working as a publicist for director Maurice Tourneur. Smith was also a close friend of Richard Barthelmess, but there is no evidence that he devoted an inordinate amount of space to the actor in his fan magazine articles.[4]

Although he was at one time western editor of *Photoplay*, Mark Larkin (1889–1963) spent much of his career as publicity director for Mary Pickford. While under contract to the actress, he wrote of "The Mother of Mary" in *Motion Picture Magazine* as early as September 1919 and of Pickford's last film, *Secrets*, in *Photoplay* in March 1933.

Joseph Henry Steele is an interesting example of a press agent/publicist who published in the fan magazines. Born in Philadelphia on September 6, 1897, Steele worked as a personal representative of silent leading man Richard Barthelmess and handled publicity for Ronald Colman, Cary Grant, and Ginger Rogers in the 1930s. He published at least two fan magazine pieces on Barthelmess: "Intimate Portrait of a Man with Black Hair" in *The New Movie Magazine* (March 1930) and "Dick" in *Photoplay* (February 1932). Steele was a production associate at Paramount in the 1930s and later a producer at RKO before taking on his biggest star, Ingrid Bergman, whose personal publicist he was from 1945 through 1952. Steele published three major pieces in *Photoplay* on the actress, "Portrait of Ingrid" (August 1945), "The Intimate Story of Ingrid" (June–August 1946), and "Swedish Homespun" (April 1949). He was also heavily involved in defending her image once news of her affair with Roberto Rossellini broke in 1949 (see chapter 8). Steele was responsible for the first biography of the star, *Ingrid Bergman: An Intimate Portrait* (1959). He died in Los Angeles on September 21, 1960.

Initially, studio publicists were accepting but also wary of too close a liaison between a writer and a star. Early on, publicists had realized that in overpromoting a star in a fan magazine they were not necessarily selling a film but inflating an ego, and with an inflated ego would come an inflated notion as to worth. In 1918, Pathé publicist P. A. Parsons complained, "The picture was lost sight of in the exploitation of the star. The business still suffers from the effects of this type of publicity. It was fine for the star. It shot salaries up from two figures to four and five, but it put the emphasis in the wrong place. The star became greater than the picture. The tail wagged the dog."[5]

Some fan magazine writers could boast of what was a close, almost intimate, relationship with individual stars, and that affinity could mean ease of access, exclusive stories, and guaranteed assignments. The stars in all probability also realized the benefits to be derived from having a personal fan magazine writer as a friend who might also serve as a personal publicist.

As William J. Mann documented in his biography of gay Hollywood star William Haines, the actor was frequently photographed at Hollywood events in the company of studio publicist Katherine Albert. In a way, she served as his "beard," although Haines made no secret of his homosexuality.[6]

On August 4, 1928, the trade paper *Motion Picture News* reported that Katherine Albert, formerly feature writer on the staff of Pete Smith, director of publicity for MGM, had been appointed feature and fiction writer at *Photoplay* by Mark Larkin. At issue was the extent to which Albert carried her loyalty to Pete Smith and MGM with her when she joined *Photoplay*. Once with the magazine, she contributed an extraordinary number of pieces on MGM players, beginning with a November 1928 article on the studio's transformation of Austrian actress Eva von Berne. Among the MGM stars that Albert promoted at *Photoplay* were Aileen Pringle (January 1929), Lupe Velez (February 1929), Nils Asther (February and March 1929), Dorothy Sebastian (July 1929), Renée Adorée (January 1930), John Gilbert (February 1930), Marie Dressler (March 1930), Ramon Novarro (April 1930 and November 1932), Greta Garbo (August 1930 and April 1931), Anita Page (September 1930), Conrad Nagel (September 1930), Norma Shearer (May 1931), Joan Crawford (August 1931), and Johnny Weissmuller (June 1932). She even contributed a piece on MGM's *Trader Horn* to the March 1930 issue. Yes, there were articles by Albert on non-MGM players, most notably a series on "The Unknown Hollywood" from October 1931 through June 1932, but they were distinctly in the minority.[7] At the least, the writer used her sources at the studio to gain access to its stars. At the most, she was working both for *Photoplay* and for MGM.

Katherine Albert was as much a member of the film industry as one of its chroniclers in the pages of the fan magazines. Born in Kentucky on October 6, 1902, she had married Dale Eunson, a prolific writer for films, theater, and later television, in 1931. Together, they cowrote many television scripts, as well as the films *On the Loose* (1951), *The Star* (1952), with Bette Davis, and *Sabre Jet* (1953), with Robert Stack, and the plays *Guest in the House* (1942) and *Loco* (1946). Their daughter, Joan Evans (born July 18, 1934), was an actress featured in *On the Loose*, and her godmother was Joan Crawford. She contributed the occasional piece to *Photoplay* in the 1950s, and, as Joan Evans Weatherly, she was editor of *Hollywood Studio Magazine*, which began publication in May 1966 as a monthly journal very obviously aimed at film buffs. Dale Eunson died in 1970, and Katherine Albert died in Santa Monica, California, on July 26, 1970.

Katherine Albert's relationship with William Haines was nothing compared to *Photoplay*'s Herbert Howe's involvement with MGM leading man Ramon Novarro. Not only did Howe write extensively about Novarro over many years, he also bedded him, becoming his lover in 1925. In print, Howe was a ladies' man, writing about an imaginary girlfriend and praising the beauty of stars such as Corinne Griffith and Pola Negri. Writing of him in the November

Herbert Howe (second from left) on the set of *The Arab* in North Africa (1924) with the director Rex Ingram (far left), Alice Terry (without her usual blonde wig) and Ramon Novarro.

1923 issue of *Photoplay*, Adela Rogers St. Johns began her piece: "He dines with Pola Negri! He reads French with Mabel Normand! He swims with Alice Terry! He teas with Mrs. Charles Ray! He escorts Florence Vidor to Bowl concerts! He dances with Corinne Griffith!" After describing Howe as a "Lothario, this playboy of the movie world," Rogers St. Johns did throw in a couple of hints as to his true personality, "He is a bachelor—from choice," and she suspiciously ended her commentary with a quote from Oscar Wilde.

Howe had a healthy interest in gay celebrities, particularly those of Hispanic background. Although likely not gay, an obvious favorite was handsome, Spanish-born leading man Antonio Moreno, the first of the "Latin lovers," whom Howe interviewed as he stepped out of his shower at the Lambs' Club. "One dry hand was extended in salutation while the wet one was employed with a Turkish towel massaging the equatorial zone." "I like action, you know!" Moreno tells Howe, glancing up "from the vigorous action of the towel upon the left leg."[8] What Antonio Moreno thought of Howe's approach to interviewing is not known, but he does not appear to have granted another interview until six years later, in the July 1926 issue of *Photoplay*. But, of course, Howe was Moreno's publicist at the time of the first interview, and not later. "Tony introduced me to Hollywood and the flowery path long ago, and for several years I was associated with him," wrote Howe in the February 1925 issue of *Picture-Play*.

Born Herbert Riley Howe in Sioux Falls, South Dakota, on September 28, 1893, he began working as a film publicist in New York in the early 1910s. After military service in World War I with the U.S. Tank Corps, Howe was hired by the *New York Telegraph* as a reporter and began writing for the fan magazines. The first star of which he wrote was vamp Louise Glaum, featured in articles in *Photo-Play Journal* (October 1917), *Motion Picture Classic* (December 1917), and *Photoplay* (August 1918). In 1921, he was under contract to Brewster Publications, while also working as a publicist for the Vitagraph Company. In 1922, Howe began a long relationship with *Photoplay*, a publication in which his name had first appeared with a story on Richard Barthelmess in April 1918.

Howe's sexual orientation was obviously well known to his employers. He was deemed the ideal reporter to interview Somerset Maugham for *Shadowland* (June 1921). A month later, the magazine featured Howe's interview with ballet dancer Hubert Stowitts, with the writer conducting the interview in his subject's dressing room while he rubs brown makeup from his muscles. William Haines was the subject of an October 1924 article in *Photoplay* and, of course, Novarro was featured in April 1925 and in an entire series in *Motion Picture Magazine* from February through May 1927, titled "On the Road with Ramon Novarro."

In 1923, Howe traveled to Europe with Novarro, working not only as a publicist for the star but also for his director, Rex Ingram, and Ingram's leading lady and wife, Alice Terry. Howe continued as publicist and promoter of Novarro into the 1930s, writing of him in "The Hollywood Boulevardier" column in the September 1930 issue of *The New Movie Magazine*, but the sexual relationship was probably at an end. Howe made several relatively specific comments about Novarro's sexual orientation in *The New Movie Magazine*, or at least remarks that might raise questions with the readership. In August 1930, he explained that "Ramon Novarro doesn't want to be a husband, he wants to be a god. Which, of course, is a far more commendable ambition." In August 1931, readers were promised that Howe "tells all about Ramon Novarro"—well, not quite all, but he did mention the star washing out "our shirts" one night. In a "Salute to Herb Howe," published in April 1934, the writer is asked if it is strange that Novarro has not married. "No," he responds, "his religion forbids divorce." A fan asks Howe why Novarro needs twin beds in his bedroom. "Hollywood hospitality, honey," replies Howe, "Hollywood hospitality." Of course, the term "gay" was not used to mean homosexual back then, but it is curious that in December 1934 Howe was described as "*New Movie*'s gay caballero."

Howe continued with *The New Movie Magazine* until its demise in 1935 and then vanished from the scene, aside from the occasional piece in *Photoplay* in the 1940s and 1950s. In the mid 1950s, Howe reappeared, again as Novarro's publicist, but died on October 12, 1959, in Los Angeles.

Photographs of Howe show him as a somewhat stolid, ordinary-looking individual. He did not have a stereotypical gay appearance, and he had none of the looks of a romantic leading man. However, he was what Ramon Novarro needed as a publicist for his career and as stability in his life. Without Herbert Howe at his side, Novarro deteriorated in terms of both a reliance on alcohol and cheap sex, both of which ultimately led to his tragic end at the hands of two Hollywood hustlers.

Novarro biographer, André Soares, wrote of Howe, "The popular image of this average-looking, heavy-drinking intellectual from Sioux Falls was that of the Hollywood Boulevardier: a sophisticated man-about-town, a reader of Nietzsche and Schopenhauer, a European—in spirit, if not in birth—lost among the sunshine and palm trees of Southern California."[9] Despite his professional and private ties to Novarro and Moreno, Herbert Howe was an honest and fair critic and commentator, often outspoken in his comments on Hollywood celebrities. "The secret of Herbert Howe's success as an interviewer," wrote Adela Rogers St. Johns, "is that he knows everybody worth knowing in pictures—and he doesn't care what he says about them."[10]

A very different relationship between a fan magazine writer and an actor was that of Samuel Richard Mook and Spencer Tracy. A good-looking man who had joined the military in World War I, Mook was born in Memphis, Tennessee, on July 24, 1894, and died there on May 10, 1948. Through a close friend, actor Neil Hamilton, Mook met Tracy at a party. As early as 1932, in his "Medals and Birds" column in *Screenland*, Mook wrote that Tracy was an actor of comparable talent to that of Paul Muni. At Tracy's request, Mook escorted the actor's wife, Louise, to premieres and parties. When Spencer Tracy began a well-publicized affair with Loretta Young in 1933, it was Mook who published Louise's side of the story in the November 1933 issue of *Movie Mirror* and Tracy's side in the January 1934 issue of *Screenland*. In all, Mook published at least twelve fan magazine articles on Spencer Tracy, with the last appearing in the October 1943 issue of *Screenland*. Probably the personal and professional relationship ended with Tracy's involvement with Katharine Hepburn and her determining with whom he could associate. Samuel Richard Mook, whom some writers have suggested was gay, remained a bachelor.

The interrelationship between the writers and the stars should come as little of a surprise. The one needed the other, and both were open to flattery either in regard to what was written about them or how wonderful that writing could be. As Larry McMurtry pointed out, "Movie magazines, for example—speaking now of the drugstore variety—are at once a by-product of the star system, and one of the system's props. Undoubtedly, many people who have all but given up going to movies still read movie magazines and fantasize about stars—relating their glory, as they imagine it, to their own unglamorous existences, an action that must involve some real, and otherwise dormant, imaginative faculties."[11]

The fan magazine writers and publishers, at least on the surface, embraced what the studios chose to reveal about their stars because that was also what the public wanted to read about those stars. "Fan book readers don't want to hear anything derogatory about the star. They want the myth," explained one fan magazine editor in 1948. "We are writing inverse statements of frustration. We paint beautiful pictures of love, excitement, wealth, prestige, security and glamour. . . . We give the reader a feeling of identification [with] the stylized intimacy of a movie star's existence. Every marriage we describe must have an

Joan Crawford never met a fan magazine writer she did not like.

idyllic, untarnished quality to it. If you want to keep on running stories about a star, you must strongly intimate that everything is just the way it was before they were married."[12]

"Joan was the queen and we were her ladies-in-waiting," said Dorothy Manners of Joan Crawford.[13] Between 1929 and 1976, Manners wrote at least fourteen fan magazine articles on the star. In the last, published in the April 1976 issue of *Photoplay*, Joan Crawford was "the girl without a past," but Manners, of all people, must have known better. It was not only Manners with whom Crawford remained friendly. She turned to fan magazine writer Jane Kesner Ardmore to coauthor her autobiography, *A Portrait of Joan*.[14]

Born in Fort Worth, Texas, on July 30, 1903, Dorothy Manners had started her career in Hollywood as an actress—she described herself as a "lousy" one—with bit parts in various films in 1921, 1922, and 1923 and as cowboy star Buck Jones' leading lady in *Snowdrift* in 1923. She contributed a monthly gossip column to *Motion Picture Magazine*, and she was hired by Louella Parsons as her main assistant in 1945. With Parsons' sink into senility, Manners took over her column on December 1, 1965, and assumed the title of motion picture editor of the syndicated Hearst Headline Service. Heavy with photographs, a gossip column by Dorothy Manners also appeared in the 1960s and 1970s in *Modern Screen*. The syndicated newspaper column ended in January 1978, and Manners died in Palm Springs on August 24, 1998.

Had he still been alive when she was working on her autobiography, Joan Crawford might well have wanted to work with Norbert Lusk, "Norbie," as she called him. Born in New Orleans in 1883, Lusk combined fan magazine writing with publicity work for Samuel Goldwyn, Thomas H. Ince, George Loane Tucker, and Hugo Ballin in the silent era, beginning his career as a writer with the Lubin Company in Philadelphia in November 1912. He had even written at least one silent screenplay, *Thrown to the Lions*, a melodrama involving a cabaret entertainer and gangsters that was filmed by Universal in 1916. While at Lubin, Lusk wrote a piece on the company's players for the July 1914 issue of *Motion Picture Story Magazine*. As a publicist at Goldwyn, he wrote a piece on one of its stars, Mabel Normand, for the February 1918 issue of *Picture-Play*.

Always working out of New York, Lusk served as film critic for the *New York Morning Telegraph* in the 1910s. Circa 1922, he became both film critic and editor of *Picture-Play*, remaining with the magazine through 1938, while also working as New York film correspondent for the *Los Angeles Times*. At *Picture-Play*, Lusk saw himself as "a liaison officer between followers of films and the world of the stars,"[15] and he claimed to have reviewed an incredible 2360 films. From 1942 to 1945, Lusk was associated with the Museum of Modern Art and the Library of Congress, helping to determine which films submitted to the latter for copyright should be retained for preservation and serving with such major academics as Siegfried Kracauer and Erwin Panofsky. He was associate editor of the National Board of Review publication *New Movies*, in which he published his autobiography, "I Love Actresses!"

As his later career indicated, Lusk was intelligent and sophisticated. A genial, avuncular bachelor known for his intimate dinner parties and his culinary skills, Lusk was a mild-mannered critic who could be bitingly sarcastic. "He has the most sardonic and at the same time the lightest sense of humor I have ever encountered," wrote fellow writer Samuel Richard Mook in 1930.[16] As he became older and work became scarcer, it was Joan Crawford who offered Lusk financial support and probably arranged for him to work as an occasional publicist for Twentieth Century–Fox and Warner Bros. in 1948. When Lusk published his autobiography in the pages of *New Movies*, the last chapter was devoted to "My Ultimate Actress," Joan Crawford. Worried that she had been unable to contact him, Crawford asked for a Warner Bros. employee to visit Lusk's apartment, where it was discovered that he had died alone a day earlier, on July 23, 1949.

Joan Crawford on the cover of the January 1934 issue of *Motion Picture.* Courtesy of Sue Slutzky.

Another close friend of Crawford was Jerry Asher, who wrote pieces on her in *Movie Mirror* (June 1934 and September 1935), *Modern Screen* (June 1936), *Silver Screen* (June 1936), and *Screenland* (February 1938). Asher was also reportedly close to Fred Astaire, writing on him in *Movie Classic* (January 1935), *Screenland* (September 1936), and *Modern Screen* (September 1941). Asher's name appeared on extensive pieces in *Photoplay* in the 1940s and 1950s while he was also working as a publicist at Warner Bros.

It was not necessarily close friendships but rather the fact that he was well-known in the industry as a homosexual that led to Asher writing several articles for *Movieland* in the 1950s on Hollywood stars who have since been identified as gay: Rock Hudson (May 1953 and November 1956), Tab Hunter (August 1956), George Nader (September 1956), and Tony Perkins (December 1956 and March 1957).

Comparing Asher to two of his contemporaries, Sara Hamilton and Howard Sharpe, "whose special province is love with a capital 'L,'" one commentator wrote in 1939, "He is completely smitten by Hollywood's make-believe, and convinced of the accuracy of his own priceless observations."[17] In later years, Gladys Hall commented, "Don Ameche said to me one day not long ago in New York, we were all a little in love with each other in those days. And we were."[18] But that love was contingent upon not merely mutual respect (which, in reality, often did not exist), but on the studio contract player and his or her representatives determining what route such love might take. It was also very much a *ménage a trois* with the subject and the writer forced to welcome an editor to the love fest.

While the casual reader might assume that it was a good life and a good living to be a fan magazine writer, such was far from the truth for many in the field. Typical of the freelance writers was Constance Palmer, who retired from magazine and newspaper writing with her 1921 marriage to actor Lucien Littlefield, whom she had met on the set of the Valentino vehicle *The Sheik*. Palmer revived her career in the 1940s as his began to wind down. As her daughter recalled, "All the editors were in New York, so she would make a list of suggested stories, send them to Delight Evans or whoever it was in New York, and maybe the editor would pick out one. Then she would go to the studio and get permission from the publicity office. Usually a publicity person would come along to the interview, maybe the star would change the content or the publicity department would change something. By the time it got back to the editor, maybe it wasn't the same angle the editor wanted. Maybe she would sell it and maybe she wouldn't."[19]

Any life or color that an article contained might be rudely removed by a studio publicist. An interview on a studio lot might have to be conducted in the presence of as many as two or three minders for the star involved. And, as one writer angrily complained, when the interview was over, she would be escorted to the studio gate to prevent her possibly wandering around the lot and discovering someone else to interview. A fan magazine writer might present herself as a friend or confidante of the subject of her interview, but such was seldom the situation.

A more accurate description of how Hollywood stars viewed fan magazine writers was provided in the 1932 RKO feature film *What Price Hollywood?*, directed by George Cukor and based on an original story by Adela Rogers St. Johns. A fan magazine writer named Miss Dupont (played by Josephine Whittell) comes to interview newlywed players Mary Evans (Constance Bennett) and Lonny Borden (Neil Hamilton). "I'm doing a series of articles on the Love Lives of the Picture Stars. I want your Love Life for the April number." After asking ludicrous question after ludicrous question, she concludes by addressing Borden, "Have you got a photograph of your marvelous physique?"

When Gladys Hall wrote a two-part article on the "Life of Charles Boyer" in 1941, she was required to have the piece approved not only by the star but also by his studio, Paramount. Sometimes, if she was lucky, Hall was able to move quickly: an article on Don Ameche was approved by Twentieth Century–Fox in April 1938 and sent on to *Modern Screen* that same month. Her article, "Mistakes My Daughter Will Never Make," written as if by actress Joan Bennett, was approved with changes on October 31, 1941, and immediately sent to *Motion Picture Magazine* that same month.

In 1939, Hall's income was one of the highest of all fan magazine writers—a reputed $10,000 a year.[20] In the late 1930s, *Photoplay* might pay as much as $200 or $300 for a story, *Movie Mirror* offered only $75, while *Modern Movies* was as low as $40 or $50. Payments for many writers were relatively small. For an article on Lizabeth Scott, titled "It's Great to Be 22!," published in the September 1945 issue of *Screenland*, Constance Palmer received $75. For a piece on Shirley Temple, "Shirley, Today," in the August issue of *Screenland*, she received $100. *Silver Screen* was slightly better, paying $100 each for "Quiet Guy," an article on John Garfield in the October 1946 issue, and for "Claudette [Colbert] Speaks Up" in the June 1947 issue. By the 1950s, payments were on average $100 an article, sometimes increasing to $125 (for *Movie Stars Parade*). In all, Constance Palmer earned $2635 in 1946 and only $1975 in 1947.[21]

Of course, it has also been suggested that there were fan magazine writers who were paid for what they decided not to cover. As Carl F. Cotter wrote in 1939, "Some of the more successful writers, it is claimed, earn a handsome income from editorial omission rather than inclusion."[22]

Omission or exclusion from the pages of the fan magazines was one thing. Exclusion from the studios, and thus from the stars, was always another way for the producers to control what appeared in the fan magazine. By resorting to what was basically censorship, the studios could deny access to their stars, forcibly tongue-tying the writers. As one publisher in the 1930s noted, without the ability to publish stories on, say, Jean Harlow, circulation could diminish by as much as ten percent.[23]

No matter their fame, all fan magazine writers were forced to deal with a New York editor, who was generally female. Norbert Lusk amusingly recalled these Boadiceas of big business in 1947,

> The lady editor is not invariably hard to deal with. She has her favorite callers and dependents, and she gives work to the deserving needy, but all are subject to replacement. However, by the very nature of her position she is never without them and they are never sure of their tenure though they swallow slights and cling as long as they can. She imposes her likes and dislikes upon them, and her whims, all pointing to a craving for prestige and preference. . . .
>
> Sometimes the lady editor is a mild sadist whose pleasure is to hurt the defenseless and watch them squirm, or to eliminate an associate for not "liking" her loudly enough. Coworkers may wryly whisper "Miss Hitler," the chorus cries

"darling!" and declares, with the gusto of persons who prefer butter on their bread, that the current number of her magazine is most wonderful of all.

"I'm more than editor," says one whose title is that. "I'm a doctor, a magazine doctor. I can tell what's wrong with a publication." Upper brackets, perhaps as a national consultant, must be the destiny of the career woman who speaks thus of movie editorship, but she continues to give her omniscience to the one magazine whose fluctuant circulation is her worry. . . .

Considering themselves mentally superior to actresses, except for the current one or two they get on with "because they are such fun," the editors sometimes are a little stagy and given to theatrical effects. A bed placed on a dais, a collection of expensive perfumes or French dolls when they were a smart fad, some high-priced books too special to be best-sellers; and a guest sometimes touches an executive hand that has been sprayed by an atomizer. On the other side, he may be welcomed into a tweedy interior where the principal décor is a half-empty bottle of Scotch, editorial legs stretched as wide apart as snug skirt will allow.[24]

As the Hollywood studios came under increasing pressure to observe a production code that would govern what could and could not be depicted on screen or face the threat of federal censorship, so did attention turn to the fan magazines and the part they played in presenting a negative image of Hollywood to the world. The studios quickly realized that it was not enough simply to present a positive image on screen, it was necessary to continue with that image on the printed page.

The Western Associated Motion Picture Advertisers (WAMPAS), founded in 1920 and best known for its selection of thirteen promising young actresses named WAMPAS Baby Stars, was a body comprised of leading professional Hollywood publicists. On a voluntary basis, it had approved the credentials of fan magazine writers, which permitted them studio access. This accreditation process worked reasonably well but had no official endorsement. The solution was for the Association of Motion Picture Producers and Distributors of America (the Hays Office) to take over.

On August 10, 1934, the Studio Publicity Executive Committee of the Motion Picture Producers and Distributors of America (later to become the Motion Picture Association of America) unanimously issued the following pronouncement:

Whereas the undersigned members of this Committee seek to curb the inaccuracies, misrepresentations and exaggeration of facts by certain fan magazine writers, which tend to create false impressions in the mind of the public in regard to motion-picture personalities, and which result in much unfavorable public reaction, the Committee herewith adopts the following resolutions, effective immediately:

That, in the future, all fan magazine interviews, stories or symposiums which involve studio contract players, whenever or wherever obtained by fan magazine representatives or free-lance writers, shall be submitted to the studio publicity director, or his properly designated representative, for approval before publication;

That each writer shall first obtain approval of the studio publicity director or his representative, of any idea upon which an interview is to be based before such an interview is granted;

That, insofar as practicable, a third party, representing the studio, shall be present during all interviews between players and writers;

That any writer violating these definite rulings of the studios shall be denied admission to the studios thereafter, and all further cooperation.

As it was explained to a *New York Times* reporter (August 11, 1934), the action was decided upon as a result of recent articles written about Jean Harlow and Mae West, "which were considered objectionable." One publicity director told the *Times* that the action was taken "to curb asserted inaccuracies, misrepresentations and exaggerations by a 'certain fan writer.'" On July 3, 1934, *The Hollywood Reporter* launched an attack on the current issue of *Modern Screen*, which contained "one of the most inexcusably vicious stories we have ever read, 'How Long Will Hollywood Protect Harlow?'"

The Jean Harlow article immediately disturbed the film fraternity by beginning with acknowledgement of husband Paul Bern's suicide. "She shouldn't have married Paul anyway," reported Rachel Benson. The gist of the piece, which was quite sincere, was that Hollywood failed to defend Clara Bow, its redhead, but should protect platinum blonde Jean Harlow. At the same time, Benson suggested that actress Dorothy Dunbar considered naming Harlow as co-respondent in a proposed divorce from her husband, Max Baer. She concluded, "I don't see why a world should not protect such a girl by a true understanding and appreciation for the thrill she gives them. . . . And since Jean, herself, is giving it to us, I, for one, hope that the world will take over the job from Hollywood of protecting this interesting person from herself, as Hollywood has done until this moment."

Aside from that article, the August 1934 issue of *Modern Screen* contained three other pieces that caused outrage within the Hollywood establishment: "If I Should Love Again" by Gladys Hall (about Miriam Hopkins), "She Ain't No Angel" by Ruth Biery (about Janet Gaynor), and "How [Jack] Oakie Gets His Women..!" by Jack Jamison. Hall reported on Hopkins' one-time husband, Austin Parker, her adopted son, and her assertion, recounted with considerable vehemence, that "Women shouldn't marry." The piece by Biery begins by suggesting that Gaynor is trying to break up the marriage between Robert Montgomery and his wife, Betty: "She is no longer a child. She's a mature woman. She's been in love with men, married and divorced." Character comedian Jack Oakie might seem a strange choice to generate controversy. The problem appeared to be that he could get a considerable number of beautiful girls, including Mary Brian, Peggy Hopkins Joyce, and Toby Wing. When Oakie telephoned the last, her sister Pat might take the call, and Jamison reported, "Whichever girl got to the phone first got the date."

Jean Harlow was presumably showing her support for *Modern Screen* when her character in *Dinner at Eight* in 1933 is seen reading a copy of the fan magazine.

On August 13, 1934, *The Hollywood Reporter* announced that the western editors of five of the leading fan magazines had agreed to cooperate with the new ruling—although, in reality, there was little else they could do. Two days later, the Hays Office suggested to the recently formed Screen Actors Guild that its members cooperate.

On August 15, the western editors of the various fan magazines met with the publicity heads of the major studios, and, according to *The Hollywood Reporter* (August 16, 1934), "the editors signed a pledge to purge their publications of false and salacious material." Signing the pledge were Elizabeth Wilson of *Silver Screen*, Elza Schallert of *Picture Play*, Ruth Waterbury of *Movie Mirror*, Walter Ramsay of *Modern Screen*, James Fidler of *Screenland*, Eugene Chrisman of Fawcett Publications, John Mitchell of *The New Movie Magazine*, Dorothy Donnell of *Motion Picture* and *Movie Classic*, and Ivan St. Johns of *Photoplay* and *Shadoplay*. The number of approved fan magazine writers was to be reduced from 300 to thirty.

Fan magazine writers were required to obtain identification cards from the Motion Picture Producers and Distributors of America, a badge of recognition that became known as the Hays Card. There is no documentation as to how the issuance and withdrawal of the cards functioned. According to Carl F. Cotter, the cards were issued for a three-month duration. The card could be withdrawn at any time, and once lost, it was virtually impossible for the writer to get it back, because the number of cards in use was severely limited.[25] The writers with cards were described as being on the "white list," consisting of some fifty or so individuals, twenty more than the number originally reported. With their cards in hand, fan magazine writers could apparently sit around the publicity departments of the studios all day, in the hope of hearing a piece of gossip that was not too scandalous to incur the wrath of the producers but juicy enough to interest the editors back east.

There is no record as to how long the Hays Card was in use. By the 1950s, however, it was supplanted by a listing of accredited writers provided to the studios by what was then the Motion Picture Association of America. Bonnie and Reba Churchill were teenagers when they began writing for the fan magazines in the early 1950s. As Bonnie recalled, "The lady at the Motion Picture Association thought we were just going to do nothing but harass the studios. We were teenagers and didn't know anything. We kept sending letters that we wanted to be accredited. My mother and I went up to the Association, and when the lady saw my mother and she saw me, we were so unlike anything that she knew. She said if we hadn't come up there, she would never have accredited us. Then, we were on the list."[26]

The Hays Card did not completely keep criticism at bay. In New York, in November 1934, for example, some 2000 men and women representing twenty fan clubs launched a drive to curb "the spurious distortion of facts by many of

Will Hays. Courtesy of
Academy of Motion Picture
Arts and Sciences.

Hollywood's gossip columnists and fan magazine writers." The Fan Club Federation, as it was called, promised to get at "the real truth about Hollywood."[27] Nor did the Hays Card prevent negative reporting. In 1939, *Photoplay's* Kirtley Baskette was identified as "being the chief exponent of dirt," based on a story titled "Hollywood's Unmarried Husbands and Wives." Reportedly, both the Hays Office and the featured stars were outraged. "The article is pretty bad," a spokesperson said, "The title is even worse. I don't know what we'll do about it, but we'll certainly take some action." What such action, if any, was is not revealed.[28]

When fan magazine writers in response to the crackdown began the practice of unauthorized interviews outside of the studio, which was nothing particularly new, the studios responded with an emphasis on the morality clauses in the contracts of its stars, writers, directors, and producers. The morality clause forbade signees from granting interviews not approved by the studio, and, it would seem, that aspect of the morality clause was more ruthlessly applied than in other areas dealing with more outrageous behavior.

In an April 1934 editorial in *Photoplay*, Kathryn Dougherty commented, "Certain motion picture publications have become more and more daringly offensive in the type of photographs they are printing. They scream with sex— sex at its worst. They hope to maintain their circulation by appealing to the most vulgar of taste. Pick up one of these sheets and you get the impression that the motion picture industry is a tangle of legs, divorce suits and scandal."

Not surprisingly, even before taking on the written word, the Motion Picture Producers and Distributors of America had ruled on the visual image. Following complaints from the Catholic organization the Legion of Decency, the Hays Office forbade what is best described as "leg art." A bathing suit continued to be respectable in that it was an item of clothing to be seen on any beach in America. Panties, garters, and the like were appropriate to the bedroom but not to the pages of the fan magazines. As with any rules, there were ways to break them, as *Modern Movies* found in May 1939, when a feature on "Hollywood's Stocking Secrets" provided it with the opportunity to display the stockinged legs of various stars, ranging from Martha Raye to Joan Crawford. There was even concern in regard to nightclub photographs showing only two stars, the implication being that the couple was having an affair. The accompanying caption was required to make very clear that this was not the situation— even if it was.

In March 1937, the Motion Picture Producers and Distributors of America expressed alarm at the number of candid shots being used in magazines and newspapers. While studio photographers were required to have their work approved by the organization's Advertising Advisory Council, the same rules did not apply to photographers shooting on assignment. *Modern Screen* was again the subject of controversy, with its August 1937 issue, when it featured Joan Blondell in various stages of undress. The magazine had hired its own photographer, Frank Muto, to take the photographs and had not submitted them for studio approval. *Modern Screen* editor from 1935 to 1939, Regina Cannon was advised that "We shall take steps to prevent the recurrence of such an incident. If it is to be the policy of your magazine to publish such pictures, it will be impossible to cooperate with either your writers or photographers."[29]

The problem of unauthorized photographs was not new. On June 27, 1933, *Variety* had reported that a photograph of Claudette Colbert and Fredric March, presumably on the set of Cecil B. DeMille's *The Sign of the Cross*, "in a more or less embarrassing position" had been published in an unidentified fan magazine. It further disturbed Paramount that the photograph was published with a suggestive caption line: "It's known in Hollywood that several fan mags are always in the market for pictures that shouldn't get out of the studios. Several times poses of an off-color nature have been traced to outside lens hounds who happened to be visiting the studios. With small candid cameras it is possible to grab pictures without the subjects or bystanders wise to the proximity of a photog." As a result, Paramount barred cameras from the studio lot. Other studios followed, and the ban has remained in effect through the present.

Sex and nudity were nothing new to the fan magazines at this time. In August 1918, *Motion Picture Magazine* had featured leading men in their bathtubs as well as photographs of Theda Bara in *Salome* displaying considerable flesh. The photographs in *Shadowland* have already been noted. The 1932–1933 release of *Goona-Goona: An Authentic Melodrama of the Isle of Bali*, with its shots of bare-breasted women, was welcomed as titillation for the readers of fan magazines. *Picture Play* (July 1933) interviewed the Balinese dancers, while *Hollywood* (December 1933) ran a piece by Harry Carr titled "New Shirtless Movie to Worry Censors." In addition, some popular periodicals traded on a Hollywood connection when there was none, as with *Hollywood Nights*, whose September 1931 cover featured an artist's visualization of a scantily-clad Hula dancer and promises a piece "for Men Lonely."

The humor magazine *Film Fun*, which lasted from 1915 through 1942, often featured cheesecake artwork in the 1930s as well as pin-ups on its covers in 1940. In the 1930s, other film-related humor magazines, such as *Screen Humor*, *Real Screen Fun*, *Reel Humor*, and *Movie Humor*, boasted pin-up covers, as did *Movie Merry-Go-Round*, whose 1937 issues promised "Lots of Gorgeous Silk-Stockinged Lovelies." All the covers were heavy on garters, stockings, and what may only be described as crotch shots. *Movie Humor*, with its promise of "Hollywood Girls and Gags!," pointedly informed its readers on the front cover that "This is NOT *Film Fun*." In a March 23, 1938, report, Lester Thompson, chairman of the Advertising Advisory Council of the Motion Picture Producers and Distributors of America, described *Reel Humor*, *Reel Screen Fun*, and *Movie Humor* as "sex magazines which trade on the industry," interspersing "motion pictures with nude or semi-nude figures."[30] Not surprisingly, the studios denied servicing the publications with still photographs.

Readers with specialist tastes might also find much to appreciate in the fan magazines. In January 1930, *Picture Play* provided a photo spread titled "Baby Behave!" featuring Hollywood leading ladies being spanked. In July 1930, it returned to the subject with "Bitter Lessons," a series of photographs of leading men being spanked. Known for his bondage and spanking photographs featuring Bettie Page and others, Irving Klaw (1910–1966) is well remembered also by film buffs for his family business Movie Star News on 14th Street in New York. Here, one could find all manner of studio publicity photographs. From the 1960s onward, Klaw and Movie Star News regularly took full-page advertisements in various fan magazines.

Writing in 1937, Clifton Fadiman pointed out that the fan magazine publishers were generally located in the eastern or midwestern United States, as far away as possible from Hollywood. But, at the same time, "the tie-up between studio and fan magazine is real, even if not directly financial."[31] By the 1970s, the connection was also, in part, very much financial. The Ideal

Publishing Corp., which owned *Movie Life*, was in turn owned by the film and television distribution company Filmways, Inc. *Movie Mirror* and *Hollywood Hot-Line* were published by Sterling Women's Group, a subsidiary of Warner Communications. (Sterling was subsequently acquired in the mid 1970s by the advertising agency, Sanford Schwartz, for two million dollars.)

For several decades, there had been agitation for the film community as a whole to publish a fan magazine. In 1929, two years after its founding, the Academy of Motion Picture Arts and Sciences announced abortive plans to start its own fan magazine, "telling the truth about motion picture people."[32] Eventually, in July 1971, the National Association of Theatre Owners published the first issue of its own fan magazine, *Movies Now*, for distribution directly to theater patrons. Two other fan magazine–like publications, aimed exclusively at theatergoers, are *In Cinema*, first published July 1980 and available free to New Yorkers, and *Movie Guide*, first published in July 1981 and sold by subscription as well as at theater concession stands. Almost twenty-five years later, on December 16, 2005, the *New York Times* launched a digest-sized magazine, *OnMovies*, featuring material from the paper and published eighteen times a year. A reported 1.25 million copies were distributed free of charge to patrons of Loews Cineplex Theaters nationwide.

CHAPTER 5

THE FAN MAGAZINE AS A LITERARY OUTLET

In January 1912, *Motion Picture Story Magazine* revealed the results of a letter-writing competition in which readers were asked to provide their opinions on a variety of film-related subjects. One of the winners, taking fifth prize, was an eleven-year-old schoolboy from Chicago named Edward Wagenknecht, "whose long and carefully prepared letter has exceptional merit." Wagenknecht went on to become emeritus professor of English at Boston University, a noted literary scholar, and the author of one of the most prominent works on silent film, *Movies in the Age of Innocence*. (He also coauthored two works with this writer.)

Edward Wagenknecht was the first in a long line of literary figures who contributed occasionally yet significantly to the fan magazines. The editors obviously welcomed major names from the world of literature, individuals whose contributions suggested endorsement of the fan magazine in its own right. They provided legitimacy to the genre, while probably adding little if any to the number of readers or subscribers. The literary giants presumably welcomed the payments made to them by the fan magazine editors and the wider audience to which they played. After all, the readership of most best-selling novels was but a fraction of that enjoyed by the fan magazines, and the writing published in the fan magazines was, on the whole, decidedly second-rate compared to the work of these individuals elsewhere. Often, the comments from the literary set are remarkably innocuous, almost amateurish, suggesting they were tossed off between breakfast and lunch for a readership that would be impressed by the name and unconcerned as to what such a name might actually write. If truth be told, what Herbert Howe or Frederick James Smith wrote was infinitely superior to that from the pen of Elinor Glyn, Avery Hopwood, or Somerset Maugham.[1]

Of course, an argument might be made that the story adaptations published in the formative years of the fan magazine are themselves literary contributions. By adapting back to the printed page the works of Charles Dickens or William Shakespeare, which had in turn been adapted for the screen, the pioneering fan magazine writers were bringing the classics of literature to the working class masses. It was very much the *Reader's Digest* approach to literature.

Generally, those from the field of literature contributed to the fan magazines because they had something to say—but not always. For those just embarking on their writing careers, an article in a fan magazine was just part of the job. So it was with the author of *Ship of Fools* (1962), Katherine Anne Porter.

In October 1920, *Motion Picture Magazine* published Porter's interview with Charles Ray, a silent leading man at the height of his success. "Charles Ray is a most difficult person to interview," wrote Porter. In fact, it was not quite as difficult as she might have led the reader to believe. As *The Moving Picture World* (March 13, 1920) reported, the Arthur S. Kane Pictures Corporation had hired a new employee to handle various aspects of the publicity and promotion of its stars, including Charles Ray: "Katherine Anne Porter, a widely known magazine and newspaper writer . . . will be in charge of feature writing for the fan publications and newspapers." In reality, Porter, like Louella Parsons, had begun her career not as a writer but as an extra with the Essanay Company in Chicago circa 1914.

Mary Roberts Rinehart was already an accomplished novelist when she contributed to *Motion Picture Magazine* in February 1921. Her editorial piece, "The New Cinema Year," attacked producers for failing to note that the average intelligence of the audience had risen steadily. "There is humor that is not cruel, comedy that is not vulgar, and love that is not vicious or abnormal," she argued. In conclusion, she praised the Lon Chaney vehicle *The Miracle Man* as "an expression of a vast longing for faith." So short is the piece that it must have taken Rinehart all of five minutes to compose.

When Rinehart again returned to the fan magazines, the contribution related to her work within the industry. In June 1919, she had signed a three-year contract with Samuel Goldwyn, who had created a subsidiary company, Eminent Authors Pictures, Inc., to promote various popular American playwrights and novelists through screen adaptations of their works along with original-scripted features. Others involved included Gertrude Atherton, Rex Beach, and Rupert Hughes. In February 1922, *Photoplay* published Rinehart's essay "Faces and Brains," in which she commented, "There will always be room for new faces in pictures, particularly where those new faces are not merely types, but have intelligence and acting ability behind them." The article was tied in with a publicity stunt organized by *Photoplay* and Goldwyn to find new screen personalities. A month earlier, Rupert Hughes had published a similar piece in *Photoplay* on the theme of "New Faces for Old."

An unusual fan magazine contributor was Booth Tarkington, hailed in 1921 as the most significant of contemporary writers. Tarkington was not exactly wordy, writing only three paragraphs on the unlikely subject of actor Thomas

Willard H. Wright, better
known as S. S. Van Dine.

Meighan. Tarkington concluded that "He is more than a 'vastly popular movie actor' and this is because his enormous public sees the *man* that he is as well as it sees the actor that he is." The one-page article in *Photoplay* (August 1924) also included a rendition of Meighan by another American icon, James Montgomery Flagg.

That same issue of *Photoplay* included an essay on actor Oscar Shaw by Sally Benson, who was later to write short stories and mystery reviews for *The New Yorker* and was responsible for three major screenplays, *Meet Me in St. Louis* (1941), *National Velvet* (1944), and *Anna and the King of Siam* (1946). In the early 1930s, she wrote a couple of pieces for *The New Movie Magazine* on comedian Benny Rubin (January 1931) and Charles Ray and his failure to make a comeback (June 1931).

Rinehart, Hughes, Tarkington, and Benson were not the only popular writers finding a home at *Photoplay* during this same period. Willard H. Wright was a literary critic and scholar and the author of volumes on Nietzsche and the syntax of aesthetics. Between September 1921 and September 1922, he wrote a series of articles for *Photoplay* on subjects as varied as *The Cabinet of Dr. Caligari* (September 1921), "Life in the Movies" (October 1921 to March 1922), Charlie Chaplin (February 1922), and "A Motion Picture Directory" (September 1922). The last is relatively amusing; for example, "omission" is defined as "The type of sin rarely committed by a motion picture director."

H. L. Mencken (center) in Hollywood, with Paul Bern, Louis B. Mayer, Aileen Pringle, Norma Shearer, Irving Thalberg, and Harry Rapf.

Perhaps as a result of his induction into the popular world of fan magazines or perhaps, as is the general opinion, because of a physical collapse, Wright ceased to write scholarly books. He adopted the pen name of S. S. Van Dine and created the character of private detective Philo Vance, who was played by William Powell in a series of Paramount features between 1929 and 1933. In 1929, Wright published the autobiographical *I Used to Be a Highbrow but Look at Me Now*. What had *Photoplay* wrought?

Between 1912 and 1914, Wright edited *The Smart Set*. The man most associated with that journal, H. L. Mencken, wrote a piece promising "The Low-Down on Hollywood" in the April 1927 issue of *Photoplay*. It is a lengthy article, running to five pages, and written in the form of a self-interview. He criticized Hollywood producers for assuming that novelists and playwrights can write competent films and offered some lukewarm praise for F. W. Murnau. He noted that in the few movies he had seen, there was nothing property identifiable as acting. Mencken described Emil Jannings as "a competent actor," and concluded by remembering Valentino as "a sad young man." "He has, in the movies, plenty of brothers and sisters." The critic did mention of attending the first night of *What Price Glory?* with Aileen Pringle, but, obviously, made no reference to her being his mistress.

Mencken's coeditor at *The Smart Set*, George Jean Nathan, contributed his first fan magazine article to *The New Movie Magazine* of June 1932, titled "Celluloid Sirens." Nathan found Hollywood's female stars "sex appeal fakes, and just a little idiotic."

Mencken visited Hollywood and came away with a mistress, actress Aileen Pringle. Elinor Glyn visited Hollywood and came away with a celebrity status she had never quite achieved earlier in her career. She had published her most famous romantic novel, *Three Weeks*, in 1907, and saw a number of her works adapted for the screen. However, it was with Paramount signing her to a contract in 1920 that she gained fame as great as many of the studio's stars. In her 1936 autobiography, *Romantic Adventure*, she wrote, "I felt there was the unique opportunity to spread the ideals of romance and glamour into the humblest homes. . . . I am always proud to think that I was never one of those who belittled the artistic possibilities of the cinematograph industry, or underestimated its enormous potential for good and evil in the life of mankind."

Glyn certainly never underestimated the potential that her films might achieve and how the fan magazines might be used to promote her career. She was a constant in the gossip columns and photographs of such periodicals in the 1920s. Frederick James Smith interviewed her in *Motion Picture Classic* in February 1921, and she was furious when he reported she had claimed, "No educated people go to the cinema in England, you know, except to those cowboy things." When *Motion Picture Classic* spoke to her again in June of the same year, she refused to discuss her work: "I am not particularly friendly to the magazine you represent. They printed a horrible story about me—horrible!"

However, Glyn was willing not only to be interviewed by but also to write for *Photoplay*. In March 1921, she considered life "In Filmdom's Boudoir," noting, "The moving picture world is a very wonderful one. In no other are there collected so many really lovely young women, for instance. But they are all so very young!" In June 1921, Glyn contributed a piece on "Sex and the Photoplay" to *Motion Picture Magazine*. "What is this Sex Bogy?" she wrote. "Analyzed down to its essence, it is the life of the world—the eternal fire which keeps the human race still inhabiting the earth. It was created by God, who presumably knew His business when He evolved the scheme of things."

Gloria Swanson starred in *The Great Moment*, a 1921 film based on an original story by Glyn, who hastened to provide a photobiography of the actress in *Photoplay*'s June 1921 issue. Again, in *Modern Screen* in July 1931, Glyn profiled the actress with a piece titled "The Gloria Swanson I Know." A couple of months earlier, she had written of "Rudolph Valentino, as I Knew Him" in the May 1931 issue of *Modern Screen*. In July 1928, Madame Glyn began a six-part series in *Photoplay* on modern sex problems, a subject somewhat removed from the magazine's basic tenet.

Somerset Maugham was another Brit with a slightly better reputation than that of Elinor Glyn, and certainly one that has safely endured. He did not appear to have considered himself superior to Hollywood and what it represented. Maugham contributed a piece on his "First Impressions" on a four-week visit to Hollywood in the January 29, 1921, issue of the trade paper *Motion Picture News*. Like Elinor Glyn, whom he described as one of his "old friends," Maugham had been signed to a Paramount contract, and he was happy to conclude that "The possibilities of the cinema completely intrigued me."

In April 1921, Maugham contributed a piece to *Motion Picture Magazine* on "The Author and the Cinema." "Nothing is impossible on the screen," he wrote. "The photoplay permits a breadth of expression, a true portrayal of dramatic incident, a faithful painting of the most gorgeous landscape that affords the maker of film drama all the scope offered by the novel and stage play combined. To a writer of sincerity and imagination this well-nigh unlimited scope of the film is a lure that in most cases has been irresistible."

Motion Picture Magazine was also able to welcome to its pages in 1921 one of America's most popular playwrights, Avery Hopwood. In October of that year, Hopwood wrote a short piece on "The Future of Screen Comedy," in which he complained that comedy lagged behind screen drama. "The motion picture fan and producer still think of screen comedy in terms of slapstick," he grumbled. "Comedy will never advance or earn the applause of intelligent people, so long as it sticks to custard pies and bathing girls. Even Charlie Chaplin abandons slapstick when he makes a picture like *The Kid*."

Janet Flanner, best known as Paris correspondent "Genet" in *The New Yorker*, described herself, incorrectly, as "the first cinema critic ever invented," based on the time she spent in 1916 and 1917 as film reviewer for her hometown newspaper, the *Indianapolis Star*. Following World War I, she spent some time traveling in Europe, prior to deciding to make her home in Paris. Flanner wrote of the filmgoing experience in Turkey in the April 1922 issue of *Filmplay Journal* and in Rome in the July 1922 issue of the same fan magazine. She also contributed a piece on minor leading man David Powell to the December 1920 issue of *Photoplay*.

The fan magazines of the 1920s did offer at least one giant of the literary field whose impact on American society is beyond question, Theodore Dreiser. His writing about the Hollywood community originated with his September 1919 meeting with Helen Richardson, a bit player and extra who often appeared in comedies and who had been married to minor actor Frank Richardson. She and Dreiser lived together in Hollywood from 1939 onward, eventually marrying in 1944.

Dreiser wrote a three-part piece in *Shadowland* (November 1921, December 1921, and January 1922) titled "Hollywood: Its Morals and Manners." He discussed the reality of life there with startling realism (as one might expect), noting that the "commonplace" director will make overtures to every attractive worker on his set, that casting directors "sell" parts to actresses, deliberately keeping down salaries. It is a depressing and original story told in an anonymous style with no reference to Hollywood glamour or stardom.

It is unclear whether it was editor James R. Quirk or Dreiser himself who headed the latter's interview with Mack Sennett, "The Best Motion Picture Interview Ever Written," when it was published in the August 1928 issue of *Photoplay*, but it is certainly the longest literary piece to be found in any fan magazine, running seven pages and providing a rare, intimate glimpse of the comedy producer. Dreiser left the reader in no doubt as to his admiration for Sennett: "For to me he is a real creative force in the cinema world—a

Elinor Glyn.

master at interpreting the crude primary impulses of the dub, the numbskull, the weakling, failure, clown, boor, coward, bully. The interpretive burlesque he achieves is no different from that of Shakespeare, Voltaire, Shaw or Dickens, when they are out to achieve humorous effects by burlesquing humanity."

In January 1932, Dreiser made his last contribution to a fan magazine, *The New Movie Magazine*, naming the six worst pictures of the year. His selection was not well received, and the next month George Arliss responded, "the talkies are not intended for people of Mr. Dreiser's mental stature."

Literary contributions declined in number in the 1930s, as the fan magazines increased in popularity. British-born Louis Goulding was at the height of his popularity during the decade, and he contributed twice to the fan magazines. The first piece in June 1936 appeared in *Photoplay* and was an interview with "The True Paul Muni." "I think the greatness of Muni belongs primarily to himself," wrote Goulding. "No director, no scenarist, no cameraman, no soundman, has had very much to do with it. It consists of a certain iron integrity combined with a certain delicate sensitiveness which can't be built up from outside. It must develop from within." It was a good piece about a great actor, and, as Ruth Waterbury commented in a preface to the article, "Only a writer as great as Louis Goulding could penetrate to the soul of the man called by many Hollywood's greatest actor."

Somerset Maugham.

Goulding's second fan magazine piece, "This Was My Hollywood," appeared in the September 1937 issue of *Cinema Arts*. It compared the city of its title to Oxford (of all places). In both, "there was the perpetual sense of beauty in the background." However, Goulding ended by noting that Hollywood "also bears quite a strong likeness to the primitive jungle of Borneo, but I will not attempt to expound the similarity now."

Another contributor to the September 1937 issue of *Cinema Arts* was Archibald MacLeish, the poet, essayist, and playwright, who also served as Librarian of Congress from 1939 to 1944. MacLeish was the unofficial producer of the 1937 documentary *The Spanish Earth*, a powerful left-wing indictment of fascism and the Spanish Civil War. In order to promote the film, "the kind of history which the historians of heavy volumes do not write," MacLeish wrote the piece for *Cinema Arts* titled simply "MacLeish on Spain."

Cinema Arts stands with the 1930 periodical *Cinema* as the most elegant and beautiful of all fan magazines. Appropriately, it is the sister publication *Cinema* that provided readers with the opportunity to read, or at least try to decipher, e. e. cummings in an article titled "Miracles and Dreams" in its June issue. The article began in much the same style as it planned to continue (like the show of shows), "The show of shows continues. A murdering mutter of profit and protest suggestingly haunts the theatre of theatres, but the curtain of curtains is conspicuous by its absence. And over and over the stage of stages monotonously marches our heroine, Industria—carefully presenting to the audience of audiences her miraculous cinematographic face which has recently learned to speak." There was a brief reference to Chaplin, but basically the piece was a tribute to Mickey Mouse, Oswald the Rabbit, and Krazy Kat (who was compared to Lady Chatterley's lover!). Unfortunately, Walt Disney failed to recognize cummings' genius and offer him a job during the poet's 1935 visit to Hollywood. His potential for being hired elsewhere was more than somewhat hindered by his reference to Hollywood as "the Christian wailing wall" and his description of MGM as a studio run by "a kike named Irving Thalberg."

Writer and critic Robert Graves compared cummings to an earlier poet Vachel Lindsay, who also had a fondness for the motion picture, authoring the seminal 1915 work *The Art of the Moving Picture*. Lindsay contributed a poem, "To Mary Pickford (on hearing she was leaving the motion-pictures for the stage)" to the December 1914 issue of *Photoplay*. The first verse reads, "Mary Pickford, doll divine, / Year by year, and every day, / At the moving-picture play, / You have been my valentine." Perhaps not surprisingly, Lindsay was never again invited to contribute to *Photoplay*. Indeed, this one offering is so insignificant as not to be even listed on the magazine's contents page.

In that same issue of *Photoplay*, there were two other verses by lesser mortals named Elmer Edmond Johnson, writing on "The Picture Show Pest," and Elizabeth Wilson, whose poem on "Those Serial Pictures" begins, "Kind heavens have mercy! What's this that I hear? / Another new series about to appear?" Unlike Vachel Lindsay, Elizabeth Wilson was invited to continue as a fan magazine contributor, in all publishing more than 120 articles in *Screenland* and *Silver Screen* in the 1920s, 1930s, and 1940s.

The one film journal welcoming the literary set in the 1930s was *The New Movie Magazine*. In its first issue of December 1929, novelist Fannie Hurst wrote on "The Battle of Hollywood," being the sound revolution. Critic Heywood Broun discussed "Mary Pickford's Ten Greatest Film Stars" in February 1932. There were no surprises except for the inclusion of Mickey Mouse. In July 1932, *The New Movie Magazine* began publication of Edgar Wallace's "Hollywood Diary." The popular British novelist was in Los Angeles working on *King Kong*, and the pieces were eventually published after his death by Hutchinson in London under the title of *My Hollywood Diary*. In 1935, *The New Movie Magazine* asked a number of writers to select their favorite players. In January, Sinclair Lewis chose Katharine Hepburn as his favorite star. In February, George Jean Nathan selected three: Loretta Young, "for her ability

to play love scenes with infinitely more effectiveness than any of her counterparts"; Jean Muir, for her performance in *Desirable*; and Sylvia Sidney, for
"substantial dramatic equipment in general."

James M. Cain was a hardboiled novelist of the Depression who found a
ready market for his work in Hollywood. Not surprisingly, he was willing and
able to help the film community promote screen adaptations of his writings.
In February 1946, in connection with MGM's release of *The Postman Always
Rings Twice*, Cain wrote an article for *Photoplay*, praising the film's star, Lana
Turner, as both a blonde beauty and an actress. The text is so bad that it could
just as easily have been written, and perhaps better so, by a studio publicist
than by Cain himself. After describing Turner as "a tasty dish," the great writer
went on to praise the actress for her portrayal of Cora, concluding, "Lana understood her [Cora] better than I did. And I wrote the book! The hunch I'd
had about Lana was completely justified. She's more than a glamour girl. She's
an actress. When she played Cora, she *was* Cora. I think she's going to make a
hit of that *Postman* book yet!"

Aside from literary figures, one cannot ignore the contributions of three
very disparate political representatives. In June 1928, *Photoplay* provided His
Imperial Highness Archduke Leopold of Austria with the opportunity to publish his "Sketches from Hollywood." In July 1938, Eleanor Roosevelt wrote in
Photoplay on "Why We Roosevelts Are Movie Fans." She noted that a trip to
Hollywood would make all moviegoers more appreciative of the films that they
saw. Like a true advocate, she noted, "From Warner Brothers I carried away
the vision of real streets with buildings—in Paris, in Spain, East Side New York
City—and of a research department where a whole wall was lined with hard-
ware of different periods and reference books that were so enticing that I would
have gladly offered myself as a candidate for a job among them! From Metro-
Goldwyn-Mayer, I think my impression was one of marked efficiency. . . . At
the Twentieth Century–Fox studio I was so taken up with Shirley Temple that
I thought of little else." A few months later, in January 1939, *Photoplay* invited
First Lady Eleanor Roosevelt to again contribute to its pages with a piece titled "Film Folk I Have Known." *The New Movie Magazine* in July 1931 hosted
Grand Duke Alexander of Russia's report on his visit to Hollywood, a reminder
of the number of Russians who had already come to the film capital, most notably the Mdivani family, supposed members of the Georgia royal family, who
made a habit of marrying Hollywood stars.

CHAPTER 6

NEW WRITERS, NEW PUBLISHERS, NEW HORIZONS

In the formative years of the fan magazines, Eugene Brewster and James R. Quirk were the two dominant publishers. In the 1920s and 1930s, several new publishing outlets arrived on the scene, taking over the earlier publications and introducing ones of their own. If there were any singular factor linking one with another, it was that the primary income of those new publishers was often from comic books.

Ultem Publications was responsible for *Star Comics*, *Modern Movies*, and *Movie Life*, all of which began in 1937. A year later, the company was acquired by Centaur Comics. Hillman Periodicals was founded in 1938 by Alex L. Hillman and had a host of comic books in the 1940s, including *Air Fighter*, *Crime Detective*, *Dead-Eye Western*, *Punch and Judy*, and *Victory*. In November 1944, it launched its most ambitious general magazine, *Pageant*, a publication similar in size to *Reader's Digest*, but filled with the type of content that would be an anathema to the competition. A year later, Hillman began publication of its first fan magazine, *Movieland*, which survived into the 1970s. *Movieland* was followed by *Screen Guide* in 1946. The company's output was taken over by Macfadden Publications in 1961.

Sometimes it was nothing more than unpaid bills that led to a fan magazine changing ownership. *Screenland*, which was first published in 1920, was acquired in 1932 by printer John Cuneo and the International Paper Company because the original publisher had failed to pay his printing and paper costs. Paul Hunter was named the new publisher, and eventually he became the majority owner of the fan magazine. In the early 1960s, *Screenland*, along with *Silver Screen*, was acquired by the Macfadden-Bartell Corporation, which continued their publication through a subsidiary, Super Market Publishing Co., Inc., with Patricia de Jager and later Micki Siegel as editors of both.

Bernarr Macfadden shows off his physique at the age of fifty-five in this 1923 photograph. Courtesy of University of Southern California, Regional History Collection.

The Ideal Publishing Company was a subsidiary of Grosset & Dunlap (founded in 1898), and familiar to film buffs for its Photoplay Editions, cheap reprints of novels that had been adapted for the screen, illustrated with still photographs from the films themselves.[1] Ideal was founded in 1937 by William M. Cotton (1904–1971), who had been with Fawcett Publications. Eventually, it was responsible for approximately twenty periodicals in the fan, teenage, and confession categories, about half of which were film oriented.

Initially, Ideal took over the Ultem fan magazines, *Movie Life* and *Modern Movies*, and they became its first publications in the genre. The latter, edited by Ruth L. Baer, ended its life in 1939. *Movie Life*, selling for fifteen cents, consisted entirely of photographs with no credited writers and was billed as "Hollywood's Only All-Picture Magazine." By the 1960s, the subtitle was gone and there was considerably more text. From August 1952, there was also a gossip column, "The Chatterbox," written by Lloyd Sloan. *Movie Life* was followed by *Movies* in 1939 and *Movie Stars Parade* in 1941, both of which had little to distinguish them from other fan magazines of the period.

Ideal did one substantive thing for its female readership. In 1948 and 1949, it led a campaign for the repeal of the twenty percent tax on cosmetics. In an editorial, published simultaneously in *Movie Stars Parade*, *Movie Life*, *Personal Romances*, and *Intimate Romances*, William Cotton urged his female readership to combat "the man-made tax on feminine necessities." The magazines ran headlines such as "Is It a Luxury to Be Attractive?" and "Protest the Tax on Your Attractiveness," while Ideal's promotion manager shipped out kits on the anti-tax movement to 40,000 women's clubs. Other fan magazines joined in the protest, including *Screenland* and *Silver Screen*. There was, for example, an article in Fawcett's *Today's Woman*, in which "an angry housewife sounds off on luxury taxes."[2] The tax was repealed in 1950.

Hunter, Hillman, Ultem, and even Ideal were relatively unimportant and lacking in eccentricity, totalitarianism, and color compared to two of the new leading publishers of the period, Macfadden and Fawcett.

"The Father of Physical Culture," as Bernarr Macfadden was called (along with a good many less charitable names), would seem an odd figure to dominate the world of fan magazine publishing. But Macfadden did just that. He advocated vegetarianism, health foods, enriched flour, and vitamins. He had all the passion of a religious fanatic when it came to healthy living, under which heading was also included a healthy sex life. To a large extent, Bernarr Macfadden was a cult figure for a half century in the world of exercise and clean living. In 1898, he founded the Physical Culture Publishing Company to publish his magazine *Physical Culture*, a publication in which he was often featured semi-nude, and he embarked on a publishing career that not only embraced all manner of periodicals and newspapers but also seventy-four self-published texts and an eight-volume reference work, *The Encyclopedia of Health and Physical Culture*.

"The liveliest, and most contentious, American of his century," as *New Yorker* writer Robert Lewis Taylor described him, was born Bernard McFadden on a Missouri farm on August 16, 1868. By the age of ten both his parents were dead, and the child appeared sickly enough to follow them sooner rather than later. However, inspired by a circus trapeze act and recalling the healthy life of a farm worker, the young man determined to become a professional wrestler and gymnast. Because there was no interest in publication of a journal to promote the lifestyle that Macfadden embraced, he founded his own publication and changed his name to something he considered more dynamic.

Other periodicals followed, most notably *True Story*, first published in May 1919 and extant through 1941, which once had the largest newsstand circulation of any magazine in the world. The first issue of ninety-six pages included interviews with Billie Burke, Douglas Fairbanks Sr., William Farnum, and Dorothy Gish from the world of entertainment. Its cover, according to Charles Fulton Oursler, who was Macfadden's supervising editor and a dominant figure in the publishing house, featured "a coarse blown-up chromo of a Hollywood blonde."[3] Macfadden's approach to publishing was influenced by a lack of commitment to the perpetuity of any of his magazines. He had no sentimental attachment to any of them, with the one exception of *Physical Culture Magazine*. *Beautiful Womanhood*, *Midnight*, *True Detective Mysteries*,

The Master Detective, *Metropolitan Magazine*, *Muscle Builder*, *Modern Life*, *Ghost Stories*, *True Experiences*, and *Model Airplane News*, they all came and went on a whim.

Macfadden had a great interest in using the motion picture to promote physical health. As early as November 1917, he began releasing a series under the title *Physical Culture Screen Magazine* through the General Film Company. The first production featured muscular poses, wrestling, deep breathing, gymnastic exercises for girls, classical dancing, and recreative exercises for children.

The first fan magazine from the physical culturist was *Movie Weekly*, a ten-cent rotogravure publication, which first appeared on the newsstands on February 12, 1921. In the early issues, the articles were on a far lower level than those found in rival publications. In the first issue Conway Tearle wrote of "Love Making on the Screen." On March 12, 1921, Billie Burke revealed "Her Many Lovers on Stage and Screen." A week later, Alice Brady discussed "Negligees for the Home." In the physical culture mode, on May 21, 1921, *Movie Weekly* began a series, "How to Obtain a Movie Figure."

There was a very basic approach to content, as revealed in an editorial on page 20 of the first issue: "*Movie Weekly* has no axe to grind. *Movie Weekly* is not tied to anything or anybody. *Movie Weekly* has one desire, to interest you and to please you. *Movie Weekly* intends to print true stories. *Movie Weekly* does not intend to accept publicity 'propaganda' that is spread over the pages of many publications. *Movie Weekly* tells the truth behind the scenes in Movieland." On April 9, 1921, and again on page 20, *Movie Weekly* announced it was the fastest growing publication in America, and, perhaps more importantly, that it was "Good Enough and Clean Enough to Go into Every Home in This Great Country."

By 1925, its last year of publication, *Movie Weekly* was looking far more like a typical fan magazine, as represented by *Photoplay*. Frequent contributors were Adele Whitley Fletcher and Gladys Hall, along with Alma Talley and Harriette Underhill. Publication ceased on September 26, 1925.

Whether Macfadden had become bored with *Movie Weekly* or whether it had ceased to perform satisfactorily is unknown. The publisher probably decided to concentrate his efforts on his most famous of publications, the daily *New York Evening Graphic*, which had begun publication in September 1924. It might be remembered as the first newspaper upon which Walter Winchell worked on a regular basis or as an outlet for then-sports commentator Ed Sullivan. But, it was for its scandalous stories and its composite photographs that the newspaper became famous—so much so that it was known as the "Porno-Graphic." The newspaper ceased publication in 1932. (Macfadden's publishing empire also included other newspapers: *The Automotive Daily News*, *Daily Investment News*, the *Detroit Daily Illustrated*, the *New Haven Times-Union*, and the *Philadelphia Daily News*.)

Macfadden's next foray into fan magazine publishing came in November 1931 with the first issue of *Movie Mirror*, subtitled, somewhat hopefully, as

"Filmland's Most Beautiful Magazine." Edited initially by Ruth Waterbury and later by Ernest V. Heyn (with the title of executive editor), *Movie Mirror* had little to differentiate it from other major fan magazines of the 1930s, such as *Photoplay* or *Motion Picture*. There were pieces by all the familiar names, including Dora Albert (who seems to be in every issue), Muriel Babcock, Marquis Busby, Maude Cheatham, Gladys Hall, Adele Whitley Fletcher, and Harriet Parsons. Harry Lang handled the film reviews, with each subdivided under the headings of "It's About" and "The Locale." Lang later went on to write "The Talkie Town Tattler" gossip column in *Motion Picture* in the mid through late 1930s, at which time the *Movie Mirror* reviews continued in the same format but with no credited critic.

An interesting section in the magazine was the "Movie Mirror Junior" column. Each issue featured a guest editor for the column, including Judy Garland (December 1937), Alfalfa Switzer of "Our Gang" (January 1938), and Marcia Mae Jones (March 1938). Macfadden appears to have used *Movie Mirror* at times to promote his public views on morality. In October 1938, Marian Rhea asked, "Hollywood Youth: How Moral Is It?," revealing that Ronald Reagan did not approve of petting, that Anne Sheridan "couldn't drink if I wanted to," and that Anne Shirley made all her own clothes.

Despite his fixation with physical fitness, Macfadden's film publications were less health-oriented than those of his predecessors, James R. Quirk and Eugene V. Brewster. As Heather Addison noted in her well-documented and little-known text, *Hollywood and the Rise of Physical Culture*, fan magazines played a prominent role in terms of fitness and dieting in the 1920s. She pointed out that in 1917 *Motion Picture Magazine* carried 16 physical culture advertisements, 59 in 1921, 116 in 1925, and 76 in 1930. In *Photoplay* in the 1920s, the Corrective Eating Society published sixteen advertisements—thirteen of them full-page—promoting a weight control course.[4]

Photoplay was very much aware that its readers saw the supposed healthy lifestyles of the stars, as depicted in its pages, and concerned that they might become fixated with weight reduction. Were both Hollywood and the movies equally responsible for a dieting craze in America, did Hollywood symbolize physical culture, and was there an overemphasis on the masculinity of the male stars? In a series titled "Wholesale Murder and Suicide," published in the July through September 1926 issues of *Photoplay*, the magazine warned, "The movies, which set standards of beauty for more people and to a far greater degree than the stage, have emphasized slightness, thinness, to such an extent that any other kind of figure looks strangely undernourished to American eyes."[5]

The dangers of "reduceomania" were discussed in *Photoplay* articles such as "The Deuce with Reducing" (July 1925), "Health—Hollywood's Greatest Asset" (November 1926), "Starving Back to Stardom" (August 1928), "Diet—the Menace of Hollywood" (January 1929), and Dr. H. B. K. Willis' "Diet for Health and Beauty" (February 1929). Nor was *Motion Picture Magazine* less concerned, with Dorothy Calhoun becoming a one-woman authority on the subject with "The 18–Day Diet" (October 1929), "Taking the Die out of Diet" (July 1930),

"Diet Quickies—Three Stars Tell How to Lose Weight Fast without Fasting" (September 1930), and "Don't Diet! Curves Are Back!" (March 1932).

In January 1941, *Movie Mirror* merged with *Photoplay*, which Bernarr Macfadden had acquired in 1934, along with *Shadoplay*. His approach to fan magazine publishing was very much hands on, an approach that he also adopted in regard to his female staff. As Ruth Waterbury, his editor at *Movie Mirror* and at *Photoplay*, recalled,

> The trouble with him was he was a very erotic old man. You had to keep out of his way. He was a personality; after all, this was a man who had no background, no breeding, nothing, who had made himself a multi-, multi-, multi-millionaire. He was the worst lecher that ever lived. God, he was a dreadful old man. You know how the files are in an office. He'd have some girl go pull out a file, and it was always crowded. So the girl would be pulling out a file here, and he'd brush against her. He hated girls to wear lipstick, so when I had to see him, I'd put on more lipstick than you ever saw. Because he wanted to kiss you, and he'd get it all over him. He got a little discouraged with me. I used to have to take up the covers to show the old man, and I remember once he said to me, "Why can't I have one girl whose butt is showing?" That was his standard! He was just awful! But he had a formula. He sure as hell did![6]

At one point, Macfadden became very enamored of actress Ann Sheridan, admiring her physical shape and demanding that her "ass" be featured on the cover of *Photoplay*. Sheridan was fitted out in a skintight bathing suit and photographed from the rear while looking back over her shoulder with a beaming smile.[7]

Ruth Waterbury had overall editorial control of the magazine, even, she claimed, when Heyn was executive editor. "Pardon my conceit," she told me. "I did something that was very daring. I remember one issue, I put the Academy Award winners in it before they were announced. It was so clear who was going to win, so we had them on the cover. I got a painting made of Gable before they had made a decision on *Gone with the Wind*. Suppose he hadn't gotten it, where I would have been, I don't know. I changed the kind of cover we used, too, and the first one I used was Shirley Temple—and we picked up 80,000 circulation on that issue."[8]

Bernarr Macfadden was forced out as company president in February 1941, at the age of seventy-three. Subsequently, he acquired *Physical Culture* and debuted a new publication, *Bernarr Macfadden's Detective Magazine*. In 1946, his former company introduced a periodical of which he would have approved, *Sport*, which eventually achieved a circulation of more than a million copies. Macfadden Publications subsequently came under the control of Irving S. Manheimer in 1951; in 1962, it was sold to the Bartell Broadcasting Corporation for $1.5 million and became the Macfadden-Bartell Corporation. At that time, the company claimed sixteen publications with a circulation of 8.5 million. Eleven of its periodicals were classified as for women: *True Story*,

Captain Wilford H. Fawcett with Harold Lloyd. Courtesy of Minneapolis Central Library.

True Confessions (which along with *Motion Picture* was acquired from Fawcett in 1963), *True Romance*, *True Experiences*, *True Love*, *Photoplay*, *TV Radio Mirror*, *Inside TV*, *Silver Screen*, and *Screenland*. Their total circulation was 6,440,400.[9]

Bernarr Macfadden died at the Jersey City Medical Center on October 12, 1955. It was his first—and last—visit to a hospital. Presumably, the end result proved his righteous opposition to organized medicine.

One of the signs of trouble in River City, Iowa, according to Professor Harold Hill in *The Music Man*, is your kid starting to memorize jokes from *Captain Billy's Whiz Bang*. There is a slight problem in that the musical is set in 1912, seven years prior to first publication of the infamous periodical. But there is no doubt that *Captain Billy's Whiz Bang* not only brought immorality and sexual innuendo to small-town America, but also helped found a publishing dynasty.

Captain Billy's Whiz Bang was described as "the most prominent comic magazine in America with its mix of racy poetry and naughty jokes and puns, aimed at a small-town audience with pretensions of 'sophistication.'"[10] It was founded and edited by Wilford H. Fawcett, who had returned home from military service in World War I and was in search of employment. Using jokes and verses that he had heard from his fellow soldiers, Fawcett began a mimeographed publication that was initially sold in local hotel lobbies. By 1923, *Captain Billy's Whiz Bang* had a circulation of 425,000. Fawcett Publications was born. A second and similar publication, *Smokehouse Monthly*, was published from 1928 through 1937.

Captain Fawcett's home was Robbinsdale, Minnesota, now a suburb of Minneapolis, and it was here that Fawcett Publications, Inc., came into being. The company was housed in a custom-built three-story building, the ground floor of which was occupied by the Security State Bank, which Fawcett also founded. Captain Fawcett had some experience in journalism, having worked prior to the war as a police reporter for the *Minneapolis Journal*. To help expand his organization, however, he brought in his brother, Captain Roscoe Fawcett, a former sports editor at the *Portland Oregonian*, as vice president and general manager. A second brother, Harvey, was named business manager. The one non-family member of the executive was managing editor Jack Smalley, who was later to head up Fawcett's Hollywood office, out of which five Fawcett magazines were published.

Fawcett's printing operation was located at a plant in Louisville, Kentucky, which later became the Fawcett-Dearing Printing Co. Many of the company's early periodicals, including the fan magazines, used the Louisville address, suggesting erroneously that they were actually published there.

Just as *Captain Billy's Whiz Bang* was modeled after a similar pocket-size publication, *Jim Jam Jems*, so did Fawcett borrow ideas from other publishers. *True Confessions* was obviously based on Macfadden's *True Story*. In 1929, when vaudeville comedian Chic Sale published his outrageous classic of outhouse humor, *The Specialist*, Fawcett commissioned Cedric Adams to write a similar volume, *The Country Plumber*.

Fawcett's first venture into fan magazine publishing also originated with his experiences in World War I. In Paris, he had acquired various issues of *La Vie Parisienne*, and from these he lifted illustrations, added suggestive captions, and came out with *So This Is Paris!* First published in March 1925, the magazine became *So This Is Paris and Hollywood* in October of the same year, with the addition of some Hollywood "leg art," and then simply *Paris and Hollywood* in January 1927.

A typical issue, that of February 1927, featured actress Jane Winton, whom readers were assured "loves to wear one-piece bathing costumes," and to prove the statement she is shown doing just that. "What Will Those Tricky Girls of Hollywood Do Next?" readers were asked. The answer is to show off their dimpled knees. There was the "Latest Gossip from Paris," along with a piece on Betty Compson who, as evidence of the French background to the magazine, readers were told "registers beaucoup sex appeal." Editor Jack Smiley was one of the first to experiment with color photographs on a regular basis, although they were only color-tinted.

The magazine became *Paris and Hollywood Screen Secrets* and then simply *Screen Secrets*, eventually merging with another Fawcett publication, *Screen Play*. As *Screen Secrets*, it was surprisingly frank in its reporting on Hollywood

The May 1932 issue of *Hollywood* magazine.

subjects and stars, well worthy of further research, if (and sadly it is a big "if") a complete run could be found. In the early 1930s *Screen Play* featured covers by prominent illustrator Henry Clive, the gossip column "So This Is Hollywood!" by Anne Howe, and an occasional gossip column by Muriel Babcock titled "A Hollywood Reporter Tells All." In January 1932, there were pieces on three European film actors, Lil Dagover, Ivan Lebedeff, and Maurice Chevalier, and in March 1932, James M. Fidler reported "Discovered!! Sex Menace."

In the 1920s, Fawcett began publication of its most prominent periodical, *Mechanix Illustrated*, founded in 1922 as *Modern Mechanics and Inventions*, which was eventually to become *Home Mechanix* in 1984 and was later acquired by Time, Inc. The success of the magazine led to the creation of a number of how-to books.

In 1930, Fawcett acquired *Hollywood* magazine from the Hartwell Publishing Corporation, and the following year it took over *Screen Book* (later combined with *Screen Play*). Frederick H. Gardener, who had been eastern editor of *Hollywood* and executive editor of *Screen Book*, became executive editor of both for Fawcett. *Hollywood* was a ten-cent magazine, with at least three gossip columns, "Through the Lens," "Speaking Confidentially," and Harry Carr's "Shooting Script." Captain Roscoe Fawcett's "Cinema Curiosities" featured unusual photographs of the stars with unusual captions. A typical issue from May 1932 had Barbara Stanwyck hating Hollywood, Sylvia Sidney revealing her strange personality, and Lupe Velez naming her Hollywood lovers. Other fan magazines were acquired, including *Motion Picture Magazine* and *Movie Story Magazine*. There was even a syndicated newspaper cartoon feature, "Screen Oddities," put out by Fawcett through the Bell Syndicate. In 1931, the fan magazines along with *True Confessions* were placed together as a unit titled Fawcett's Women's Group. As of 1934, that group reported a guaranteed monthly circulation of 1.7 million.

In 1930, Fawcett and its 150 employees relocated to Minneapolis. Four years later, the company moved to Greenwich, Connecticut, with editorial, advertising, and art operations in New York, from where the book publishing division, Fawcett World Library, operated. Printing was centered in Louisville. Captain Billy died suddenly in Los Angeles on February 7, 1940, at the age of sixty-three. He was a colorful character, who, aside from his publishing empire, had found time for three wives, the creation of a summer resort, Breezy Point, in Peqoit, Minnesota, and leading the American rifle shooting team at the 1924 Olympic Games. Son Roger was apparently equally flamboyant, noted for serving drinks to guests at the publishing house, dispensed through the gold penis of a nude male statue.[11]

Fawcett's sons, Wilford, Roger, Roscoe, and Gordon, took over the company, which included additional publications such as *Battle Stories*, *Daring Detective*, *Family Circle*, *Triple-X Western*, and *True*. In 1940, they launched Fawcett Comics, introducing the character of Captain Marvel in *Whiz Comics* No. 2 (February 1940). Because of a paper shortage during World War II, Fawcett was forced to close down forty-nine of its magazines, retaining only fourteen. In the late 1940s, the company took over distribution of Mentor and Signet paperbacks and introduced its own line of Gold Medal Books. One of the last magazines from the company was *Woman's Day*, which would boast over six million in circulation in 1958. In the 1960s, Fawcett sold its confession and fan magazines to Macfadden. Fawcett Publications was acquired by CBS in 1977 for a reported $50 million. All the fan magazines had ceased publication by this time.

Although he took over publication of *Film Fun*, with its youthful humor and suggestive still photographs, in the 1930s, George T. (Thomas) Delacorte Jr. has far more gravitas than his two chief rivals in the field, Macfadden and

MY CHRISTMAS STORY by Bing Crosby

JAN.
15¢

modern screen

DELL

read
how I feel about love
by Shirley Temple

The January 1951 issue of
Modern Screen.

Fawcett. Not that he was lacking an entertaining background, having quit Harvard in 1910 because it was "too sedate." Born in Brooklyn, New York, on June 20, 1894, Delacorte eventually attended and graduated from Columbia University in 1913 and promptly took a job with the New Fiction Publishing Company. He would hand out cigars to newsstand owners to promote their publications' circulation, and so successful was he that he became president of the company. In 1921, Delacorte was fired, but he used the contractual severance pay to found the Dell Publishing Company, which was to become one of the largest mass-market publishers in the world.

Delacorte used Bernarr Macfadden as a role model, publishing confession-type periodicals such as *Sweetheart Stories*, his first, and *I Confess*. Taking the

lead from Tower Magazines, sold only at F. W. Woolworth, Delacorte began selling his magazines, beginning with *Modern Romances*, *Radio Stars*, and *Modern
Screen*, at S. S. Kresge and S. H. Kress stores. According to *Time* (November
3, 1930), "the Dell Company is emphatic that its magazines 'stand on their own
feet,' that they are offered just like any other merchandise in Kress and Kresge
stores, which do not guarantee their sales. Also, . . . the Dell magazines already
give promise of gathering bountiful advertising from makers of goods retailed
by Kress and Kresge. E.g.: An inside cover advertisement for hair nets with the
legend, 'Sold exclusively at S. S. Kresge Co.'" Copies were sold at newsstands
only in communities without these two chains. Dell's early fan magazines included *Screen Romances* and *Screen Stories*, both established in 1929, but its
most important and longest-lasting fan journal was *Modern Screen*.

Founded as *The Modern Screen Magazine* in November 1930, with publication initially credited through late 1932 to the Syndicate Publishing Company,
this ten-cent periodical contained all the standard fare, including reviews and
gossip. The magazine boasted writers of the caliber of Adele Whitley Fletcher,
Faith Baldwin, Harriet Parsons, Grace Kingsley, Dorothy Manners, Gladys
Hall, Maude Latham, Ruth Biery, Katherine Albert, Dora Albert, and Ida Zeitlin, and the first cover featured Kay Francis.

The first editor was Ernest V. Heyn, but the individual most associated with
Modern Screen on the editorial side was Regina Cannon (1900–1992), who had
the title of associate editor, western representative, and Hollywood editor in
the early 1930s, until becoming its full-fledged editor by the end of 1935 and
remaining in that position through the end of the decade. According to Carl F.
Cotter, Cannon had the lowest of standards and was the hardest to please, was
lax about answering her mail, and played favorites with New York writers. "She
publishes the worst stories of the entire lot."[12]

Among the more unusual articles in the early years were "How [Russ] Co-
lombo Discovered America—and Vice Versa" (December 1933) by Jerry Wald,
who was to become a major Hollywood producer in the 1940s and is said to
have been the role model for Budd Schulberg's *What Makes Sammy Run*. Silent screen star Blanche Sweet contributed "A Tribute to Ginger [Rogers]" in
November 1935. In August 1936, a piece on Lionel Stander, titled "One of the
Biggies," was authored by Philip K. Scheuer, who became film critic for the
Los Angeles *Times*.

By 1933, *Modern Screen* had established itself as the only major competitor
to *Photoplay*, boasting the "Largest Circulation of Any Screen Magazine." In
its September 1933 issue, *Modern Screen* featured the most famous photographic name to emerge from the golden age of Hollywood, George Hurrell,
displaying nine of his photographs under the heading "A Great Photographer's
Greatest Portraits." Included were Jean Harlow, Constance Bennett, Douglas
Fairbanks Jr., Sally Eilers, Johnny Weismuller, Joan Crawford, Helen Hayes,
Carole Lombard, and Joe E. Brown and his son.

In the 1940s, *Modern Screen* increased its price to fifteen cents, but little
changed in content or quality of writing. Louella Parsons had a regular gossip

column, titled variously "Good News" and "Louella Parsons in Hollywood," that continued well into the 1970s. Film reviews were handled by Christopher Kane and later by Florence Epstein. In addition, outside reviewers were asked to select a "Picture of the Month." For example, novelist Fannie Hurst chose *Caesar and Cleopatra* in August 1946 and *Henry V* in November 1946. In 1947 and 1948, columnist Dorothy Kilgallen was making the selections, which included *The Bachelor and the Bobby Soxer* (August 1947), *Road to Rio* (March 1948), and *Rope* (September 1948). As early as April 1937, Kilgallen had contributed a piece on Rosalind Russell, titled "That Complaining Roz."

Modern Screen had some surprising contributions. The *New York Times* critic Bosley Crowther had an article on "My Academy Award Selections" in March 1948. Playwright Moss Hart wrote an editorial on *Gentlemen's Agreement*, which looked at anti-Semitism in America, with "A Turkey Leg to Mr. Zanuck" in December 1947. Even Herbert Howe reappeared on the scene with a piece on Audrey Hepburn, "Dutch Treat," in April 1954. There were at least two advice columns per issue in the early 1950s: Joan Evans spoke out for teenagers with "Tell It to Joan" and Ann Blyth was "Your Hollywood Shopper." Blyth was not the only Hollywood star lending her name to a fan magazine column. Claudette Colbert was in *Photoplay*, and from February 1948 through March 1952 Irene Dunne had a regular feature, "Have You a Problem," in *Silver Screen*.

In the early 1950s *Modern Screen* featured several articles supposedly written by the stars, without credit to a collaborator, but presumably the work of anonymous publicists. There was "An Open Letter from Judy Garland" (November 1950), "Sex Is Not Enough" by Lana Turner (September 1951), "What Men Have Done to Me" by Joan Crawford (November 1951), and two pieces from Marilyn Monroe, "I Am an Orphan" (February 1951) and "Who'd Marry Me?" (September 1951).

In the 1930s, *Modern Screen* had presented its Award for Exceptional Merit to individual films, aping *Photoplay*'s Medal of Honor. On April 16, 1952, *Modern Screen* introduced its Golden Key Awards to various players, voted in a continuing poll of the magazine's readers. The fifteen "promising winners," only two of whom held much promise, were Suzan Ball, Anne Bancroft, Eileen Christy, Penny Edwards, Virginia Gibson, Gloria Greenwood, Dorothy Hart, Peggy King, Lucille Knoch, Kathy Phillips, Barbara Ruick, Karen Sharpe, Mary Sinclair, Joan Taylor, and Ursula Thiess.

The best known of later figures associated with the magazine was Helen Weller (1911–1993), who became West Coast editor of both *Modern Screen* and *Screen Stories* in the spring of 1958. Under her maiden name of Helen Hover, she had written for *Radio Stars* and *Radio Guide* in New York in the 1930s. In the 1940s, based in Hollywood, she wrote the gossip columns "Filmland Whispers" for *Screen Book* and, later, "Intimate Gossip" for *Screen Life*. Her husband was a neurosurgeon and her brother was owner of the legendary nightclub Ciro's.[13]

Once subtitled "The Friendly Magazine," by the 1960s, *Modern Screen* was billing itself as "America's Greatest Movie Magazine," and to a large extent it was, running neck-and-neck with *Photoplay* in terms of circulation.

By 1931, Delacorte had fourteen magazines under his control, including the satirical weekly *Ballyhoo*, edited by Norman H. Anthony, who had been editor of the old humor magazines *Life* and *Judge*. *Ballyhoo* initially sold an incredible two million copies, but it ceased publication in 1939.

Like Macfadden, Delacorte adopted a cavalier attitude toward the periodicals under his control. John Tebbel noted that, "He bought and sold magazines solely on the basis of their immediate popularity, and in a period of a quarter-century had owned more than 200 of them."[14] By 1942, Dell was the single largest supplier of periodicals to the American News Company, selling 160 million magazines a year. Delacorte's son Albert P. Delacorte was generally credited in an editorial capacity with many of the fan magazines, but his actual contribution to the journals is not known.

Aside from his periodicals, Delacorte began a series of comic books featuring Gene Autry, Mickey Mouse, Tom and Jerry, the Lone Ranger, Roy Rogers, and others, along with a series of crossword puzzle books. The comic books were all carefully family-oriented, and Delacorte would publish nothing in any way offensive. It had been claimed that Dell's comic books featuring Disney cartoon characters helped keep the film studio financially solvent for many years. In 1942, with a new subsidiary, Dell Books, Delacorte embarked on the publication of paperback novels, which were sold through newsstands, drugstores, and supermarkets, the same outlets as for his periodicals. The publisher boasted a paperback sale of nine million copies of *Peyton Place*. As Ken McKenna wrote in the New York *Herald Tribune* (July 1, 1962), Delacorte was "the man who made money guessing what the lowbrows wanted."

Dell was a mass magazine business with the emphasis on mass. It was also an organization with a strong female executive. In the 1960s, its president was Helen Meyer, who noted, "Our philosophy is to gamble. We are the largest mass-market publisher in the world. We are the only publisher with mass-market paperbacks, higher-priced quality paperbacks, hard cover books, magazines, comics, and even purse books [volumes small enough to be carried in a woman's purse]."[15]

In 1976, Delacorte retired and sold Dell to Doubleday, and it subsequently became the Bantam Dell Publishing Group of Random House. Several years earlier, he had explained to a reporter from *Time* (June 27, 1969) that, "I was born and raised in New York, made my money in New York, and now I want to give my money back to New York." Through the George and Margarita Delacorte Foundation, he gave the city a group of bronze statues of characters from *Alice's Adventures in Wonderland*, erected in Central Park, and also funded the park's open-air theater. In addition, he gave more than $6 million to Columbia University. The publisher who would also go down in history as a philanthropist died on May 4, 1991.

By 1939, all of the fan magazines were published out of New York, except for *Screen Guide*, published out of Chicago. At one point, Fawcett Publications had moved its operation from Minneapolis to Los Angeles, under the management of Jack Smalley, but by the late 1930s it also was headquartered in New York. Most of the magazines maintained offices in the Hollywood area, but sometimes these would be nothing more than the homes of one of their writers.

The Hollywood representatives reportedly earned as much as $200 a week (*Screenland* and *Silver Screen*) or as little as $40 (*Modern Movies*).[16] Fan magazine writers could earn between $25 and $125 for a story, and as *Daily Variety* reported on July 24, 1936, "Fan mags provide a living for a surprisingly large number of writers in addition to the salaried staffs maintained by the various publishing concerns. There are probably 30 writers who make a fair living each month on a freelance basis. There are another 50 who sell one or two stories and get enough to pay the rent, make a payment on the car and have a few dollars left over for beans and coffee. Most of these are either lazy or just struggling for a living while writing the Great American novel or the next Cecil DeMille picture. Usually they hang on for a year or two and fade from the picture, to be followed by a new crop."

The new crop of fan magazine writers arriving on the scene in the 1930s did hang around for later decades, their names becoming as familiar as those of the pioneers in the field. Those discussed below had names guaranteeing both reliability and assurance. There were, of course, other fan magazine writers with decidedly lower credentials. Ezra Goodman in *The Fifty Year Decline and Fall of Hollywood* noted that "The people who write fan-magazine stories are a baroque lot." He continued,

There was one fan-magazine authoress who rarely left her room in Hollywood for years. According to an in-the-know fan-magazine publicist: "She didn't come to the studios. She had a great, protruding abdomen. Maybe she was pregnant? Actually, it was some kind of tumor. She was a wino and she had a horrible apartment. We preferred to take people there if we had to rather than have her at the studios. We never took really important stars there, but usually someone on the way up." The material for most of this writer's articles was delivered to her by messengers from the various publicity departments, who handed it to her through a shuttered window, and she usually wrote her stories without even meeting her subjects.

This press agent also tells of another prominent fan-magazine writer who "was 8,000 years old. She had a bladder condition. She would come to the studio and bring her stinking, lousy little dog with her. If a star gave her a lovely story, she always cried. If a star refused to give her good copy, she always peed. You always had water on either occasion."[17]

If anyone had a name ideally suited to the craft of fan magazine writing, it was Delight Evans—and it really was her name. Born in Fort Wayne, Indiana, she left school at the age of fifteen—"education was mostly informal," she once noted—and spent her entire life working with just two fan magazines, *Photoplay* and *Screenland*. Her first articles in the former, on Douglas Fairbanks Sr. and Mary McAllister, were published in December 1917, and Evans wrote a further seventy-six stories for *Photoplay* through 1923. Her last piece for *Photoplay*, on Mae Marsh, appeared in March of that year. In 1924 she joined *Screenland* as a feature writer, reviewer, and eventually editor from 1929 through June 1948, tripling the magazine's circulation in her first two years there. Evans was for many years married to Herbert Crooker, eastern publicity manager for Warner Bros. and MGM.

While Delight Evans was editing *Screenland*, Ida Zeitlin was writing for it, contributing at least twenty-five feature stories between 1931 and 1942. She also wrote forty articles for *Photoplay* from 1930 to 1952, at least fifty-seven for *Modern Screen* from 1937 to 1956, and occasional pieces in the 1930s for *Motion Picture*, *Movie Classic*, and *Movie Mirror*.

Dora Albert never seemed to stop working from the early 1930s into the 1970s. I was a young researcher in the Margaret Herrick Library of the Academy of Motion Picture Arts and Sciences in 1971, and I can recall Dora's appearance in the library and our arguments as to whom would have use of its one manual typewriter, available to the public. Having lost the battle, she would subsequently appear, extremely and permanently bad-tempered, looking very ancient, followed by an equally aged husband, carrying an equally ancient typewriter. Once the typewriter was placed to Dora's satisfaction, her husband would be dismissed to return at the end of the day. Somehow, Dora Albert was everything one might imagine a stereotypical fan magazine writer to be.

In her family autobiography, *Dancing at Ciro's*, Sheila Weller wrote of Dora Albert, "She had a voice like a loud, raspy Minnie Mouse and she practically invented the concept of eating with your mouth open." Weller identified Albert's husband as Sam Heend, a television repairman.[18]

Born in New York in December 1906, Dora Albert's name first appeared in *Silver Screen* in 1931. By 1933, she was also contributing to *Screen Book*. There were much longer engagements. She had articles in *Movie Mirror* from 1932 to 1940, in *Screenland* from 1938 to 1948, and in *Movieland* from 1944 to 1959. The two most prominent writing assignments were with *Modern Screen*, from 1934 with a piece on Mary Carlisle to 1973 with an article on Laraine Day, and with *Photoplay*, from 1937 with a piece on Gracie Allen to 1978 with an article on Kristy McNichol. Like so many other fan magazine contributors, Albert also found time to author two self-help books, *You're Better Than You Think* (1957) and *How to Cash in on Your Abilities* (1961). Dora Albert died in Los Angeles in December 1997.

Another fan magazine writer whom I met when I first came to Los Angeles was Ivy Crane Wilson, who seemed incredibly old and was very irritated at her deafness, but who always enjoyed company. She was probably better known to Brits than to Americans in that she had served for many years as Hollywood correspondent to London's *Star* newspaper and edited an annual, *Ivy Crane*

Delight Evans with Alma Tally and Greer Garson. Courtesy of Academy of Motion Picture Arts and Sciences.

Wilson's Hollywood Album, the fourteenth edition of which appeared in 1962. The *Album* contained articles, such as "Swimming Is a Great Idea" by Esther Williams and "Thank You Miss Shearer" by Janet Leigh, supposedly written in the first person by Hollywood stars, but all the responsibility of press agents (although I have seen evidence that the stars at least read and approved the copy). One fan magazine adopted this same pattern, the annual *Hollywood Diaries*, edited by Ira Peck, all of whose articles were supposedly written by the stars, ranging from Jeff Chandler to Debbie Reynolds. Issue no. 2 from 1956 included a piece by Rock Hudson reminding himself, "Rock Hudson, You're a Married Man!"

Born in Australia, as Ivy Payne, she introduced South Sea Island dancing to New York, and in 1912 and 1913 she toured with Otis Skinner as the featured dancer in the original production of *Kismet*. As Mrs. Douglas Crane, she and her husband popularized the tango on the Orpheum vaudeville circuit. Through her third husband, Harry Wilson, she began her career as a motion picture publicist, which led, naturally, to fan magazine writing. Two of her earliest feature articles were on Glenda Farrell in the June 1933 issue of *The New Movie Magazine* and Frances Dee and Joel McCrea in the January 1934 issue of *Silver Screen*. Ivy Crane Wilson died in Los Angeles on December 7, 1977, at the age of ninety.

A somewhat later arrival on the scene was Fredda Dudley Balling, who contributed to *Movieland* in the early through mid 1940s, with feature articles on Robert Walker (July 1944) and George Sanders (September 1945) and an

Ivy Crane Wilson (center) greets a group of visiting French film personalities in the 1950s.

"Inside Hollywood" gossip column, which appeared in 1944 and 1945 and perhaps later. She helped Bette Davis with an advice column in *Photoplay* in the 1940s and was a columnist for *Screen Stars* in the 1960s. Balling was also coauthor of director Tay Garnett's amusing 1973 autobiography, *Light Your Torches and Pull Up Your Tights*. Born in Longmont, Colorado, on May 29, 1905, Fredda Dudley Balling died in Los Angeles on February 24, 1990.

Ernest V. Heyn, who succeeded Ruth Waterbury at *Photoplay*, was described by her as someone who "didn't have the mood. With him it was a job. They say this is dated, that is not dated. If things were as dated as people say, there wouldn't be any Christmas. Sentimentality [is what] I believe people want."[19] Heyn may have lacked sentimentality and nostalgia, but he took over *Photoplay* in a new and changing decade—and he certainly had a lengthy résumé as a fan magazine editor.

A 1925 graduate of Princeton who did postgraduate work at the University of Berlin, Heyn seems an odd choice to be editor of *Film Fun*, probably his first editorial appointment circa 1929. He was founding editor of *Modern Screen* in 1930, a position he held until 1934, and later in the decade Heyn edited *Screen Guide* and *Movie Mirror*. When the latter merged with *Photoplay*, Heyn took over as editor, a position he held until May 1942. Carl F. Cotter described him as about the hardest editor to please and the one with the highest editorial standard. In the same article, Cotter cited Eliot Keen at *Silver Screen* and Bill Hartley at *Screen Book* as the friendliest and the promptest to reply.[20]

From 1949 to 1951, Heyn was editor-in-chief of *True Story*, and from 1964 to 1971 he was editor of *Popular Science*. He also authored a history of the magazine, *One Hundred Years of Popular Science* (1972). Ernest Victor Heyn died in New York on June 28, 1995, at the age of ninety.

A familiar figure as editor, but less well documented than Ernest V. Heyn, was Lester C. Grady, whose name appeared on the masthead of *Film Fun* (circa 1930–1938), *Silver Screen* (circa 1939–1953), *Movie Show Magazine* (circa 1942–1943 and 1947), and *Screenland* (circa 1948–1953).

Were these writers, editors, and their peers talented or were they hacks? It is a difficult question to answer in that obviously few, if any, fan magazine writers devoted much thought to what they were churning out month after month. The energy and time that they expanded was considerable, but, ultimately, there was probably little respect for the end product. A few fan magazine writers, such as Jane Ardmore and Gladys Hall, retained copies of their draft articles and the published results. Myrtle Gebhart pasted her clippings into oversized scrapbooks. However, many fan magazine writers simply had no interest in what they had contributed to American popular culture. If Ruth Waterbury needed to look up a piece she had written twenty years earlier in *Photoplay*, she didn't go to her nonexistent files, but rather paid a rushed visit to the Margaret Herrick Library of the Academy of Motion Picture Arts and Sciences. In all probability, she was in the majority.

The disparagement of the craft of fan magazine writing is no more apparent than in a 1943 article written by an anonymous exponent, "Yes, some of us can write. We have occasionally made the better magazines of general circulation. But that only makes the majority of us pathetic. For fan magazine writing is insidious. It is so simple, for the most part, that a dull high school boy could do it. The result is that we tend to take the easiest way: we manufacture drivel at so much a word."[21]

CHAPTER 7

THE GOLDEN AGE OF THE FAN MAGAZINE

The "golden age" of the fan magazine embraced three decades, the 1920s through the 1940s, an era when Americans acknowledged the motion picture as their primary source of entertainment and when interest from the general public in anything movie-related was at its height. In the 1930s, America was suffering through the Great Depression, film companies were faltering, and Paramount was in receivership, but the fan magazines kept on going.

In May 1933, *The Hollywood Reporter* noted a slight slump in fan magazine sales the previous year, aligning it with the inability of both the periodicals and the studios to attract sufficient fans at a time of fiscal crisis. *Photoplay* suffered the most, in part because of James R. Quirk's death and Kathryn Dougherty's appointment as editor, but also because its two major rivals, *Modern Screen* and *Silver Screen*, offered more of what the public wanted to read and at a lower price—ten cents versus twenty-five cents. At this point, newsstand sales were as follows: *Modern Screen* 556,421; *Silver Screen* 471,806; *Photoplay* 461,842; *Motion Picture* 456,002; *Picture Play* 341,218; *Movie Classic* 326,852; *Screen Book* 267,573; *Screenland* 262,611; *Screen Play* 211,132; *Hollywood* 181,694; *Screen Romances* 137,141; and *Film Fun* 130,097.[1]

A little over a year later, on August 15, 1934, *The Hollywood Reporter* returned to the subject of fan magazine circulation and pointed out that those periodicals specializing in sensationalism the previous year had lost circulation, while the opposing group had gained. Both *Photoplay* and *Screen Play* reported increased circulation. *Modern Screen* lost 100,000 in circulation, while *Photoplay* gained about the same number. "It looks as if the movie fans are wearying of sensationalism and salaciousness in their reading matter. After all, why not?" asked *The Hollywood Reporter*'s hopeful if somewhat optimistic Frank Pope. "The element that made fan magazine readers, that increased them to millions a month, was the glamour that surrounded their favorite stars."[2]

Paramount production chief
Jesse L. Lasky keeps up-to-date
on the current fan magazines.
Courtesy of Academy of
Motion Picture Arts and
Sciences.

Aside from the newsstand sales, there was little, in reality, to distinguish one fan magazine from another. As Clifton Fadiman wrote, "The thinnest ones cost a nickel, the fattest ones cost a quarter. That's how you tell them apart."[3] A price war of sorts developed after the first publication in December 1929 by the Tower group of *The New Movie Magazine*, distributed at the five-and-dime stores, most notably Woolworth's, at ten cents a copy. *Time* magazine (October 15, 1934) described Tower's magazines, its rival publishing house, as the "gum-chewers" magazines, to which Tower promotion manager Lucile Babcock responded, on November 12, 1934, "gum chewing is no longer merely a ruminative agitation of the jaws. It now has purpose, character, and style direction." By 1933, *The New Movie Magazine* was probably the biggest selling of fan magazines, with an estimated circulation of 650,000 copies. (Exact figures were unavailable because the Tower group reported the sales of its three periodicals, two of which were unrelated to film, as a group.) Within a short space of time, eight of the leading fan magazines had followed *The New Movie Magazine*'s lead and sold their issues for ten cents.

The editorial director of Tower magazines was Hugh Weir, who obviously fancied himself as an Americanized version of Noel Coward, managing to look both stolid and effete in photographs, showing him in profile with his lips clasped around a cigarette holder. According to the 1931 edition of *The Motion Picture Almanac*, Weir was a reporter, a newspaper feature writer, newspaper editor, a scenario writer, a film editor, a writer for and editor of magazines, and an author of books, who "has kept in touch with the changing times." He certainly had a magic touch when it came to popular magazines, claiming a record sale of 22,230,706 copies of Tower magazines purchased by "shopping women" between 1929 and 1931.

The New Movie Magazine disproved suggestions that the fan magazine deteriorated in the 1930s. It certainly contained fewer pages than *Photoplay* and its other, more expensive rivals, and the quality of the reproduction of the illustrations was somewhat inferior, but the content was excellent and on a par with the best that James R. Quirk had to offer. The cover illustrations for almost all of the first year were by the highly regarded artist Penrhyn Stanlaws, beginning in December 1929 with Nancy Carroll and including Bebe Daniels in April 1930 and Lila Lee in July 1930. Another prominent illustrator associated with *The New Movie Magazine* was McClelland Barclay. Catherine McNelis, president of Tower, deserves credit for negotiating a wide circulation for the magazine, which by September 1930 announced in each issue on its contents page, "On sale the 15th of each month in Woolworth stores." Credit for the content itself belongs to the first editor, Frederick James Smith, who also reviewed films to the same high standard and in similar format to the *Photoplay* approach.

Also from *Photoplay*, *The New Movie Magazine* took its two principal writers, Adela Rogers St. Johns and Herbert Howe, whose name was often featured on the cover. Both contributed original articles, and Howe also wrote "The Hollywood Boulevardier" column. There was also a general gossip column, and Walter Winchell was represented for the first few months by a regular column, initially titled "Snappy Comebacks Untold Stories of the Movies." Other regular contributors, familiar to readers of *Photoplay*, included Ruth Biery, Regina Cannon, Homer Croy, and Ruth Waterbury. It is not surprising that in November 1930, *The New Movie Magazine* proudly proclaimed on the front cover, "The Largest Circulation of Any Screen Magazine in the World."

Throughout its short existence—it ceased publication in 1935—*The New Movie Magazine* maintained a high standard of writing, inviting many literary figures to contribute pieces and opinion. At some point, Smith departed as editor and there was no formal replacement, although the reviews were handled by Frederic F. Van de Water, described as a "noted author and critic," whose

The December 1931 issue of *The New Movie Magazine*; Herbert Howe is important enough to have his name on the cover.

approach to the films was "from the angle of the audience." Van de Water (1890–1968) was, in fact, a reporter, newspaper editor, book critic, and specialist writer, who had authored more than thirty-five books, including a biography of General Custer. Herbert Howe continued his column, but it was now signed "Nemo" (Nobody), described as a man-about-town.

Henry Willson began writing a "Junior Hollywood Gossip" column in 1933; he was later to become infamous for his discovery, naming of, and sometimes relationships with Rock Hudson, Rory Calhoun, Troy Donahue, Tab Hunter, and others. Sidney Skolsky, famous for his tintypes in the *New York Daily*

Members of the Tower Magazine group wish success to Nelson Eddy (standing) in 1935, just as their own publication, *The New Movie Magazine*, is about to cease publication. From left to right: James Featherstone, executive; Frank McNelis, editor; Miriam Gibson, assistant editor of *Tower Radio*; Mrs. James Featherston; and Frederick James Smith, editor of *Tower Radio*. Courtesy of Academy of Motion Picture Arts and Sciences.

News, made his first appearance in December 1931 with an article on Edward G. Robinson titled "Putting Little Caesar on the Spot." As late as November 1935, Skolsky contributed a piece on Jimmy Durante. (He had contributed to *Screen Play* in January 1934 with a series of articles, beginning with a piece on Mae West. In the 1950s, he fronted a fan magazine–like nostalgia publication titled *Sidney Skolsky's This Was Hollywood*.)

The biggest change to *The New Movie Magazine* came in February 1935, when the page size was dramatically increased to a size that was to be adopted a year later for the first and all future issues of *Life* magazine. Two years later, in October 1937, *Photoplay* followed suit, with a similar page size, as well as a "natural color photograph" by George Hurrell of Joan Crawford on the cover and major articles by Gilbert Seldes, Lowell Thomas, and novelist Faith Baldwin.

The New Movie Magazine briefly experimented with a complementary publication, *The New Movie Album: A New Who's Who of the Screen*, first (and probably last) published in October 1930. Joan Crawford graced the cover, and each page was devoted to an individual star with a photograph and biography.

If *The New Movie Magazine* was in the tradition of *Photoplay* at its best, there were two other, short-lived fan magazines in the 1930s that lived up to *Photoplay*'s editorial standards but were also artistically and stylishly the most elegant fan magazines ever produced.

The first, titled simply *Cinema*, was an oversized publication, foreshadowing the dimensions of *Life* magazine, which billed itself as "The Magazine of the Photoplay." Published for only one year, from January through December

1930, *Cinema* boasted beautifully reproduced photographs on the highest quality art paper. The cover art was of an equally high standard, and the May 1930 issue depicted a youthful Jean Arthur, sketched by Alberto Vargas, decades before he was to become familiar to *Playboy* readers.

Some major names from the early years of serious film criticism were represented in the pages of *Cinema*. Harry Alan Potamkin wrote on "The Rise and Fall of the German Film" (April), "The Cinema in Great Britain" (May), "Film Beginnings in Belgium and Holland" (June), and "Cinema Iberia" (December). Wilton A. Barrett contributed a piece on art cinemas to the April issue. In June, S. M. Eisenstein and G. V. Alexandrov discussed "Doing without Actors." Pare Lorentz wrote on "Screen Comedy" in May and on "Good, Bad and Corporate Test," being the mix of art and business in the making of motion pictures, in June.

The dramatic reviewer was Creighton Peet, while editor James Shelley Hamilton handled film reviews. Hamilton was a pioneering screenwriter, supposedly responsible for *The Perils of Pauline*, who had been an editor at *McClure's* and *Romance*. A graduate of Amherst College in 1906, he was responsible for its famed ballad, "Lord Jeffrey Amherst." From 1934 until 1945, he served as executive director of the National Board of Review. At his death, in Rutland, Vermont, on June 5, 1953, at the age of sixty-nine, Terry Ramsaye described Hamilton in *Motion Picture Herald* (June 13, 1953) as a "scholar and author of quiet distinction," adding he was "much a friend of the movies. He was also a good gardener, in retirement up in Vermont."

Cinema Arts was certainly the most sumptuous film magazine ever produced in any genre or type. A prototype edition, "for private circulation and not for sale," appeared in September 1936 as an oversized, spiral-bound edition. A year later, in June, July, and September 1937, three additional issues were published. All were oversized with hard covers featuring caricatures by Jaro Fabry. (The June issue contained some pieces that had earlier appeared in the prototype edition.) On par with the quality of the artwork was the quality of the articles, written by critics such as Mordaunt Hall, Frank Nugent, Richard Watts Jr., and Archer Winsten; filmmakers such as Bella and Samuel Spewack, Kenneth Macgowan, and Rouben Mamoulian; and socialites such as Helena Rubinstein. Paul F. Husserl was credited as editor of the three 1937 issues.

The 1930s saw the introduction of many other new fan magazines. Typical was *Modern Movies*, first published in July 1937 under the editorship of William T. Walsh, who was succeeded a year later by May C. Kelly. The emphasis here was on gossip with the "It Happens in Hollywood" column, later retitled "Hollywood Happenings." *Modern Movies* had an initial cover price of fifteen cents, but in April 1939 it lowered the cost to ten cents.

The golden age was very much a good golden age for the consumer, as fan magazines lowered their prices. For example, a month after *Modern Movies*' decision, *Screen Romances* lowered its cover price from twenty-five to ten cents. Good value does not always reflect honesty and integrity, and while there are many commentators who criticized the ethical standards of the articles and interviews therein, the film reviews have been subject to little appraisal. Because of a publication schedule far in advance of the release of many films, it is obvious that the fan magazines did not necessarily see the films under review. Generally, they got away with it. Sometimes they were caught out.

On September 8, 1933, *Daily Variety* published a front-page story concerning ten films reviewed in the new, October, issue of *The New Movie Magazine*. It was reported that five of the films were still being edited, one completed production the previous day, one was still in production, and another had not even finished shooting. *Only Yesterday*, which finished shooting three days earlier, was described by *The New Movie Magazine* as "slow and somewhat stodgy." Of *Dancing Lady*, still in production, the fan magazine reported, "The story is the same general type as *Dancing Daughters*. Robert Z. Leonard has directed a fast moving show." Of *Ann Vickers*, still being edited, *The New Movie Magazine* commented, "From the moment when she gives in to her first man to the time she stills the unrest of her last man, there is no moment when Miss [Irene] Dunne is not at her ease." Lillian Harvey had made two films for Fox, one of which remained unreleased and the other finished the previous week. *The New Movie Magazine* commented, "*My Lips Betray* was okay . . . or seemed to me . . . but *My Weakness* is going to put her right on the top. Harry Langdon gets a pretty good break and Lew Ayres does exceptionally well. I'd like to see someone taller than Lew work opposite Miss Harvey in her next picture."

The New Movie Magazine was not the only fan journal caught out. Three years later, a gossip column in the December 9, 1936, issue of *The Hollywood Reporter* revealed that *Photoplay* routinely reviewed films that had not as yet even been previewed, "Something funny about the whole thing somewhere!"

Because of the lack of extant complete runs for most fan magazines from this period, it is virtually impossible to determine just which star dominated the cover art at any one time. However, thanks to a 1933–1934 survey by *The Hollywood Reporter*, such information is available for that period. The results are both surprising and expected. Topping the list with ten covers were Joan Crawford and Mae West. Tied in second place with nine each were Katharine Hepburn and Greta Garbo. Surprisingly, next came Ruby Keeler with seven, beating out Jean Harlow with six covers, and Myrna Loy, Kay Francis, Norma Shearer, and Lillian Harvey with five each. Fox was trying hard to make Lillian Harvey a Hollywood star, but failed, and she soon returned to a career in German films. Another Fox star, Janet Gaynor, had four covers, reminding us that she was a prominent star in the early through mid 1930s. She tied with Carole Lombard. Astonishingly, Marlene Dietrich had only three, along with Claudette Colbert and Constance Bennett. Clara Bow, at the end of her career, still managed to garner two covers, as did Sally Eilers, Helen Hayes, Miriam Hopkins, Jean Parker, Margaret Sullavan, Sylvia Sidney, and Gloria Stuart. With one each were some big names and some completely forgotten figures: Lillian Bond, Glenda Farrell, Frances Dee, Mary Pickford (thanks to her last film, *Secrets*), Dorothy Jordan, Marion Davies, Adrienne Ames, Ginger

On the set of *Polly of the Circus* (1932), Clark Gable and Marion Davies enjoy the latest issue of *Motion Picture*. Courtesy of Academy of Motion Picture Arts and Sciences.

Rogers, Lupe Velez, Bette Davis, Ann Harding, Lona Andre, Loretta Young, Anna Sten, Madge Evans, Alice White, Heather Angel, Constance Cummings, Patricia Ellis, and Dolores Del Rio.

No men made the covers unless accompanied by a female star. Clark Gable was on the cover of *Hollywood Movie Novels*, supporting Jean Harlow, and on the cover of *Modern Screen* with Mae West, despite their being under contract to different studios. (That same issue, August 1933, also ran a competition offering cash prizes for the best answer to "Why Not Clark Gable as Mae West's Screen Lover?") John Gilbert made it onto the cover of *Picture Parade* thanks to Garbo, and, of all people, James Dunne was featured on the cover of *Hollywood Movie Novels*, alongside Sally Eilers.

Shirley Temple on the cover of *Screenland*.

Inside the magazines there was little new on offer, but Greta Garbo dominated. Despite an obvious lack of personal interviews, *Screen Book* (July 1933) reported on what she ate, said, and did on a trip from Sweden to San Diego. That same month, *Hollywood Movie Novels* reported that her uncle was a taxicab driver in Stockholm. In August 1933, *Screen Play* began running "The Only True Story of Garbo's Private Life" by her former private secretary, Sven-Hugo Borg. An "imaginative" meeting between Garbo and Mae West generated commentary in a number of fan magazines early in 1933.

Mickey Mouse got more coverage than some stars, with pieces in *Screenland* (July 1933), *The New Movie Magazine* (August 1933), and *Movie Classic* (November 1933), along with an exposé by Walt Disney in *Screen Book* (January 1934). With so much coverage, it is little wonder that in May 1934 *Photoplay* published "Is Walt Disney a Menace to Our Children" by David Frederick McCord, which worried over the nightmares that the Big Bad Wolf in *Three Little Pigs* might cause.

It is surprising how many confessional stories were featured and just how many relatively forgotten stars were featured in a typical issue. For example, in October 1933 *Screenland* had Dixie Lee Crosby writing on "What I Think of Bing," character comedian Charlie Ruggles with "My Confessions," Joe E. Brown's life story, interviews with Paul Robeson and Ginger Rogers, Constance Cummings on her marriage to British playwright (and later politician) Benn Levy, and a joint article on brothers Frank and Ralph Morgan.

Which star had the most cover art from the 1930s through the 1950s? An argument might certainly be made on behalf of Shirley Temple, who graced 138 covers from that period. She could be seen on fifteen from *Modern Screen* (1935–1951), twelve from *Photoplay* (1935–1950), and eleven from *Screenland* (1934–1958).[4] In comparison, Kay Francis, who had starred in the Warner Bros. film *Mandalay* (1934), while Temple supported, appeared on the covers of thirty-eight American fan magazines, beginning with *Motion Picture* in July 1930 and ending with *Picture Play* in November 1937.

According to *Variety*, Shirley Temple was the subject of the most space given to female stars in the fan magazines in 1935.[5] She also beat out Clark Gable, who came first in the male division. Runners-up in the female field were Joan Crawford, Claudette Colbert, Ginger Rogers, Greta Garbo, Jean Harlow, Carole Lombard, Katharine Hepburn, Mae West, and Marlene Dietrich. Trailing Gable were Fred Astaire, Gary Cooper, Bing Crosby, Dick Powell, Will Rogers, Franchot Tone, Nelson Eddy, William Powell, and John Boles. Of approximately 2500 established players, only 330 were found on the covers, in full-page and half-page photographs, and in individual interviews and feature stories in the fan magazines.

In 1935, *Variety* surveyed twelve publications: *Photoplay, Picture Play, Silver Screen, Screenland, Motion Picture, Classic, Screen Play, Screen Book, Hollywood, Movie Mirror,* and *Modern Screen.* Of the 132 covers represented by these magazines, Claudette Colbert was seen on ten; Shirley Temple on nine; Ginger Rogers on eight; Carole Lombard and Jean Harlow on seven; Janet Gaynor, Joan Crawford, Myrna Loy, and Ruby Keeler on six; Miriam Hopkins, Mae West, Greta Garbo, and Katharine Hepburn on four; Kay Francis, Dolores Del Rio, Alice Faye, Ann Sothern, Marion Davies, Bette Davis, and Loretta Young on three; Marlene Dietrich, Gloria Stuart, Virginia Bruce, Merle Oberon, Jeanette MacDonald, Margaret Sullavan, Joan Bennett, Grace Moore, and Ann Harding on two; and Irene Dunne, Lillian Harvey, Anna Sten, Madge Evans, Mary Carlisle, and Elizabeth Allen on one. There were no male stars on any of the covers.

The fan magazines were willing and able to provide moviegoers with everything they needed to know on the subject despite increasing competition from other published sources. Popular periodicals devoted increasing space to Hollywood, and by the 1930s, for example, *Ladies' Home Journal* had its own correspondent reporting back from the film studios. Relatively serious film reviews began to appear. *Life*, the old humor magazine, had paid scant attention to films in the 1910s, but a decade later it was publishing on a regular basis reviews by the distinguished theater critic Robert E. Sherwood (who was to become its editor from 1924–1928). As of 1931, *The Motion Picture Almanac* reported a total of 181 motion picture editors at various American newspapers.[6] Of that number thirty-five were female.

One popular magazine with major coverage of the Hollywood scene, along with film reviews, was *Liberty*, which began life on May 10, 1924, as a weekly, five-cent publication. It became biweekly on February 1, 1947 (the beginning of the end) and monthly from September 1947 through July 1950, when it ceased publication. Adela Rogers St. Johns was its leading contributor of stories on Hollywood. Other fan magazine writers found in its pages include Kirtley Baskette (1936–1941), Margaret E. Sangster (1932–1940), Frederick James Smith (1924–1941), Ruth Waterbury (1926–1942), and Elizabeth Wilson (1944–1949). However, *Liberty* used fewer fan magazine writers than might be expected; for example, Adele Whitley Fletcher was represented in its pages by only one piece, "Does Your Job Fit You," in July 1942.

As early as March 14, 1927, *Liberty* had aligned itself strongly with the film industry, launching a $50,000 competition to find a story from its readers that would be serialized in the magazine and produced as a feature-length film by Famous Players–Lasky Corporation. Bernarr Macfadden took over publication of *Liberty* from its founders, Col. Robert Rutherford McCormick and Capt. Joseph Medill Patterson, in 1931, after it had lost them $12 million.

Another of Macfadden's publications, *True Confessions*, which had commenced publication in 1922, by the 1930s had the look of one of his fan magazines. Selling for ten cents a copy, *True Confessions* provided readers with such unsigned features as "The Cinderella Career of Barbara Stanwyck" (March 1934) and "The Men in Garbo's Glamorous Life" (February 1935), with the stars' faces on the cover very obviously helping to sell the magazine on the newsstand. Dating back to 1919, *True Story Magazine* was Macfadden's most popular periodical, selling for twenty-five cents in the 1920s and for fifteen cents in the 1930s. Billie Dove graced the cover of its March 1929 issue and Ginger Rogers was on the cover of the June 1937 issue, with "Ginger Rogers Own Story" inside. There was even a hint of nostalgia in April 1934 as Pola Negri wrote on "Rudy Valentino and I."

Two new magazines came along in the 1930s, both of which would impact the circulation of the fan magazines. The first, and most important, was *Life*, first published on November 23, 1936. In cover size it resembled the later issues of *The New Movie Magazine*, but there the resemblance ended. The emphasis at *Life* was on current news, in which Hollywood was not a major player.

It was not until May 3, 1937, that a Hollywood star, Jean Harlow, made the front cover, followed by Harpo Marx (September 6, 1937), Nelson Eddy (September 27, 1937), and Greta Garbo (November 8, 1937). In later years, *Life* was to average on its covers four or five movie stars a year. Similar in format, but more Hollywood-oriented was *Look* magazine, first published in January 1937. Its first issue featured Dolores Del Rio and Joan Crawford, followed in issue no. 2 by Myrna Loy and Greta Garbo, and in issue no. 3 by Marlene Dietrich and Jean Harlow. The major difference between *Look* and the fan magazines was that that latter catered to women, whereas *Look* was promoted as a magazine for a male readership.

By the 1930s, fan magazines routinely carried advertising from the major studios. For example, in March 1929 *Motion Picture* carried one page of advertising each from Fox Movietone News, Paramount, First National, and Warner Bros. In September 1931, the magazine had one page of advertising from Paramount and MGM and two pages from Fox. *Modern Screen* for October 1932 had one page of advertising each from Fox, Paramount, and Universal and two pages from MGM. A decade later little had changed, with *Modern Screen* for September 1949 carrying one page each of advertising from MGM, Paramount, Universal-International, and Warner Bros., two-thirds of a page of advertising from Walt Disney, all promoting individual productions and a number of movie star and studio-connected product advertising.

It had not always been so. Initially, the studios had concentrated on the popular, nonspecific periodicals. Educational, the first company to consistently advertise short films in national magazines, began its general advertising with the 1921–1922 season, taking space first of all in the *Saturday Evening Post* and *Ladies' Home Journal*. It was not until the mid 1920s that Educational began to advertise in the fan magazines. Pathé took out its first magazine advertising in the *Saturday Evening Post* in 1916, but by the late 1920s it was concentrating on advertising in fan magazines only. The company made no secret that it went out of its way to provide the fan magazines with whatever they wanted. Writing in 1918, its publicity manager P. A. Parsons noted, "As they are important and decidedly worth catering to, each of them should be studied to meet their requirements. Specially taken photographs, clear-cut and snappy, gossipy interviews of real interest, exclusive articles on subjects worthwhile, 'personality stuff' which is different—one will find these in the fan magazines, and such should be the character of the material furnished. Truly it is a far cry from the old days when the same old bunk went to every publication regardless of its nature and requirements."[7]

The *Saturday Evening Post*, along with *Ladies Home Journal, Literary Digest*, and the old *Life* humor magazine, were the periodicals of choice when United Artists embarked on a $75,000 advertising campaign for Douglas Fairbanks' *Robin Hood* in 1922. As late as 1927, *Photoplay* was the only fan magazine routinely used for advertising purposes by Universal. The thrust of its advertising campaigns was directed at the *Saturday Evening Post, Boys' Life, American Boy*, and various farm journals.[8]

Arguably, during the so-called golden age for both the fan magazines and the Hollywood film industry, the magazines were more attractive to a female audience and more determinedly marketed toward such a readership. At least two contemporary writers tried to analyze the relationship between the fan magazine and its reader, Margaret Farrand Thorp in 1939 and Leo A. Handel in the 1950s.

Thorp noted that in Hollywood at the time of her study there are more than 300 correspondents representing the fan magazines, the "quality" periodicals, and the newspaper syndicates. These writers "make it possible for the worshiper to identify herself with the glamorous star as she can do with no other character in fiction."[9] "The imitative fan is almost always feminine,"[10] and the writer helped the identification process with information as to how to dress as the stars do, to color hair and apply makeup as they do, to eat what they eat, and to furnish their homes in a replicative fashion. "Everything is superlative, surprising, exciting."[11]

Writing a decade later, Handel cited a 1948 *Seventeen* magazine survey, "Teenage Girls and Their Motion Picture Habits." The survey linked the female approach of the fan magazines with financial considerations. Families always followed their daughters' choices in the selection of motion picture.[12] Thus, what the fan magazines had to say to their female readership equated to revenue at the box office. A 1948 study by Dr. Paul Lazarsfeld of Columbia University came up with a similar opinion. His contention was that fan magazine readers were the "opinion leaders" among moviegoers, and thus, they could make or break a film at the box office.[13]

What might a fan expect to read in her magazine of choice during this golden age? As already noted, there were rules governing content, and *Picture Play*'s Norbert Lusk identified some of them:

> Enough for a writer to remember he must not bring up the subject of clothes to Kay Francis, must not infer Irene Dunne is cultivated and well-mannered, even though it is obvious in all she says and does; must not write of Nelson Eddy and Jeanette MacDonald in the same paragraph. Mention of Mae West's business acumen is taboo, and Sonia Henie's enormous earnings as a skating star of rink and screen must be ignored. Marriage and fatherhood are forbidden topics in interviews with Gary Cooper and Fred Astaire, nor must the latter's real name of Austerlitz be given, while Ginger Rogers' union with Lew Ayres was a nonexistent fact which the compliant reporter shunned till divorce routed the hobgoblin.
>
> George Raft's choice of fisticuffs as the quickest means of settling a difference of opinion was a virtue never to be extolled in the fan magazines; but the remaining catalogue of his good points might be repeated any number of times. Melvyn Douglas's friends and outside interests, except for his wife and son, were banished from articles about him. House furnishings of glazed chintz offended Douglas Fairbanks Jr., whose relationship to his famous father was something else he would just as like be left out. Attempt was made to safeguard the good

behavior of Simone Simon when reporters were cautioned not to let fall the name of Janet Gaynor in her presence. [Gaynor had starred in the silent version of *7th Heaven* and Simon in the sound remake.] The face of Joe E. Brown was under protection, too. It must never be described as funny. But he could make funny faces.[14]

The fan magazines presented the stars as approachable when, in reality, they were not. They were real in that they found love and happiness—often on a monthly basis—and they thought long and hard before embarking on marriage. Would Barbara Stanwyck marry Robert Taylor or not? The more she thought about it, the more copy she provided as fan magazine fodder—and the longer her name and her face would be in public view. In 1937, *Motion Picture* magazine managed to publish six pieces relative to Stanwyck and Taylor and their romance, a full two years before they actually married: "I'm Not Ready for Marriage Yet," Robert Taylor to Leon Surmelian (January); "Eleanor Powell Writes a Letter to Your Bob," Bunny Russell (March); "What! No Bob Taylor!," a pictorial feature (April); "The Taylor Harlow 'Romance,'" Carol Craig (May); "I'm in No Mood for Marriage," Barbara Stanwyck to Molly Gardner (May); and "This Is Their Affair," a pictorial feature (June).

Perhaps Hollywood stars did right to worry about marriage and take their time, based on the number of articles the fan magazines were publishing on divorce. In late 1933, there was Eric L. Ergenbright's "The Divorce Epidemic Strikes Hollywood" in *Motion Picture* (September 1933), Harriet Parsons' "Behind the Scenes of the Divorce Epidemic" in *Modern Screen* (October 1933), Dr. Louis E. Bisch's "Psycho-Analyzing the Hollywood Divorce Epidemic" in *Screen Book* (October 1933), and, on a calmer note, "Secrets of Hollywood Happy Divorces" by Herbert Howe in *The New Movie Magazine* (November 1933). On a personal note, Ruth Biery reported "Carole Lombard Admits the Truth about Her Divorce" in *Screen Play* (December 1933).

Between June 1933 and June 1934, *The Hollywood Reporter* published a series titled "Reviewing the Fan Mags." Not only did it report on the content of each, but it also recorded the number of square inches devoted to each studio in each issue. An analysis of these findings reveals little that is unexpected. Eighteen fan magazines were included in the survey: *Hollywood, Hollywood Mirror, Hollywood Movie Novels, Modern Screen, Motion Picture, Movie Classic, Movie Mirror, Movies, The New Movie Magazine, Photoplay, Picture Parade, Picture Play, Screen Book, Screen Play, Screen Romances, Screenland, Shadoplay,* and *Silver Screen,* some probably on a selective basis.

The most important studio in Hollywood, MGM, had the most coverage in the year, a total of 75,841 square inches. In second place was Paramount, which most would rate as Hollywood's second major studio, with 62,696 square inches. Warner Bros. came third with 39,429 square inches; fourth was RKO with 34,447 square inches. United Artists boasted 15,852 square inches, Universal had 11,008 square inches, and Columbia garnered 6134 square inches. Last came Twentieth Century Pictures, which only entered the list halfway

A 1938 theater exhibitor displays a wall of fan magazine covers. Courtesy of Academy of Motion Picture Arts and Sciences.

through the process and had yet to merge with the Fox Film Corporation. It had 2182 square inches.

The amount of space could often be linked to a specific cause and effect. In July 1933, *Screenland* featured ten photographs of Katharine Hepburn, primarily from *Morning Glory*, which helped move RKO into second place behind MGM. The latter had the largest amount of space in the August 1933 issue of *Movie Mirror* thanks to the fictionalized story of *Tugboat Annie* and contract star Lee Tracy's autobiography. Warner Bros. garnered the most space in the November issue of *Movie Mirror* thanks to a story on choreographer Busby Berkeley and a fictionalization of the Barbara Stanwyck vehicle, *Ever in My Heart*. Paramount easily gained the top space in the May 1934 issue of

Photoplay with pieces on four of its contract players—Sylvia Sidney, George Raft, Bing Crosby, and Richard Arlen—as well as an article on showmen Earl Carroll, then associated with the studio. Universal's coverage was relatively low because the studio lot was closed during the first part of 1933.

Some claim the 1920s was the decade in which the fan magazines displayed the most intelligent coverage of the industry, but there was little to differentiate the 1930s and the 1940s. The advent of World War II and the more realistic films that ensued had little impact on the fan magazine reader. She still wanted escapist fare, and the magazines were willing and able to provide it. What the war did accomplish was to reduce still further the male readership of the fan magazines. The likes of *Photoplay* and *Modern Screen* were read at the hairdresser or beauty salon, not in an army barracks or aboard a battleship.

The fan magazines had taken note of Hitler not in regard to his anti-Semitism or in horror at his march into Austria and Czechoslovakia, but rather his infatuation with Marlene Dietrich. In December 1933, *Modern Screen* ran a piece by Princess Catherine Radziwill on that theme, titled "The Strange Case of Hitler and Dietrich." A similar piece by Dorothy Calhoun appeared in the January 1934 issue of *Motion Picture*, with the title "Hitler Demands Return of German Stars." Dietrich did not return to Germany, and both Hitler and the fan magazines got over it.

Prior to America's entry into World War II, at least one fan magazine, *Movie-Radio Guide*, took up the issue of the country's neutrality with its readers in the summer of 1941. First they were asked to consider Charles A. Lindbergh and his isolationist policy, and then on August 23 whether they approved of President Roosevelt's foreign policy. Lindberg and Roosevelt and the politics of the day received less space than articles devoted to Garbo's glamour and Cesar Romero picking Hollywood best dancers.

It was *Movie-Radio Guide* that also published, on April 5, 1941, an article by Norman Kerry titled "I Saw the Fall of France." The piece might be dismissed as one of many on this major catastrophe for the allied cause except that the author had been a silent screen star, the leading man in the Lon Chaney vehicle *The Phantom of the Opera*. In 1939, Kerry had joined the French Foreign Legion after many years of semi-retirement in Europe.

Benito Mussolini's propaganda activities came to the attention of *Photoplay* in September 1941, when he addressed a letter to Deanna Durbin, published in the daily press. The Italian leader wrote that "in the past we always had a soft spot in our heart for you," but feared that, like the remainder of American youth, she was now controlled by the president. He implored, "If you only knew how good and beautiful are the children of Rome and Berlin and how much poetry there is in the youth of Europe, then you wouldn't listen to your and our enemies." While *Photoplay* was in the process of obtaining a comment from the star, or concocting one of its own, H. I. Phillips of the New York *Sun* replied on her behalf, and *Photoplay* gladly reprinted the response on its editorial page. It concluded,

Anyhow, Mister Mussolini, you are not half so sorry about me as I am about you. I know you are unhappy with Adolf. I know you would rather play in somebody else's yard.

I'll bet you would like to be a little boy or girl and come right out and give your honest opinion about Nazism, Hitler and German aggressiveness. I'll bet that if you could do it without anybody's knowing it you would love to go into a movie theater and boo newsreels of Hitler.

You're sorry for little girls like me, mister! Well, am I sorry for big boys like you!

There are numerous books dealing with the motion picture and World War II, but one will look in vain in their pages for references to the fan magazines and the situation in Europe and the Pacific. It was as if America deliberately ignored what the fan magazines might accomplish for the war effort. The War Activities Committee of the Motion Picture Industry was created immediately after the outbreak of the war in order that the screen might most effectively serve the all-out victory program.[15] The editors of *The Hollywood Reporter* and *Daily Variety* were appointed members of the committee, and there was even a Trade Press Division. The fan magazines were excluded.

The December 1941 issues of the fan magazines had, of course, already appeared prior to the attack on Pearl Harbor, and it was not until January or February 1942 that the fan magazines caught up with the war. The initial coverage was primarily devoted to photographs of movie stars in uniform. For its August 1942 issue, *Photoplay* published a cover of the Stars and Stripes, with photographs of various male stars in the armed forces. Efforts were made to cover all branches of the military. In February 1942, *Photoplay* reported on a young contract player named Peter Ashley, training at California's March Field air corps base. A two-page spread in *Photoplay* (April 1943) featured 120 Hollywood players then in the military, from Hardie Albright to Lewis Howard. Twentieth Century–Fox production head, Col. Darryl F. Zanuck, wrote in *Photoplay*'s June 1943 issue of the war on the North African battle front. *Movie Stars Parade* ran a regular "Stars 'n' Stripes" column, featuring photographs of movie stars in uniform on furlough. In December 1943, *Modern Screen* honored a group of young actors who had joined the Army Air Force, including George Reeves, Edmond O'Brien, and Ray Middleton, and who had then returned to Hollywood to appear in a screen adaptation of Moss Hart's salute to the Force, *Winged Victory*.

It was not an easy life for a Hollywood actor in the military, as a lengthy article titled "The Truth about the Stars in Service," written by "Fearless," explained in the May 1944 issue of *Photoplay*. It was reported that Tony Martin, while in the Navy, was the subject of innuendo that he had accepted presents from young Navy men whose careers he might influence. Victor Mature, in the Coast Guard, was assigned to carry the ship's garbage ashore each day for disposition. Glenn Ford found it hard to be "one of the guys" after one of his movies was shown while he was in boot camp. The piece provided a fascinating

MOVIE-RADIO GUIDE

TEN CENTS • CANADA—12c   PROGRAMS FOR APRIL 5—11

BETTY GRABLE
Next to be seen in
the 20th Century-
Fox picture "Miami"

"I Saw the Fall of France," by Norman Kerry
Special! Complete New Radio Log of All Stations Listed by Wave-Length Locations!

The April 5, 1941, issue of *Movie-Radio Guide* features a piece by former silent leading man Norman Kerry on the fall of France.

record of the far-from-easy life in the military for a Hollywood star. "Fearless" lived up to his reputation, as promised in a January 1941 editorial, of "a writer who disproves the suspicion, which I have often heard, that motion-picture magazines don't really print the truth about Hollywood."

Hollywood's most famous conscientious objector, Lew Ayres, was the subject of a critical but not openly hostile piece in the July 1942 issue of *Photoplay* by Adele Whitely Fletcher, titled "The Strange Case of Lew Ayres." The magazine tried to restore Ayres' credibility in June 1945, with a "Letter from Lew Ayres," writing from the South Pacific to Adela Rogers St. Johns, discussing his incredible bravery under fire with the medical corps, and asking "only that you read with an open heart."

To explain away why many in Hollywood were not in the military, as early as May 1942 *Photoplay* published a piece by Walter Winchell, titled "Keep 'em Rolling, Hollywood," in which the gossip columnist and lieutenant commander in the Naval Reserve explained that it was more important to have the stars making movies to boost morale than donning uniforms. He wrote of the three days of devastating bombing suffered by the British city of Coventry:

> The people of Coventry were ripe for any rabble-rouser or government over-thrower. They had buried their dead. They had gone without milk for their children—without food and without shelter. To them life seemed at an end.
>
> A few days after the bombings, someone dug up a movie from Hollywood. It was shown to the people of Coventry and other near-by towns night and day for a week, twenty-four hours a day.
>
> It was so funny it made them laugh for ninety minutes, or at least took their minds from their personal misery.
>
> The star was Bob Hope. The picture was *The Ghost Busters*.

In a similar vein, another newspaper columnist, Ed Sullivan, wrote of "Bob Hope, Hero without Uniform" in the December 1943 issue of *Photoplay*. Asked why some stars were not drafted, in January 1944 *Movie Stars Parade* explained that many, including Spencer Tracy, Humphrey Bogart, Walter Pidgeon, and Cary Grant, were over the age limit. Some, including Don Ameche and Bing Crosby, had Class A dependents. And then there was the 4F brigade: Mickey Rooney, Orson Welles, Errol Flynn, Laird Cregar, and Sonny Tufts, among others. Sadly, *Movie Stars Parade* did not reveal the individual reasons for the 4F label, signifying their unacceptability for the military.

At least one fan magazine writer did her bit for the armed forces. Myrtle Gebhart maintained a wartime correspondence with Corporal William Leonard Eury of the Army Air Force, routinely sending him and his fellow soldiers copies of fan magazines and pin-up photographs supplied by the studios. Eury, in response, gave his opinion as to some of the Hollywood stars contributing to the war effort. "John Payne is still a private in the air corps, and that's the rarest thing in the army," he wrote on September 19, 1944. Eury was also highly critical, noting, in that same letter, "*Photoplay* spoke of Major James Stewart as being a 'veteran of 17 combat missions.' That seems such a small number to be bragging about when compared to the 50 or more missions which all our boys have to do before they can even hope to go back home. I do think that some of the writers should be a little more reticent in roof-topping the awards of the film great, for it really stirs up resentment in the boys."[16]

The fan magazines did not ignore those on the home front. As early as September 1940, *Photoplay* published a "Code for American Girls," written by Bette Davis. Based on the sincere and unpretentious writing style, it seems reasonable to assume that the actress did indeed author or at the least closely oversee its writing. Davis urged an end to such foolishness as concern over the length of one's skirt or the color of one's lipstick: "I think girls and young women should be reminded that the world is not coming to an end, that the values that really count in the long run will not be fundamentally changed. I have little patience with convention for convention's sake, but until a better code is generally accepted, the conventional values are a good guide post to the young."

The September 1943 cover of *Modern Screen* pointed out to its readers that "Women at Work Will Win the War," with a photograph of Deanna Durbin in nurse's uniform. In January 1944, *Movie Life* reminded readers that "Uncle Sam Needs Women in War Work" and featured a photograph of Judy Garland selling war bonds. Garland was back on the cover of the December 1944 issue, urging readers to buy Sixth War Loan Bonds at their favorite movie theater. The July 1944 cover of *Photoplay* featured just one item, a $100 U.S. savings bond. Novelist James Hilton, active in Hollywood as a screenwriter, wrote a "Salute to the Hollywood Canteen" in the November 1943 issue of *Photoplay*, and the October 1944 issue of *Movie Life* contained a photo spread of Private Joe Miller, a paratrooper convalescing at Birmingham Hospital, being entertained by Ellen Drew and Rochelle Hudson.

With the men away, an editorial in the July 1942 issue of *Photoplay* promised that Hollywood producers would be casting all-women films. Joan Crawford had persuaded MGM to allow her to direct a short subject that would be followed by a feature-length production. *Photoplay* reported, "Eventually her contract will have her working one-third as actress and two-thirds as director." Soon, Lana Turner, Joan Bennett, and Hedy Lamarr would be starring in parts calling for them to do men's jobs. "There will be no turning back," *Photoplay* promised. "When the war is won—and there can be no alternative no matter what the agony—women must go on from this new position. They will bring forth the new generation, and will share equally in its destinies." The article read like wonderful feminist propaganda, and there was not a word of truth to it, although the fault lay more with the film industry than with *Photoplay*.

"Are American Women Good Wartime Wives?" asked Kathryn Grayson in *Photoplay* (March 1944). A few months later, Ann Sothern wondered "What Kind of Woman Will Your Man Come Home to?" in *Photoplay* (November 1944). There was no need for anxiety, the wives of the Hollywood stars in uniform and their Hollywood fans were ready to welcome back their loved ones once the conflict was over.

Clark Gable was welcomed back in the December 1945 issue of *Modern Screen*, "a major in memory only," with "his temples a little greyer" and "his appeal very much the same." That same month, Clark Gable was also featured by May Mann and Glenn Ford by Richard Steele in *Screen Stars*.

Where the fan magazines failed in World War II was in providing the troops with photographs of pin-up girls. The cover photographs were incredibly austere, lacking in sex appeal and the leg shots associated with Betty Grable. In *Photoplay* in 1942 there were head-and-shoulder shots only, with no skin visible below the neckline. The April 1943 cover featured an actress with major sex appeal, Veronica Lake, but she shared equal space with a large black dog, with whom she appeared, if possible, both emotionless and loving. It was not until June 1943, when Betty Grable was featured, actually showing a hint of cleavage, that the covers got a little sexier. *Modern Screen* was somewhat more adventuresome than *Photoplay*, and as early as May 1942 it featured a cover of Ann Sheridan in a low-cut evening gown.

During the war years, for the first time some male members of the film community got to appear on the covers. Frank Sinatra was on the August 1944 cover of *Movie Stars Parade*. *Movieland* featured several male stars: Sonny Tufts (August 1944), Van Johnson (December 1944), Gregory Peck (March 1945), John Hodiak (June 1945), Helmut Dantine (October 1945), and Cornel Wilde (December 1945). What was even more remarkable was that the covers were not dedicated to the stars in uniform but primarily feature players designated 4F.

One of the most amazing pieces from World War II to be found in the pages of *Photoplay* was a January 1945 article by Humphrey Bogart, buried in the middle of the magazine and not even given a full page to itself, titled "Medal from Hitler." Here the star wrote, in part,

> There are no "superior races." There are only people who for a time happen to be luckier or better situated than other people.
>
> There are no "inferior races." There are only people who've had bad luck, or poor education, or maybe live in a tough climate.
>
> For example, there's no such thing as a "Jewish Race." There are Negro Jews, there are Chinese Jews. If you believe in the Jewish religion, you're a Jew. That's all there is to it—although the Germans want you to believe differently. . . .
>
> So—if you want to be a German or a Jap stooge, you know how to go about it. Just get out in the street or talk to your neighbor and preach race prejudice.
>
> Hitler will bless you. Hirohito will applaud you.
>
> In fact, you'll be a mighty good Jap, a mighty good German.
>
> There's only one thing you won't be.
>
> You won't be a good American.[17]

With a return to normality after World War II, the fan magazines settled back into what might be described as the same old regime. There seem to be more photographs than a decade earlier, with illustrations often intruding into text, which was, of necessity, shortened. Authors were at times as much writers of photo captions as they were chroniclers of the industry. It has been claimed, without substantiation, that fan magazine sales rose four hundred percent between 1931 (which was, of course, the height of the Depression) and 1946, when America was returning to normalcy. Certainly, verified sales remained high a year after the end of World War II, with two boasting circulation above a million copies: *Modern Screen* 1,328,051; *Photoplay* 1,002,929; *Motion Picture* 830,878; *Movie Story Magazine* 612,176; *Movieland* 589,191; *Screen Guide* 587,067; *Screen Star* 566,942; *Screen Romances* 519,661; *Movie Life* 381,097; *Movies* 370,297; *Movie Stars Parade* 353,055; and *Movie Show* 209,751.[18]

The post-war years were dominated by a new realism in Hollywood film-making and the rise of film noir. Such trends had little if any relevance to the fan magazines that marketed glamour to a female audience. The new genres in Hollywood were male dominated both on screen and in the audience. They might be, and were, safely ignored by fan magazine writers and editors.

One male player who was regularly featured on fan magazine covers in the 1940s and early 1950s was Van Johnson, an MGM studio-manufactured star. He was the idealized, youthful heartthrob to whom the female readership might relate. Johnson scored twenty-four feature articles in *Photoplay* between 1944 and 1954 and six in *Movieland* between 1944 and 1956, as well as pieces in *Screen Album*, *Screen Guide*, *Screenland*, and *Silver Screen*. The two female stars competing with Van Johnson for coverage in the mid through late 1940s were also from MGM: June Allyson and Esther Williams. It was even claimed that *Motion Picture* would rotate these two on its covers, issue after issue. This is probably an exaggeration, just as is a claim by June Allyson that she appeared on 2000 covers between 1943 and 1959.[19] She may have posed for as many as fifty-five photographs at one sitting, but that does not necessarily equate to fifty-five covers.

While discussing the 1940s with Ruth Waterbury in 1972, I described them—to my shame—as the dead years, the years of Victor Mature. She responded, "Up in the [Louella] Parsons office, Dorothy Manners, Louella, and myself, we all hated Victor Mature. They'd call up and say, could we print something on Victor Mature, and Louella said to me, 'Ruthie?' And I said, 'To Hell. Fire me. I'm not going to interview Victor Mature.' He never could get in the paper. . . . I think physical beauty has an awful lot to do with it. The Marilyn Monroe era. Here was this chick came along, and, wow, you got something going for her."[20] For the fan magazines, the 1950s was Marilyn Monroe, and it was much else besides.

GOSSIP, SCANDAL, AND INNUENDO

The fan magazines were not without their gossip columnists, the most notable, most respectful, and most reliable of which was the pseudonymous Cal York in *Photoplay*. Generally, the columns were free of innuendo and the type of cheap gossip most associated with the better known practitioners of the craft. Contributors to the Cal York column might chastise those in the film industry, but they were seldom if ever revealing "facts" unknown to readers of the daily newspapers. By the 1950s, Cal York was fighting for space in the pages of *Photoplay* with several other gossip columnists, including Sidney Skolsky ("That's Hollywood for You"), Edith Gwynn ("Hollywood Party Line"), Herb Stein ("What's Hollywood Whispering About"), and Mike Connolly with a semi-gossip column titled "Impertinent Interview."

The most famous of the gossip columnists active in the newspaper world could be found within the pages of the fan magazine, but their contributions were generally lightweight, often in reality written by staffers, and very obviously secondary to and probably based on the items found in their daily outlets. If anything, the power of gossip columnists in the non-fan magazine world proves Larry McMurtry's argument that they were the only successful writers in Hollywood.[1]

Hearst columnist Louella Parsons was an early contributor to *Photoplay*, publishing a piece in September 1918 titled "Propaganda," in which she discussed the role of the motion picture in World War I. As she recalled in her autobiography, *The Gay Illiterate*, she had lost her film column in the Chicago *Herald*: "The one bright spot in the whole mess was the encouragement that James Quirk, editor of *Photoplay* . . . gave me. Jimmie was a lovable Irishman with a devastating wit. He had been my friend for many months, so when he telephoned and asked me to come and see him I hastened to keep the appointment."[2] Quirk paid Parsons $25 for the piece, "a wonderful lift to my morale."

In January 1942, *Photoplay* again approached Parsons for an article on the same subject, relevant to World War II. "The fat check I received didn't look half as big to me as that $25 many years ago." It is ironic that the same issue of *Photoplay* should also contain a piece by Hedda Hopper on "Resolutions the Stars Should Make," which the editor hastened to assure readers "by no means expresses the opinions of this publication or its editor. Her comments express her own personal view and should be read as such."[3]

In fact, Hopper began her column with an attack on a senate committee that had investigated the film industry's anti-Nazi bias:

> I'm hoping the first person put on the witness stand will stand up, when accused of making propaganda pictures, and have courage enough to say, "Sure we made 'em. We make pictures to please all the people. And inasmuch as all our books, radio, short stories, newspapers were filled with the atrocities of Hitler, we put a few of them on the screen. What would you have us do—close our eyes and pretend a war isn't going on?" But when the public proved that they didn't want war pictures, no industry ever turned about-face more quickly to go into musicals, comedies, and give the public what it wanted. Let's stand up to our obligations and when accused of something we had every right to do, say, "Sure we did it. You can't shoot a man for aiming to please—or can you?"[4]

A year after Parsons' first contribution to *Photoplay*, Quirk gave her twelve-year-old daughter an assignment to write a piece, "From Four to Twelve" (September 1919), on the son of actor George Beban, famous for his Italian characterizations. When Harriet received a copy of the magazine and a check for $15, her mother asked if she was thrilled with her first byline. "No, they changed my ending," was supposedly the response.[5]

Harriet Parsons returned to *Photoplay* as a staff writer in 1929, interviewing singer John McCormack in May 1930 and writing a series of pieces titled "Studio Ramblings" in September through December 1930. "I worked my tail off," she recalled in 1980. "I never considered what I did fan magazine stuff. I took it all very seriously."[6] In 1934, she was writing for *Movie Mirror* and *Silver Screen* prior to becoming a short subject director at Columbia and a film producer, in the 1940s, at Republic and RKO.

"I think it is very rude to have had a love affair with an important man, like F. Scott Fitzgerald, and then write a piece about him, what a mess he was at the end of his life."[7] The comment came from Ruth Waterbury, and the subject of her criticism was Sheilah Graham. She was "the last of the unholy trio," as Graham called herself, rather cleverly placing herself on the same level as Louella Parsons and Hedda Hopper.

Much of what Graham did was exemplary of skilful publicity and promotion. She was a self-invented woman, of whom *Variety* (November 23, 1988) wrote in its obituary, her "own life was as vivid and storied as those she wrote about." Certainly, Graham had to work hard to build up a career and life that started in the charity ward of a London orphanage, with the real name of Lily

Louella Parsons.

Sheil. She embraced work as a chorus girl in the 1920s, and in June 1933 she moved to the United States and a new career as a newspaper woman. Four years later, Graham began a relationship with F. Scott Fitzgerald, which lasted until his death and about which she wrote in several books, most notably *Beloved Infidel* (1958, coauthored with Gerold Frank). The book became a 1959 film, in which Graham was portrayed by Deborah Kerr, whom the writer had interviewed for *Photoplay* in November 1947.

A story is famously told of Graham's making the fatal mistake of criticizing in print the Café Trocadero, owned by Billy Wilkerson Jr., publisher of *The Hollywood Reporter*. Wilkerson would vehemently attack his perceived opposition, as he did in the mid 1930s with his reporting on the fan magazines. So successful was he in his efforts to damage or destroy Sheilah Graham's career in retaliation for her comments that her lover, Fitzgerald, challenged Wilkerson to a duel.

Sheilah Graham wrote a number of books, including a 1969 memoir, *Confessions of a Hollywood Columnist*. Her syndicated column was published from the 1930s onward, and when the contract with North American Newspaper Alliance expired on November 30, 1970, it was still appearing in 150

Harriet Parsons (left) and Radie Harris, circa 1945. Courtesy of Academy of Motion Picture Arts and Sciences.

newspapers. She was a frequent radio and television performer and a busy fan magazine writer for *Photoplay* from December 1944 (with a piece on Jeanne Crain) through December 1963 (with a piece on Anthony Quinn). In all, she published at least forty-nine articles in that one magazine, many having to do with marriage and divorce (something about which she knew a good deal, having been married and divorced three times). Graham had at least one article in *Modern Screen* (June 1949 on Peter Lawford), and her work likely appeared elsewhere. She fronted several fan magazines in the 1950s; her name appeared as part of the cover title, but it seems unlikely that Graham actually contributed much, if anything, to them.

A gossip columnist who was a major force in his day but who is virtually forgotten is James M. (Marion) Fidler, better known as Jimmy Fidler, whose career embraced the fan magazines, newspapers, radio, and television. Born in St. Louis on August 24, 1900, Fidler had come to Hollywood after military service in World War I and worked as an extra in a handful of silent films. Circa 1920, he became motion picture editor of the *Hollywood News*, a four-page insert for the Los Angeles *Express*. From there, he advanced to press agent for Gloria Swanson and others. In July 1933, he had pieces on Janet Gaynor in both *Silver Screen* and *Screenland*. In 1933 and 1934, he wrote regularly for the latter, with pieces on Katharine Hepburn (September 1933), Greta Garbo and John Gilbert (November 1933), Lillian Harvey (December 1933 and January 1934) and Clark Gable (June 1934). Fidler also wrote on Garbo for *Motion Picture* in April 1934 and on Jean Harlow for *Silver Screen* in June 1934. As

Sheilah Graham
and Sidney Skolsky.
Courtesy of Academy
of Motion Picture Arts
and Sciences.

late as June 1945, he had a piece in *Modern Screen*, in which he remembered
"favorites of yesteryear," a popular and ongoing topic with the fan magazines.

More importantly, in 1933 Fidler made his first radio broadcast, interviewing Dorothy Jordan. By the late 1940s, he was heard on 486 stations, ending
each broadcast with the once well-known phrase, "Good night to you, and you,
and I do mean *you!*" His gossip column appeared in 360 newspapers. Fidler
was also featured weekly on the *Movietone News* from Twentieth Century–
Fox. He had a high-pitched, intense voice, unsuited to the broadcast media,
and he thrived on being unpopular. "He seeks, ferrets, pries, peeps, snoops,
collects, conjectures, prognosticates, and interprets the more savory and news-
worthy events of the film colony for palpitating readers and listeners," noted
one critic in 1939.[8]

Fidler was perhaps most notorious for his campaign against anti-Nazi films
made in Hollywood in the late 1930s. As a result, he was summoned to appear
before an Interstate Commerce Commission Senate Subcommittee in September 1941. He expressed no remorse and shocked his audience by admitting
to reviewing films without seeing them.

Fidler continued unabated into the 1950s, introducing a syndicated television program, *Jimmy Fidler in Hollywood*. Fidler retired in 1983 and died in
Westlake, California, on August 9, 1988.

Jimmy Fidler.

Less outrageous than Jimmy Fiddler was Jimmy Starr (1904–1990). He came to Hollywood in 1919, working as a messenger boy at Metro and then a screenwriter at Warner Bros., before embarking on a new career as a gossip columnist. In fact, while still at Warner Bros., Starr became motion picture editor of the Los Angeles *Record* in 1923. He worked for various Los Angeles newspapers in the 1930s and began a regular "Starr Dust" column that ran in various publications through December 1961. Starr's writing for the fan magazines was relatively minor and, ultimately, unimportant to his career.

Radie Harris wrote the "Broadway Ballyhoo" column for *The Hollywood Reporter* from 1940 through 1988. From January through May 1930, she contributed a series of articles to *Picture Play* with titles such as "Is Marriage Like That Now?" and "Orgies You'd Love to Find," which gave more than a hint of the gossip columnist she was to become.[9] Harris became a gossip columnist proper in 1933 with her "Movie Eavesdropping" column in *Screen Book*, billed

Hedda Hopper.

as "The Newsmagazine of the Movies." In the September 1933 issue, not only did Harris have her gossip column, sharing space with three other gossip columns, but she also had a feature article on Douglas Fairbanks Jr., titled "Doug, Jr. Wins." In November 1933 she contributed a piece titled "Who Is Frances Fuller?" to *Screen Book*, and in January 1938 she wrote in *Modern Movies* on "Stars of the Future."

Another writer from *The Hollywood Reporter* was George Christie, whose "The Great Life" column chronicled Hollywood society from 1975 through 2001. Earlier, he had been a frequent fan magazine contributor, writing twenty articles for *Photoplay* between 1958 and 1964 and interviewing various younger Hollywood celebrities in the pages of *Modern Screen* from 1959 through

1963, including Tommy Sands (March 1959), Edd Byrnes (May 1959), Mitzi Gaynor (September 1959), Sal Mineo (June 1960), Annette Funicello (September 1960), Deborah Walley (August 1961), and Fabian (March 1962).

May Mann was an anorexic blonde, born in Salt Lake City and named Miss Utah of 1938, who obviously considered herself as much of a celebrity as the individuals about whom she wrote. Known as the "Hollywood Date Girl" because of the number of parties she attended and reported upon, Mann married heavyweight boxer "Buddy" Baer in 1948. As early as May 1938, she had written on Clark Gable in *Screenland* and that same month profiled Wallace Beery in *Movie Mirror*. She contributed to *Photoplay* on a regular basis from 1972 to 1977, and at one time her syndicated column appeared in a reported 400 newspapers. Ezra Goodman reprinted an item from Mann's Hollywood diary in *Popular Screen*, which he described as of a complexity that beggars Marcel Proust: "Tuesday: Honestly, Troy Donahue has me confused. He introduced Nan Morris, a twenty-two-year-old secretary, to me at a big party and before I could item it, Warners told me it was all off for good. Nan started dating John Ireland since he and Tuesday Weld are splitto. So I caddy out to Warners to lunch with Troy and he says he is dating Diane McBain, a contract pretty at Warners. Then I go to this big party for Connie Francis last night—and there's Troy and Nan again!"[10] May Mann died—age of course unknown—in Los Angeles on April 15, 1995.

Louella Parsons' bitter rival, Hedda Hopper, was good at ferreting out stories but incapable of writing about them. Despite such inability, she was a frequent fan magazine contributor, featured in *Photoplay* in the 1940s with stories on Joan Crawford (June 1941) and Orson Welles (May 1944) and most frequently in the 1950s and 1960s. She also "wrote" for *Modern Screen* from 1944 through 1950 and in 1953. The pieces were semi-gossip items, such as "Why Dan Dailey's Marriage Failed" in September 1949. Prior to her career as a writer, Hopper had used the fan magazines in July 1933 to promote a "fashion war" between herself and actress Lilyan Tashman; *The Hollywood Reporter* (June 3, 1933) described it as "too vitriolic to do either side any good, and its relative unimportance only adds to its bad taste."

In May 1951, Hopper was paid $1000 apiece for four stories a year in *Photoplay*, beginning with one on Elizabeth Taylor in August of that year. However, Hopper's main source of fan magazine revenue came from *Motion Picture*. In the 1950s, she was paid $650 for a thirteen- to fifteen-page story and $12,000 a year for her gossip column. In June 1961, the editorial director at Fawcett Publications, then the publisher of *Motion Picture*, told Hopper that between 1943 and 1961 it had paid her a grand total of $100,980.80.[11]

Modern Screen used present-day gossip columnist Liz Smith from 1949 into the early 1950s. Another contributor was Mike Connolly (1913–1966), who wrote the "Rambling Reporter" column in *The Hollywood Reporter*. Connolly also wrote for *Screen Stories*, with his last piece, "Elizabeth Montgomery: The Risks I Take with My Marriage," appearing in the February 1967 issue, three months after his death.

The gossip columnists to be found routinely in newspapers, along with new stories in the daily press, kept Americans informed of and outraged at what was going on in wilder Hollywood circles. Over the breakfast table, Americans read of the 1922 murder of director William Desmond Taylor, the implication that drugs and illicit sex might be involved, and certainly the association of two Hollywood stars, Mary Miles Minter and Mabel Normand. They read of the 1920 drug-related suicide of actress Olive Thomas in Paris, a city closely linked with sin in the minds of most Americans, and, more tragically, as far as the moviegoing public was concerned, of the drug-related death of matinee idol Wallace Reid in 1923. They read of comedian Roscoe "Fatty" Arbuckle being accused of the 1921 rape and murder of a Hollywood starlet in San Francisco. They also read of plans to clean up the film community, led by women's and church groups across the United States, and within the industry itself through the appointment of Will Hays, former postmaster general in the Harding administration, as an ersatz film czar. Americans read all about these tragedies and scandals in their newspapers, but they found little on the subject in any of the fan magazines. These types of happenings had no place in the Hollywood that the fan magazines represented. Their world was insular and secure from subjects such as these.

The appointment of Will Hays was given the full support of *Photoplay*. Bernarr Macfadden, a long-time combatant against censorship, was less enthusiastic in the pages of *Movie Weekly*. As early as 1905, in response to his publication in *Physical Culture* of photographs of scantily clothed athletes, his offices had been raided by the police as a result of complaints from Anthony Comstock and the New York Society for the Suppression of Vice. In 1907, Macfadden had been convicted of sending lewd and obscene matter through the mail, after *Physical Culture* had published a serial in which venereal disease was discussed. It was left to President William Howard Taft to pardon Macfadden, and it is certain that the publisher held a grudge against the mail service and anyone who had been its postmaster general.

On October 14, 1922, *Movie Weekly* published a two-page diatribe on "The Vampire of Censorship." "The way to reform the movies is to get rid of the reformers!" author James Craig Gordon proclaimed: "Nothing more sinister has ever menaced a civilized art than the imbecile autocracy of the political jakes and the frowsy old maids who want to decide what you and I may see in a picture play." If the tide of censorship was not stemmed, Gordon warned, William S. Hart would not be allowed to hate the villain, Ruth Roland could not show fear when trapped by a gang of counterfeiters, Mary Pickford in *Tess of the Storm Country* would not be permitted to be envious of richer girls, because it will be illegal to be envious. No crime of any kind would be permitted on screen. "It will be violation punishable by fine or imprisonment to make fun of a social worker, a member of the Board of Censors, a moralist, a reformer, in moving pictures." There would be no killings, no guns, no fun, no Shakespearian adaptations, not even The Passion Play.

"Will Hays may clean up Hollywood," Gordon concluded. "He may restore financial stability among the producers. But neither Will Hays nor a thousand like him can breathe the breath of life into the picture drama after all its blood, all its vitality has been sucked dry by the vulture of censorship. We don't need this czardom. The laws against indecency in this country are sufficient to destroy any producer who panders to immorality. We can protect ourselves against obscenity. These self-styled reformers cry, 'To clean up the screen you must get rid of the vampires!' The most sinister vampire that ever spread its brooding wings across the shining radiance of the screen is the vampire of political censorship."

The following week, vampire Will Hays responded, also in two pages. He wanted "the films to offer the highest type of dramatic entertainment to the millions who find enjoyment and diversion in the motion picture theaters." He wrote of the motion picture as "the greatest of all media for the education of mankind at large." And he believed "the motion picture screen may someday become a universal language for all races from the ice-choked regions of the Arctic to the sun-blistered waste of the Sahara." It all sounded rather familiar, as indeed it was, borrowing heavily from Thomas Alva Edison's initial views on the motion picture and D. W. Griffith's lofty ideals.

"The people of this country, of course, are against censorship fundamentally," Hays proclaimed. "But, just as certainly, my friends, is this country against wrong-doing—and the demand for censorship will fail when the reason for the demand is removed." The bottom line was that if the readership of *Movie Weekly* supported "good pictures," there would be no call for censorship.[12]

The next week, James Craig Gordon returned to his theme, noting that Massachusetts was voting for or against motion picture censorship as that issue was being produced. *Movie Weekly* "hopes that censorship is licked finally and decisively," but, just as Hays called on the public for support, the magazine called on the producer not to pander to the salacious and the lewd, and "to put up the bars against the dirty moving pictures."[13]

Movie Weekly was the only fan magazine to exploit the February 1922, still unsolved, murder of director William Desmond Taylor. There had been about a dozen references to the director during his lifetime, beginning with a short piece in *Motion Picture* in January 1915 on how he got into films and a longer article, by Richard Willis, describing Taylor in considerably overblown fashion as a "Master Producer of Masterpieces" in the December 1915 issue of *Movie Pictorial*.

Following his murder, *Movie Weekly* published an editorial in its March 4, 1922, issue, in which it announced, "*Movie Weekly* will not cast opprobium [*sic*] on the motion picture players or upon the picture colony. . . . We ask our readers not to turn radically against Hollywood and the motion picture people there. Keep your heads during this crisis and don't say anything against any man or woman that will shame you when the Taylor mystery is finally solved." A week later, the fan magazine quoted screenwriter John Emerson, "Is murder so uncommon a crime that a whole community and an honorable profession shall be besmirched when a man is killed, as the police authorities of Los Angeles agree, by a vicious and probably insane criminal? And is there anything so remarkably extraordinary in the fact that a man as kindly, as lovable as William Taylor should have women admirers?" These two editorials were followed by Truman B. Handy's "The Colorful and Romantic Story of William D. Taylor's Remarkable Life," which was so colorful and romantic that it needed five issues to document it, beginning on March 18 and concluding on April 15, 1922.

The death of William Taylor led to the demise of the career of Mary Miles Minter, who was romantically linked to the director and whose mother was considered the chief murder suspect. Edward Wagenknecht, who first appeared in print as an eleven-year-old in *Motion Picture Story Magazine*, was disturbed by the caustic comments about Minter appearing on a regular basis in the pages of *Photoplay*. He was pleased at the least to get a letter in her support published in that magazine.

While *Movie Weekly* was exploiting the Taylor murder, James R. Quirk and *Photoplay* were demanding action from movie czar Will Hays. In an open letter, headed "Moral House-Cleaning in Hollywood," Quirk defended Hollywood, noting, "Vice is to be found everywhere—in every profession and in every city in the world. The motion-picture profession is neither better nor worse than any other. *Photoplay* asks nothing for motion pictures but justice—that simple, fine justice which the American public knows so well how to exercise."

At the same time, Quirk pointed out to Hays that "In motion pictures, as in all great industries, there are undesirables—selfish vicious persons who work injury to everyone with whom they are associated." As an example, and obviously referencing Mary Miles Minter, "There is the actor and the actress who live loose, immoral lives, and who thrive on scandal and lurid notoriety." Quirk concluded, "*Photoplay*, for its part, will refuse to print any personality story about any motion-picture star, who is notoriously immoral, or whose actions are such as to reflect unfavorably on the industry."[14]

One actor who *Photoplay* obviously decided was not immoral and who had received a raw deal was Roscoe "Fatty" Arbuckle, accused in the 1921 rape and murder of a Hollywood starlet, Virginia Rappe. Despite being found not guilty, the opprobrium led to public disgrace and his studio, Paramount, canceling his contract, as it had done with Mary Miles Minter.

Quirk published four editorials in defense of Arbuckle, dating from 1923 through 1931. "Hollywood's greatest vice is the vice of a fanatical Puritan village," opined Quirk in February 1923. Noting that Valentino had once been described as a "lounge lizard" and that Pola Negri had been attacked for her aloofness and refusal to permit prying into her private life—a jealous leading lady had supposedly written "To Hell with the Hun" across her dressing room—Quirk pointed out that "Whenever one of the important members of the movie colony suffers misfortune his fellows devour him." Arbuckle was not mentioned by name, but was very obviously the star assigned to "The Ducking Stool for Hollywood."

Roscoe "Fatty" Arbuckle.

In March 1923, Quirk criticized Hays for initially banning Arbuckle from
the screen and then lifting the ban in obvious response to Paramount's need
to put into distribution the comedian's last unreleased productions for its own
financial gain. Unfortunately, as Quirk noted, the public does not forget so
quickly: "If Arbuckle ever had a chance to come back, Mr. Hays has killed it.
Instead of 'Fatty' giving us an old time healthy laugh, Mr. Hays has given us a
cynical one. Let us have a little less bunk and a little more sincerity."

Two years later, in August 1925, Quirk demanded "fair play," announcing
that "I would like to see Roscoe Arbuckle come back to the screen." The editorial was surprisingly frank in its suggestion that Virginia Rappe had a dubious
past and that it was impossible to present evidence to the jury reflecting on her
character. It was pointed out that Arbuckle was $200,000 in debt and yet had
not taken advantage of bankruptcy: "Arbuckle made clean pictures always. He

was never guilty of vulgarity. Children could see them with safety. Aside from his screen personality, there isn't a better comedy director in the world. I hold that he is today entitled to a chance to earn the money which his talents are worth, in order that he may pay off the debt incurred in defending himself." In conclusion, Quirk asked readers who agreed with his opinion to write Will Hays and say so.

Quirk made his last public statement about Arbuckle in May 1931: "During a radio talk a few days ago, I made a casual reference to the response accorded a story in a recent issue of *Photoplay*. The story was about Roscoe Arbuckle. It was entitled 'Just Let Me Work.' We have already received two thousand letters from men and women who want to see Arbuckle given a chance to earn a living. Poor Fatty, declared innocent by a jury of his peers, has suffered enough. But the good club women and organized professional reformers who stoned him into oblivion show no signs of putting into practice the precepts they mouth so glibly on Sabbath morn."

A couple of months earlier, in March 1931, *Photoplay* had carried a pitiful, three-page article by Tom Ellis, "Just Let Me Work," in which the comedian noted that people were entitled to their opinions, that they even had the right to oppose him, but "My conscience is clear, my heart is clean. I refuse to worry. I feel that I have atoned for everything." Ellis pointed out that Arbuckle was working as a director but that the name he was using could not be revealed, that the shorts he was directing were better than many feature-length productions (a somewhat exaggerated claim): "Today then, 'Fatty' Arbuckle, the hilarious comedian, is gone. Instead, there is a big fat fellow behind a director's desk in Hollywood. . . . There's no grin on his face. It's almost always serious. There are lines there that weren't on the cherubically asinine countenance that beamed from the screen in the old 'Fatty' comedies."

Other fan magazines took up the fight to rehabilitate Arbuckle. In March 1929, *Motion Picture* reported on the stars helping to make his nightclub, The Plantation, a success, including Al Jolson, who sang there for nothing. In September 1931, the magazine asked if a sign in front of a theater announcing "Fatty Arbuckle Talks!" would cause as much of a sensation as the sign "Garbo Talks." Positive quotes were printed from a curious group of celebrities, including director James Cruze, Buster Keaton, Ann Harding, Laurel and Hardy, Conrad Nagel, and former silent star Lois Wilson. Two months later, in November 1931, *Motion Picture* published six pages of letters from readers wanting Arbuckle back on the screen. In October 1932, *Modern Screen* entered the fray, with writer Edward J. Doherty commenting, "I say nothing of the fans forgiving Fatty because it is my belief there is nothing to be forgiven." With Arbuckle's June 29, 1933, death, *Screen Book* (September 1933) published a five-page tribute, headed "The Tragic Comedian Passes."[15]

Arbuckle had also received support from an unlikely source. In November 1921, novelist and short story writer Gouverneur Morris had published an open letter in *Screenland*. Morris was outraged that the comedian was to be subjected to a second trial after the first resulted in a hung jury. He attacked both the press and the man in the street and demanded to know more about the background of the murdered woman. "It may be that Virginia Rappe was afflicted before she went to the famous party, and that Arbuckle is no more responsible for her death than the policeman who arrested her." In conclusion, Morris wrote, "I do not know Arbuckle, but, because of the laughs he has given my kiddies and me, I am his friend until there are better reasons (than now exist) for believing that no man should be his friend. And surely it can't be so bad as that."[16]

The fan magazine was very obviously nervous about publishing the piece, and Morris certainly showed considerable courage in that he was at the time under contract as a screenwriter to Samuel Goldwyn and he was also potentially jeopardizing his writing career in the newspapers of William Randolph Hearst, which had long been on the attack against Arbuckle. *Screenland* explained, "In presenting Mr. Morris' letter, the Editors of *Screenland* are thoroughly cognizant of the prudish caution that would argue suppression of such a daringly frank arraignment. Mr. Morris, however, is not only one of the leaders of American contemporary fiction, but he is a student of criminology, as expressed in many of his fiction works. This distinguishes Mr. Morris' contribution from any mere morbid analysis of the Arbuckle case and removes any hesitancy *Screenland* might feel in presenting such a discussion before its readers."

In the case of Roscoe "Fatty" Arbuckle, it was very much the fan magazines, led by *Photoplay*, against public opinion. Such was not the situation with the handsome leading man Wallace Reid, whose death of drug addiction in January 1923 induced an outpouring of public grief and sympathy. Through no fault of his own, Reid had become addicted to morphine, provided to ease his painful recovery from an accident. He was seen as a brave man, with a courageous wife at his side, fighting demons over which he had no control.

Within two months of his death, in March 1923, *Photoplay* published an emotional and loving tribute from Herbert Howe, in which Reid was described as "the exemplar of American youth. Reckless genial, carefree and democratic, with an unfailing sense of humor and a spirit that never said die." Howe concluded, "He died with the whispered hope that he might save at least a few from the agony that was his. His last role was the greatest he ever played. Never on the screen did he wage such a brave and splendid fight. The loyal love of millions will follow the star that is forever—just Wally."[17]

Wallace Reid continued to appear in the pages of the fan magazines, which were equally supportive of the efforts of his wife, Dorothy Davenport Reid, to exploit his memory, advance her own career, and raise his son. He was honored by *Motion Picture* in June 1923, with a tribute, "Lest We Forget," which also included reference to the death of Olive Thomas. Letters to Wally Reid's memory were published from readers in the June 1925 issue of *Photoplay*. As late as December 1930, Dorothy Calhoun asked the readers of *Motion Picture*, "What If They Had Lived," in reference to Reid, Rudolph Valentino, and Barbara La Marr.

Politically, fan magazines remained steadfastly neutral. They would seldom take positions that might offend the readership, which had no interest in politics anyway. Prohibition, dating from the Volstead Act in 1918, was of little relevance to the fan magazines. It was pretty much disregarded by the studios, with films routinely depicting characters enjoying illicit booze and bootleggers welcome guests on the lots. In the course of interviews and in celebrity articles, stars never discussed their career over a martini or a highball but, rather, over an iced tea, lemonade, or a cup of coffee. Fan magazines had no problem in reviewing films ridiculing prohibition, such as *Blonde Crazy* (1932) from Warner Bros., and when MGM used a shot of Norma Shearer with a glass of champagne in her hand in the advertising for *The Divorcee* (1930), the fan magazines were happy to accept payment to publish the copy.

Surprisingly, one article on the subject made it into a fan magazine, the November 1932 issue of *Screen Play*, under the heading "The Stars Vote on Prohibition." Writer J. Eugene Chrisman discovered, not surprisingly, that "Hollywood is *wet*." He reported that Hollywood had fewer speakeasies in proportion to its population than any community in the United States, that there were fewer raids on drinking places than in ninety percent of the communities in the country, and fewer deaths from alcoholism. Stars coming out in print in favor of the repeal of prohibition included Pat O'Brien, Ralph Forbes, Jack Holt, Tom Brown, Jimmie Gleason, Ina Claire, and Walter Byron. Supporting prohibition, Colleen Moore pointed out that movie stars did not dare drink too much because of the demand for clear minds, clear eyes, clear skin, and clear voices. Among the missing were any major stars and any major contract players.[18]

What are today so often described as Hollywood scandals, such as the deaths in the 1930s of actress Thelma Todd and Paul Bern, husband of Jean Harlow, were ignored by the fan magazines or just mentioned in passing. News stories on such tragedies were more than sufficient. Charlie Chaplin also escaped relatively unscathed from negative attention by the fan magazines. There were, of course, pieces on his marriage to and divorce from Lita Grey and Paulette Goddard. Once Chaplin had left the country and been refused permission to return, he was of no interest—after all, his career was in decline and by the 1950s there were newer and far more exciting celebrities on which the fan magazines might salivate. Surprisingly, Chaplin was the subject of an "Open Letter" by editor Delight Evans in the March 1941 issue of *Screenland*. New York–based Evans was angered that the comedian had refused to accept an award from the New York Film Critics' Circle for *The Great Dictator*: "Can it be that you aren't Charlie any longer, but a Genius above all evaluation? If that's so, then goodbye to the great little man who has done so much to make millions happier. We'll miss you."

The late 1940s and 1950s claimed two Hollywood stars in the name of scandal, Ingrid Bergman and Lana Turner. The 1949 affair between Bergman and her director, Roberto Rossellini, genuinely shocked Hollywood, which, along with the moviegoing public, had great affection for the actress. As Louella

Parsons wrote in *Photoplay* (June 1949), "Whenever anyone in Hollywood has become involved in any great scandal, always we have said, 'Well, thank goodness there are those stars upon whom you can count.' And, invariably, we had added, 'Stars who live with the greatest personal dignity and propriety—Ingrid Bergman, for instance.'" *Photoplay* never went after Bergman in a derogatory fashion. For instance, in July 1949 Cal York was defensive of the actress, pointing out she had suffered through a negative response to two recent films, *Arch of Triumph* and *Joan of Arc*, and that husband Dr. Petter Lindström "controlled her professional and private life with too firm a hand."

Joseph Henry Steele, who was Bergman's personal publicist from 1945 to 1952 and who had been writing about her in the fan magazines throughout the 1940s, took again to the pages of *Photoplay* in December 1949 to present "The Bergman Love Story," explaining, "This has been the toughest assignment of my life. Because of my very intimate relationship to the whole affair I was truly afraid that I was disqualified to write it. I hate to say that this story is yours conditionally, but it simply has to be that way. It is too vital and important to the happiness of the principals involved in this cause célèbre. It was only on my word that *Photoplay* would keep faith with me that Ingrid agreed to let me do it. She has okayed every word of it, and every word of it must be a must." In reality, neither Bergman nor publicist Steele had too much to worry about. In December 1952, *Photoplay* announced to the world "Your Verdict on Ingrid: 4 to 1 in Her Favor."

Facing harsher treatment than Ingrid Bergman was Lana Turner a few years later. But Bergman had only deserted her husband and daughter for another man, while Turner's daughter, Cheryl Crane, had killed her mother's lover, Johnny Stompanato, on the night of April 4, 1958. There were pieces in *Photoplay* with such lurid headings as "The Untold Story of Lana's Shame" (July 1958), "Cheryl Crane Pleads, 'Mummy, How Can I Choose between You and Daddy?'" (October 1958), and "Why Lana Let Them Put Her Daughter Away" (June 1960).[19]

The greatest scandal affecting the film industry concerned not a single individual but a vast number of innocent Hollywood workers who were blacklisted because of real or perceived Communist sympathies. The hearings of the House Un-American Activities Committee in the late 1940s and early 1950s, and the subsequent blacklisting of many within the entertainment industry, is one of the most shameful episodes in American political history. It is a period that has been well covered by critics and scholars—and it was virtually ignored by the fan magazines.

In May 1952, *Photoplay* made reference to "Hollywood Reds" in its Cal York column, but the story concerned Van Johnson's penchant for red socks, Lana Turner wearing a corsage of blood-red carnations, and Gary Cooper sporting a red flannel vest. Of a film under review that might be described as a problem, *The Boy with Green Hair*, which is generally considered to have leftist undertones, critic Elsa Branden noted in February 1949, "But whether you interpret this as a film fraught with social significance or merely an imaginative

fable, you'll agree it is way off the beaten track." When dealing with pure period propaganda, Branden would simply state the facts subject to the mores of
the time. Thus, "Communism rears its hateful head in this exciting movie," she
wrote in December 1949 of *I Married a Communist*.

There was little direct reference to what was going on in Washington and
Hollywood, in part, one suspects, because the fan magazines knew that their
readers had little interest in politics, leftwing or rightwing. There was undoubtedly a subtle influence at work, as with Edward G. Robinson, the subject of
more than nineteen fan magazine articles in the 1930s, being ignored in the
1940s and 1950s as a result of his name being linked to Communist-front orga-
nizations. On the whole, however, an Iron Curtain descending on Europe and
a war in faraway Korea was less important than whether the Shirley Temple–
John Agar marriage would survive (it didn't) or whether Deborah Kerr would
be typecast (she wasn't).

Prior to the blacklist, *Photoplay* did stand up against attacks on members
of the film industry by anti-Communist agitators. In September 1940, it published a piece titled "Is Melvyn Douglas a Communist?" by Sally Reid. After
noting that the actor had been branded by certain factions "as a radical, a
Red, a Communist, an enemy to these United States of America," Reid confronted Douglas on the set of his latest film. Responding to a specific attack
by the American Legion, he complained, "Their insinuations as to my Com-
munistic activities are not only baseless, but vicious to a degree. Even a casual
investigation would have clearly established that I have as little regard for the
Communists as I have for the Nazis and that I have been quick to condemn
their influence wherever I have found it in operation. This has earned me the
attack of Communists as well. In the interest of all liberals and for my own
good name, I have requested from the Attorney General a thorough and immediate investigation of me and my connections by the Federal Bureau of
Investigation."

Once the House Un-American Activities Committee had begun its work,
Photoplay did ask writer James M. Cain to contribute an editorial titled "Is
Hollywood Red?" to its August 1947 edition. The piece was surprisingly thorough and well considered, discussing both sides of the question. Despite a
supposed liberal bent, Cain did not dismiss the notion that there were party
members at work in Hollywood. However, he noted, "In the long run the film
will be exempt from subversion in any particular direction, as it must remain
entertainment if it is to remain profitable, so that any imbalance here must
inevitably right itself."

Did the *Photoplay* readers pay any attention to what Cain had to say? With
such more appealing stories as what took place on a date with Tyrone Power
and Lana Turner, a discussion of Joan Leslie's mind, and a revealing piece
by Maria Montez on husband Jean Pierre Aumont, not to mention features
on Laraine Day, Peter Lawford, Peggy Cummins, June Haver, and James
Stewart, along with a problem-solving column hosted by Claudette Colbert, it
seems unlikely.

In objection to the House committee hearings, fifty prominent members of the film industry, led by Humphrey Bogart, flew to Washington, D.C., on October 26, 1947. Careerwise, it was a bad decision by Bogart and his colleagues, some of whom were blacklisted. Bogart was forced to explain his actions in a March 1948 *Photoplay* article, "I'm No Communist." While the title might, in hindsight, suggest that Bogart was taking a coward's way out of a controversy, in truth, he was surprising outspoken. He questioned why the politicians were singling out Hollywood rather than the auto industry or the Newspaper Guild. He asserted that Hollywood liberals were devoted to "our" democracy. Finally, he asked that others not be dissuaded from protest because of the reaction against him and his fellow travelers to Washington, "Though headlines may have screamed of the Red menace in movies," he wrote, "all the wind and fury actually proved that there's been no Communism injected on America's movie screens. As I said, I'm no Communist. If you thought so, you were dead wrong. But, brother, in this democracy no one's going to shoot you for having thought so!"

Obviously, with the continuing newspaper coverage of the work of the House Un-American Activities Committee, *Modern Screen* was somewhat concerned at how its readership perceived Hollywood. It had, after all, spent a great many pages through the years reporting on extramarital affairs and divorces. So, in September 1949, it determined to expose "Why Stars Turn to Prayer." In what was promised as the first in a series, Bing Crosby, Ricardo Montalban, Betty Hutton, Esther Williams, Pat O'Brien, Al Jolson, Loretta Young, Barbara Stanwyck, Doris Day, Maureen O'Hara, and others revealed the power of prayer. *Modern Screen* might have made much of the breakup of the John Payne–Gloria de Haven marriage, but instead it chose to reveal that the only belonging that Payne took with him, aside from a change of clothing, when he moved out of their home to a hotel was his Bible.

Similarly, *Photoplay* went on the record in defense of the Hollywood community with a July 1950 editorial, "Let the Hollywood Record Speak," in which it attacked Senator Edwin C. Johnson, chairman of the Senate Commerce Committee, who had made "sensational charges" against various stars and proposed a federal censorship of Hollywood's morals. Proudly, *Photoplay* noted that there was only a 29.9 percent divorce rate in Hollywood, compared to a national divorce rate of 40 percent. The following month, *Photoplay* published a four-page listing, titled "The Other Side of the Hollywood Story," providing information on the marriage record, the home life, and the community service and honors of more than 140 Hollywood players.

At least these pieces made a welcome change from typical nonresponses to the blacklist era, such as "Gable's Mystery Romance" (*Modern Screen*, October 1953), "Screenland Salutes Ingrid Bergman" (*Screenland*, February 1949) and, a real crowd-pleaser I am sure, "I Was Slapped—and Liked It" by Joan Crawford (*Screenland*, May 1950).

Fan magazines were able to deal with the murder of an American president, but the August 9, 1969, killing of actress Sharon Tate by Charles Manson and his "family" was a little too close for comfort. The brutality of the murder of Tate, who was nearly nine months pregnant at the time, and others was particularly disturbing, yet the vast amount of publicity generated in the national and local press determined the need of the fan magazines to respond. Utilizing a publicity photograph of Sharon Tate on the ground and spread across two pages, *Photoplay* revealed in November 1969 that "Sharon Tate Handed Her Killer the Murder Weapon." In a piece totally devoid of sensibility, it announced, "Waiting for new life to be born, Sharon was struck down. The girl who feared nothing and wanted to experience everything—finally did." It was explained that the "starry-eyed girl who came to the film colony at 16" had the misfortune to meet Roman Polanski, whose every action (not the least his being born outside of the United States) seemed at fault. It was Polanksi who taught Tate that "'games' could be fun," who had "purged her of inhibition."

Photoplay returned briefly to the murder scene in February 1970 with a half-page, unsigned article titled "Sharon Tate Killed by Love Cult." Roman Polanski was not mentioned as the magazine recounted the story of Charles Manson and his followers: "For them, 'love' was 'death' and men were beasts huddled in a valley for slaughter." It was positively Biblical in its exposition.

In 1948, it was reported that there were currently only eight "absolutely safe" cover girls: Ingrid Bergman, Rita Hayworth, Lana Turner, June Allyson, Betty Grable, Shirley Temple, June Haver, and Esther Williams. The only "safe" male star was Alan Ladd, whose presence on a fan magazine cover would not reduce its newsstand sales by as much as twenty percent.[20] Within a matter of a few years, several of the "absolutely safe" cover girls would be tinged by scandal, most notably Ingrid Bergman, Rita Hayworth, and Lana Turner. From a modern viewpoint, perhaps the only "safe" cover girl was Shirley Temple, and even she was involved in a divorce. If anything, the object lesson here is that nothing is forever in both the world of Hollywood and the world of the fan magazines.

If the fan magazines were limited by studio control as to what they might openly discuss, to what extent could they indulge in innuendo? There were obviously certain key words and phrases used by gossip columnists and fan magazine writers that went far beyond the dictionary definition. An "engagement" between two players generally implied that sexual intercourse had taken place, particularly if the actress in question was someone like Clara Bow, exuding sexuality. An actress having "her appendix removed" usually meant that she was having an abortion.

There was little or no innuendo to be found in Kirtley Baskette's "Hollywood's Unmarried Husbands and Wives," published in the January 1939 issue of *Photoplay*. While not categorically stating that the various stars under discussion were actually living together, it is very much clear to the reader that they were. "Carole Lombard is not Clark Gable's wife . . . [but] still she has remodeled her whole Hollywood life for him," wrote Baskette. George Raft was linked to Virginia Pine: "She is not George's wife, although there's little doubt that she would be if George's long-estranged wife would give him a divorce." Others identified in the same predicament were Constance Bennett and Gilbert Roland. Robert Taylor and Barbara Stanwyck were identified as having purchased two ranches side by side in the Northridge area of the San Fernando Valley: "The occupants ride together and work together and play there together." The implication of "play there together" was clear.

Writers might occasionally tease the reader with a hint of something of which only an insider could know. It was generally of a sexual nature and, more explicitly, dealt with an actor being gay or lesbian. Obviously, some care must be taken in translation. When Kirtley Baskette wrote in *Modern Screen* (August 1939) that Robert Cummings was "The Gay Deceiver," he was using "gay" in the old-fashioned sense of the word. When a photo spread in the January 1939 issue of *Photoplay* showed Cesar Romero skating and identified him as a "gay blade," there must be some suspicion as to the true meaning of the phrase. However, when *Movie Life* (November 1950) printed a photograph of Farley Granger with two women and described it as a "Gay Trio," there was little question that "gay" was being used in the modern sense in reference to the actor's homosexuality.

One of the queerest—in any sense of the word—fan magazine articles was written by Martha Kerr and published in the November 1939 issue of *Modern Screen*. Titled "Vincent's Priceless Hat," it was subtitled as "Being the revelations of a very gay Fedora on his even gayer boss." The hat wrote that it and Price were inseparable and that only after the actor had met and married Edith Barrett was it retired.

Hints at homosexuality were generally veiled. Only those in the know would figure out the hidden meaning behind the title, "Janet Gaynor's Great Friendship," heading an article by Virginia T. Love about the actress and her assumed lover Margaret Lindsay in *Movie Mirror* (April 1934). Similarly, a limited number of readers would understand a gossip item in *Shadoplay* (October 1934) linking Gaynor and "her pal" Margaret Lindsay as the best hula dancers in Hollywood.

Rumors of a homosexual relationship between Cary Grant and Randolph Scott are prevalent today, but what did readers of *Hollywood* magazine (October 1933) make of a story headed "We Can't Afford a Hollywood Marriage," in which the couple deplored the necessity of the "Hollywood front"? The couple was transparent in stories of their lives together and the homes they shared. "They Keep Bachelors' Hall" wrote Ben Maddox in *Silver Screen* (March 1933), explaining that Grant and Scott met on the Paramount lot and decided to pool their rent. Grant married Virginia Cherrill, but Esther Meade explained in *Modern Screen* (September 1934) that he and Scott were "still pals." Scott was interviewed in Grant's dressing room. He and Grant had gone to England together for the wedding, and the "three often go places together." After announcing the divorce from Cherrill, Maude Cheatham was able again to report on "Movie Bachelors at Home" in *Screenland* (January 1936). There was a photograph of Grant and Scott side by side in the pool, and the former explained, "Every morning when we aren't working, we jump out of bed into

Rock Hudson is featured on the cover of *Hollywood Playtime* (1956).

our bathing trunks, make a run for the surf." Just what Grant and Scott got up to at the beach was revealed by *Modern Screen* in September 1937 with a two-page photo spread, "Batching It," with shots of the two bathing suit–clad bachelors swimming, working out, racing through the surf, and in the showers. Again, there was the problem with that word, when Ruth Waterbury wrote in *Photoplay* (April 1939) of "The Gay Romance of Cary Grant." It was all very odd, not the least because it was all very open. The two men, the writers, and the readers were either incredibly naïve or the actors were willing to risk the readers not guessing the truth of the relationship. Perhaps it was the sheer transparency of the couple's life together, as reported in the fan magazines, that kept it from ever becoming identified as a homosexual relationship.

Fan magazines were certainly willing and able to offer space to Hollywood's gay bachelors, keen to prove to the fans that they were still looking for the right woman. *Silver Screen* (July 1945) revealed that Hurd Hatfield was dating a female dancer he met in the MGM commissary. In March 1952, Rock Hudson wrote in *Screenland* on "Dates I Won't Forget!" "I think I shouldn't marry for three more years, not until I'm thirty," he explained to questioning fans. Similarly, Farley Granger told *Screenland* (May 1952) readers "What I Want from Love," and assured them that "I don't mind waiting now for the right girl."

Even in the early years, fan magazine writers and editors used innuendo when confronted by gay Hollywood. John Ten Eyck, profiling Eugene O'Brien in the November 1918 issue of *Photoplay*, dropped a number of hints as to the actor's sexual orientation, noting the French novel, the huge blue bowl of yellow flowers, and the faint suggestion of the tang of sandalwood in bachelor O'Brien's apartment. "The photographer, a person of no imagination, looked at the flowers and the pictures and the tea, as much to say, 'I wonder where he hides her—when he has company?'" Later, O'Brien drew a handkerchief from his pocket and "A faint scent of lilac floated on the air."

When J. Warren Kerrigan told *Shadowland* (October 1919) of "leading a double life," he was referencing his Irish heritage demanding a life of wandering, fighting, and adventure when, in reality, he longed for a quiet home life. As the first major gay star in Hollywood, Kerrigan might just as easily have been discussing the need to hide his sexuality with endless talk of his love and devotion for his mother. His career was almost ruined in 1917, when he told a local Denver newspaper that he would not go to war and that first America should take "the great mass of men who aren't good for anything." He argued that those who brought beauty to the world, such as the actor, should not be drafted. In August 1917, *Photoplay*'s James R. Quirk brought Kerrigan's outlook to his readership, branding the actor as "one of the beautiful slackers." While the link between Kerrigan's attitude toward war and his homosexuality is tenuous, it is certainly there—and doubtless Quirk was fully aware of the actor's sexual orientation.

As early as November 1929, Katharine Albert explained in *Photoplay* "How Bachelors Manage Their Homes." William Haines, described as a "playboy," appeared in a photograph captioned "At home, fastidious housekeeper and host, art connoisseur. The commode is Venetian; the portrait a Sir Peter Lely." I don't think any more clues are necessary. Tea with Ramon Novarro was served by his "man" and consisted of "tiny finger sandwiches, cut in hearts and shamrocks, and luscious little petit fours." Albert explained that Gary Cooper lived with his mother and noted a baking ham in the kitchen, a gift from Andy Lawlor's mother in Virginia. Modern research suggests overwhelmingly that Cooper was involved in a long-term gay relationship with Lawlor, a minor actor virtually unknown today, whom Katharine Albert did not bother to identify.

Gary Cooper was featured in a November 1930 *Picture Play* photo section headed "Boys Will Be Coy," in which, it was explained, our virile heroes assume expressions that belong to ingénues. The photograph published must be

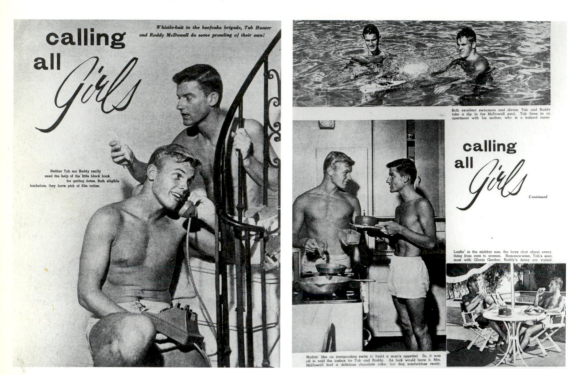

The "Calling All Girls" article in the June 1953 issue of *Movies*.

the most effeminate ever taken of the rugged leading man. Coming a close second was David Rollins, known to have been gay, of whom it was explained, he "has been coy and coquettish in so many photographs that this is no novelty."

Dorothy Manners' gossip column in *Modern Screen* would occasionally feature a Hollywood wedding, but when the magazine decided to feature "Hollywood's First Homosexual Marriage" in June 1971, it was the subject of a special article by Celeste Lenoir. In two pages, devoid of photographs but heavy with breathless prose, Lenoir documented the happy event. "We at *Modern Screen* know who these two men are," she explained. "However, while we do think it is too startling a story to remain untold, we will not disclose the identities of these men as we do not wish to bring hurt and embarrassment to their relatives."

There were clues galore. One was supposedly a television actor who had just achieved stardom, while the other was an aging once-major film star. "His looks were fast fading; his once-strong muscular body was getting flabby. . . . He was middle-aged, and the years were flying by fast." The latter would "occasionally see his mentor in a restaurant—old, alcoholic, ugly, slobbering over some young paid stud—a laughing stock to everyone in the film industry." It does not take too much detective work now, and presumably then, to identify the mentor as Henry Willson, the film star as Rock Hudson, and the television actor as Jim Nabors. The *Modern Screen* article was perhaps most extraordinary in the effort it made to explain homosexuality to its readers and the sympathy that it bestowed upon the two central characters.

calling all *Girls*
Continued

Though Tab and Roddy had just recently met, they both struck it off immediately and became good friends. Above, Tab pulls up into the driveway of the McDowall home, near 20th, in his light blue Ford.

Roddy introduces his pal to his mother and dad. Rod has an older sister, Virginia; Tab, an older brother. Close in age, Rod is 23; Tab will be that on July 1st.

Tab was fascinated with Roddy's tape recorder. Both boys are very conscientious about their careers. A true movie fan, Tab sees about five films per week, plus legit plays.

No, Tab isn't singing, he's reading a French script as Rod records same. Not a linguist, Mr. Hunter "fractured" the language. Tab's next picture is UA's Wells Fargo Express.

A very talented artist, Roddy spent seven years organizing, producing and directing a movie studio. He called it Imperial Eagle Productions, did his own camera, art and publicity work, but abandoned project when it became impractical.

As with women, the fellows finally got around to discussing their clothes. Tab admires newest suit in Roddy's wardrobe. They have similar builds, but Tab's 2" taller.

Roddy's combination bedroom-sitting room is decorated in a very masculine way. Though he makes frequent trips home, Rod is presently living in New York, doing theater and TV work.

Prior to his becoming a Hollywood agent, Willson had written a series of articles in *The New Movie Magazine*. One of the most open in September 1933 was titled "Tom Brown's Buddy Looks Him Over," in which Willson wrote of "living with him the past six weeks," but was quick to point out, "He likes all of the girls, respects and admires them." (An occasional article by Willson also appears in *Photoplay* in the 1930s.)

Arguably, the most famous of suggestive gay photo spreads was "Calling All Girls," which appeared in the June 1953 issue of *Movies*. Here, wearing only shorts, Roddy McDowall and Tab Hunter were shown at the Hollywood home of the former. "Though Tab and Roddy had just recently met, they both struck it off immediately and became good friends," readers were advised. The two men telephone for dates using their little black books, take a dip in the pool, and raid the icebox in the kitchen. "Romance-wise, Tab's seen with Gloria Gordon; Roddy's dates are varied," the piece concluded. Yes indeed!

Movies, which was first published in February 1951 by Ideal, was one of the more outrageous fan magazines of the period. With lots of photographs and few signed articles, it covered television and recording as well as the motion picture, and there was very obviously someone involved in the publication with a gay perspective. The covers featured male stars as often as female ones, and there was considerable beefcake, with the magazine being especially fond of Scott Brady, John Derek, Aldo Ray, and Robert Wagner—particularly when they were shirtless.

Aside from the "Calling All Girls" piece, the reader was invited to view photographs of the New York apartment shared by Roddy McDowall and Merv Griffin, including a shot of the two of them sitting together on a bed while supposedly telephoning their respective girlfriends. While in New York, Roddy, along with Danny Stradella, found time to show Tab Hunter the city in an August 1952 photo spread titled "The Bachelors Step Out." Certainly, *Movies* outed the bachelors before they were outed to a wider audience.

Farley Granger wrote "This Is My Private Life" in the August 1953 issue of *Movies*, and the same issue featured "The Laughs on Me" by Rock Hudson. Hudson was featured in the December 1952 issue with "This Is What I Like" on what he looks for in a woman; in the April 1953 issue with Ben Maddox's "Who Has Rock's Heart," which included photographs of the actor and his roommate Bob Preble; and in the December 1953 issue with "The Rise of Rock!," written by Henry Willson, which advised, "it's best to stay single."

Again, it was Farley Granger featured in a January 1950 issue of *Movie Stars Parade*, bare-chested, along with Howard Duff and John Payne, in a photo spread titled "Their Torsos Are More So." It was the type of piece that could easily appeal to a closeted gay fan magazine reader as well as a healthy, red-blooded American female. The most blatant photo spread aimed at those two disparate readers was "Stag Night at the Steam Room," published in the October 1950 issue of *Modern Screen*. Here, not only was Rock Hudson naked except for a towel over his genitals, but joining him at the Finlandia bath house and similarly unattired were Hugh O'Brian, Scott Brady, John Bromfield (showing the most skin), and Tony Curtis.

The one fan magazine writer who could have easily identified members of the Hollywood gay community was Hedda Hopper, but even she was stifled by the threat of libel. In 1958, Hopper asked *Motion Picture*'s Jack Podell if he would like a story on Rock Hudson's new wife: "Do you want me to do a special story for you on Phyllis Hudson? She won't give it to anybody else. Of course, she won't say he is a fag, and name his lover, but we can hint at that."[21]

In his groundbreaking study, *Behind the Screen: How Gays and Lesbians Shaped Hollywood, 1910–1969*, William J. Mann identified a number of fan magazine writers whom he believed to be gay, aside from the obvious Herbert Howe. Included on Mann's list were Ben Maddox, Samuel Richard Mook, and, possibly, John Ten Eyck and Richard Willis. I am inclined to add Norbert Lusk to their number. Most intriguing of the group was [John] Marquis Busby, a graduate of the University of Southern California, who began his career with the *Los Angeles Times*. He was western representative of *The New Movie Magazine* and a contributor to *Motion Picture*, *Movie Classic*, *Silver Screen*, and *Movie Mirror* (at least twelve articles). He wrote some thirty pieces for *Photoplay* between 1929 and 1931, including a highly intriguing two-part life story of William Haines, "The Wisecracker Reveals Himself" in the September and October 1929 issues. Busby lived with his mother and died tragically young of scarlet fever at the age of thirty-one in Los Angeles in March 1934.

Mann's intuition was matched by the opinion of Ezra Goodman, writing in *The Fifty Year Decline and Fall of Hollywood*, quoting one anonymous fan magazine writer: "There are about a hundred of us, roughly three quarters of us women and the rest men, or at least people who wear trousers." Goodman also wrote of the problems facing fan magazines in writing of closeted gay actors: "The fan magazines are afflicted with some rather special editorial problems. One of these has to do with the appreciable number of gaudy young movie actors who are quite disinterested in girls. How are the fan magazines to keep presenting these profiles to their swooning, girlish readers as ardent, romantic personalities, and how are they to explain the fact that these movie idols seem so oblivious of the opposite sex? The fan magazines turn themselves inside out trying to drum up romances for these susceptible swains, and they trot out such tricky and evasive verbiage as 'Trying to escape from any romantic involvement'; 'He wants a free life'; and 'Few women have been able to get really close to him.'"[22]

Almost twenty years earlier, an anonymous fan magazine writer had provided a description of a typical male member of the community, "He is a delicate-looking male creature who just *loves* the theatre. Since there isn't any theatre to speak of in Hollywood, he just *loves* 'the industry.' He feels that in his way he is part of the movie universe, making and breaking careers, and he simply loves it, the dear fellow."[23]

Could gay writers have insinuated a gay agenda into the pages of the fan magazines? It seems unlikely. Patrick O'Connor, who edited *Silver Screen* and *Screenland* in the 1960s, denied the suggestion most vigorously. "Absolutely not! I was very busy hiding my own gayness, so I would have been very sympathetic to anyone else who was hiding theirs. No, I would cut it out if somebody tried to imply or hint at it—cut it right out."[24]

An argument might certainly be made that just as the fan magazines appealed to young women, they also held a fascination for a gay readership, anxious to revel in Hollywood glamour and thrilled to find a suggestion that the film industry might very well be home to many of their orientation. As Patrick O'Connor recalled, "When I was a boy, I used to read the girl-next-door's fan magazine. I wouldn't want to be seen with one as a boy—it would have been considered sissy—but I read hers."[25]

CHAPTER 9

THE 1950S AND THE INFLUENCE OF TELEVISION

Fan magazines devoted to the motion picture had experienced little competition from similarly audience-oriented radio publications, the earliest of which were *Radio Art* (founded in 1923) and *Radio Broadcast* (founded in 1922 and merged with *Radio Digest* in 1930). Both ceased publication in 1939. Other prominent radio fan magazines include *Radio Stars* (first published 1932), *Radio Romances* (1945), *Radio Album* (first published in 1948), and *Radio Best* (first published in 1947 and later *Radio and Television Best*). They were never as numerous or as widely circulated as their film counterparts, but radio fan magazines, particularly those carrying program schedules, did find a market. Walter Annenberg's *Radio Guide*, founded in 1931, with its seventeen regional editions each with program listings, sold a reported 420,000 copies in 1936. It ceased publication in November 1943, by which time it was known as *Movie and Radio Guide*. (It was resurrected in 1953 as *TV Guide* by Annenberg's Triangle Publications, an early publishing executive of which was named, coincidentally, James Quirk.)

Walter's father, Moses Annenberg, founded the fan magazine *Screen Guide*, published out of Los Angeles, in 1932. According to his biographer, Walter Annenberg "did not think much of the magazine, but he loved the fact that it gave him a regular excuse to take the train to California."[1] A second fan magazine, *Stardom*, followed, but it ceased publication in 1944, replaced by *Seventeen*, the first popular magazine specifically aimed at teenage girls but one of which their parents could approve. It was to be influential later in encouraging the fan magazines to more actively aim their content at that same market.

Radio Mirror had found a relatively substantial audience from its inception in 1933, and it continued publication into the 1950s with a new title *Radio and Television Mirror*, ending its life in 1954 as *TV Radio Mirror*. The title change was emblematic of a change in interest of the core readership of the fan magazines. Just as television in the 1950s provided the film industry with its biggest challenge in terms of audience and revenue, so did television create a new audience for a new type of fan magazine—one in which the motion picture, if not taking a back seat, had at least to compete with the new medium for space and publicity. Within five years, between 1961 and 1966, fan magazines suddenly discovered that television stars sold as many issues as did many of their movie counterparts. *Peyton Place* and *The Man from U.N.C.L.E.* were as intriguing as Frank Sinatra and Sean Connery, particularly when *Peyton Place* boasted such stars as Ryan O'Neal, Mia Farrow, Dorothy Malone, Barbara Parkins, and Chris Connelly.

By the mid 1950s, television fan magazines, all published out of New York, included *TV People*, *TV Star Parade*, and *TV World*. Television and the motion picture shared an awkward relationship in many fan magazines, with the titles promising something from both media, as with *TV and Movie Screen*, *TV and Screen Life*, and *True Movie and Television* in the 1950s and *TV Movie Parade*, *TV and Screenworld*, and *TV-Film Stars* in the 1960s. Some fan magazines added TV to their titles, with *Screenland*, for example, becoming *Screenland plus TV-Land*.

However, the impact of television, surprisingly, was felt less by the fan magazines and more by the mass market periodicals. By the early 1970s, half a dozen leading magazines were no more, including *Collier's* (ceased publication 1956), *The Saturday Evening Post* (ceased publication 1969), *Look* (ceased publication in 1971), and *Life* (ceased publication in its original format in 1972). There was no evidence that the movie-oriented fan magazines were losing circulation at the start of the 1950s. Audit Bureau Circulation figures for 1950 indicate sales as follows: *Modern Screen* 1,168,445[2]; *Photoplay* 1,211,644; *Screenland* and *Silver Screen* 924,430; *Motion Picture* 795,173; and *Movieland* 290,221.

In that each copy was probably read by at least three individuals, it was estimated that fan magazines attracted a total audience of fifteen million, in other words one-fifth of all those attending movies on a weekly basis.[3] The film industry still needed the fan magazines, the fan magazines still needed the film industry, and fifteen million Americans needed both.

At the same time, some of the studios were growing concerned that fan magazines were skimming the gloss and glamour off their stars by reporting too much on their home lives. The aura of mystery attached to a movie star was disappearing fast. Whereas the studios might want to promote Van Johnson as clean-cut, all-American boy, the fan magazines in the 1950s had little interest in someone as wholesome. It was Ava Gardner, Rita Hayworth, Marilyn Monroe, and Elizabeth Taylor with whom their readers were obsessed. Even the likes of Jane Powell and Doris Day promised a hint of glamour. After what was described as years of discussion over the loss of glamour in Hollywood, MGM announced in May 1953 that it would no longer authorize stories about its stars and their children. It would be okay to publish "glamour" pieces on Esther Williams, Jane Powell, or Elizabeth Taylor, but there could be no acknowledgment that they had a family life.

Flair magazine reported that the fan magazines in 1950 represented a multimillion dollar business.[4] In his 1950 report on audience research, Leo A. Handel noted that thirty percent of audience members at the New York opening of a major production had read of the film in a movie magazine.[5] In 1952, John Danz, president of the Sterling Theatres in Oregon, Washington, and California, stated that "Movie magazines are the 'Dun and Bradstreet' rating on movie stars, and invaluable to the exhibitor." Earl Hudson, president of the Detroit United Theatres, claimed "Fan magazines helped make Van Johnson a movie star. Marlon Brando and Shelley Winters quickly became new favorites through youthful theatre audiences."[6]

In 1954, the Dell Publishing company asserted that it printed more than one million magazines each day, including not only the acknowledged fan magazines, but also *Who's Who in Hollywood*, the *Hollywood Family Album*, and comics devoted to Walt Disney characters and Western stars such as Roy Rogers, Gene Autry, Rex Allen, Johnny Mack Brown, and Buck Jones.

In October 1955 at a luncheon of studio publicity directors in Beverly Hills, Irving S. Manheimer, president of Macfadden Publications, publisher of *Photoplay* and others, claimed that fan magazine sales now totaled more than 8.5 million copies per issue, a substantial increase over five years earlier. The fan magazines were increasing in popularity while sales of the four leading general weekly magazines declined by 2,300,000 copies and newsstand sales of four women's service magazines dropped by one million copies.[7]

What was happening to the fan magazines in the 1950s was a dumbing down of stories and a noncritical approach to the reviewing process. Certainly, in the 1940s film criticism in the fan magazines had reached a low level. By the 1950s, it was at rock bottom. Since the 1930s, film reviews in the fan magazines had not been overly critical. For example, *Movie Mirror* used a tick in rating the new releases. One tick signified a "good picture," two ticks an "extraordinary" one. There were no tick designations for average, weak, or poor films— Hollywood just did not make productions of such a low quality as far as the fan magazines were concerned. In the 1950s, *Modern Screen*, like its competitors, rated the new films from a high of four stars (excellent) to a low of two stars (fair). The fan magazines refused to recognize that there was such a category as poor. One contemporary writer noted that of forty-five films reviewed in a single issue of *Modern Screen*, only one title actually fell to the level of fair.[8]

There was also a recognition that the fan magazine readership, while still devoutly female, was decreasing in age. More teenagers were reading fan magazines than were their mothers. *Seventeen* magazine had begun publication on September 1, 1944, and eventually it boasted an average readership of 6.5 million—a far greater number than read all of the fan magazines combined. When *Teen* began publication in 1959, its circulation quickly increased to one million copies a month. Later periodicals such as *Tiger Beat* (1965) and *Teen Beat* (1976) were further recognition of a youth market.

There was a vast teenage market out there, and fan magazines had to capture that audience. One approach was an emphasis on romance, with new

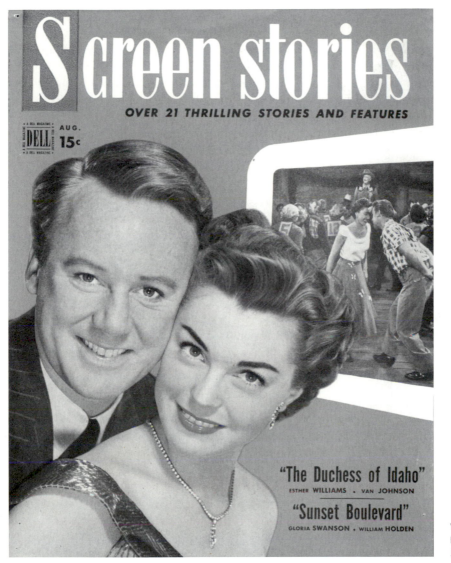

Screen stories

OVER 21 THRILLING STORIES AND FEATURES

DELL   AUG. 15¢

"The Duchess of Idaho"
ESTHER WILLIAMS . VAN JOHNSON

"Sunset Boulevard"
GLORIA SWANSON . WILLIAM HOLDEN

Van Johnson is featured with
Esther Williams on the cover of
Screen Stories (August 1950).

periodicals such as *Sheilah Graham's Hollywood Romances*, earlier titled *Hollywood Romances*. Issues of these fan magazines from 1953 and 1957 had one thing in common—Elizabeth Taylor. For the next two decades, Taylor was one actress guaranteed a fan magazine cover because her image and her love affairs assured the magazines of an avid readership. She was beautiful, she could gain reader sympathy with the various tragedies in her life, she was charitable, she was "a bad girl," and "she's always good for a breakup story."[9] Liz Taylor was on the cover of *Sheilah Graham's Hollywood Yearbook* in 1953 and again in 1955, and she appeared on the cover of the September 1957 issue of *Hear Hollywood*, a decidedly odd fan magazine that provided its readers with a phonograph recording of some of its printed interviews.

In 1958, Dell published a fan magazine, which is assumed to be a one-off, titled *Liz and Mike. Modern Screen* featured Elizabeth Taylor on the cover in July 1958, with husband Mike Todd and the promise of an article titled "The Most Tender and Tragic Love Story of Our Time." She was featured again in October 1958 and in December 1958, with a composite of her, Eddie Fisher, and Debbie Reynolds, with the last pleading, "Don't Hurt Eddie . . . Don't Hurt My Husband." Ironically, the 1959 breakup of Reynolds' marriage to Fisher and his leaving her for Elizabeth Taylor helped ensure Reynolds appearance on the covers of countless fan magazines. "They're running out of stills of Debbie," reported Ezra Goodman. "They are taking old black-and-white pictures and tinting them for color. Debbie sells books. It's a horrible thing they call reader identification."[10] (A few years earlier, in November 1952, Reynolds had been one of the "Targets for Scandal" in a piece by Marta Jensen in *Movie Stars Parade*. The scandal: the actress had announced her choice of Stanley Donen as her next director!)

As Goodman described it, the Debbie-Liz-Eddie saga was "the most explosive triangle of the past decade." In a 1958 readers' poll, *Motion Picture* reported that Taylor came first in interest, followed at number two by Debbie Reynolds, whose career was suddenly of major import. In 1959, Reynolds was the wronged wife, and all the stories were in her support. In April 1960, *Motion Picture* reported that she was afraid she would not find love, but a month later, it announced her fears were unfounded, she had found a wealthy suitor named Harry Karl. It was "the incredible story of the romance Hollywood said couldn't happen, wouldn't happen, mustn't happen," explaining why Debbie went from Glenn Ford to Harry Karl. In fact, while Debbie was fearful of love in *Motion Picture*, that same month she had already found it, and Harry Karl, in *Modern Screen*. Elizabeth Taylor appeared five times on the cover of *Modern Screen* in 1959, announcing in March, "I Was Betrayed" and giving her side of the story, in July pledging "I Will Be Faithful," and in November with the magazine revealing "The Tragic Facts about Liz' and Debbie's Fatherless Children."

Citing some of the headlines in which their names had appeared, Taylor and Fisher began lawsuits in November 1960 against the publishers of seven fan magazines: *Modern Screen, Screen Stars, Movie World, Movie TV Secrets, Movie Mirror, Movie Stars-TV Close-Ups,* and *TV-Film Stars.* What the suit alleged was pretty explicit and obvious, at least in hindsight,

Defendants acted maliciously, irresponsibly and wickedly, for the crass commercial purpose of stimulating circulation of motion picture fan magazines, in flagrant disregard of the truth and of resulting injury and distress inflicted on the plaintiffs and their infant children. Among devices used by defendants to accomplish their objective was lurid display of front cover teaser headlines, leading the public to believe that articles in said magazines would reveal scandalous conduct on the part of plaintiffs, thereby exciting prurient curiosity of the public and inciting it to purchase the magazines—whereas the articles themselves in no way substantiated those headlines and often belied them. By such sensational, yellow journalism—in subversion of every standard of honest, responsible reporting— the defendants acted in furtherance of continuing campaign calculated to exploit for profit and popularity the prominence of the plaintiffs and other motion picture and performing artists, to the grave impairment of their professional and family lives.[11]

Marilyn Monroe should have dominated fan magazine covers in the 1950s, but there were only an estimated seventy-five, beginning with *Silver Screen* in February 1952. Monroe's first *Photoplay* article, "Make It for Keeps," and the first I have found, dates from July 1951. Fan magazine editors could be quite demanding in terms of what they expected from a Monroe story, even if the writer was Hedda Hopper. *Motion Picture* magazine's Jack Podell had the following detailed questions for Hopper: "Does she honestly think she's capable of a happy marriage considering her life as a star and the demands made on her as a woman and individual? Does she think marriage is the thing for her? She'll say yes, but ask Hedda to keep on posing the question and exploring it. See if Monroe wonders if any actress can handle marriage successfully. She is a sex queen, symbolically the mistress of the nation. Does she think any woman under these circumstances can be a good wife to only one man? I don't want this thought answered with a yes or no—I want it explored fully. I want the inside on Monroe, not what makes her tick."[12]

The actress was very much a glamorous star in the classic sense, belonging more to the "golden age" of Hollywood beauty than to the 1950s. In a curious way, while she might have been the "mistress of the nation," Monroe was old-fashioned, as far as the fan magazine readers of the 1950s and 1960s were concerned. As one fan magazine publisher explained it, "Liz is a stronger woman, more independent, and doesn't need public sympathy. Marilyn was too sensitive, too human. People don't want to read about stars with the same hang-ups they have."[13]

Monroe's farewell to the fan magazines covers came with her death. In October 1962, *Modern Screen* announced "Goodbye Marilyn." In February 1963, *Photoplay* disingenuously announced, "We Grant Marilyn's Last Wish and present for the first time the nude photos she wanted published after her death." Even in death, with the promise of nudity, the poor woman was still forced to share a cover with the actress who had usurped her in the fan magazines. Above a photograph of Monroe was the promise of more than her nude photographs inside: "How Liz Broke Her Love Deal with the Burtons." While she did not have another cover story in *Photoplay* in 1963, Monroe was featured in the June, August, and September issues.

Elvis Presley made his first feature film appearance in 1956 and his first fan magazine appearance that same year. Coverage of major names in the recording industry can be dated back to the 1940s, however, with many fan magazines providing a separate, relatively small amount of space in the rear portions of the journals. Presley was the subject of ninety-five stories in *Photoplay*, beginning

Muriel Babcock (far left) with various members of the staff from Ideal Publications is hosted by Frank Sinatra at Toots Shor's restaurant in New York.

with Laura Lane's "From Brando to Presley—Why the 'Rebel' Craze Is Here to Stay" in November 1956. A month later, *Modern Screen* asked its readers to vote for the king of rock 'n' roll with the choice between Presley and Pat Boone. The former was not a prominent selection for a cover photograph, although he was featured as early as February 1957 on the cover of *Movieland*.

Elvis Presley was of most value to *Photoplay* with his death. David Ragan recalled "On August 19, 1977, two and a half days after the death of Elvis Presley, a 128–page one-shot magazine about the star's life and career entitled *A Photoplay Tribute to Elvis Presley*, was assembled, edited, and completed by me. Duplicate plates were made and flown by charter planes to three U.S. cities and went to press over the weekend. The magazine went on sale, first in New York City and Los Angeles, on August 22 and was an instant success. Peter Callahan, chairman of Macfadden Holdings, gave an interview to the New York *Times* in which it was stated that the Presley tribute earned upwards of $750,000 in two weeks. 'That capital infusion,' said Callahan, 'made this company. Elvis was very good to us.'"[14]

Not all stars welcomed the attention from the fan magazines. Natalie Wood, whose career, along with that of her husband Robert Wagner, had relied to a large extent on fan magazine coverage, launched a campaign against such publications in the fall of 1958. She was generous in acknowledging that perhaps they "helped boost me to stardom," but she told the Los Angeles *Times* (October 7, 1958) that "now they are becoming a liability, alienating a good portion of the public for Hollywood. . . . Our big beef is that the fan mags not only insult the intelligence of the personalities they cover but of the readers as well."

While the readership was young in the 1950s and the coverage was generally youth-oriented, the magazines remained under the editorial control of an older generation. All the fan magazines published by Ideal were supervised by Muriel Babcock, a woman decidedly lacking in Hollywood glamour and in her fifties.

Born on March 19, 1900, Babcock had been writing for the fan magazines since 1929, when she first appeared in *Photoplay*. In the 1930s, she had a major body of work in *Modern Screen*, *Motion Picture*, *Movie Classic*, *Movie Mirror*, *Screen Book*, *Screenland*, and *Silver Screen*. She edited *Picture Play* for the last three years of its life, and in the 1940s fan magazines under her command included *Movie Life*, *Movie Stars*, *Movie Stars Album*, and *Movie Stars Parade*. As late as 1960, Babcock introduced a new fan magazine at Ideal, *Star Album*, which, recognizing that modern readers lacked the ability or the interest in reading, consisted basically of one-page photographs of the stars. In 1953, Babcock and Ideal had introduced *Movie Pin-Ups*, a twenty-five-cent publication containing nothing more than full-page photographs of stars, along with their vital statistics, grouped in categories such as cheesecake, sweater girls, beefcake, and "for the girls." Female stars dominated, and the choice of headings such as "cheesecake" and "sweater girls" throws into question the determination that the readership was primarily female. The increase in the number of photographs per issue and the decrease in reading matter appear to be in direct proportion to the lowering in age and sophistication of the readership. Muriel Babcock died in Huntington, New York, in January 1988.

Competing with Ideal's output in the 1950s was a relatively new company, Skye Publishing Co., which had primarily been involved in publication of Macfadden-type journals such as *True Crime Cases*, *Crime Confessions*, and *Cavalcade*. Its fan magazines from the 1950s were all edited by Joan Curtis, heavy on photographs and light on text, and included *Hollywood Stars*, *Movie & TV Album*, *Screen Annual*, and *Screen Life*. Curtis also edited *Movie Fan*, *Movie Pix*, and *Screen Fan*, which may well have been published by Skye through a subsidiary company. In acknowledgement of the age of the readership, another entity was Screen Teen Co., responsible for *Movie Teen* as well as *Movie Pix*, whose publisher was also identified as Astro Distributing Corp. Destined to a longer life and prominence was Sterling and Company, founded in 1953, publishing *TV Picture Life* and *TV and Movie Screen*, titles indicative of the upcoming prominence of television.

Only one fan magazine publisher realized that a young readership demanded a younger editorial hand, and that was J. Fred Henry, publisher of *Screenland* and *Silver Screen*. In August 1952, he took the unprecedented decision to hire two teenagers, Reba and Bonnie Churchill, as coeditors of his magazines. Not only were Reba and Bonnie Churchill the only sister writing team in Hollywood, at a reported age of eighteen and fourteen, respectively, they were also the youngest. "It seemed like it was in tune with the times," said Bonnie Churchill. "We were the age of the people we were interviewing. He [Henry] was very forward thinking, and his idea was that we were the age of the people who were reading the books, and what they wanted to read was what we wanted to read."[15]

Reba Churchill joined the *Hollywood Citizen-News* in 1946 and graduated from cub reporter to assistant women's editor. Bonnie left school early to join her sister in writing a syndicated column, "Hollywood Earfuls," which was published in *Silver Screen* and contained short, pithy gossip items, such as: "Margaret Truman and Robert Merrill are the latest twosome—on records, that is. The two have recorded a semi-classical album plus some popular disks."

It was all very innocuous, and throughout their careers neither woman could be accused of publishing anything negative on Hollywood. Typical of their fan magazine articles was one from the September 1949 issue of *Modern Screen*, in which they reported on Roy Rogers and Dale Evans and which contains both black-and-white and color photographs of the two intrepid reporters. They were young enough to be considered copy in their own right, and doubtless their photographs helped sell the magazine to a youthful readership. With their youthful exuberance, the Churchills brought an informality to reporting on the more mature members of the Hollywood community. Thus it was in *Screenland* (December 1952) that it was not Granger discusses Hayworth, but rather "Stewart Discusses Rita."

At sixteen, Bonnie got her license as well as a new and unusual automobile: "I think the first interview we went to that I drove was Roy Rogers and Dale Evans. We went out to their ranch. I drove so slow because I was afraid I was going to do something wrong and get a ticket." When she was able to purchase her first car, a Chrysler, she told the dealer that as a writer she had specific requirements. After a telephone call to Detroit, the company presented her with a custom-built vehicle, a Chrysler New Yorker with a white leather top and a typewriter that could be pulled out of the glove compartment and a plug-in device allowing for the sending of telegraphic wires.

The sisters, who never married, did everything together, including the actual writing of the pieces. "I'd sit at the typewriter, and she would be over my shoulder," said Bonnie. "My sister was working at the *Hollywood Citizen-News*—she was working specific hours—so whenever we would have an interview, I would call by and see if she could come. The times she couldn't come, I would have to do it myself." Until the pair acquired a tape recorder, notes were taken in longhand.

The Churchills' boss, J. Fred Henry, died suddenly in New York at the age of fifty-three on August 7, 1952, almost simultaneous with their appointment as coeditors. Henry had entered publishing with Dell in 1929, remaining there for ten years, during which time he helped found *Modern Screen* and *Modern Romances*. He left Dell to join Ziff-Davis as vice-president, and in 1948 purchased *Silver Screen* and *Screenland* from the Liberty Publishing Company.

Henry's wife, who inherited the magazines, decided to reinstate the previous editor, Lester C. Grady, feeling more at ease with a veteran in charge. However, Grady did continue to give the sisters assignments, as well as the monthly gossip column (which Bonnie Churchill insisted was not a gossip column but a Hollywood column: "We never wrote gossip"). There were also other assign-ments, most notably from *Modern Screen*, which Bonnie remembered paid the most. The magazine commissioned a series of articles on Hollywood par-ties and teenagers.

Sometimes, the Churchills' age, naiveté, and girlish enthusiasm worked in their favor. As Bonnie recalled,

> Robert Mitchum was one of the first people we interviewed. We had an assign-ment from Lester Grady. We didn't know that he was so hard to get. We had lunch with him [and] he gave us a fabulous story. We were so happy and we were writing away. Just as he finished his dessert, he said, "Did you like the story?" "Oh yes, Mr. Mitchum." I was so happy because Mr. Grady said if we got it, he'd put it on the cover of the magazine with our names. He said, "I want to tell you now, be sure and listen. You can't print a word I said. I just made the whole thing up." And he just laughed and laughed.
>
> Then he looked at me, and I'd never been one to hide my feelings like my sister. He saw this tear well over and run down my cheek. And he got kind of em-barrassed and left. The woman who was there from the studio, Muriel Hill, said she was so sorry we'd wasted all this time and we'd missed the paycheck. The next day, the phone rang, "Can you be out here at RKO in two hours? Robert Mitchum is going to do the interview. He saw that tear going down your cheek. He will give you a story and you can print it." He never spoke about his folks or his children, and he spoke about everything like that. My mother said, "You see, the good Lord was with you." From that moment on, we always liked him.

Reba Churchill died in Los Angeles on April 29, 1985, at the age of fif-ty-three. Bonnie continued to write a column, syndicated by National News Syndicate, and today she does a daily show and a Sunday show, heard on 135 CBS-affiliated radio stations and with twenty-five million listeners. The sisters also wrote *Reba and Bonnie Churchill's Guide to Glamour and Personality* (1962).

In December 1952, the world of the fan magazines changed forever, when the first issue of *Confidential* appeared. What was it? "It is a scandal sheet. It is the gossip columnist with dementia praecox. It is expertly written; its sto-ries are usually amusing (except to the subject). Its editors are masters of the double entendre, the sly innuendo, the literary leer, and it has, largely through its success, littered the newsstands with 25 or so competitors."[16] *Confidential* did to Hollywood stars what the fan magazines even before the Hays Office could not do. It revealed them in all their scandalous modes, without apology and without restraint. It "tells the facts and names the names," as its masthead promised—and generally the facts were accurate and the names well known. *Confidential* should not be confused with a fan magazine, even if its influ-ence on the fan magazines would ultimately be devastating. If nothing else, it taught the fan magazine editors how to use a cover line to grab the attention of a potential reader.

Confidential magazine was founded by Robert Harrison (1904–1978), a publisher of "girlie" magazines, such as *Whisper, Parade, Titter*, and *Flirt*, who had worked for the *New York Graphic* and for the Quigley Publishing Company (responsible for the trade paper *Motion Picture Herald*). It was a good combination—the *New York Graphic*, a newspaper noted for its sleaze, and a conservative, Catholic, film-related publisher with close ties to the Hays Office. Harrison knew what a publisher could get away with and what the film industry wanted kept under wraps.

The initial print run of 150,000 would eventually rise to 4.6 million. It was not until the third issue, August 1953, that *Confidential* began to emphasize Hollywood, with a piece on Robert Mitchum appearing naked at a party hosted by Charles Laughton and covering himself in ketchup. The gay subtext to the piece was typical of the magazine's thrust; in its first issue, it had published an article on a gay wedding in Paris, titled "World's Queerest Wedding." *Confidential* was to out a number of Hollywood celebrities, with damning stories on Lizabeth Scott, Marlene Dietrich, Dan Dailey, Tab Hunter, and others. In July 1957, it explained to its readers "Why Liberace's Theme Song Should Be Mad about the Boy."

If nothing else, *Confidential* was decidedly more entertaining that any of the fan magazines of the period on offer, with stories such as "Why Sinatra Is the Tarzan of the Boudoir" (May 1956), "Joan Crawford's Back Street Romance with a Bartender" (January 1957), and "Louella Parsons: Hollywood Hatchet Woman" (April 1959), complete with a photograph of the gossip columnist picking her nose. There was genuine wit here, for example, a photograph of the Gabor family in November 1953, headed "Mama Gabor and the Three Little Bores." At least one fan magazine publisher, Fawcett, came out with a parody, *Cockeyed*, in July 1955, with a cover story "Liberace's Wig Maker Tells All!!!"

There were lawsuits, which *Confidential* was generally able to overcome, and its July 1957 issue was banned from California distribution by the state's attorney general. In September 1957, the magazine carried a two-page statement, headed "Hollywood vs. *Confidential*," in which it announced, "California has accused us of a crime—the crime of telling the truth." However, it was the lawsuits that eventually forced Harrison's sale of *Confidential* in July 1958, and the new owner, Hy Steirman, tried to keep away from Hollywood gossip. In reality, the magazine was about to be overcome by a new publication, the *National Inquirer*. Both *Confidential* and its founder died in the same year, 1978.

At least two famous gossip columnists had ties to *Confidential*. Mike Connolly provided it with material he could not use in his column in *The Hollywood Reporter*. Walter Winchell promoted *Confidential* on the air and in his newspaper columns. In return, *Confidential* published a series of articles exposing his enemies and praising his achievements.[17]

Hollywood being Hollywood, the film industry produced a feature film about the publisher of a gossip magazine titled *Real Truth* who prints an exposé of a movie actor's long-past prison record, much as *Confidential* had exposed Rory Calhoun having served time in jail in its May 1955 issue. Produced

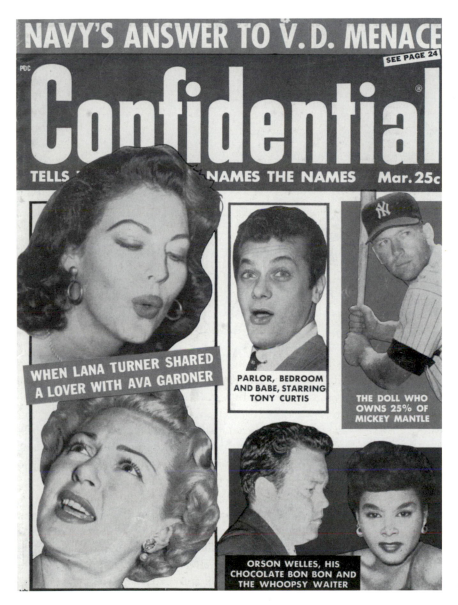

The March 1957 issue of *Confidential*.

by Armand Deutsch for MGM release in 1956 and titled *Slander*, the film stars Steve Cochran as the publisher and Van Johnson, outed as gay by *Confidential*, as the ex-con. The film concludes with the publisher being killed by his own mother and the actor going on television to warn the public against buying these types of fan magazines. The Hollywood solution is obviously either to shoot the publishers or for the readership to take action. As Bosley Crowther wrote in the *New York Times* (January 17, 1957), "It makes scandal-mongering the menace of free enterprise, parental love and the American home. . . . The fact that the comfortable inhabitants of several million American homes support these magazines is not inspected."

Ruth Waterbury interviews
Henry Fonda on the set of *War
and Peace* (1956).

"*Confidential* in the fifties was totally responsible for changing the movie magazines," asserted Rona Barrett. "They didn't know how to get those kinds of stories that *Confidential* had. But what they tried to do, they changed the headlines of every story to make them far more sleazy. They never had sleazy titles on those movie magazines, and now they were doing very suggestive titles. In a way, *Confidential* was for the more sophisticated people out there, who began to believe. Because many of the stories that they did run, even though they may have paid for those sources, were really accurate."[18]

The success of *Confidential* proved that studio cooperation was not necessary. Editors and writers had no need for the film companies for artwork, for story confirmation, for anything. "The whole basis of *Confidential* was to cut people down," commented Warner Bros. chief of publicity Max Bercutt.[19] The end result was a huge circulation. It is ironic that fan magazine publishers, with journals such as *True Confession* and *True Story*, were unwilling to risk the wrath of the film industry by including stories similar to those found in *True Story* in the pages of their sister publications. As one fan magazine editor put it, vis-à-vis the relationship between the stars and the periodicals: "They tell the truth about them to hurt them. We tell lies about them to help them."[20]

Confidential may have changed the makeup and outlook of the fan magazines, but it had no impact on their sales. At the end of the 1950s, the circulation figures for the fan magazines were on the whole slightly up from the figures reported at the beginning of the decade: *Photoplay* 1,295,723; *Modern Screen* 1,267,420; *Motion Picture* 986,896; *Screen Stories* 375,242; *Silver Screen* 340,193; *Screenland plus TV-Land* 300,476; *Movie Stars-TV Closeups* (a new entrant) 260,012; *Movie Life* 253,137; *Movie Mirror* 200,758.

Aside from the omnivorous readers, there were still those who believed fervently and passionately in the need for fan magazines. One such supporter, whose view was somewhat biased in that her job was at stake, was Margaret Hinxman, review editor of the British fan magazine *Picturegoer*. In the summer of 1959, she wrote, "I refuse incidentally to be offended by the fact that we're usually and sometimes patronizingly referred to as a 'fan paper.' The dictionary describes a 'fan' as an enthusiastic devotee and an ardent admirer. And if there were a few million more such picturegoing 'devotees' and 'admirers' the Rank Organization wouldn't be turning cinemas into skittle [bowling] alleys and Laurence Olivier probably wouldn't have to shelve *Macbeth* for lack of financial backing."[21]

CHAPTER 10

THE 1960S

In 1937, Clifton Fadiman made an astute observation: "My guess is that the film mags are selling each year to a lower and lower stratum, speaking purely in intellectual terms, of American society. Eventually the bottom will be reached. Then the magazines will have to alter in an upward direction the straight moron approach to which they have unswervingly held for twenty-five years."[1]

The "slop," as Fadiman called it, of the fan magazines continued unabated and relatively unchanged into the 1950s. The circulation curve remained constant. If the fan magazines became less literate—as they did—it was because the audience was younger and less literate. Then came the 1960s; the studio system was dying, and their publicists were no longer peddling stories to the fan magazines. Editors and writers were on their own in unearthing stories and unchecked as to the content of such stories. Press agents were still active, but stars dictated to whom they could and could not speak. "Why should all fan magazines be judged poison?" asked one editor. "If publicity outfits, movie companies and networks continue to give such poor cooperation in arranging interviews, I think I'll stop cooperating with them."[2] This comment is almost pathetic in its naiveté, as if the fan magazines still believed they wielded any power. In the same *Variety* article, a press agent responded, "The fan magazines were all right when they printed nothing but Cinderella stories. Now that they don't print those stories anymore, who needs them?"

Just as the press agents were suggesting that the fan magazines be ignored, so briefly in 1973 did the Producers Guild of America suggest in its journal that moviegoers boycott the fan magazines. Exhibitors reported that audiences read of a star jilting his pregnant girlfriend, branded him a "louse," and refused to see any more of his films. It is all incredibly simplistic to infer that publicists would reject potential publicity for their clients, readers could stop being titillated by fan magazine trash, and they believed every unsourced item that was written. Knowing that a star is a louse is going to increase his audience, not decrease it.[3]

Patrick O'Connor, who was editor-in-chief of *Silver Screen* and *Screenland* in the 1960s, found the situation ludicrous. "These guys from the studios thought that we had power, that we made a difference," he recalled. "And the editors of these magazines thought that they had power too. It was bullshit. There was a cultural gap. The editors of *Photoplay* and *Modern Screen* thought they had power. The guy who was editor-in-chief of *Photoplay* was so paranoid about people stealing his ideas that he spoke in Yiddish. They had no power at all. They were lost."[4]

It was not just the living providing the fan magazines with fodder to raise the ire of the reader. One industry-affiliated writer complained that "with so many journalistic termites operating in the film capital, it's a wonder the film structure has not yet been destroyed." The cause of his anger? A headline announcing, "Now It Can Be Told: Why Al Jolson Was the Most Hated Man in Show Business."[5]

Once, fan magazine writers had been required to get advance and then final approval from the studio with which a star was under contract prior to publication. By the 1960s, it was no longer the producer whose permission was needed but the personal press agent. Even if the story was approved, the fan magazine editors realized that the title could easily be changed to suggest a more scurrilous content. Thus, Gale Storm might write of "My Baby's Four Fathers," but the story itself was nothing more than an account of how her three brothers helped her and her husband raise the child.

With the independent filmmaker came a new brand of films and a new brand of stars, uninterested in furnishing the fan magazines with the same old guff. Fan magazines complained that stars now wanted to talk about the environment, women's liberation, and liberal politics—themes that held no interest for their readers. "We ran a story on Jane Fonda," *Modern Screen*'s editor-in-chief told *Cosmopolitan*'s Arnold Bell, "and no one was interested. Our readers are basically conservative, but they don't want to read about John Wayne's politics, either, though they're basically interested in John Wayne."[6]

Who readers most wanted to read about in the entertainment world was Lucille Ball. As one fan magazine writers explained it, "Lucy comes across as being very gracious. Housewives identify with her as the all-American woman. They grew up with Lucy in the movies and on T.V. They went through birth pangs with her and through her divorce from Desi Arnaz. They were happy when she remarried and sad when Desi Jr. took up with 'bad' Patty Duke and fathered Patty's baby. Now they're with Lucy again in her comeback as Mame. With Lucy, the fans relive their own joys and sorrows."[7]

Interest in Lucille Ball is understandable. Her television show *I Love Lucy* is still popular. Perhaps it should, therefore, be no surprise that the comedienne was eclipsed in fan magazine coverage by none other than Lawrence Welk. After all, his television show still continues in syndication on public television, if not quite as popular as it was on the ABC network between 1955 and

STILL ONLY 35¢

THOSE SHAMELESS NUDE SCENES: Bonus
The Women Who Do Them... and the Women Who Don't

MOVIE STARS

AUGUST

PDC

JACKIE'S SECRET LITTLE BLACK BOOK
Why so many are afraid of what's inside it!

Ideal MAGAZINE

HOW WELK FINALLY FORCED THE LENNONS OFF TV
WILL THEY EVER FORGIVE HIM?

LAWRENCE WELK

LENNON SISTERS

Lawrence Welk is featured on the covers of *Movie Stars* (August 1970) and *TV and Movie Screen* (March 1971).

1971. "Lawrence Welk Is a Happening," announced *Photoplay* in December 1969. "It's all gone straight to the maestro's head and we don't just mean the champagne." The story was about Welk's skit on the "Now Generation," performed for night club audiences, but the headline might just as well describe the entertainer as far as the fan magazines were concerned. He even made it into *Confidential* magazine on January 15, 1960, after his firing of Alice Lon, the first champagne lady, with the story, "What the Bully with the Baton Did to the Champagne Lady."

Perhaps fan magazine readers were looking for a father figure and found him in Lawrence Welk, or perhaps they wanted someone as solid, reliable,

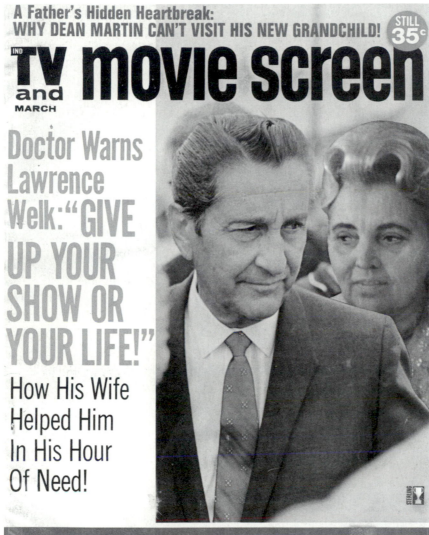

A Father's Hidden Heartbreak:
WHY DEAN MARTIN CAN'T VISIT HIS NEW GRANDCHILD!

STILL 35¢

IND
TV and **MARCH** **movie screen**

Doctor Warns Lawrence Welk: "GIVE UP YOUR SHOW OR YOUR LIFE!"

How His Wife Helped Him In His Hour Of Need!

UNWED PEGGY LIPTON TELLS WHY "MARRIAGE CAN BE A BUM TRIP!"

and unchanging as the American Midwest. The fan magazines were happy to oblige their readership with stories such as "Doctor Warns Lawrence Welk: 'Give Up Your Show or Your Life!'" (*TV and Movie Screen*, March 1971).

Undoubtedly, there was collusion between the Welk organization and *Modern Screen*, which featured the entertainer in three stories in 1971. Suspiciously, all are written by Bernice McGeehan, who was later to cowrite Welk's various books, and a May 1971 photo spread of the wedding of Welk dancer Bobby Burgess and Kristie Floren (daughter of Welk's accordionist Myron Floren) just happens to include a photograph of *Modern Screen*'s west coast editor, Helen Weller.

Cast members of *The Lawrence Welk Show* were also popular with fan magazine readers, most notably Jo Ann Castle and the Lennon Sisters. The latter, particularly Kathy, were a constant source of interest. When there was an overabundance of Liz or Jackie coverage, then the fan magazines would turn to the Lennon Sisters with cover stories such as "How They Lost Their Innocence" in *Silver Screen* (July 1968), in which fans voiced their disgust that two of the four had married divorced men: "I think they're hypocrites." *Screenland* in 1967 featured the Lennon Sisters in seven of its twelve issues, including four cover stories. The most entertaining article was titled "The Girls Talk about Dating! Drinking! Dope!" It might just as well have consisted of a one-line response: They don't.

Welk and the Lennon Sisters were on the cover of *Motion Picture* in January 1970, with the story "Why Kathy's Grief for Her Dad Is the Greatest—How Welk Is Trying to Help Out—But Can't." In 1968, the Lennon Sisters left *The Lawrence Welk Show*, and in June of that year they were featured on the cover of *Photoplay* with the story "Lennons Fight Welk: Are They Mistreated by Him—or Ungrateful? Why Two of Their Husbands Quit the Band. Why They Won't Pose with Welk for Pictures." In August 1970, a cover story in *Movie Stars* revealed "How Welk Finally Forced the Lennons off TV: Will They Ever Forgive Him?" The story related to the cancellation of *Jimmy Durante Presents the Lennon Sisters*, which had been airing on Saturday nights after *The Lawrence Welk Show*. Both shows appealed to the same "Geritol set" and, as a result, there were only enough sponsors for one show.

Regardless of what the pundits might have to say and all the negative publicity, fan magazines could still fill fifty percent of all theater seats in the late 1960s. A survey by Communications Research Center in Chicago reported in the January 3, 1967, issue of *The Film Daily* revealed that the fan magazines stimulated greater movie attendance than *Reader's Digest*, *Life*, *Look*, *Time*, *Newsweek*, the *Saturday Evening Post*, and seventeen other mass circulation periodicals. *Modern Screen* and *Photoplay* accounted statistically for the sale of more than one of every two theater tickets. Richard Heller, editorial director of *Modern Screen*, told *The Film Daily*,

> I was flabbergasted and delighted. I have always maintained that fan magazines sell a great many more tickets to movies than any other publications. I am absolutely certain that people who make movies and those who sell and distribute them have little inkling of how important fan books are to the success of their films.
>
> This report was not designed to elicit these figures, but they clearly show that a movie maker may derive some prestige from promoting features in books like *Mc-Calls*, *Redbook*, *Seventeen*, *Good Housekeeping*, *Ladies Home Journal*, *Life*, *Look*, but they sure sell a hell of a lot more tickets through fan magazines.

The response of the movie makers was indifference. In the same issue of *The Film Daily*, the producers were reported to have reduced or cancelled advertising in the fan magazines because of a question as to effectiveness and because of the allegedly deteriorating moral tone of the publications. A vice-president at Columbia asserted, "They've hurt the industry as a whole . . . in effect to cater to the cheapest elements in the country." The fan magazines might sell tickets, increase profits, but they would not save the industry but rather help close it down. As usual, those within a dying industry were out of touch with the viewers and with potentially highly viable advertising outlets. The response of the Hollywood community to the fan magazines was a throwback to the 1930s. Fan magazines could not be trusted, and they should not be supported unless they were under the close control of the industry.

The fan magazines did fight back. Alice Schoninger, editor of *Motion Picture*, editorialized,

> At one time "kick the can" was a popular game with kids—today, "kick the fan magazines" is popular, even considered chic, with talk show folks. Now, some of them have legitimate gripes. But they complain about the inaccurate reporting and then indulge in inaccurate complaining. If you have complaints, Barbara Anderson, Johnny Carson, Irving Shulman, Lennon Sisters and all the rest, then name names. Tell us which movie magazines injured you . . . I know there are some magazines that do commit editorial atrocities and I deplore them as much as the talk showers. But let's be fair—don't lump us all together. I don't like being thrown in with that company and neither do the other responsible editors in this field.[8]

A similar stance had been taken a few years earlier by Frederick A. Klein, executive vice-president of Macfadden-Bartel. He resented the five, fifty-or-so-year-old magazines that he published being uttered in the same breath as the "shoe-string nonentities that hit the newsstands."

> Would you hold a respectable newspaper responsible because of material published by cheap tabloids? As entertainment publishers, we certainly would not condemn the entire film industry because of some producers who cater to the sexually aberrated. . . .
>
> Responsible fan magazines such as those published by Macfadden-Bartell are, in effect, a bridge. They make actors and actresses come alive—apart from the world of celluloid. The public not only wants to be entertained by the stars on screen, but they enjoy following the lives of the stars off screen.
>
> We do not invent what the stars do; we merely reflect their lives. . . . So, in essence, what the responsible fan magazines do is to act as monthly news magazines showing the stars in the full gambit of their lives, from raising Cain to raising children.
>
> Anybody who knows this business knows how often entertainment magazines protect the stars who need protection from their excesses.[9]

One actress who had reason to disbelieve this notion was Julie Andrews. In January 1969, *Screenland* published a story suggesting she was romantically involved with actor Sidney Poitier. That same month, *Modern Movies* published a story alleging that she was indifferent and unconcerned about the welfare of her six-year-old daughter, Emma, and that Emma had been involved in emotional scenes relative to Andrews' friendship with director Blake Edwards (whom she married in November 1969). Julie Andrews sued the publishers of each magazine, Macfadden-Bartell and Magazine Management Company, the editors, and the story writers for a total of $6 million, $4 million of which was for punitive damages.[10] The suit was settled out of court for an undisclosed sum and publication of a retraction in both magazines.

David Ragan was editor of *TV and Movie Screen* in 1957–1961 and managing editor of *Motion Picture* in 1961–1964. He recalled,

> Writers—almost all in Hollywood—almost never came to us with story ideas. But they read the magazines and knew well what had already been done. So as the editor you dared to parcel out assignments by star name alone, unless there was some particular angle you wanted covered. I had a stable of ten or twelve writers that I could count on. Three of my special pets were Fredda Dudley Balling, Dora Albert, and Marcia Borie. Ruth Waterbury would come to town on occasion and make the fan mag rounds. More regularly, at least annually, Jane Ardmore would do the same. [She was a] talented, prolific writer, well liked at all studios and networks.
>
> The TV network publicity people could not have been more cooperative. The same was true of the movie companies' publicists, as I learned when I broke into the fan mag business as the editor of a combined-title magazine *TV and Movie Screen*, at Sterling Group. Every week, publicity folk would bring actors and actresses to my office, especially the young ones, for meet-greet visits. Just a few of the many: Warren Beatty (just before he started work on *Splendor in the Grass*), Steven McQueen (prior to the debut of his TV series *Wanted: Dead or Alive*), Dennis Hopper, Carol Lynley, Dolores Hart, Dick Chamberlain, Troy Donahue, Annette Funicello, Jean Seberg (just before her French period), Hugh O'Brian, and George Hamilton.
>
> I had a one-word yardstick that I used to determine which stars were worthy of coverage. That word: *lovable*. And I had a device that unfailingly determined that.
>
> In every issue of *TV Radio Mirror*, where I first used it, there appeared a small coupon inviting readers to make their favorites known. The inducement was a free paperback book to the first 500 who submitted a filled-in coupon. More than 2000 coupons were received each month. I'm forgetting to mention that Macfadden had its own paperback book division. So the cost was minimal. All coupons were carefully tabulated, but the results were never published. Why help my fan mag competitors?
>
> Readers were not asked simply, Who are your favorite stars? Instead, a carefully worded headline, changed each month, appeared on each month's coupon. Another might be: The star I would like for a friend. It was designed to get down to the nitty-gritty: Who do you really *love*? It worked. Those coupons served me well. And they provided surprises.

Who knew that Dean Martin, then headlining in the TV variety show bearing his name, was a *lovable*? But the numbers didn't lie. Americans had fallen in love with his music and casual charm. And month after month, as long as his show lasted, Dean Martin was at the top of the Favorite Stars list. Absolutely number one. And we, on the editorial staff, were stuck with coming up with fresh articles on the world's dullest interview subject.[11]

Ragan (b. 1925) had begun his career as a syndicated columnist in 1951 and had his first editorial assignment as managing editor of *Tele-Views* the following year. However, most of the legendary fan magazine editors and writers were either gone or in decline, replaced by a new breed, including Patrick O'Connor, who recalled,

> I wanted to be in the book business, but I was too old—I think I was thirty-five—and I finally got a job at Popular Library, a paperback publishing company, which published *Silver Screen*, *Screenland*, *Ranch Romance*, and puzzle and paperback books. There were the puzzle people and the Western people and the sexy detective people—they weren't very sexy. I got a job as a sub-assistant editor. I had to work as a bartender at night to support myself because the pay was so awful. My office was next to Ira Peck, who was editor of *Silver Screen* and *Screenland*, assisted by a woman named Ruth Fountain. He was friendly enough, but he was not an easy guy. Anyway, he quit after I had been there a couple of years. He was making twice what I was making. So I ran down the hall to the publisher and said, "I want that job." He said to me, "You don't know the difference between Annette Funicello and Frankie Avalon." I was not into popular film. I was the usual snotty film person. I didn't even have a television set. Anyway, he said, "I'll give you a trial."
>
> In hindsight, Ira Peck was a very lazy man. It was just a job. But Ruth, who worked for him, was fantastic. She laid it out, she bought the stuff, she read it, she wrote the blurbs. She was never offered the job. She was never even considered because she was a woman. Ruth knew how to do it and she taught me how to do the layouts and write the cover lines. [There was] just the two of us.[12]

Ruth Fountain was eventually named managing editor; a couple of decades earlier, she had been assistant editor of *Silver Screen*.

While Patrick O'Connor was a newcomer in the 1960s, Jack J. Podell (1927–1997), a graduate of the University of Missouri Journalism School, had been making a name for himself in the field since the early 1950s, when he was editor of *Television Life Magazine*. In 1954, he was appointed editor of *Motion Picture Magazine* and later became Fawcett's editorial director. In 1961, Podell moved on to Macfadden-Bartell, becoming editorial director of its women's group of magazines. Later that same year, he was named editor-in-chief of *Photoplay* and *TV Radio Mirror* and successfully lured Hedda Hopper as a gossip columnist for *Photoplay* away from *Motion Picture Magazine* as of October 1961. "He was very creative and had a distinct penchant for promotion," recalled Larry Thomas, who replaced Podell at *Motion Picture Magazine*; he had been with the magazine since 1954, serving as associate editor and film reviewer.

Thomas explained that most chain publishers had a similar structure, namely an editor and a managing editor for each publication, with an editorial director supervising them overall: "In most cases, the managing editor is responsible for the physical production of the magazine, that is, the end-of-month putting together of the product, measuring the copy, sizing and placing it, sending it to the printer, and acting as liaison. During the rest of the month, he serves creatively as part of the team."[13]

Within two years of Podell moving to Macfadden-Bartell, he was able to persuade his new employer to acquire *Motion Picture Magazine* and *True Confessions* from Fawcett. Once the purchase had taken place, Macfadden-Bartell stripped the subscriptions from its two acquisitions, added them to *Photoplay* and *True Story*, increased the ad rates accordingly, and limited sales of *Motion Picture Magazine* and *True Confessions* to newsstands only.

While Podell was editorial director at Macfadden-Bartell, David Ragan was editor-in-chief of *TV Radio Mirror*, the country's number one television monthly. The two were close friends who dined together once a week, discussing what was important to them—not their magazines, but rather their wives, children (three to each), and their favorites in the world of classical music. Ragan preferred contraltos, while Podell opted for sopranos and the violin, which he also played. Ragan recalled,

Jack had a risky but successful way of doing his job. He hired three editors with extreme caution and trusted their judgment implicitly. Halfway through an issue an editor would meet with Jack for a specific purpose. Jack believed totally that a magazine's cover was all-important. Newsstand sales were more profitable than subscription, and the potential buyer had to be reeled in. So the cover subject and captions had to be enticing. Once these were set, Jack never looked over an editor's shoulder, never asked to see layouts, never read articles or looked at photos. With the arrival of the first bound copies he would go over the issue with a fine-tooth comb. Then, he would call a meeting for a gentle critique. Once I used a full-page photo of a young TV star giving a soul kiss to his beautiful fiancée. All Jack said of this was, "Tsk, tsk." For a few months at one point, Jack was confined to a tuberculosis sanatorium about five miles north of Manhattan. He continued to work from there. Editors would bring to him potential covers and cover lines for a meeting just like at 205 East 42nd Street, New York.[14]

When Macfadden-Bartel president Frederick Klein retired, a new and arrogant president was appointed and Podell was out. Podell moved to Chicago, heading the editorial department at the University of Chicago Press, a position he held until his death in 1997.

Paying $150 a story, *Silver Screen* and *Screenland* had no lack of contributors, including Bob Thomas, legendary entertainment reporter with the Associated

Press. Thomas had contributed at least three pieces to *Modern Screen* in the past, "The Lies They Tell about Bob Wagner" in October 1953, an interview with Debbie Reynolds in June 1959, and a piece on Victoria Shaw and Roger Smith in November of the same year. As he recalled, "Around 1960, I moved to Encino, and I found myself with a mortgage, a wife, two daughters, and one on the way. I had trouble meeting requirements on my Associated Press salary. The only escape was writing for the fan magazines. I avoided *Photoplay* and *Modern Screen*, because their demands were too difficult. The second-string fan magazines were very receptive. I did a lot of stories on newcomers. They liked new faces, and I hunted them down. I never used my own byline, but a variety of noms de plume. I wrote them as professionally as I could, but I didn't want anyone learning I was a fan magazine writer."

Thomas was not ashamed of writing for the fan magazines, but as he pointed out, "An AP story was a lot more work. There had to be a real approach to an AP story, after all it was going out to hundreds, thousands of newspapers, to radio and television. It had to be thoroughly well documented. The fan magazine stories could be fluffy."[15]

Bob Thomas might have continued to write for the fan magazines much longer had he not found, as he described it, "another racket," that of writing best-selling show business biographies, beginning with *King Cohn* on the life of Columbia Pictures head, Harry Cohn.

Army Archerd began his career as an associate of Thomas before becoming a reporter for the *Los Angeles Herald-Examiner*. He was to replace Sheilah Graham as *Daily Variety*'s gossip and entertainment reporter, publishing his first "Just for Variety" column on April 27, 1953, and his last on September 1, 2005. While working for *Daily Variety*, Army Archerd also found time to write for *Photoplay*, contributing some seventeen pieces on stars such as Yul Brynner (his first in February 1957), John Travolta, and Jon Voight between 1957 and 1979.

Another writer who published in fan magazines of the 1960s is Aljean Harmetz, with five pieces in *Photoplay* between 1964 and 1967, including an unusual religious essay, "Prayer That Changed My Life" (April 1967), and various pieces in *Motion Picture*. Harmetz went on to be Los Angeles entertainment correspondent for the *New York Times* from 1978 to 1990 and authored important volumes on *The Wizard of Oz* (1977), *Casablanca* (1992), and *Gone with the Wind* (1996), as well as a volume of interviews and profiles, *Rolling Breaks and Other Movie Business* (1983). "I do not in any way try to hide or turn my back on my fan magazine heritage," Harmetz told Katharine Lowrie in 1980. As David Ragan recalled, "Aljean was a Hollywood kid. Her mother worked as a seamstress in MGM's costume department. And when the studio was making the dress for Grace Kelly's wedding to Prince Rainier, guess who got the scoop for *Motion Picture*!"[16]

Typical of the new breed of fan magazines was *Modern Movies*, first published in June 1968 with Carol Finkelstein as editorial director, and with no connection—historical, financial, artistic, or otherwise—with the 1930s

On the set of *Father's Little Dividend* (1951), Elizabeth Taylor and Don Taylor peruse the latest issue of *Silver Screen*. Courtesy of Academy of Motion Picture Arts and Sciences.

publication of the same name. It was "The Magazine You Can Believe In," to become within the year "The 'In' Magazine of the Movie-TV World," with "Stories You'll Never Forget!" In that first issue, such stories included "Mia, Frank & Dean: The Story Behind Their Break-up!," "The Lennons: The First Divorce in Their Family!," "Carol Burnett: The Clown Who Was Accused of Home-Wrecking!," and "Janet Leigh: The 'Pyscho' Who Threatens Her!" The overuse of the exclamation mark provides enough information as to relative truth of the stories.

It was the cover as well as the cover blurb that sold a fan magazine at the newsstand. According to fan magazine writer Jane Wilkie, an editor at *Modern Screen* initiated the cover lines, which are today so very much a part of tabloid journalism. In a way, as Patrick O'Connor insisted, it was all very innocent. "The cover lines, selling lines, were not innocent, but inside the magazine was innocent. My favorite cover line was 'What did Sammy and Liz and Richard do that night at the Dorchester.' They had tea."

Despite fan magazines often having the same publisher, competition was encouraged between them. Most of the major publishing houses had monthly conferences at which it was determined which magazines sold best, which cover lines were the most popular, and which cover stars sold magazines.

100 glamorous picture pages

SCREEN ALBUM

MAGAZINE

SPRING 25c

DELL MAGAZINE

LIZ TAYLOR

DEBBIE REYNOLD'S SNAPSHOT ALBUM

"The 10 most wonderful days of my life"

Elizabeth Taylor on the cover of *Screen Album* (Spring 1954).

The publisher of Popular Library would not allow Jackie Kennedy on the cover of either *Silver Screen* or *Screenland*. "He loathed Jackie Kennedy," said O'Connor. "Everyone else was using her. It was bad taste." Kennedy's presence, of course, was indicative of a move by the fan magazines away from the Hollywood personalities toward a new breed of celebrity. Elvis Presley was a cover presence as much because he was a major recording artist as because he was a movie star. Elizabeth Taylor was always present.

A casual examination of various fan magazines reveals Taylor on the covers of *Stardom* (July 1960), *Fan-Fare* (March 1964), and *Popular Movie* (March 1966), featured in a composite photograph with Mia Farrow and the question "Is Mia More Shameless Than Liz?" She was on the cover of the

DELL
20-740-609

screen stories®

a complete guide to the movies!

SEPT. 35c

SOPHIA LOREN and **PAUL NEWMAN** in "Lady L"

MARLON BRANDO stars in "The Appaloosa"

LIZ FACES A NEW CHALLENGE!

LIZ TAYLOR: *Now it's her turn to fear a lovely, young rival!*

SAMANTHA EGGAR: *She's the bright, new star Burton prefers to his wife!*

AUDREY HEPBURN and **PETER O'TOOLE** star in *"How To Steal A Million"*

Elizabeth Taylor and Samantha Eggar on the cover of *Silver Screen Stories* (September 1966).

February–April 1954 issues of *Hollywood Family Album*, and on issues, without months of publication, from 1961, 1962, and 1963. It is virtually impossible to look through *Inside Movies* without finding Elizabeth Taylor and appropriate cover lines: "A Baby for Liz and Burton" (October 1962), "Liz on Her Honeymoon!" (June 1963), "Liz Unfaithful to Burton" (September 1963), "Liz Taylor & Peter O'Toole Caught in the Act" (January 1964), "What Liz Runs Away from, What Jackie Runs to" (May 1965), and "Why Burton's Failing Liz as a Lover" (December 1965).

Elizabeth Taylor began the 1960s as Hollywood's top box-office star. It is far from surprising that in 1961 she is on the cover of *Modern Screen* four times.

In October 1963, Mike Connolly, writing in *Screen Stories*, managed to link Elizabeth Taylor with the John Profumo scandal, which was riveting attention in the United Kingdom and throughout the world. The scandal developed after Cabinet Minister Profumo (who was married to actress Valerie Hobson) had a brief relationship with a woman named Christine Keeler, who was also sleeping with a KGB agent, and then lied in the House of Commons when questioned about it. It transpired that Taylor had been a patient of an osteopath, Dr. Stephen Ward (who subsequently committed suicide), linked with the introduction of Keeler to Profumo. At the least it was worth a cover story, particularly as it tied in with the new Taylor and Burton release, *The V.I.P.s.*

By 1967, Taylor was considered "overexposed." "As the plump seemingly contented wife of Richard Burton she no longer makes the lurid headlines of the days of their romance and the breakup of her marriage to Eddie Fisher and of Mr. Burton's to Sybil Burton," commented the *Wall Street Journal*.[17] Hedda Hopper held strong views on the fan magazine coverage of Richard Burton and Elizabeth Taylor. On June 21, 1963, she wrote to Jack Podell, then editorial director of the Macfadden-Bartell Group, "I don't think you will increase circulation by continuing to write about them. He has made himself a joke by making the sacred bond of matrimony a laughing matter. It is not. No matter how he continues to drag it down and laugh at it, personally I have stopped laughing at him and I believe the real people are doing the same."[18]

It was Mia Farrow who was stealing the limelight away from Taylor, with some thirty-six articles in *Photoplay* between 1965 and 1972. In January 1969, *Silver Screen* featured the two women on its cover, with a story "How Mia Felt Making Love to Liz Taylor in *Secret Ceremony*" that also helped promote their latest film.

Regardless, Taylor was still the dominant cover star from the world of movies. *Screen Stories* was a periodical devoted to publishing the "Best Movies of the Month in Story Form," and yet it found space, issue after issue, for cover stories on Liz. Between 1962 and 1973, she is featured on at least twenty-six occasions. She was destroyed by love (August 1962), fighting against drugs (April 1968), facing being a cripple (April 1969), undergoing secret surgery (September 1970), and explaining what being forty really meant to her (June 1972). So important was Taylor coverage to *Screen Stories* that in 1967 it demoted the adaptations that were its reason for being to the rear of the magazine and featured Taylor, and, to a lesser extent, other stars at the front.

Richard Burton's own screen career and his leading ladies could generate cover speculation. When he starred opposite Genevieve Bujold in *Anne of the Thousand Days*, *Screen Stories* (January 1970) reported on Liz having to watch the couple do a love scene on the set. In September 1966, *Screen Stories* reported on its cover that Samantha Eggar was "the bright new star Burton prefers to his wife." The story inside related to Eggar being signed to play Mrs. Chips opposite Burton in a musical remake of *Goodbye, Mr. Chips*. The musical was made with Peter O'Toole and Petula Clark, although Eggar was actually contracted and paid for the female lead.

"I'm not sure if at that time I was upset," Eggar commented, "because I didn't want anyone to think I had come between Elizabeth Taylor and her husband. I'm sure I didn't laugh at the time. I'm too well brought up. I would have been pretty devastated and nervous. I was probably scared of what she might do to me. She could not possibly have thought that I was in any way competition to her whatsoever. It would be chalk and cheese, and I'll be the cheese." In fact, Samantha Eggar's response to the cover was to have it perma-plaqued and hung for thirty years in the guest bathroom at her Los Angeles home. "It caused the most laughter when people went into the bathroom."[19]

Between 1967 and 1975, Taylor was on the cover of *Screen and TV Album* on at least sixteen occasions. In the May–July 1969 issue, she was promising "I Will Survive!" In the August–October 1970 issue, she revealed what she "has learned about life from her teenage children." Serious illness forced her into seclusion in October 1973. In May 1974, she was "raped" while filming in Rome. In July 1974, she lost her baby, and in March 1975 a jail sentence was hanging over her head.

As Patrick O'Connor explained to me, it was up to the editors to find new cover concepts: "I had someone airbrush the Beatles and give them Marine haircuts. I took them to the Beatles on the first trip [to the U.S.] and they thought they were wonderful. They were falling on the floor. Then Brian Epstein said No. I put Ringo on the cover. I raised the circulation about eight percent, which was incredible for those days. I tried to be innovative, and I had a beautiful black female writer write a piece about Sidney Poitier. That was the first time he had been in."

Sidney Poitier was the subject of only two major articles in *Photoplay*. The first, in August 1968, was titled "The Night He Cried for His Mother." The second, a month later, explained "Why He's Loved and Sammy [Davis Jr.] Isn't." *Photoplay* claimed to have surveyed the opinions of twenty-two million black Americans who go to the movies or watch television, "just as other Americans do." Most of the quoted respondents spoke in what can only be described as a white American's idea of African-American patois. The opinions were not exactly as biased as the headline, "Why Negroes Love Sidney Poitier—but Not Sammy Davis," suggested, with the main reason for the dislike being the latter's history of falling in love with white women.

Sammy Davis Jr. may have been unloved, but he was certainly not unpublicized, generating considerable fan magazine promotion, as with an April 1967 piece in *Screenland plus TV-Land* on "Color-Blind Couples," with the other half of the couple being May Britt. Just as *Confidential* in September 1963 had asked, "Are White Stars Switching to Negroes," so did the fan magazines begin to show an interest in biracial couples, as with David Frost and Diahann Carroll. "Should She Tell Her Daughter to Marry a White Man?" asked *TV Movie Scene* of Carroll in December 1970. Interracial relationships had been featured earlier in *Confidential*, including those between Ava Gardner and Sammy Davis Jr. and Eartha Kitt and Arthur Loew Jr.

In 1968, America was hit with two tragic political assassinations, those of Martin Luther King Jr. and Bobby Kennedy. The death of Martin Luther King was ignored, while the death of Kennedy can only be described as a gift to the fan magazines, assuring them of the opportunity to continue to feature the Kennedy name on their covers. Far more important was, for example, a Hollywood actress such as Mia Farrow, whom *Photoplay* quoted with a headline in October 1968 of "Someone's Trying to Kill Me."

Lena Horne was the first African-American to be featured on the cover of a fan magazine, *Motion Picture* in October 1944. Executive editor Laurence Reid took the gamble, which was considered a high-risk one, and it resulted in a sales slump. The experiment was never repeated. There had certainly been earlier coverage of black entertainers, as noted elsewhere. Stepin Fetchit was first profiled in *Motion Picture* in July 1929, with a piece by Elizabeth Goldbeck titled "Step Tells All." He was also the subject of three *Photoplay* articles in 1929 and 1930. Hattie McDaniel was featured twice in *Modern Screen*, in October 1934 and February 1941. In the latter article, as Scarlett O'Hara's "Mammy," she tells how to make her favorite Southern specialties. Paul Robeson was basically too radical for fan magazine representation, although an interview with him did appear in *Screenland* in 1933. Often when an African-American was the subject of a fan magazine piece, it was a patronizing or derogatory commentary, as with Jerry Asher's "Pat's Pal 'Banksy,'" in the April 1936 issue of *Modern Screen*. "Banksy," who is never identified by her real name, was Patricia Ellis' "colored maid."

This same attitude is apparent in what must be the first fan magazine article devoted to an African-American. "Hattie the Hairdresser Speaks" appeared in the April 1922 issue of *Filmplay Journal* and purported to be the comments of the hairdresser (but based on the piece more accurately hair stylist) at the Famous Players-Lasky lot. Hattie, who has no last name and writes in stereotypical Negro patois, discusses the hairstyles that she has created for Gloria Swanson, Agnes Ayres, Lois Wilson, and others.

Ray Charles made it to the cover of *Modern Screen* in August 1961, sharing space with four other celebrities. Inside, readers were introduced to his "Black World" in a lengthy article, bordering on the patronizing but certainly informative. A few months later, in September 1961, *Modern Screen* discussed "Negroes & Whites in the New Generation" through an interview with singer Johnny Nash. The basic premise was "Americans are Americans—regardless of skin color or religious affiliation."

While it is obviously based on and intended to be an African-American response to *Life* magazine, there can be no question that *Ebony*, first published in November 1945, owes much to the fan magazines in terms of style and appearance. Like *Photoplay*, *Ebony* was published out of Chicago and it was a pioneering publication. As founded by John H. Johnson, *Ebony* was to report on everyday achievements of African-Americans from Harlem to Hollywood. Hollywood was not featured on the first cover nor on many later covers, in

"Are Negroes Getting a Raw Deal from Hollywood?" asked *Movie TV Tattler* (October 1960). "It's time for a Negro to be shown as a human being first—a Negro incidentally," argued writer Abbey Stewart.

large part because the film industry had no African-American stars. What *Ebony* did accomplish was to honor those outside of the celebrity fields both in Hollywood and elsewhere who were African-Americans. Thus, the September 1948 issue contained a cover story on Dr. Lois Evens, the studio podiatrist at MGM and thus identified as "Foot Doctor to the Stars."

In July 1963, *Photoplay* provided Hedda Hopper with a long list of personalities on which it was interested in stories. It is a fascinating group, including the famous, the forgotten, a handful of legends, and a few surprises. The listing as reprinted here is in the order in which it was given to Hopper: Richard Chamberlain, Vince Edwards, Rock Hudson, Elvis Presley, Troy Donahue, Paul Newman, Ricky Nelson, George Maharis, Gregory Peck, Jerry

Lewis, John Wayne, Tony Curtis, Robert Mitchum, Cary Grant, Frank Sinatra, Pat Boone, Charlton Heston, Eddie Fisher, Marlon Brando, Michael Landon, Paul Petersen, Dick Van Dyke, Jack Lemmon, Glenn Ford, Jack Lord, George Chakiris, Bobby Darin, James Darren, Richard Beymer, Burt Lancaster, Warren Beatty, and Bobby Rydell. On the distaff side, the list consists of Connie Stevens, Debbie Reynolds, Elizabeth Taylor, Sandra Dee, Doris Day, Suzanne Pleshette, Annette Funicello, Hayley Mills, Sophia Loren, Natalie Wood, Donna Reed, Deborah Walley, Ann-Margret, Bette Davis, Connie Francis, Carol Lynley, Joan Crawford, Carol Burnett, Lucille Ball, Audrey Hepburn, Kim Novak, Donna Douglas, Loretta Young, Janet Leigh, Shelley Fabares, Susan Hayward, Joanne Woodward, Tuesday Weld, Shirley MacLaine, June Allyson, Judy Garland, Lynn Loring, and Patty Duke.[20]

On the whole, the younger readership of the fan magazines did not want to know about Cary Grant, Bette Davis, Joan Crawford, or Claudette Colbert. Cary Grant made it into the fan magazines by becoming part of the drug culture with his use of LSD. As Grant explained to Don Graham in *Photoplay* (August 1967), in a piece titled "What LSD Is Doing to Him," the actor used the drug strictly for therapeutic purposes. From the 1960s onward, the fan magazines did pay some attention to drug use within the film community; for example in February 1971, *Hollywood Screen Parade* published a special report, "Inside the Hollywood Sex & Drug Scene." Curiously, the only name mentioned was the deceased Janis Joplin.

Moral content was obviously no longer relevant to either the editors or many of the stars—with the one exception of Joan Crawford. The star had obvious affection for the "golden age" of the fan magazine and little respect for the new generation of leading men and women and their relationship to the fans and the fan magazines. In December 1963, Crawford spoke with *Screen Stories'* Helen Weller on the subject of "Hollywood Girls Are Killing Their Own Glamor." She urged that stars today dress appropriately, fix their makeup, and always stop to sign autographs and blow the fans kisses. "I wouldn't dream of being seen publicly in slacks," she commented. "I think that any actress who makes an appearance in public without being beautifully groomed is digging her own grave. If only one fan sees you looking less than perfect, it can be the beginning of the end." There was praise for Elizabeth Taylor, weak and ill after a bout with death and being wheeled out of the hospital. "She would not permit herself to be wheeled out until her hairdresser had been summoned and done her hair, her makeup woman fixed her face, and a French designer had sent her a beautiful, new outfit to wear." It was tough being a Crawford-approved movie star, and *Screen Stories* was anxious to let its readership know the hardships of stardom.

A couple of years earlier, *Modern Screen* had run a series by Lawrence J. Quirk, billed as "Vintage Years . . . Portraits of Hollywood Greatest Ladies." One such lady who did not take kindly to her profile was Bette Davis. In a sad but inoffensive piece, published in the May 1961 issue of *Modern Screen*, the actress was described as a star in decline who cried when she was offered the leading role in Frank Capra's *Pocketful of Miracles*. In October of the same year, Davis filed a million dollar lawsuit against the fan magazine's publisher, Dell Publishing Co., claiming she had been described as "washed up" and that the article had "subjected her to ridicule, shame, contempt and disgrace" in suggesting that her services were no longer sought in the entertainment field. The case was settled out of court. Curiously, Quirk was later to write a biography of the actress, *Fasten Your Seat Belts: The Passionate Life of Bette Davis* (1990), in which he made frequent references to himself but no mention of the lawsuit or the article.

Writing in *What Price Fame?*, Tyler Cowen noted that "quests for fame influence culture, business, politics, and everyday life. . . . Fame influences the behavior of fans no less powerfully."[21] When she married John F. Kennedy, Jacqueline Bouvier became famous. When Kennedy died and his widow married Aristotle Onassis, she became infamous. Jackie Kennedy became the first major non-entertainment celebrity to adorn the covers of the fan magazines on a regular, and monotonous, basis. Jackie Kennedy accomplished what would have been unthinkable for Woodrow Wilson's wife, Edith, in the late 1910s: she became an American icon. Fame has nothing to do with merit, and there really is little meritorious about Jackie Kennedy apart from her restrained behavior at her husband's funeral. And just as television audiences tuned in to that event in the capacity of voyeurs, so did fan magazine readers desert their standard Hollywood heroines and heroes in favor of a new figure, whose lifestyle and love life they might salivate over. "She broke the public mold of what had come to characterize the ideally desirable American woman," wrote biographer Donald Spoto. "The buxom blonde had been America's fantasy in the 1940s and 1950s, but here was a tall, almost flat-chested brunette whose features were slightly out of proportion."

Jacqueline Kennedy was the first female megastar not created by the entertainment industry. As such, she was a welcome diversion for fan magazine editors and readers at a time when the film industry was losing its star power, when the star system had basically broken down and was close to its demise. There might have been other non-film stars in the past, but they were generally male and from the world of sport. As already documented, male stars did not belong on fan magazine covers, and sport was not a subject that would appeal to a feminine readership. Eleanor Roosevelt was a star, but she was not an attractive star in the style and fashion of Jacqueline Kennedy. Amelia Earhart was, arguably, the only female celebrity outside of the industry deserving of a fan magazine cover—but while a character similar to her was played by Katharine Hepburn in the 1933 RKO film *Christopher Strong*, the aviatrix never caught the attention of the fan magazine editors.

With the ascendancy of Jacqueline Kennedy, the fan magazines reinvented themselves. The content had generally emphasized teenage stars. Now, here was a lady—not a woman—whose elegance and style easily surpassed that of any new breed of movie star. According to David Ragan, it was Jack J. Podell who perceived that the fan magazines needed a shot in the arm, "that Jackie

Kennedy, who never made a movie, was a winner as a cover subject of fan magazines. She was."[22]

On March 22, 1961, the *New York Times* reported a visit by Kennedy to the New York City Ballet the previous night, and, perhaps for the first time, described her as a "star." "Movie stars lost their meaning when Jackie became a faux star," opined Gore Vidal.[23] In October 1961, *Photoplay*'s cover story on the First Lady carried the description, "Jacqueline Kennedy, America's Newest Star." It was official—stars were no longer limited to the motion picture and television. As Jim Hoffman's article explained, "No matter which definition of the word 'star' you choose, they all fit Jacqueline Kennedy and Jacqueline Kennedy fits each and every one of them." Hoffman went on to quote a July 2 report from Associated Press, "For the first time in memory, the nation's top feminine star is not from Hollywood, nor is she an actress. She is of course, Jacqueline Kennedy. . . . The chic First Lady has supplanted Elizabeth Taylor, Marilyn Monroe and other movie queens as the idol of young girls."

Looking through *Modern Screen* from 1962, Jacqueline Kennedy was featured on four covers (January, June, September, and December), with accompanying stories, and there are feature articles in the February, April, October, and November issues. In February readers were treated to "Hints from Jacqueline Kennedy's Paris Hair Stylist." In June Florence Epstein provided "Jacqueline Kennedy's Complete Life Story," which takes only seven pages to record, and in October the reader was confronted by "Jackie's Daring Photos That Started Talk," a series of images of the First Lady in a one-piece, far from revealing, bathing suit.

In 1963, *Modern Screen* had only one cover story on Kennedy—in February—and one feature article in the January issue. The cover story was titled "The Night Jackie Almost Lost Her Husband." The content concerns the Cuban Missile Crisis, during which most wives might have lost their husbands and vice versa. For the remainder of the year, Jackie was supplanted by Liz, with six of the ten covers featuring Taylor.

On November 22, 1963, President John F. Kennedy was assassinated in Dallas, Texas. Because of their printing schedules, the fan magazines took more than two months to acknowledge the change in Jacqueline Kennedy's status. It was business as usual at *Photoplay* with a cover story in November 1963 by, of all people, novelist Fannie Hurst on "The Kennedys: Marriage & Taste." The following month, the magazine announced, "We Answer the Critics Who Say Caroline Kennedy Is Being Spoiled." Eventually, in February 1964, *Photoplay* broke the news to its readership with the cover story, "Daddy Is Gone." However, in order to prove that even in mourning there was still fan magazine life, the caption and the photograph of Jackie shared space with two other headlines, "We Say Elvis Is Married! Proof on Page 6" and "The Night Debbie [Reynolds] Prayed with Billy Graham."

Inside, there was a five-page tribute by Ella Ormandy, which managed to identify what Jacqueline Kennedy was thinking as her husband was shot and how she would speak of his "courage" to their children. As befitting such a tragic moment, Gerald A. Bartell, chairman of the board of the Macfadden-Bartell Corporation, publisher of *Photoplay*, offered his own tribute: "We mourn for his bereft family; we grieve for his troubled world. But we rejoice in the sure knowledge that the judgment of history will be that John Kennedy was a man among men."

Equally, I am sure *Photoplay* rejoiced in the promise of continued coverage of the First Lady, coverage that would not be diminished by anything as tragic as an assassination. The following month, there was a twelve-page special memento, "The Courtship of Jack and Jackie." In July, *Photoplay* reported on "The Miracle That Made Jackie Laugh Again." In September, it was "The Love Jackie Doesn't Want—But Needs!" And in December there was a fourteen-page tribute, "As We Will Always Remember Them." Basically, Jackie alternated cover stories and extensive interior coverage with Liz. The world of the fan magazines was very much back to normal.

When William Manchester published *Death of a President* in 1967, the fan magazines rushed to defend the First Lady against criticism. "We Back Jackie," wrote *Motion Picture* in May 1967. Without irony, the magazine pointed out, "Jackie is being attacked unfairly and has suffered enough . . . it's time she knew how many of us sympathize with her." *Screenland* was incessant in its coverage. In February 1967, James Gregory wrote on "That Day in Dallas: The Shocking New Theories That Won't Let Jackie Rest." In April it was revealed that "The Only Johnson Jackie Considers Her Friend" was Ladybird. In June *Screenland* ran a cover story on "How JFK Would Have Stopped the Vicious Attacks." The following month, Kennedy shared the cover with Barbara Stanwyck, Dorothy Malone, and Lucille Ball, with the story "How Each Has Been Made to Suffer as a Mother." In October she again shared a cover, this time with Robert and Ethel Kennedy, and in December, she was playing a secondary role to "Lynda Bird's Love Diary."

Mrs. Kennedy was reported in the *Wall Street Journal* always to have ignored the fan magazines. A press secretary commented, "She feels that people who buy them realize they aren't news magazines." In response, Jack Podell, then editorial director at Macfadden-Bartell, commented that sales of issues with Jackie on the cover "are good, but not so great as they used to be."[24] However, refusing to feature the First Lady on the cover was often a bad step, as Donald E. Gibbons, publisher of *TV Radio Movie Guide* discovered. After twelve issues without Jackie Kennedy, sales had fallen from 115,000 to 43,000.

The June 1968 assassination of Robert Kennedy gave the fan magazines excuse to again feature his sister-in-law. In October 1968, the cover story in *Silver Screen* was "How Jackie Is Giving Ethel Courage to Go on." In January 1969, *Photoplay* reported on "Jackie & Onassis: How He Won Her Love." The cover featured a photograph of the First Lady, along with two extremely audience-captivating headlines, "How He Got Jackie to Love Him!: Why Jackie Wept When She Told Her Children about Their New Daddy" and "How Jackie Borrows Husbands the Way Some Women Borrow a Cup of Sugar: Kennedys

WHY SINGLE GIRLS ARE SCARED OF TOM JONES ONLY 25¢

STREISAND TAILED by a PRIVATE DETECTIVE!

SCREEN secrets

ONLY 25¢   OCT.   *Scoop!* WHAT LIZ AND JACKIE DID TO GET THEIR HUSBANDS BACK!

WHY BURTON AND ONASSIS WERE FORCED TO GIVE IN!

30¢ IN CANADA

EXCLUSIVE!
• STORIES • GOSSIP
• PARTIES • PHOTOS
• TV SECTION

Elizabeth Taylor and Jacqueline Kennedy Onassis share equal space on the cover of *Screen Secrets* (October 1969).

Secretly Furious?" There was more of the same multiple-headlines in August 1970, with "Servant Tells All About Jackie & Onassis! The Night Maria Callas Found Unwed Jackie in His Apartment. Jackie Begged Onassis to Marry Her. How They Quarrel and Make Up."

"Am I Cursed?" asked Jackie on the July 1973 cover of *Screen and TV Album*. Perhaps so, if she chose to read the cover story in the March 1975 issue of the same fan magazine, with Angie Dickinson confessing, "I Was JFK's Party Girl!" Sometimes, it was possible to link the two most famous of cover stars, as with "Have Jackie and Liz Ruined Their Daughters for Love?" in the October 1974 issue of *Silver Screen* or the unrelated "Church Condemns New Onassis

Marriage Plans!" and "Liz's Son Arrested in Secret Drug Raid" in the January 1975 issue of *Screen and TV Album*.

In *Meditations in Times of War*, W. B. Yeats had written "We had fed the heart of fantasies." There was a fan magazine war going on between the old Hollywood approach to the genre, with its basis in reality, and a new iconic movement based on fame in the supposed real world, outside of the movies, which might salve a reader's need for fantasy and escape from the reality of everyday American life. The fan magazine writers and readers might not see it on that profound level, but it was happening. This was not a world in which Adele Whitely Fletcher or Ruth Waterbury might feel comfortable, but a new environment welcoming to writers with potential beyond the fan magazines and their fluff.

CHAPTER 11

MS. RONA

"They [the Hollywood producers] were in control, and then there came along a very independent person. Her name was Rona Barrett."[1] That is the lady herself speaking, and with an autonomous approach to her craft, along with intelligence, a sense of honesty and fair play, comparable to that of James R. Quirk some forty years earlier, she revolutionized not only the fan magazines but the entire coverage of entertainment news. Barrett's style was not that of Quirk, and certainly the periodicals that carry her name lack the intellectual balance that was so much a part of *Photoplay* in the 1920s and 1930s. But the linkage is there in the dedication to the craft, the belief in and love of Hollywood, good or bad, and the desire to document what it is all about. Do not be misled by the colorful, overblown appearance of a Rona Barrett publication. The humor was less biting than that adopted by Quirk, but it was just as devastating, if far more saucy and low level. Times had changed drastically and the approach could not be similar—but it was comparable.

Rona Barrett was the first fan magazine writer to mature from the genre to become a full-fledged media reporter, with a style, personality, and appearance that was unique. Once she had conquered the new territory, she returned to the fan magazines and introduced her own brand, which competed with and complemented her television work.

As one contemporary fan magazine contributor and editor commented, "Then a chubby little brunette with a decided Brooklyn accent, Rona announced that she was going to be the next Louella Parsons. We laughed. But the laugh was on us. Rona completely redid herself. She dieted, got a nose job, changed her hair color and worked with a speech coach. Everything worked to her advantage. More than anything else, she proved to be a brilliant business woman in L.A."[2]

Rona Barrett.

Barrett is often described as primarily a gossip columnist. It is a term that she strongly resents and a description she equally forcefully denies: "I thought I was a real good reporter, covering the entertainment industry. Yes, I was a columnist, but I was also an interviewer. I had many exclusive interviews. I think it's because people have often demeaned what gossip has meant. It has implied over the years that you're always talking about people's boudoir activities. That's not necessarily what I did. When you're a woman, you're called a gossip columnist. When you're a man, you are just called a columnist. I do think it has a sexist situation that probably still exists today."

However one chooses to describe her, Rona Barrett was Hollywood's leading entertainment reporter from 1960 through 1980, more a journalist than a commentator, rightly described by *Cosmopolitan* magazine as "The mistress of the genre, the principal heir to Hedda Hopper and Louella Parsons,"[3] Barrett is actually closer in style to Walter Winchell. She once had his power and, in all honesty, some of his arrogance, although I am sure she would be outraged at the comparison if directed at his political thinking or intellect. She met both Hedda Hopper and Louella Parsons. One immediately demonstrated her animosity toward her competitor, while the other provided Barrett with an example of her staying power.

Hedda Hopper was so nasty to me when I first came on the scene. We were at an opening at the Ambassador Hotel. I went to the ladies room, and there was Hedda Hopper. I touched her on the shoulder and said, "I'd like to introduce myself, Miss Hopper. My name is Rona Barrett and we both write for the same magazines." She said, "That's your problem."

I was at a party with [record executive] Robert Marcucci, who was known as "the idol maker." It was a big party that Louella Parsons was giving for Jimmy McHugh, and at this party in his backyard, there must have been 200 or better people. There was every name you could think of. I had already met Mike Connolly, who I just adored, and he was standing where we were, near one of the little bar stands. And Mike is feeling no pain at this point. Suddenly, up walks Louella, says "May I have two Scotch and water," and starts walking away. And she is wobbling, she is near the pool. Mike Connolly jabs me in the side and he says, "See that woman over there. Everybody's eyes are on her. See all those people over there. I want you to remember one thing. Those people come and go, but that woman stays forever."

Suddenly I realized that the role of a reporter was far more important than what any artist had to say.

Born Rona Burstein in New York on October 8, 1936, as a child Barrett preferred comic books to fan magazines. When she was thirteen, Rona established what was to become the official Eddie Fisher Fan Club. She became increasingly interested in the music business and, as a result, began to read all publications on the subject, both trade and fan. "I began reading the *Photoplays* and the *Modern Screens*, just like millions of others, because they were the only real sources to find out what was going on in Hollywood. Didn't everyone believe that what was printed in a magazine or newspaper was the truth?"

In 1951, she began working for a public relations company, putting out a newsletter for some 10,000 disk jockeys around the country, providing them with information on the firm's clients. As she recalled,

Right as I went into college, I was working part-time at a big magazine company for a woman named Bessie Little. Bess was one of those first women to crack the glass ceiling. She was in charge of more than thirty-five different magazines, including dozens of movie magazines, men's magazines. I started as her secretary, and she said, "I hope you have no intention of writing or doing anything like that. I'm sick and tired of my secretaries leaving me for another writing job." I said,

"No, I'm going to college and I don't have time, so I'm not interested." Three weeks later, she threw on my desk brownlines and said, "Here, edit the captions of all the photos and make sure the spellings and the names are right," Before I knew it, half my job was editing. She then started a whole group of magazines, and, after I had been in Hollywood several years, she called me one day and said, "You've got to come and write for me. I'm going to pay you $150 for ever column and you'll have three to five magazines that you'll write for every month."

In her raw, revealing, and not particularly attractive autobiography, Barrett described Bessie Little as having the voice of Katharine Hepburn or Lauren Bacall and wearing high-platformed, open-toed shoes of which Joan Crawford would approve.[4]

The company at which Barrett began her fan magazines career was Magazine Management Company. It is coincidental that there was a Quirk back in the editorial seat at that same company: Lawrence J. Quirk editing *Screen Stars* and other magazines. Patricia Bosworth, who went on to write major biographies of Diane Arbus, Marlon Brando, and Montgomery Clift, remembered, "It occupied one low-ceilinged floor of dingy offices off East 58th Street."[5] From here, other fan magazines, such as *Movie World* and *Movie Album* were published, along with romance magazines, Marvel comic books, and men's magazines, including *Stag*, *For Men Only*, and *Male*. The last were edited by novelist Bruce Jay Friedman, sharing space with Ernest Tidyman, who would win an Academy Award in 1971 for his screenplay of *The French Connection*. Chief writer for *True Action* was Mario Puzo, who in 1969 would publish *The Godfather*. Thanks to the steady income from the various magazines, Puzo told Patricia Bosworth, "Magazine Management made it possible for me to write *The Godfather*."

Magazine Management Co., Inc. traces its origins back to Martin Goodman, publisher of Marvel Comics as well as various periodicals. In the autumn of 1968, Goodman sold his publishing business to the Perfect Film and Chemical Corporation, which continued Goodman's operation under the name of Magazine Management Company. Goodman was retained as publisher until 1976, by which time Perfect Film and Chemical Corporation had become Cadence Industries.

Earlier in the 1960s, Barrett had commenced her career as a fan magazine writer, always with pieces on younger celebrities, first in *Movieland and TV Time* and later in *Photoplay*. For the former, she profiled Michael Landon (April 1959), Dwayne Hickman (March 1960), and Tommy Rettig (April 1960). For *Photoplay* she wrote on Dodie Stevens (February 1960), Troy Donahue and Dorothy Provine (June 1960), and Tommy Sands (November 1960). "We'd come into a new generation, and I knew what was happening. I knew that there were all these young, Hollywood, about-to-be stars, who were really far more meaningful to this baby boomer bunch. I concentrated on them, and I was right." Also in 1960, associate editor Lawrence B. Thomas suggested to editor Jack Podell that he give Barrett her own column, "Rona Barrett's

Young Hollywood," in *Motion Picture*, the idea according to Thomas being that she would be a junior gossip columnist to Hedda Hopper and Sheilah Graham, both of whom were under contract. A year later, Barrett was writing a column for the Bell-McClure-NANA newspaper syndicate with one hundred outlets. Barrett was obviously not popular with other columnists syndicated by the same group. When Graham was asked to comment on her in 1972, she responded, "Let's not talk about her. She means nothing to me."[6]

It is ironic that while Barrett is such a prominent figure in the resurgence of the fan magazines, it was not these that made her famous. Hollywood insiders knew who she was, the character of her work and style, but the public probably paid little heed of the name of the woman providing them with entertainment news on a regular basis. It was ABC-owned and operated affiliated KABC in Los Angeles that first introduced her face and her personality to a wider, if local audience, through appearances on its nightly news broadcasts, hosted by Baxter Ward.

Barrett found it difficult reporting on an actor or actress who had just signed a $10 million contract when the previous news item had dealt with a local tragedy or the latest casualties in Vietnam. Determined somehow to leave her viewers with a pleasant thought, she decided to borrow from a book of witticisms of Mae West. "That's what I did. My cameraman started laughing so hard that the camera started shaking as if there had been an earthquake in the studio. Baxter Ward had a smile on his face wider than a mile. It was the beginning of my using a softer story, something that had humor, because we were coming out of a report where we had suddenly seen three young soldiers murdered or a whole clan of Vietnamese children slaughtered."

From the local ABC station, Barrett was promoted in 1969 to nightly television reports on the other outlets owned and operated by the network. She appeared with Joanna Barnes, hosting *Dateline: Hollywood*, an ABC daytime program. That same year, she moved to Metromedia, syndicating under the name of *Rona Barrett's Hollywood*. In 1974, she was signed to host a series of hour-long specials, which were a big success on CBS, and the following year she returned to ABC as Hollywood reporter for *Good Morning America*. Barrett ended her television career hosting the Hollywood segment of *Tomorrow Coast to Coast* with Tom Snyder in 1980–1981 and her own prime-time series *Television: Inside and Out* on NBC. The 1981 show garnered the highest ratings in its time period, but NBC constantly changed that time slot, and despite Barrett's popularity and success, it was cancelled after only four weeks.

As a result of her new-found nationwide fame, Rona Barrett was lampooned as Mona Blarit on *Rowan and Martin's Laugh-In* and as Rona Rumor on *The Carol Burnett Show*. By the very nature of her profession, she was not always popular or looked upon kindly. A critic in the *Washington Post* described her as having "all the warmth of a self-service gas station at 2 a.m."[7] Her cohost on *Tomorrow Coast to Coast* was far from supportive, suggesting that many of the men with whom she came into contact were nervous around a female with obvious talent and not unwilling to espouse a feminist cause where appropriate.

"When I came to ABC for *Good Morning, America*, . . . I hoped they'd let me be a female Edward R. Murrow, capable of handling every story." It was not to be. She was basically typecast in the role of a gossip columnist who preferred to be identified as an entertainment reporter.

While at the height of her television fame in 1972, Barrett found time to publish a novel titled *Lovomaniacs*, which took its title from a psychological term invented by Barrett in reference to individuals incapable of having a one-on-one relationship. Two years later, she published her autobiography and recorded an album, "Miss Rona Sings Hollywood's Greatest Hits." In 1978, she published *Rona Barrett Tells You How You Can Look Rich and Achieve Sexual Ecstasy*.

Without a major television career, few individuals would have achieved the celebrity necessary to persuade anyone to sign a contract with them for such personality-oriented works. Equally, the television career provided the opportunity for a transition back to the world of fan magazines—a new world and a new, very prominent, position. The agent for this was an entrepreneur who understood the teenage market. His name was Chuck Laufer.

Working with his brother, Ira, who served as senior vice-president of the company, Chuck Laufer was a former Beverly Hills High School journalism teacher, whose philosophy was described as "make pennies, but make millions of pennies."[8] It was a philosophy that paid off as his company expanded from four employees at its founding in 1965 to eighty-five employees fifteen years later. Because of his background, on the surface Laufer was not only an expert in the field of journalism but also an expert at what teenagers and "tweens" wanted to read. He even had some practical experience in the field, having worked for Los Angeles–based Petersen Publication. In 1965, Laufer founded *Tiger Beat* as a fan magazine for girls ranging in age from nine to eighteen. The emphasis was on teen music idols, as varied as the Beatles, the Monkees, Donnie and Marie Osmond, David and Shaun Cassidy, Michael Jackson, and John Travolta (all of whom have appeared on its covers), with stories on their careers, music, and fashion tastes.

Impressed by the impact that Barrett was having in the world of entertainment reporting, Chuck Laufer approached her with a proposal for a series of Rona Barrett magazines, although it is possible that Ralph Benner, managing editor of *Teen* magazine, may have been the catalyst for the idea. The first was *Rona Barrett's Hollywood*, the premiere issue of which was dated November 1969: "Chuck Laufer was an interesting guy. Chuck was a bright man. He was always intimidated by me for reasons I never understood. Chuck knew what the trend was. He was about the same age as I was, so he wasn't an old, stuffy guy from another world or another lifetime. He was sort of with it. He understood where I was coming from. He understood that truth meant a great deal to me. I'd much rather not run a story if we couldn't verify it, and I was the one who demanded if we were going to do a story, it really needed checking and we needed two sources or don't bother. We were the first to do anything big with the Jackson family. I've known Michael ever since he's been, what, five or six."

With its subtitle "TV Secrets, Scoop Photos, Whispers, Radio," *Rona Barrett's Hollywood* had all the appearance of a typical fan magazine except that there was a preponderance of color photographs and, aside from a handful of feature articles, the emphasis was on short, pithy paragraphs that can be designated either as "news" or "gossip" depending upon one's point of view. Elizabeth Taylor and Jacqueline Kennedy Onassis were, of course, major players, and, as one might expect from the exposure in other fan magazines, *The Lawrence Welk Show* offered up both the Lennon Sisters and dancer Bobby Burgess for coverage in the second issue.

"The sad part about it, and this is a very sad story for me," noted Barrett, is that "my friend Bessie Little always dreamed that her greatest success would be if she could come to Hollywood and write. So when I had the opportunity to start this magazine, I insisted that Bessie Little come to be its editor. I made a mistake because Bessie was stuck in the other world, and after about eighteen months, it was over. I brought in a whole new staff of young people, people who were more interested in what was really happening."

Bessie Little turned out a fan magazine that was very much in the style of the old-fashioned, New York–published journals, and, unfortunately, not necessarily a copy of the best of the genre. Because of *Tiger Beat*, the Laufer brothers were used to young editors. They did not want to use established fan magazine writers, not wishing to pay the determined rate for stories. It was cheaper to hire unknowns who might not be able to write, let alone spell, but whose work could be cleaned up by a good editor.

Among those young people brought in to replace Little were editors Bonnie Rogers and, most importantly, Bill Royce. When Diane Dalbey became editor, Royce was named managing editor. He is generally credited for the tongue-in-cheek style of many of the photo captions and the amount of innuendo found in the gossip items. A typical comment, appearing in the October 1972 issue of *Rona Barrett's Gossip*, told of a certain very well known television host (assumed to be Merv Griffin), "swishing the gender of his affections before our eyes." Another item, two months later, reported on a male porno star and a best-selling male author summering together.

"I adored Bill. I loved his sense of humor. I loved his wonderful little ways of turning a phrase. If you knew how to read the magazine, you knew what he was saying. Innuendo based on fact."

While *Rona Barrett's Hollywood* and its successors might bear her name, Barrett was not the editor and nor did she have total editorial control over the contents: "I fought with my partners, the Laufer brothers, on many occasions about the stories that they were writing that were fluff and ridiculous. They gave me an advance copy. I often went to their office, though I didn't work from their office, and I trusted Bill and Bonnie Rogers, who preceded him, to let me know all the time what was going on. And if they thought things were not going the way they wanted, they would, needless to say, fill me in."

Bill Royce is an interesting character. Born in Mexico, he learned English from reading fan magazines such as *Photoplay* and *Modern Screen*. As a student at the University of California at Berkeley, he had attended an extension class on film criticism, where he met the sister of Bonnie Rogers. It was the latter, who, in November 1971, hired Royce as managing editor of *Rona Barrett's Hollywood*. As Royce recalled,

> What I did essentially was take the formula of *Screen Stories*, my favorite magazine. They used to have a column called "To Tell the Truth." I had a column called "Nothing But the Truth," a way of telling the truth without coming right out and saying it. You see, I loved Rona. Then, when the magazine first came out, it didn't reflect her. It wasn't campy. It looked made up. When I took over, I ramped up the tongue-in-cheek flavor, but I also tried a classier approach.
>
> The Laufers' attitude towards women was, in my opinion, traditionally sexist. It was like take your money and be a good girl. I never made that mistake with Rona. My relationship with her was mostly on the phone, with her going over the brown or blue lines. She'd have her corrections. I'd have my corrections. I knew her well enough that if they were going for something that was inappropriate, I could usually kill it.[9]

Reading *Rona Barrett's Hollywood*, one is very much struck by the astounding amount of content. The emphasis was on contemporary Hollywood, but there was still room for affectionate nostalgia, as with a May 1975 piece by Maureen Donaldson (a frequent and important contributor) on "Jack Benny: His 80 Years of Laughter." By 1981, the magazine was less a fan publication and more a glossy periodical in the style of *People* magazine. Barrett's face no longer was pictured on the cover, and it was titled *New Rona Barrett's Hollywood*. The only aspect that had not changed was the presence of Elizabeth Taylor, now billed as "Broadway New 'Foxy' Lady" in the August 1981 issue. That same issue included "The Stars Who Like to Sweat," featuring Arnold Schwarzenegger. Bill Royce was gone, replaced by John Peter Nugent, and so, almost, was Rona, limited in space to "Rona Barrett's Special Feature."

There was a surprising, uncredited, and very famous coeditor at *Rona Barrett's Hollywood*: Cary Grant. The actor had formed a relationship with Maureen Donaldson, who was on staff for some five years, encouraging her to become a photographer.[10] Royce first came into contact with Grant when the latter telephoned to correct a story that he had been discovered by Mae West, pointing out that he had made a number of earlier films at Paramount. The two men became good friends, and Royce would show him the blue lines and listen to his comments: "As press shy as he was, his best friends were [entertainment journalist] Roderick Mann and Henry Grice of the *National Inquirer*. That was Cary. There was always yin and yang with him. Cary took a great interest in the book because he identified with me. We both had tragic relations with our birth mothers. He was the unofficial editor. Rona didn't know this. The Laufers never knew."

In December 1972, Laufer launched *Rona Barrett's Gossip*, which was very similar in content to the previous publication except for few articles and more gossip. Barrett was not pleased with the title, having argued for *Rona Bar-rett's People*, which would, of course, have predated and secured the title reg-istration for *People* magazine. The periodical certainly lived up to its title with "Rona's Guess Who of the Month," and its clues to celebrities with something sleazy in their lives. The gossip could be unkind, as with a line suggesting an actress has undergone cosmetic surgery: "Bea Arthur is Sporting an *Uplifting* Look These Days" (September 1974).

There was even a *Rona Barrett's Gossip Super Special* spring annual, pub-lished at least in 1974 and 1975, consisting of more than 100 pages and "extra photos" (if that was even possible). The 1975 issue included the "You're Not Getting Better You're Getting Older" award to Frank Sinatra and the "When Did You First Realize You Were a Ninny" award to Peter Bogdanovich.

The last film-oriented fan magazine from Chuck Laufer was *Preview*, first published in September 1976. While it is often described as a Rona Barrett publication, her name did not appear in the title and the only two individuals identified in the first editorial page were publisher Roland Hinz and editor-in-chief Bill Royce. (Tim Hawkins was the actual editor.) According to Royce, Roland Hinz was an unusual staff member, being a born-again Christian, but he recognized something in Royce; it was Hinz who approved the outline for each issue. In the first issue, Hinz and Royce explained, "we're going to live up to our name by bringing you *first* glimpses of everything that's happening in the entertainment world—and we don't just mean Hollywood either. . . . Whether it's Hollywood . . . or down in Arizona . . . or across the world in London . . . *Preview* will be there—*first*. . . . With the same top reporters, columnists, and photographers who brought you the top-selling newsstand magazines in the en-tertainment field, we're going to bring you *more*. *More* photos. *More* in-depth interviews. *More* on-the-set and on-location visits. *More* at-home glimpses of the stars. *More* behind-the-scenes news."

In fact, it was *more* of the same except that not only was Rona Barrett's name missing, but also her face with its cheeky grin peering out from the O of her name, as on the other publications. Bill Royce handled gossip, as he had obviously done in tandem with Barrett on the other fan magazines. The first issue featured articles on three legendary stars, Elvis Presley, Barbra Streisand on location for *A Star Is Born*, and Paul Newman on location for *Slapshot*. Probably the only truly worthwhile piece in *Preview*, from a modern perspec-tive, was a two-part lengthy interview with Barrett, published in the May and June issues of 1977. Curiously, the first part of the interview included a photo-graph of Barrett with Chuck Laufer and the identification of her as executive editor not only of the fan magazines bearing her name but also *Preview*.

In fact, the magazine became *Rona Barrett's Preview* when it ceased to sell well. Royce described the magazine as his version of *Screen Stories*, with four-page layouts with photographs on five or six films and "real" interviews. His earlier complaint had been that the Rona Barrett publications were the only fan magazines published out of Hollywood, and yet the interviews were often made-up stories. For the first edition, he interviewed Lee Majors, and when a star, such as Elizabeth Taylor or Robert Redford, would not give interviews, "clip" stories would be created.

While the typical fan magazine had a young, female readership, the Rona Barrett periodicals appealed as much to a gay audience as to a female one. "I always thought it was a conglomeration," said Royce. "I think I unknowingly catered to all of them." The gay readership got all the little implications in the text, all the innuendo, and they were just as happy to read about Lucille Ball as they were to learn the latest on Barbra Streisand.

In 1977, Laufer began publication of *Rona Barrett's Daytimers*, a daytime soap opera–oriented fan magazine primarily of relevance because it was the only West Coast periodical of its type. Billed as "The Inside Channel to Daytime TV," the publication's content was very different than the film periodicals, as editor Lorraine Zenka Smith explained, "We're always trying to find a common ground to reflect the audience's normality. This makes for certain taboos, a playing down of such subjects as women's lib and abortion in the dramas themselves. The flip side of this fixation is a phenomenal emphasis on *family*, a preoccupation apparent not only in the daily drama but in the magazine's coverage of the stars' off-stage selves."[11]

In April 1978, the Laufer brothers sold eighty percent of their company to Canadian-based Harlequin, Inc., publisher of the popular paperback romance novels, for a reported $12 million. Harlequin planned to acquire the remaining stock over the next four years, while allowing the Laufers to remain as heads of the company. Subsequently, Sterling-Macfadden acquired the Laufer publications, selling *Tiger Beat* to Primedia in 1998. *Tiger Beat* was eventually purchased in 2003 by Chuck's son, Scott Laufer, whose Laufer Media also published *Bop*.

In May 1980, Laufer changed the name of *Rona Barrett's Gossip* to *Gossip*. "They have finally removed my name from a magazine I never sanctioned," Barrett told the *Los Angeles Times*, thus revealing that she and Laufer were openly feuding about the periodical.[12] Certainly, Barrett's name had helped gain the Laufer publications not only instant fan recognition, through her television work, but also easy access to the stars and, of course, gossip thereof. At the same time, it was reported that Barrett received a six-figure income for the use of her name. While denying that money was her primary consideration, Barrett claimed that she had invested her time and reputation in the magazines in the hope that they would eventually reflect the contents of her television broadcasts.

Barrett did not renew her contract with the Laufer brothers, and, after a desperate effort to take on a new direction, all the film-oriented magazines ceased publication. Bill Royce left to work directly with Barrett, and later spent three years with *The Arsenio Hall Show*, before joining *The Tonight Show* as coproducer when Jay Leno took over. He won an Emmy for his work on *The Tonight Show* in 1995.

As if to prove to Chuck Laufer that there was far more to her than a fan magazine persona, in September 1982 Barrett began publication of a journal that was strictly under her control. *The Barrett Report* was an expensive entertainment newsletter, published forty-eight times a year, with a subscription price of $1200. Bill Royce was one of a reported ten individuals who worked on her staff, providing news that was as new as news could be. It is almost as if Barrett had come full circle, beginning by writing fan magazine articles for the masses and ending by creating a new, elitist fan magazine for the wealthiest of Hollywood subscribers.

Rona Barrett's magazines had some competition, but it was only minor. There was *Rona January's Gossip World*, published in the spring of 1977, featuring "Rona's Fabulous Feast of Gossip" (except it was the wrong Rona), and there was *Toni Holt's Movie Life*, which with the lady's smiling face appearing out of the O was too close to the look of the Rona Barrett magazines to be coincidental. Toni Holt had written a couple of pieces for *Photoplay*, "This Is His Baby" on Cary Grant (October 1970) and "Weeps as Death Takes Best Friend" on Elizabeth Taylor (April 1971), and she had a one-page gossip column, "Happenings," in the magazine, beginning in July 1970. She had been an actress in daytime soap operas, a model, and a syndicated newspaper columnist with shows on local southern California television. While Carol Torney was cited as editor, Toni Holt at least received the title of executive editor on *Toni Holt's Movie Life*. A reported feud with Rona Barrett was certainly good publicity for Toni Holt, if an irrelevancy from Barrett's position and viewpoint.

CHAPTER 12

THE *PEOPLE* GENERATION

By the 1970s, the fan magazines had long since passed their zenith of influence both within the film industry and among their readership. With an overemphasis on Jacqueline Kennedy, the fan magazines acknowledged that nobody who was part of the entertainment community had the celebrity of the former First Lady. Audiences wanted to read not about specific people, but about all people—as Rona Barrett had recognized when she tried to persuade Chuck Laufer to publish a magazine titled *Rona Barrett's People*—and what the fan magazines were serving up was much from the same, tired, old menu. In its final issues, *Photoplay* acknowledged that its focus was no longer on the world of movies; it was "All about the celebrity world: who, what, when, and where." But, unfortunately, the "who" were primarily television celebrities, with a heavy emphasis on the stars of *Dallas*, the "where" of the gossip world was still under the name of Cal York from the past, and the "when" was not always the present. In its final issue, *Photoplay* reprinted a December 1938 story on Tyrone Power.

Timeliness had always been an issue for the fan magazines. They could be caught with their deadlines and their romances down, as one commentator put it. For example, in 1933 Joan Crawford revealed in advance to *Modern Screen*'s Katharine Albert that she would divorce Douglas Fairbanks Jr., and the magazine went to press with the story. However, before *Modern Screen* hit the newsstands, Fairbanks was sued by an angry husband for alienation of his wife's affection. Fearing that her fans might be offended by her response, Crawford decided it would be inappropriate to divorce her husband. Subsequently, at the end of April 1933, the actress did decide to go ahead with the divorce, and simultaneously *Modern Screen* came out with the story in its May issue. "It was one of the most extraordinary instances of journalistic jiu-jitsu on record," commented Ezra Goodman.[1]

With instant television and daily newspaper coverage only a few hours old, fan magazines could not even pretend topicality. But a periodical was on the horizon that could, one that had a major news magazine behind it and that would borrow heavily from the fan magazines. *People* magazine was to prove to be the most successful personality-oriented publication on the market. It was never heavy-handed in its coverage. The emphasis was on the lightweight and trivial, and its content was very much picture-oriented. *People* was, and is, a fan magazine—but one with a weekly relevance and a strong understanding of its audience. Lawrence B. Thomas said, "While I was at *Motion Picture*, I recall the furor in the fan field when we heard that Time-Life Corp. was bringing out a fan magazine."[2]

As one commentator described it, *People* was "big pictures, few words, short takes, fast pace." While the fan magazines had been playing for years with a mix of color and black-and-white photographs, *People* offered only the latter. Its first director of advertising sales, Dick Thomas, explained, "black-and-white photos of people are more revealing, much more immediate and much more intimate than color." Color photographs belonged in the advertising section.[3]

The people in *People* were, not surprisingly, selected on a somewhat different principle than that adopted by the fan magazines, with their overemphasis on Liz and Jackie. "Young is better than old. Pretty is better than ugly. Rich is better than poor. TV is better than music. Music is better than movies. Movies are better than sports. And anything is better than politics," explained the magazine's first managing editor, Richard Stolley,[4] who had previously been assistant managing editor of *Life* magazine.

Credit for the original concept belongs to Marian Heiskill, wife of Time's chairman of the board, Andrew Heiskill. The magazine was two years in development and test-marketed as *People of the Week* with Richard Burton and Elizabeth Taylor on the cover in August 1973. The first issue finally appeared on February 25, 1974, with Mia Farrow on the cover and an initial print run of 1.4 million copies. It was the first national weekly publication to be launched since *Sports Illustrated* in 1954.

As with the fan magazines, the primary readership at first was female. They were not teenagers, but generally women in their thirties and forties. Such readership rejected the issue with Howard Cosell on the cover, but eagerly purchased early issues featuring Cher, Grace Kelly, Elizabeth Taylor, Jacqueline Kennedy Onassis, and Michael Jackson. The best-selling issues were both memorial ones: the highest for John Lennon in 1980 and the second highest for Princess Grace [Kelly] of Monaco in 1982.

Unlike the fan magazines, *People* boasted a major news organization, Time, Inc., as its parent company. Many of the fan magazines did not even bother to maintain a Hollywood office, while *People* had a network of contributors across the United States. As of 2006, when *People*'s reported circulation was 3.73 million, it maintained bureaus in Los Angeles, New York, Washington, D.C., Chicago, Miami, Austin, and London. *People* employed fact checkers to read stories prior to publication, something unheard of with fan magazines. It had a large budget for the acquisition of celebrity photographs; most notoriously, the magazine reportedly paid $4.1 million for the baby photographs of Brad Pitt and Angelina Jolie's first child. It was even suggested that *People* paid $75,000 for photographs of Jennifer Lopez reading *Us* magazine to prevent the latter from purchasing them.[5]

Once it had been a cover line, determined by the editor, that sold the fan magazine. Now, stars, or rather their agents, were negotiating with the new style publications for full-cover photographs or, at the least, "cover chips," small picture blocks promising more coverage inside.

People, or more correctly *People Weekly*, was not the first celebrity-oriented publication outside of the fan magazine arena. In 1969, *Andy Warhol's Interview Magazine* began publication on an irregular basis and quickly took on cult magazine status. It continued beyond Warhol's death in 1987, but the circulation never rose above 100,000. There was competition to *People* from its own sister publication, *InStyle*, and from *Celebrity*, *In the Know*, and *New Times*, but the most prominent rival was *Us*, founded by the New York Times Company. Under the initial editorship of William H. Davis, *Us* began publication as a fortnightly periodical on April 17, 1977, with Paul Newman on the cover and a print run of 750,000 copies.

Not surprisingly, *Time* rival *Newsweek* was disparaging of both publications, noting a couple of months after the debut of *Us*: "The doleful fact is that the celebrity industry has reached the point at which the demand is outstripping the supply, and past and present stars alike are being endlessly recycled. There is hardly a major newspaper in the nation that hasn't launched its own gossip or names-in-the-news column. . . . Anyone who doubts the existence of a People shortage need only contemplate the media's relentless focus on Robert Redford, the Fonz [Henry Winkler from the television series *Happy Days*] and, most nauseously, Farrah Fawcett-Majors, whose visage has decorated the covers of twelve different periodicals."[6]

It was as if the mass circulation magazines had as little relevant content as the fan magazines. They had replaced or were replacing the latter, but they were not improving upon them. Ridiculing *Us* and reminding its readership of the similarity between that periodical and the fan magazines, *Newsweek* reported on an *Us* update on Kim Novak, who had found a new husband, Robert Malloy, but lost her favorite pet, a raccoon named Ume. "Ume was probably closer to me, and needed me more, than any living creature until I met Bob." Meanwhile, *People* had an eight-page story on the merchants who served Jackie Onassis, including her butcher, baker, and favorite waiter.

Tragically, the fan magazines could not even compete with this level of mediocrity, let alone with the gossip tabloids such as the *National Inquirer* or *The Star*. "In the great days of fan magazines," commented *Modern Screen*'s editor Joan Thursh, "when you had dozens of beautiful, glamorous people and this elaborate studio system that really cooperated hand-in-glove with the fan magazines—and so did the actors, in a way no movie actor does today—it was totally different. It wasn't at odds with the magazines. Perhaps an average reader would think there is still a lot of glamor to this business. There used to be, certainly—the editor of *Modern Screen* or *Photoplay* was treated like a queen. That's no longer the case."[7] Major new movie stars, such as Robert De Niro or Robert Redford, could not sell a fan magazine as well as Ted Shackleford from *Knots Landing* or Gary Coleman from *Diff'rent Strokes*. Talent was not relevant. Nor was factual accuracy, as fan magazine readers rejected the statistic of Elvis Presley being forty years old. No fan magazine would report on Roman Polanksi's arrest on charges of raping an underage girl. As *Movie World's* editor explained it, "First of all, some of our readers wouldn't even know who Roman Polanski is. Second, that does not sell. It's very ugly and you have a substantial young readership, so you have to exercise some discretion."[8]

In response to the new competition, the fan magazines would often turn retrospective, believing, perhaps with some cause, that their readership was nostalgic for the golden age of not only moviemaking but also of the fan magazines. As early as 1956, Bessie Little had edited a publication titled *Old Hollywood*, which promised "Movieland's Mad Past" on its cover but was deferential in its approach to eras long gone. That same year, Literary Enterprises, Inc., in New York, under the editorship of Ira Peck, produced *This Was Show Business* in a fan magazine format. Sections on the movies, vaudeville, the stage, musical comedy, radio, burlesque, and night clubs were heavily illustrated with photographs and boasted a first-rate text by publicist John Springer. Peck was also editor of another fan magazine–like publication, *Sidney Skolsky's This Was Hollywood*, an annual first published in 1955 by Affiliated Magazines, Inc. The implication was that Skolsky wrote all of the extensive text, which seems somewhat doubtful. There was a giant 1940 "Nostalgia" issue of *Screen Stories* in August 1971, with tributes to Lana Turner, Clark Gable, Judy Garland, and Bette Davis.

In its dying days, *Motion Picture* devoted its December 1976 issue to nostalgia, reprinting pieces on stars such as Marlon Brando, Rudolph Valentino, Humphrey Bogart, Greta Garbo, and W. C. Fields, from its earlier issues under the editorship of Patricia Sellers. Rex Reed contributed a two-page introduction, in which he confessed that as a child he rushed once a month to the local malt shop for the newest issue of *Motion Picture*: "Each month I would thrill to the articles about Hollywood, dream capital of the world, the city I longed to be part of. *Motion Picture* never failed me. . . . In the 1960s, when I got my first 'inside' look at the industry I had once cherished, I realized all the old stories were manufactured by press agents. . . . The sanctity of sacred institutions was at an end. Movies had been raped and pillaged by television." One can only wonder what the devoted readership of *Motion Picture* thought at being told that everything it had believed in was a lie.

In January 1980, *Us* was acquired by Peter J. Callahan of Macfadden Holdings. With Richard Kaplan as editor, he was able to raise circulation to over one million. Another Macfadden publication was floundering. With a combined December–January 1980 issue, it was obvious that *Photoplay* was nearing the end of its life, no longer able to meet a monthly publishing schedule. A final issue appeared in May–June 1980, and those readers bothering to scan the contents page were advised to see page twenty-nine for a special announcement. Here, the end was revealed as subscribers were promised they would receive *Us* for the remaining portion of their *Photoplay* subscription:

> Join *Us* as we expand our horizons. So much has been happening in the exciting celebrity world that *Photoplay* can no longer limit itself to just one monthly issue. Now, *Photoplay* has teamed up with the personality magazine *Us*, and *Us*, incorporating *Photoplay*, will be covering all the action in the fascinating world of stars every two weeks!
>
> That's right—all the exclusive interviews, photos, special features, nostalgia, and gossip that you enjoyed reading every month in *Photoplay* will now appear in *Us* magazine every two weeks! That means readers will be getting twice as much celebrity coverage every month!

How could *Photoplay* subscribers refuse such an offer? An old fan magazine was gone, but it was replaced by a new one, available more frequently and with more of the same coverage. But was it really a fan magazine? When *Us* was taken over by Jann S. Wenner of *Rolling Stone* in 1985, he did not use that term: "Call it what you want—gossip journalism, celebrity journalism, human-interest journalism. By any name, this has become the dominant theme of American journalism over the last five years." As the *Washington Post* (June 17, 1985) commented, "It's New! It's Old! It's *Us*!" The fan magazine was again reborn not particularly in the old mold, but, equally, not entirely in a new mold.

Because we tend to apply the term "fan magazine" to a very specific type of publication, limited to coverage of the motion picture industry, and because *People*, *Us*, and all the rest do not have the look or appeal of a fan magazine, it is difficult to justify such a description in their regard. Film buffs are willing to pay as high as $75 for a fan magazine from Hollywood's golden era and as much as $15 for one of the last issues of the original fan magazines. The only issue of *People* worth that amount is the first, with Mia Farrow on the cover. All remaining issues are generally valued at between $1 and $5 each.[9] Nobody cares about *People* a week after its publication, let alone decades later.

Photoplay died in 1980, but that did not mean that the public stopped reading fan magazines. A reported three million were still sold each month. *Modern Screen* and *Picture Life* described their readership as ninety percent female and "youngish" (under forty-five). A 1979 Magazine Research, Inc., study found readers to be "younger, brighter, more affluent" and sometimes even male. Fan magazines had become the "junk reading" of the masses.[10] Similar to the *National Inquirer*, they were the periodicals that nobody would admit to reading, but everybody did.

Joan Thursh, then editor of *Modern Screen*, commented in a 1975 interview, "Fan magazines are read at home, in doctors' waiting rooms, washeterias, beauty salons, and—can you believe?—prisons. We get tons of mail from prisoners. The movie stars themselves, though—and I don't want to cite examples—have funny attitudes. They may knock the magazines, but they're the first to buy them to see if they get mentioned."[11]

Fan magazines were also the subject of open ridicule, as with the May 1971 first issue of the quarterly parody *Movie Lies*, edited by Robert Amsel. Promising "all the poop from Hollywood," *Movie Lies* offered a cover story titled "Will Jackie Lose Lawrence Welk to Tiny Tim?" There was also a Special Women's Lib Report, featuring "The Day the Lennon Sisters Burned Their Bras" and "The Truth behind Liz's Toenail Transplant! Will She Ever Walk Again?"

In 1975, there was a comedy record album from Lily Tomlin parodying the fan magazines under the title of "Modern Scream." Years earlier, and working on a higher plane, S. J. Perelman contributed a play titled *Nirvana Small by a Waterfall* to the June 2, 1951, issue of *The New Yorker*. Based on Louella Parsons' column in *Modern Screen*, it had the lady, along with Hedda Hopper and Sidney Skolsky, overhearing "the trials and tribulations in launching the matrimonial bark of two screen players: Rhonda St. Cyr and Stewart Fels-Natchez."

How did the fan magazine writers respond to the new era? Lawrence B. Thomas noted, "It was a turbulent period in our publishing world . . . made more so by the inroads made to the field by such trashy publications as *Confidential* and the racier tabloids. As their circulation grew at our expense, it became difficult not to counter-punch by increasingly hotter cover lines (though admittedly mild ones compared to what came afterward). Eventually this led to an increase in power wielded by the public relations firms, who controlled access to their star-clients and often barred it." Thomas was quick to defend the quality of the editors themselves: "The fan magazines had been a respectable segment of the publishing world, producing some splendid editors that could compete in any field. Wade Nichols came from *Modern Screen* to the editorship of *Redbook*, Ernie Heyn from *Photoplay* to *American Weekly*, I to become editor of *Pageant* magazine."[12] Basically, fan magazine editors turned their backs on the genre, moving on to unrelated positions.

Micki Siegel's name appears as editor on many of the last fan magazines, including *Movies Illustrated* and *Inside Movies*, of which she assured me she had "absolutely no memory." She succeeded Patricia de Jager as editor-in-chief of both *Silver Screen* and *Screenland* in 1968 and remained with them until 1972, by which time *Screenland* had merged with its sister publication to become a new, larger, slick magazine. Siegel recalled,

I left because I was primarily a writer and wanted to freelance. Also in the early 1970s, Macfadden-Bartell had had a change in management. Macfadden had gone from being one of the biggest companies to one of the smallest. Just as I wanted to freelance, several of my fellow editors also wanted out. All those editors went to better jobs in other fields and to important jobs on the women's magazines. Even though they were still being published, this was probably the start of the end of the fan magazines. It was a long, lingering death.

It wasn't just *People* that killed the fan magazines, all the national magazines were doing more and more celebrity stories—and doing them more expensively than we ever could. I don't know of any editor who went from a fan magazine to either *People* or *Us*. By 1980, I was covering the Atlanta child murders fulltime for *Us*. I went on to write for other mass market magazines and was only dimly aware that the fan magazines were dying. I can't speak for my fellow editors, but I'm still close with several of them and I do know they, too, went on to more successful careers.

A former editor of *Photoplay* moved to the executive editor spot at *Good Housekeeping*, then the editor of *Modern Screen* left to become articles editor also of *Good Housekeeping*, and she brought me with her as a feature writer.

The fan magazines were a great training ground. But, I guess because they'd become so diminished over such a long period, I don't believe any of us mourned their loss.[13]

The fan magazine did not end with *Photoplay*'s passing in 1980. There were still fan magazines out there, including *Modern Screen*, which was to continue publication for another five years; this despite *The New York Times* reporting that *Modern Screen* was to cease publication late in 1977. In fact, it might be argued that *Modern Screen* continued for much longer, changing its name first to *Modern Screen's Country Music Special*, and then, in 1993, to *Modern Screen's Country Music*. *Movie Mirror* was also still extant as of 1998.

The other fan magazine that survived almost to the beginning of the new millennium was *TV and Movie Screen*, a little-remembered addition to the genre that had commenced publication in 1956, under the editorial direction of Richard Heller. (Heller held that same position on all of the periodicals published by the Sterling Group and had earlier been editor of *Modern Screen*.) *TV and Movie Screen* was quick to embrace color photographs, heavily featured Elizabeth Taylor on its covers in the 1970s, and even found religion in 1974 with a piece by Tom Netherton from *The Lawrence Welk Show* reporting on "The Day I Saw God," while serving in the military in Panama. "I'm a Christian, and I wanted to do Christian entertainment," he proclaimed, and presumably the Christian readership of *TV and Movie Screen* was in full support.

TV and Movie Screen was a monthly at publication, but it had become bimonthly by October 1987, when it published a special issue, "Elvis: An Intimate Heartwarming Tribute to the King!" When it ceased publication, the fan magazine had been renamed *TVMS Tiger Beat*, indicating its merger with the teen journal, but promising coverage of "film, television, and pop music admired by teenagers."

When *TV and Movie Screen* first started, the cover price was twenty-five cents, rising to thirty-five, fifty, and then sixty cents in the 1970s. The steady increase in price, while probably justified in terms of production and distribution costs, was a further deterrent in the war of reader attrition. Just how many teenage readers, of example, could afford the $3.75 cover price for *Inside Hollywood* when it first began publication in 1991?

Based on price alone, it is little wonder that by the mid 1980s those original fan magazines that were left had sales of under 100,000 per issue. *Movie Mirror*, published bimonthly, averaged 95,066, while the monthly *Modern Screen* reported 84,008. The highest ranked *TV and Movie Screen*, bimonthly, sold 122,378. In comparison, the adult entertainment's picture monthly, *Adam World*, sold 200,000 copies, and the American Film Institute's *American Film* boasted sales of 135,732 copies.

THE END OF THE LINE AND A NEW BEGINNING

The old-style fan magazines did not so much end as change subject matter.
The old fan magazine titles were discarded and new ones created, but the
reinvention process had little impact on the approach or the content style.
Movies might have been steadily losing their audience, along with the need
for fan magazine coverage, but in the 1980s the television soap operas were
expanding their viewership—a reported fifty million a day—and their audience was intrigued by any coverage available. Again, as in the entire history of
fan magazines, it is the female audience for whom these new magazines are
published. The viewers of the daytime soap operas were, almost of necessity,
women, and it was these same women who wanted to learn more of the series
and the stars involved.

In 1967, Paul Denis, a former radio columnist for the *New York Post* and
gossip columnist for *Screen Stars* and *Movie World*, founded what was the first
modern soap opera publication, the annual *Who's Who in Daytime TV*. Two
years later, Denis became editor of the first monthly soap opera journal, *Daytime TV*, which was, in turn, followed by *Soap Opera Special*.

Some years later, Denis was asked by NBC to prepare a survey of the soap
opera journals, and he discovered the number had risen to twenty-eight. The
majority were published by Sterling Magazines, Inc., for whom Denis claimed
in his book *Inside the Soaps* that he founded a dozen soap opera fan magazines
in the 1970s.[14] As fan magazine writer Dora Albert explained,

> Some of the magazines are a curious mixture of questions (which aren't always
> answered) about the plots of the current soaps and stories about the personal
> lives of the star. For instance, *Daylight TV* . . . asks such questions as "General
> Hospital: Who Will Rich Choose Now?" "One Life to Live: What's Ahead for

Pat?" "Search for Tomorrow: Can Travis Save Liza?" "Young and Restless: Will Jill & Brock Reunite?" "Another World: Will Steve Return to Haunt Rachel?"

On the personal side, there are stories similar to those the movie magazines used to run: Josh Taylor, "The Woman I've Loved and Lost"; Julie Barr, "I Don't Feel Guilty about My Divorce," and Sharon Gabet, "Why She Won't Marry Her Boy Friend."

In addition, the magazine runs cast lists of the various current soaps.[15]

The soap opera was not the only genre to which the fan magazines turned in the last decades of the twentieth century. There was *Fighting Stars*, devoted to celebrities who practice the art of self-defense, first published in October 1973. If fan magazines were often read by women at the beauty parlor while having their hair done, then why not concentrate on that aspect of a star's appearance. What better place than the beauty parlor in the mid 1960s was there to read *Latest Hollywood and TV Hairdos* from Modern Guide Publications, *Celebrity Hairdos* from Better Books, Inc., and a periodical suggesting it was actually a book, *Hairdo Ideas*, published by Herald House, Inc.?

Just as these specialist fan magazines were generally short-lived, ultimately the fan magazines directed at soap opera viewers will have a limited lifespan. The daytime soap operas are losing their audience. The nighttime soap operas are being replaced by reality shows. It is just a matter of time before the soap opera fan magazines vanish from the newsstands—but I guarantee there will be no replacement fan magazines devoted to reality programming. The reality of modern life is that the world cannot wait for a fan magazine to meet its publishing schedule.

Three entertainment journals of the late 1980s and 1990s are best identified as the "new" fan magazines, glossy, literate, and aimed at a far more intelligent and affluent audience than their ancestors. The first, and most prominent, was *Premiere*, which had originated in France in 1976 and was introduced to the U.S. market by Hachette Publications, Inc., and News Corporation in July–August 1987. Edited by Susan Lyne, and with Dan Akroyd and Tom Hanks featured on the first cover, *Premiere* heavily emphasized film, with feature articles on Woody Allen, director Chris Columbus, and Kevin Costner in its first issue. Reverting to a monthly with the second issue, it was very obvious that *Premiere*, with a cover price of $1.95, was cheap enough to appeal to the *People* generation but offered more substance, more gloss, and a determination that its readership, even if only by default, was sophisticated and superior to anybody who had once read *Photoplay* or *Modern Screen*.

There is something singularly unappealing about the name *Movieline*. It is a title more suited to the Internet than the glossy, $2.00 publication that first appeared in September 1989. (It had an earlier life as a free publication distributed to moviegoers in southern California.) By featuring Jane Fonda on the cover, perhaps editors Laurie Halpern Smith and Virginia Campbell were deliberately appealing to a feminist audience, but again a readership far removed from that for the old-style fan magazines. *Movieline* disappeared from the cover and contents page in May–June 2003, replaced by *Movieline's Hollywood Life*. The emphasis also changed from film to the Los Angeles lifestyle. An article in that first renamed issue, "To Live & Date in L.A.," introduced readers to the Chateau Marmont hotel, "Hollywood's Secret Hideout." In January–February 2006, the name changed completely to *Hollywood Life*, and the cover price of $3.99 was evidence that this was no fan magazine for the film enthusiast but rather a publication for the would-be rich and the would-be famous living primarily in Los Angeles. The paid circulation was down to 251,000 when *Hollywood Life* ended its life with the March–April 2007 issue, featuring a provocative-looking Chloe Sevigny on the cover.

Richard B. Stolley, largely responsible for the success of *People* magazine, knew what he was doing as editorial director of *Entertainment Weekly*, which first hit the newsstands on February 16, 1990, with a cover featuring record stars Neneh Cherry and K. D. Lang and a price of $1.95. Publisher Time, Inc., introduced a timely publication intended to cover all media, including television, movies, books, and the record industry, with news items and feature articles. Again, as with *Premiere*, *Entertainment Weekly* was a publication aimed at a more literate and educated audience. Can one truly imagine a contemporary fan magazine reviewing or even discussing a book?

Each year, *Entertainment Weekly* publishes a selection of specialty issues, previewing future attractions, featuring celebrity-approved photographs, and honoring the Academy Awards. Aping its parent magazine's man or woman of the year, the last issue of each year honors the entertainer of the year, chosen by readers at the magazine's official website. While film and television stars predominate, in 2007 the title was bestowed on novelist J. K. Rowling. The website www.ew.com serves to keep *Entertainment Weekly* absolutely current with the latest programming information and an archive of the publication's past issues.

To a large extent the fan magazine audience had lived in small American towns; housewives had read them at the beauty parlor and teenage girls had been engrossed with them at the counter of the local drugstore. *Premiere*, *Movieline*, and *Entertainment Weekly* might be found at the office of the doctor or dentist, but they would be read by a large, general audience, who acquired the periodicals by subscription and took them into their homes along, and on an equal footing, with *Time* and *Newsweek*. By 2003, *Entertainment Weekly* reported an average weekly circulation of 1.7 million, far more than any fan magazine had reached.

All was not well at *Premiere* with its buyout from Hachette by the News Corporation and its subsequent sale to K-III Holdings. In May 1995, Hachette again acquired the magazine in partnership with New World Communications Group. Circulation was never as high as that for *Entertainment Weekly* and in the new millennium it was around 500,000 to 600,000. Perhaps *Premiere* was too good for the industry and its readership, which was turning more and more to the Internet for its entertainment news. Perhaps the magazine overestimated the intelligence of its readership, concentrating on the entire filmmaking process rather than just those in front of the camera. The *Wall Street Journal* (March 9, 2005) actually reported that *Premiere* had been "weeding out less-desirable readers even though that meant a drop in circulation." Had it become like one of those big-city "in" nightclubs with bouncers denying access to the likes of this writer and his readers? Perhaps the publisher exerted too much pressure on the editorial staff in terms of what the content should be. Or perhaps, in all honesty, at its end *Premiere* might still be glossy, but it was far less vibrant, unexciting compared to the way it had been. Whatever the reason, the magazine published its final issue, with Will Ferrell on the cover, in April 2007.

The "big three" of the new-style fan magazines had their competitors—*Silver Screen* to their *Photoplay*. Dennis Publishing, publisher of *Maxim*, released two newsstand-only specials titled *Maxim Goes to the Movies* in 2003, but decided it was impractical to publish the new journal on a regular basis. In March 2005, *Entertainment Weekly* mailed out a test issue of *Look* to some of its subscribers. Named after the photographic magazine, *Look* was aimed at a male readership of "rabid" movie fans, with a profile of Morgan Freeman and a story on the screen adaptation of the comic book *Sin City*. The approach was singularly flawed in that the most avid of movie fans are film buffs, few of whom would want to read about Morgan Freeman.

Arguably more of a general interest periodical than a film or fan magazine, *Talk Magazine* was launched in September 1999 by Tina Brown, the former editor of *Vanity Fair* and *The New Yorker*, with financial support from Miramax and the Hearst Corporation. It was those two financial backers who suspended publication of the magazine in January 2002 despite a circulation of 650,000 as of June 2001. Recalling the last years of the fan magazines, *Talk Magazine* began its run with a high-profile, political piece—not Jacqueline Kennedy Onassis, but Hillary Clinton claiming that the abuse her husband had suffered as a child led to his chronic infidelity.

Other periodicals that were not fan magazines but were celebrity oriented include *In Touch*, launched in 2002, and *Radar*, combining gossip, news, fashion, and beauty tips. In the summer of 2003, American Media moved the editorial staff of its tabloid *The Star* to New York, promising to transform the favorite newspaper at the checkout counter into a more respectable magazine. It was, as the *New York Times* (August 4, 2003) noted, an upgrade from newsprint to glossy paper. It was not necessarily an upgrade in quality reporting. The individual generally credited with turning *The Star* "from a frowzy supermarket tabloid to a glossy magazine that dished plenty of celeb gossip,"[16] is Bonnie Fuller, a former editor at *Cosmopolitan*, who was *The Star*'s editorial director from 2003 through 2008.

What *The Star* and other recent periodicals had over the fan magazines was that they were on display and accessible at the supermarket checkout counter. They did not have to rely on subscriptions, nor did they have to concern themselves with prominent placement on the newsstands. What has never been considered fully from the first fan magazine in 1911 through the present is the cost of postage to subscribers, who generally receive a healthy discount on the cover price. Subscriptions sales boost advertising revenues, but if the same sales figures can be realized through direct marketing and sales, then advertisers will respond.

"The goldfish bowl," as Adela Rogers St. Johns characterized the early Hollywood community, has grown to become a veritable ocean of celebrities, embracing the sports and political arenas as much as the entertainment industry. Personalities are no longer the end result of hard work in the movies or on television, but rather the pathetic choices of a public obsessed with celebrity, rather than personality, over substance and/or creativity. *Time* magazine's "digital democracy" has evened the playing field, making everyone a star.com and every outlet a potential replacement to the fan magazine.

"Showbiz junkies," as *Variety* described them, can no longer wait patiently for a monthly magazine, be it *Premiere* or a fan publication. With all manner of entertainment on line, including motion pictures, why wait for the printed word when the digital word can be instantaneous. As *Variety*'s Anne Thompson put it, "At a time when the likes of celebrity Web site TMZ.com, Defamer, and People.com rush amateur photos of the Hollywood Hills brush fire and news of Mel Gibson's latest indiscretion to the Web at the speed of thought, writers and editors who once specialized in crafting polished, in-depth insider features about Hollywood stars and filmmakers are learning the mantra of the Web: Write fast—and write short."[17]

The Internet has changed the world, not always for the better, but certainly in terms of immediate access to news and information. Those seeking motion picture credits and the like can go at once to the International Movie Data Base, founded in 1990 by Col Needham, where documentation is relatively correct but not totally so. Those seeking to buy or wishing to sell fan magazines can advertise on eBay and elsewhere with varying results. Those actually wishing to find the twenty-first-century equivalent of a first-half-of-the-twentieth-century fan magazine will have limited success based on their expectations. Are blogs sites comparable to the fan magazines of old? Obviously, they are not, although some, such as AintItCoolNews.com, run by Harry Knowles out of Austin, Texas, will provide web surfers studio press releases and commentary from some filmmakers. The studios cooperate up to a point, but publicists are quick to point out that it is far easier to sell a film today with trailers online via YouTube, MySpace, or Apple Movies. While once the fan magazine readership had perhaps a dozen or so journals from which to select, today they (and now it is equally those of both sexes) are faced with hundreds of outlets, just as studio publicists must determine which best suits their needs.

No longer is America divided between those who are readers of fan magazines and those who are not, but rather between those who think they are film critics and that the Internet offers them an outlet for their commentary and those who know they are neither critics nor fans of the Internet. Endless numbers of forums on the Internet allow for the posting of reviews. Even the International Movie Data Base allows for the posting of reviews and gossip, generally from the United Kingdom. Sites such as RottenTomatoes.com and

Metacritic.com provide the user, provided he or she is "accredited" in some fashion, with ample opportunity to voice an opinion on movies, DVDs, video games, CDs, television programming, and everything else that was once restricted to those with access to the printing press. PerezHilton.com (web site of Mario Lavandeira) is, according to *The Hollywood Reporter* (April 9, 2008), a "salacious salon for celebrity gossip," a site that appeals to the same female age group who twenty or more years earlier would have been avariciously reading the fan magazines. Indeed, with its photographs and its one-line, generally outrageous, captions, PerezHilton.com is reminiscent of the fan magazines in their failing years. The photographs at PerezHilton.com are a sad reminder that generally, in the twenty-first century, most people do not care about reading. The Internet is visual, and photographs are what web surfers want to see. What commentary there is has to be brief and quickly readable.

Closest perhaps to what the fan magazines represented is a recently created site, Film in Focus, launched in December 2007, the result of a liaison between publishers Faber & Faber and Random House and Focus Features, in partnership with *Filmmaker* magazine. It provides users with promos, trailers, and links to other sites and articles. Concentrating on non-mainstream cinema and providing most of the departments found in the fan magazines of old are such Internet sites as the Alternative Film Guide, GreenCine Daily, and Like Anna Karina's Sweater.

But are such Internet sites comparable in any true sense to the fan magazines? An argument might certainly be made that it is the Internet itself that has replaced the fan magazines, just as it has replaced a library of books or an archives of papers, providing potential moviegoers with the opportunity to research which of the new films or the new stars are of appeal to them. They use search engines such as Google, sites such as Movies and Moviefone, and, of course, the distributors' own websites. According to *Daily Variety* (September 19, 2006), a study by MarketCast on behalf of Google found that eighty-nine percent of moviegoers initially heard about a film from traditional sources, while only eight percent used online sites. "Among all forms of advertising, the study found that online trailers and Web ads are the third and fourth most influential on moviegoers, trailing far behind TV commercials and in-theater trailers but ahead of billboards and radio."

Is it the Internet itself that is the ultimate fan magazine for all fans? No matter what your interest, the Internet will serve it—with speed and efficiency if not always factual accuracy. But then did the fan magazines worry too much about accuracy in their stories? The studio gloss that was applied is comparable to the veneer of trust offered by Wikipedia, an encyclopedia for the people written by the people with little regard for anything more than minimal fact checking. The studio trailers give the producers and distributors ultimate control over what the public sees and reads. It is a far more satisfying solution than any formal agreement with the fan magazine publishers. Sure, there will be uncontrollable elements on the Internet, but there were similar elements at work within the fan magazines. Is what is available on the Internet any worse than what *Confidential* magazine might publish?

It was the time element—the distance between the story and publication—that fatally hurt the fan magazines and may well have been a factor in the demise of *Premiere* and *Movieline*. The Internet provides immediate gratification in terms of news delivery. There is no waiting period for the fan between the story hitting the daily newspapers and the story reaching the glossy magazines. In fact, the story will generally hit the Internet before the daily press can publish it.

There is, of course, an unspoken and unacknowledged distinction between the fan magazines and anything on the Internet—and that is the appeal, talent, and charisma of the individuals involved. Once there were legends, ranging from Rudolph Valentino and Greta Garbo in the silent era to Joan Crawford, Clark Gable, and Bette Davis in the 1930s. A contemporary legend can sell a contemporary fan magazine. What passes for stardom and celebrity today is neither. The instantaneous gratification that can result from an Internet moment with a Paris Hilton or a Britney Spears will not extend beyond half an hour. Nobody should want to go back and relive what are ultimately tragic moments in the lives of these excuses for celebrity. It was tragic when Anna Nicole Smith died at such a young age, but a year or more from her passing, does anyone outside of her immediate friends and family care? However, fans did want to continue a liaison, a relationship, a love affair, a fantasy with the stars that once peopled the fan magazines.

One of the greatest of fan magazine writers, Ruth Waterbury, whose spirit seems at times to be watching over this book, and not always approving of what I have to say, discussed the difference in Hollywood between then and now back in 1972. Nothing has really much changed in the intervening years. Once there were stars.

> Valentino was an extremely handsome man, but [Ronald] Colman was a handsome man in a different way. Physical beauty of the males in Hollywood at that time was really a thing. Neil Hamilton, who was a very good-looking man, but nothing up here—nothing. I was invited down to Malibu by Neil Hamilton, and all of a sudden I fainted dead away. It was just Joel McCrea walking down the beach. I'd never seen anything like that. Gable, I think was the man of the thirties, definitely. Of course, there's nothing the matter with John Wayne to this day. [Errol] Flynn was very handsome, very charming, very amusing and [a] very aesthetic man. He was an extraordinarily beautiful man.
>
> Really, the ugliness of people in pictures today is something awful. Generally speaking, I can get to almost anybody. But, also, I don't have to get to anybody. So I will not take any back talk from any little punks. I don't talk to people like that. I say great, good, and walk out.[18]

The stars stopped talking to the fan magazine contributors. The fan magazine writers walked out on the stars. And the public walked out on the fan magazines. It was a vicious circle that led to a sad, pathetic end of the fan magazine.

U.S. FAN MAGAZINES

Because of the ephemeral nature of fan magazines, it is difficult to determine exact beginning and end dates of many publications. This listing provides the most definitive information available, but is, of necessity, incomplete. Reference sources used include the annual listings in the *Film Daily Year Book of Motion Pictures* from 1926 to 1969; N. W. Ayer and Sons' *Directory of Newspapers and Periodicals* (later the *Gale Directory of Publications and Broadcast Media*); *Ulrich's International Periodicals Directory*; the five-volume *Union List of Serials in Libraries of the United States and Canada*, edited by Edna Brown Titus (H. W. Wilson Co., 1965); the published Library of Congress Copyright Office *Catalog of Copyright Entries: Periodicals, 1946–1977*; and the reported holdings of various U.S. libraries. Most documentation on fan magazines is incredibly incomplete; for example, the 1932 edition of *The Motion Picture Almanac* lists only eleven fan publications, and yet there were almost double that number published at that time.

Where the month of publication is given, it is the date appearing on the fan magazine itself. Often, the copyright date appears inside the magazine and it is different, usually a month earlier, from the date on the cover or contents page. Also, fan magazines were generally available for sale two or three weeks prior to the date on the cover.

It should be noted that there is misnumbering in many fan magazines, both in terms of issues and volumes. With fan magazines published from the 1950s onward, it is virtually impossible to base a date of first issue on the volume and number quoted in the publication. Unless indicated, the fan magazines listed here were published on a monthly basis and out of New York. Some fan magazines described themselves as "bimonthly," and this appears, correctly, to mean they were published every two months, not, as the term is loosely used today, twice a month. If a fan magazine is the subject of substantial coverage in the text, the information here is limited to basic years of publication only. Some 268 fan magazines are listed, but it may well be that there are many more.

Television fan magazines that do not contain a reference to film in their titles are not included. Some of the listed periodicals may not rightly be designated "fan magazines" but are listed here in an effort to aid readers who might expect their inclusion based on information found elsewhere. Additionally, some annuals are included in that they resemble fan magazines and have the same publishers.

Best Screen Stories: first published 1942; annual; editors: Evelyn Van Horne and Gwen Campbell; no longer extant as of 1950; published by Dell

Bijou: first published April 1977; bimonthly; subtitled "the magazine of the movies"; editor-in-chief: Ted Sennett; published by Baronet Publishing Co. out of New York

Buck Jones Western Stories: November 1936–September 1937; three issues only published

Castle of Frankenstein: 1962–1975; published by Gothic Castle Publishing Co.

Celebrity: first published Winter 1958; editor: Jack Podell; number 3, and last, is dated Winter 1960, suggesting an annual publication schedule; published by Fawcett

Celebrity Hairdos: circa 1963–1965; published by Better Books, Inc.

Cinema: first published January 1930; last issue believed published December 1930; published by Cinema Magazine Publishing Co. out of East Stroudsburg, Pennsylvania

Cinema Art: first published 1921; volume 1, number 5 is dated March 1922; published by Downs Publishing Co., out of Philadelphia

Cinema Art: circa 1926–circa 1929; the *Union List of Serials* gives publication years as 1923–1927; edited by Mrs. John [Marie] Mckee; published out of New York and not believed associated with the earlier publication of the same name

Cinema Arts: 1936–1937; only three issues (June, July, September 1937) and a "preview" issue (September 1936) were published; editor: Paul F. Husserl (no editor identified for preview issue); published by Cinema Magazine, Inc., out of New York

Cinema Review: circa 1926; a weekly publication out of Hollywood

Classic, see *Motion Picture Classic*

Cowboy Movie Thrillers: December 1941–March 1942; four issues only published; published by Red Star News Co.

Elsa Maxwell's Café Society: first, and assumed to be only issue, published 1953; editor: Christopher Kane; published by Dell

Famous Monsters of Filmland: 1958–1978; published by Warren Publishing Co., out of New York

Famous Monsters of Filmland Yearbook: 1962–1972; published by Warren Publishing Co., out of New York

Fan-Fare: volume 1, number 2 is dated March 1964; bimonthly; published by American Periodicals Corp.

Fangoria: first published 1979; editors: Robert Martin, David Everitt, and Anthony Timpone; devoted to the horror genre; first published by Starlog Group and later Creative Group out of New York

Fantastic Films: 1978–1985; published by Blake Publishing Corp.

Feature Movie Magazine: first published March 1915; semi-monthly; published by Features Publishing Co. out of Chicago

Fighting Stars: first published October 1973; extant as of December 1985; bimonthly; published by Rainbow Publications, Inc., out of Burbank, California

Film Album: volume 1, number 1 is dated Summer 1948; extant as of Winter 1949; editor: Dorothy Votsis; published by Select Publications, Inc., out of New York

Film and T.V. Careers: first published Fall 1963 with each issue devoted to an individual star, beginning with Elizabeth Taylor; number 3 and last is dated May 1964

Film Arts Monthly: circa 1926; published out of New York; no copies known to exist in public institutions

Film Fun: 1915–1942; editors: Elizabeth Sears (beginning in 1916), George Mitchell (1924–1928), Curtis Mitchell (1928–1930), Ernest V. Heyn (1930), Lester C. Grady (1931–1938), Victor Bloom (1939–1941), George Saxon (1942); published by Leslie-Judge Co., out of New York (1915–1925), Film Humor, Inc./Dell out of New York (1926–1938), and Film Publishing Co., out of Dunellen, New Jersey (1939–1942)

Film Humor: 1948–circa 1949; volume 1, number 4 is dated Spring 1949

Film Kiddies' Herald: circa 1927; both a fan and trade publication issued twice a month out of Hollywood and edited by Frederick

F. Paul and Grace Kerwin; no copies known to exist in public institutions

Film Players Herald: first published March 1915; editor: Lloyd Kenyon Jones; as of February 1916 merged with *Movie Pictorial* (see that entry); published by Photoplaywrights' Association of America

Film Stories: first published March 26, 1921; extant as of November 10, 1921; weekly; published by Street and Smith

Film Truth: first published April 1920 and still extant in May 1921; published out of New York by Photoplay Associates, which may have been a fan-related organization

Filmplay Journal: first published July 1921; extant as of 1922; billed as "A Monthly Magazine of Film Folk"

Glamour of Hollywood: April 1939–April 1941; as of May 1941 became *Glamour* and no longer classified as a fan magazine; absorbed *Charm* magazine 1959; first editor-in-chief: Alice Thompson; initially published by Condé Nast out of Greenwich, Connecticut

Golden Screen: August 1934–November 1934; merged with *Motion Picture Magazine*

Gossip, see *Rona Barrett's Gossip*

Hairdo Ideas: circa 1966; published by Herald House, Inc.

Hear Hollywood: billed as "The World First Talking Magazine"; volume 2, number 2 dated September 1957, includes a phonograph record inside of James Dean and Tony Perkins in an exclusive, intimate interview; published by Hear, Inc., out of Beverly Hills, California

Hi-Hat: first published September 1927; published out of Hollywood and, while not a trade paper, intended as much for members of the film industry as for movie fans and billed as "The Round Table of the Film Fraternity"; editor and reviewer: Eddy Eckels; extant as of January 1928

Hollywood: September 20, 1924–June 1928; known as *Holly Leaves*, 1913–1924; *Hollywood Movie Novels*, June–August 1933; *Hollywood Screen Life*, February 1939–February 1940; merged into *Motion Picture*. (This information is taken from

the *Union List of Serials*, and I am not convinced that it is correct.)

Hollywood Album of Love: number 1, dated 1961, is believed to be only issue published; editor: Terry Brennan; published by Romance Publishing Co.

Hollywood Diaries: first published 1956; only one other issue, 1957, believed published; annual; editor: Ira Peck; published by Popular Library, Inc.

Hollywood Family Album: circa 1948–circa 1961; published by Dell

Hollywood Family Album: not necessarily associated with the above, earlier magazine; volume 1, number 4 is dated July–September 1950; volume 1, number 12 is dated 1963; quarterly; between 1961 and 1963, only three issues appear to have been published; became *Sheilah Graham's Hollywood Family Album*; editor: Jean Ramer; published by Dell

Hollywood Guys and Gals: first published 1955; editor: Mary Callahan; published by Fawcett

Hollywood Hi-Hat, see *Hi-Hat*

Hollywood Hot-Line: extant in 1974 and 1975

Hollywood Life: first published 1925; volume 1, number 5 is dated March 1926; editor: Douglas Z. Doty; published by Wheeler-Reid Publications, Inc., out of Hollywood

Hollywood Life Stories: 1951–circa 1966; number 10 is dated 1960; editor: Jean Ramer; published by Dell

Hollywood Love and Tragedy: first published November 1956; number 2 is dated August 1957; editor: Diana Lurvey; published by Ideal

Hollywood Love Life: number 1, dated 1955, is believed to be only issue published; editor: Ira Peck; published by Affiliated Magazines, Inc.

Hollywood Low-Down: circa 1933–circa 1941; edited and published out of Hollywood by Jimmy Valentine, becoming the official magazine of the Fan Club Federation (founded in 1934); the Fan Club Federation should not be confused with the Fan Club League, which operated out of Indianapolis, Indiana, around the same time

Hollywood Men: no copyright notice or year of publication, but based on content, first year of publication assumed to be 1953; number 2 is copyrighted 1954; editor: Maxine Arnold; published by Maco Magazine Corp.

Hollywood Mirror: first published April 1934; published out of Los Angeles, but with special sections for franchisees in each major city; available by subscription only

Hollywood Movie Fan: extant as of December 1924; editor: Leonard C. Boyd; published out of Los Angeles

Hollywood Movie Nights: extant as of October 1931

Hollywood Movie Novels: an Internet source lists volume 22, number 8 as August 1933

Hollywood Movie Parade: a 1956 issue has been identified; some connection prior or later to *Movie Parade*

Hollywood Movie Novel Magazine: first published January 1929; published by Jacobsen Publishing Co.

Hollywood Picture Life: first published 1955; volume 1, number 2 is dated Winter 1955–1956; quarterly; published by Non-Pareil Publishing Corp. out of New York

Hollywood Playtime: first published 1955; annual; editor: Ira Peck; published by Literary Enterprises, Inc.

Hollywood Rebels: number 1, dated 1957, is believed to be only issue published; advertised as an annual; editor: Diana Lurvey; published by Ideal

Hollywood Romances: first published 1948; number 11 is dated 1957; extant as of 1964; annual; editor: Jean Ramer; published by Dell; became *Sheilah Graham's Hollywood Romances*

Hollywood Screen Life, see *Hollywood*

Hollywood Screen Parade: 1957–circa 1971, but March 1958 is listed as volume 12, number 2; bimonthly; published by Actual Publishing Co., Inc.; formerly *Movie Play* and some connection prior or later to *Movie Parade*

Hollywood Screenland: extant as of 1923

Hollywood Secrets Annual: first published 1955; last issue is believed to be number 5, dated May 1960; editor: Richard Heller; published by Publication House, Inc.; must have some connection to *Hollywood Secrets Yearbook*

Hollywood Secrets Yearbook: first published 1955; last issue is believed to be number 9, dated 1962; annual; editors: Richard Heller and Bessie Little; published by Dell

Hollywood Sex Queens: first published October 1966; annual; editor: G. T. von Aspe; published by Sari Publishing Co., out of North Hollywood

Hollywood Star News: 1935–1942; published by Associated Mimeo Publications out of Hollywood; a curious, mimeographed publication, produced privately for nonprofit by "hi-school boys," but still worthy of the title of fan magazine

Hollywood Stars: 1956–1958; unable to verify possible merger with *Movie Pix* and *Screen* as of December 1956; bimonthly; editor: Joan Curtis

Hollywood Talent Parade: first published 1944

Hollywood Teen Agers: first published February 1960; number 2 is dated 1961; editor: Jean Ramer; published by Dell

Hollywood Teen Album: numbers 1 and 2 are both dated 1962; editor: Bob Lucas; published by Hanro Corp.

Hollywood Yearbook: first published 1950; extant as of 1957; editors: Christopher Kane and later Florence Epstein; later became *Sheilah Graham's Hollywood Yearbook*; published by Dell

Ingenue: New Hollywood at Work and Play: first published 2003

Inside Hollywood: first published 1991; extant as of 1992; bimonthly; published by World Publishing Corp., out of Evanston, Illinois

Inside Movies: volume 2, number 4 is dated October 1962; volume 13, number 4 is dated December 1965; editors include Milburn Smith and Micki Siegel; published by Countrywide Publications, Inc.

Latest Hollywood and TV Hairdos: circa 1963–1965; published out of New York by Modern Guide Publications

Liz and Mike: first published 1958 (believed to be only issue); published by Dell

Mediascene, see *Prevue*

Modern Movies: July 1937–July 1939; editors: William T. Walsh and later Ruth L. Baer;

published by Bilbara Publishing Co., later Ideal, out of Mount Morris, Illinois; absorbed by *Movies* (see that entry)

Modern Movies: first published June 1968; last issue seen is dated March 1974 and listed as volume 1, number 2; became *Modern Movies Hollywood Exposed* in May 1975; believed to have ceased publication in May 1976; editorial directors: Carol Finkelstein, Harry Matetsky, and Diane Robbens; initially published out of New York by Zenith Publishing Corp., and then Magazine Management Co.

Modern Screen: first published November 1930; until June 1931 titled *The Modern Screen Magazine*; ceased publication 1985, ending its days as a bimonthly publication

Modern Screen's Hollywood Yearbook: first published 1957 and extant as of 1962

Modern Stars: volume 1, number 4 is dated November 1960; published by Besscal Publications, Inc.; identified as "formerly *Movie TV and Record Time*"

Monsters Unlimited: 1965–1966; formerly *Monsters to Laugh With*, 1964–1965; published by Non-Pareil Publishing Co.

Motion Picture and Television Magazine, see *Motion Picture Story Magazine*

Motion Picture Classic: September 1915–August 1931; began publication as *Motion Picture Supplement* (September–November 1915); name changed 1931 to *Movie Classic* (see that entry); available on microfilm

Motion Picture Magazine, see *Motion Picture Story Magazine*

Motion Picture Story Magazine: 1911–1977; name changed 1914 to *Motion Picture Magazine*; September 1951–September 1954 known as *Motion Picture and Television Magazine*; 1911–1941 issues available on microfilm

Motion Picture Supplement, see *Motion Picture Classic*

Movie Action Magazine: November 1935–June 1936; editor: John L. Nanovic; published by Street and Smith

Movie Adventures: November 1924–December 1924; editor: Ellen McIvaine; published by Brewster Publications Inc., out of Brooklyn, New York

The September 1925 issue of *Movie Digest*.

Movie Album: first published 1941; volume 1, number 4 is dated December 16, 1942; quarterly; editor: Sara Corpening; published by Fawcett

Movie Album: 1955–1966; volume 1, number 2 is dated Winter 1955–1956; quarterly; editor: Bessie Little; published by Select Publications, Inc.; no connection to earlier title of same name

Movie and Radio Guide: 1940–1943; formerly *Radio Guide* (1931–1940)

Movie and TV Album: circa 1956; editor: Joan Curtis

Movie and TV Fan-Fare, see *Fan-Fare*

Movie and TV Gossip: volume 8, number 5 is dated March 1974; became *Movie and TV Tattler* in May 1974; published by Star Guidance, Inc., out of New York

Movie and TV Gossip Album: circa 1957

Movie and TV Tattler, see *Movie and TV Gossip*

Movie Classic: September 1931–February 1937; subtitled "The Newsreel of the Newsstands"; editor: Laurence Reid; published by Motion Picture Publications, Inc., out of Chicago; absorbed by *Motion Picture Magazine*

Movie Digest: first published June 1925; published by John D. Foley out of Hollywood

Movie Digest: first published January 1972; extant as of May 1973; bimonthly; editor: David Ragan

Movie Fan: extant as of 1922

The Movie Fan: first published May 1936; extant as of December 1936; editor and publisher: E. M. Orowitz; newspaper-style fan magazine published by the Emo Movie Club out of New York

Movie Fan: number 2 is dated July 1946; last issue is dated November 1954; quarterly and then bimonthly; edited in last six years by Joan Curtis, and earlier by Abby Sundell and James Stewart-Gordon; published by Magazine Productions, Inc. (later Monthly Magazine Productions, Inc.) and then Skye Publishing Co., Inc.; combined with *Screen Life* as of January 1955

Movie Fun: first published September 1940; published by Crestwood Publishing Co. out of New York

Movie Glamor Guys: first published 1950; editor: Joan Curtis; published by Fawcett

Movie Glamour: first published 1945; bimonthly

Movie Humor: circa 1934–circa 1942; subtitled "Hollywood Girls and Gags"; editor: M. R. Reese; published by Ultem Publications out of New York

Movie Life: first published 1937; extant as of January 1980; billed initially as "Hollywood's Only All-Picture Magazine"; became *Toni Holt's Movie Life* in late 1970s; later editors include Marsha Daly and Carol Tormey; published by Ideal

Movie Life Yearbook: first published 1944; first editor: Betty Etter; published by Bilbara Publishing Co. (believed to be a subsidiary of Ideal) out of New York; became biannual in 1950; extant as of 1975

Movie Love Stories: June 1, 1941–January 1942; editor: Jerry Albert; published by Albing Publications

Movie Magazine: March–December 1915

Movie Magazine: first published September 1925; continued as *Pictures* in 1926

Movie Melody Magazine: first published July 1921

Movie Merry-Go-Round: July 1936–June 1939; editor: Frederick Gardener; published by Periodical House, Inc., out of New York

Movie Mirror: November 1931–December 1940 (when merged with *Photoplay*)

Movie Mirror: first published March 1956; extant as of 1998; bimonthly; editor: Joan Goldstein; published by Sterling Group, Inc.; no connection to earlier publication of same name

Movie Mirror Yearbook: first published 1960; annual; editors include David Ragan and Madeline Eller; published by Sterling Group, Inc.

Movie Monthly: first published March 1924

Movie Parade: volume 10, number 15 is dated March 1971; published by Actual Publishing Co., Inc.; some connection to *Hollywood Parade* and *Hollywood Screen Parade*

Movie Pictorial: volume 1, number 9 is dated July 4, 1914; extant as of 1916; weekly then monthly as of September 1915; editor: Roy S. Hanford; published out of Chicago; merged with *Film Players Herald* (see that entry)

Movie Pin-Ups: volume 1, number 3 is dated Fall 1952; extant as of 1953; published by Ideal

Movie Pix: circa 1951–circa 1958; volume 4, number 5 is dated August 1953; edited for last six years by Joan Curtis and earlier by Abby Sundell and James Stewart-Gordon; unable to verify possible merger with *Hollywood Stars* and *Screen* as of December 1956; bimonthly; published by Astro Distributing Corp. out of New York

Movie Play: first published Winter 1944; number 2 is dated January 1946; extant as of 1955; quarterly; published by Buse Publications, Inc., out of Chicago; possibly became *Hollywood Screen Parade*

Movie Play: volume 1, number 2 is dated August 1966; bimonthly; editor: Robert Arnold; published by Normandy Associates, Inc.; not believed to be associated with earlier periodical of the same name

Movie Radio Guide: 1940–1943; formerly *Radio Guide*; supervising editor: Carl A.

Schroeder; published by Triangle Publications, Inc., out of Philadelphia.

Movie Show Magazine: first published September 1942; some sources indicate last published circa 1947, but believed to be still extant in 1970; edited by Lester C. Grady (first two and later years) and Ruth Taylor (other years); published by Hunter Publications out of New York

Movie Songs Magazine: first published April 1946, editor: Charles Reed Jones

Movie Spotlight: first published early 1950; volume 5, number 3 is dated June 1954; bimonthly; editor: Ruth Ericson; published by Spotlight Publishing Co., Inc., and then Actual Publishing Co., Inc.

Movie Stars, see *Movie Stars Parade*

Movie Stars Parade: first published 1940 or 1941; volume 4, number 2 is dated January 1944; renamed *Movie Stars TV Close Ups*, circa January 1959; as of March 1961 renamed *Movie Stars*; later renamed *Movie Stars TV Close-Ups Parade*; extant as of June 1976; editors include Pat Murphy and Diana Lurvey; published by Ideal, originally using name of Bilbara Publishing Co., Inc., out of Chicago

Movie Stars Parade Album: first published 1946; extant as of 1948; editor: Pat Murphy; published by Ideal

Movie Stars TV Close-Ups, see *Movie Stars Parade*

Movie Story Magazine: May 1934–July 1951; formerly *Romantic Movie Stories*; published by Fawcett; absorbed by *Motion Picture*

Movie Story Yearbook: first published 1942; editor: Dorothy Hosking; published by Fawcett

Movie Tattler: volume 1, number 7 is dated March 1964; editor: Clark Willard; published by Flight Plan, Inc., out of New York (possibly related to *Movie TV Tattler*)

Movie Teen: circa 1947–circa 1953; volume 2, number 3 is dated April–May 1949; bimonthly; edited in final years by Abby Sundell and James Stewart-Gordon; published by Screen-Teen Co. out of New York

Movie Teen Illustrated: circa 1955–circa 1963; volume 5, number 3 is dated August 1963; quarterly; published by Dodsmith Publishing Co., Inc., out of Malibu, California

Movie Thrillers: circa 1925; published by Brewster Publications, Inc., out of Brooklyn, New York

Movie Thrills: first published February 1950; with *Movies*, added to magazine list of Ideal Publishing Corp., with promised policy of publisher W. M. Cotton, "Give them only glamour, no scandal"

Movie Time: circa 1952–circa 1956; in 1959, the Library of Congress recorded a curious copyright registration by Loretta G. Fillion for volume 1, number 36, dated November 8, 1936

Movie Today: first published 1961

Movie TV and Record Time, see *Modern Stars*

Movie TV Confidential: first published July 1969; extant as of 1970; published by Stanley Publications, Inc., out of New York

Movie TV Secrets: circa 1960–circa 1966

Movie TV Tattler: first published January 1960; bimonthly; editorial director: Nina Finkelstein; published by Meteor Publications, Inc., out of New York; there are references to a *Movie TV Tattler*, first published in 1953

Movie Weekly: 1921–1925; available on microfilm, but many pages are missing or damaged

Movie Weekly: circa 1951–circa 1957; editor and publisher: H. G. Odza

Movie Weekly: first published 1987; a tabloid publication; editor: Kevin Brown; published by E. W. A. Publications out of Brooklyn, New York

Movie Western: only three issues published in July, October, and December 1941; published by Albing Publishing, out of Holyoke, Massachusetts

Movie World Annual: first published 1974 by Magazine Management Co., Inc.

Movieland: first published 1943; name changed to *Movieland and T.V. Time*, May 1958; extant as of December 1974; editors include Doris Cline, Kay Sullivan,

Dorothy Lee McEvoy, James Gregory, and Lillian Smith

Moviepix: first published February 1938; published by Dell

Movies: May 1930–September 1935

Movies: first published August 1939; extant as of October 1947; editors include Muriel Babcock and Mary C. Kelley; formerly *Modern Movies*; published by Ideal

Movies: first published February 1950; last issue seen August 1954; believed to have ceased publication in April 1956; editor: Pat Campbell; with *Movie Thrills*, added to magazine list of Ideal Publishing Corp. with promised policy of publisher, W. M. Cotton, "Give them only glamour, no scandal"

Movies Illustrated: circa 1960–circa 1966; identified as "formerly *TV, Movie and Record Stars*"; editor: Micki Siegel; published by Atlas Magazines

Movies in Review: May 1945–November 1948

Movies International: first published September–October 1965; editor: James R. Silke; published by Challenge, Inc., out of North Hollywood

Movies Now: premiere issue dated 1970; volume 1, number 1 dated July 1971

Moving Picture Monthly: 1929–1933

Moving Picture Stories: first published January 3, 1913; extant as of February 18, 1930; weekly, then biweekly; editor: Ethel Rosemon; originally published by Frank Tousey out of New York and later M. Clifford Pardec out of Springfield, Ohio; available on microfilm

The New Movie Album: A Who's Who of the Screen: first published October 1930; possibly no further issues

The New Movie Magazine: December 1929–September 1935; no issue for June 1931

New Stars: no information available; possibly an alternative title for *New Stars over Hollywood*

New Stars over Hollywood: number 4 is dated October 1946; bimonthly; published by D. S. Publishing Co., Inc., out of New York

Old Hollywood: first published 1956; editor: Bessie Little; published by Warwick

The February 1934 issue of *New Movie*.

Publications, Inc. (Martin Goodman), out of New York

One Woman: first published Fall 1983, with each issue devoted to a single female personality, beginning with Morgan Fairchild; extant as of Spring 1984

Pantomime: September 28, 1921–March 18, 1922; weekly; editor-in-chief: Victor C. Olmsted; published by Movie Topics, Inc., out of New York

Paris and Hollywood, see *So This Is Paris and Hollywood*

Paris and Hollywood Screen Secrets, see *So This Is Paris and Hollywood*

Photo Dramatist: circa 1926, published out of Hollywood; not believed to be associated with *The Photo-Drama Magazine*, first published in 1919 as *Photoplaywright*, and not a fan magazine

Photo-Era: circa 1898–1932; referenced in the *Film Daily Year Book of Motion Pictures* as a motion picture–related technical, fan, and trade publication, edited by A. H. Beardsley out of Wolfeboro, New Hampshire, but, in reality, devoted to photography; merged into *American Photography*

Photo Play Topics, see *Photoplay Vogue*

Photo Screen: first published October 1965; extant as of February 1978; published by Sterling House, Inc.

Photo Story Book: circa 1929

Photoplay: 1911–1980; available on microfilm, but all issues from 1911 are missing

Photoplay Annual: first published 1952; extant as of 1962; editors: Fred Rutledge Sammis, Tony Gray, Ann Higginbotham, Isabel Moore, and Betty Etter

The Photoplay Author: volume 4, number 2 is dated August 1914; published by Independent Publishing Co., out of Cicopee, Massachusetts

Photoplay's Directory of Stars: 1957 may be only edition published; editor: Betty Etter; published by Macfadden

Photo-Play Journal: May 1916–February 1921; published by La Verne Publishing Co. and then Central Press Co., out of Philadelphia

Photoplay Pinups: first published 1952; number 4 is dated 1953; editor: Fred Rutledge Sammis; published by Bartholomew House, Inc.

Photo-Play Review: March 16, 1915–November 13, 1915; published out of Philadelphia

Photoplay Vogue: first published August 26, 1915; biweekly; also known as *Photo Play Topics*; published out of Buffalo, New York

Photoplay Weekly Mirror: September 1916–March 19, 1917; promoted as "an illustrated magazine"; published by Photoplay Mirror Publishing Corp. out of New York

Photo-Play World: September 1917–May 1920; no issues published for January–June and November 1918 and March–April 1919; published out of Philadelphia

Photoplayers Weekly: 1914–1917; published by Western Film Publishing Co., out of Los Angeles

Photostar: volume 1, number 2 is dated March 1971; bimonthly; editor: Lars Beck; published out of New York

Pic: Hollywood-Sport-Broadway: May 1937–December 1948; weekly; editors include A. Laurance Holmes; promoted to "Cover the Entire Field of Entertainment"; published by Street and Smith Publications, Inc.

Pictorial Movie Fun: first published September 1940; extant as of 1942; published by Getwood Publications

Picture Parade: first published January 1934; published ten times a year and available only by subscription

Picture Play: first published as *Picture-Play Weekly*, April 10, 1915; as of December 1915, became a semi-monthly titled *Picture-Play Magazine*; as of March 10, 1916, began monthly publication; title changed to *Picture Play*, May 1927; ceased publication in 1941 when merged with *Charm* magazine

Picture-Wise: no copies known to exist in public institutions; an Internet source lists number 5 with a date of 1946

Pictures, see *Movie Magazine*

Popular Movie: volume 1, number 11 is dated March 1966; published by Flightplan, Inc.

Popular Screen: first published September 1934

Popular Screen: first published October 1959

Preview: first published September 1976; named changed to *Rona Barrett's Preview*

Prevue: first published 1981 out of Reading, Pennsylvania

Prevue: founded 1973 as *Mediascene*, number 25 is dated May–June 1977; circa 1979 became *Mediascene Prevue* and later *Prevue*, volume 2, number 30 of which is dated December/March 1988; last issue seen is volume 3, number 2, dated August/October 1994 and devoted entirely to pin-ups; initially bimonthly but later appears to have been a quarterly publication; editor/publisher/designer: [James] Steranko; possibly same as previous publication

Questar: 1978–1981; published by W. G. Wilson/MW Communications

Real Screen Fun: August 1934–November 1942; bimonthly; editors include Franklyn Lippincott and George Shute; published by Tilsam Publishing Co.; no copies known to exist in public institutions

Reel Humor: August 1937–July 1939; bimonthly; editor: Frederick Gardener;

published by Periodical House out of Mount Morris, Illinois

Romances of Hollywood: circa 1934–circa 1936; name changed in last year to *Romances of Hollywood Movies*

Romantic Movie Stories: December 1933–February 1937; published by Graphic Arts Corp. (1933–1934) and then Fawcett; became *Movie Story Magazine*

Rona Barrett's Gossip: first published December 1972; title changed May 1980 to *Gossip*

Rona Barrett's Hollywood: first published November 1969

Rona Barrett's Preview, see *Preview*

Rona January's Gossip World: volume 1, number 2 is dated April 1977; published by EGO Enterprises of New York, Inc.

Saucy Movie Tales: December 1935–February 1938; published by Movie Digest, Inc.

SBI: Show Business Illustrated, see *Show Business Illustrated*

Screen: 1921–1922; advertised as "A Journal of Motion Pictures for Business, School and Church," and may not have been a fan magazine

Screen: circa 1953–circa 1956; unable to verify possible merger with *Hollywood Stars* and *Movie Pix* as of December 1956

Screen Album: first published May 1931; extant as of March 1975; appears to be annual or semi-annual as of 1938; became *Screen and TV Album* and extant under that title as of October 1978; published by Dell

Screen and Radio Weekly: circa 1936–circa 1948; weekly; published by Detroit Free Press Weekly

Screen and TV Album, see *Screen Album*

Screen Annual: 1954 issue is described as "Summer Fun Issue"; published by Skye Publishing Co., Inc., out of New York

Screen Book Magazine: 1928–1940; volume 8, number 5 is dated June 1932; by 1940, incorporated *Screen Play Magazine*; editors: Captain Roscoe Fawcett and later William Hartley; later became *Screen Life*; published by Fawcett

Screen Comedy: number 2 is dated October 1931

The September 1937 issue of *Screen Romances*.

Screen Fan: 1953–circa 1958; bimonthly; editor: Joan Curtis; published by Screen Teen Co. out of New York

Screen Greats: first published 1970; volume 1, number 8 is dated 1972, featuring Greta Garbo; published by Barven Publications out of New York

Screen Guide: May 1936–circa 1951; became *Screen and Television Guide* as of 1948; absorbed by *Motion Picture*; first editor: Ernest V. Heyn; initially published by Regal Press, Inc., and then Hillman Periodicals, Inc., out of Dunellen, New Jersey

Screen Hits Annual: number 8 is dated 1953, suggesting 1946 as first year of publication; editor: Evelyn Van Horne; published by Dell

Screen Humor: first published January 1934

Screen Legends: first published May 1965, with first issue featuring James Dean and Carroll Baker; bimonthly; published by Associated Professional Service, Inc.

Screen Life: generally assumed to have been first published 1928, but volume 23, number 5 is dated December 1940; extant as of November 1941; combined with *Screen Play* and *Screen Book Magazine*; editors include William Hartley and Llewellyn Miller; published by Fawcett

Screen Life: circa 1953–circa 1958; bimonthly; first published by 20th Century Books, Inc., and later by Skye Publishing, Inc.; edited by Joan Curtis except for a brief period when Patricia Grubbs is identified as editor; merged with *Movie Fan* as of January 1954

Screen Mirror: circa 1930–circa 1931; editor: Albert Margolies; published out of Los Angeles

Screen Mirror: first published September 1970; extant as of 1972; published by Captain Publications out of New York

Screen Play: circa 1934–circa 1937; published by Fawcett

Screen Play Secrets, see *So This Is Paris and Hollywood*

Screen Romances: first published June 1929; extant as of March 1947; editors include May Ninomíya and Evelyn Van Horne; published by Dell

Screen Romances Album: first published February 1931

Screen Secrets, see *So This Is Paris and Hollywood*

Screen Secrets: first published October 1969 (only issue seen); possibly only one other issue in 1970; editor: Amanda Murah; published by Magazine Management Co. out of New York

Screen Snapshots: circa 1926; published out of New York and maintained Hollywood office; no copies known to exist in public institutions

Screen Star Stories: September 1931–1937; published by Motion Picture Publications, Inc.; merged with *Movie Classic* October 1934

Screen Stars: 1944–circa February 1978; combined with *TV and Record Stars* 1959; published by Interstate Publishing Corp., out of Dunellen, New Jersey, and later Margood Publishing Corp., Official Magazine Corp., and Magazine Management Co., Inc.

Screen Stars Yearbook: first published 1974

Screen Stories: first published May 1929; monthly except January each year through 1978 and then bimonthly; published by Dell and later Ideal; May 1948–1975 available on microfilm

Screen Stories Annual: first published circa 1946; number 14, believed to be last, is dated 1960; published by Dell

Screen Weekly: July 1932–September 1932; a five-cent magazine;

Screen World and TV: volume 8, number 4 is dated July 1960; bimonthly; published by Official Magazine Corp. out of New York

Screenland: A Weekly Magazine for Photoplay Patrons: January 24, 1916–January 1, 1917?; editor: A. M. Gunst; published out of Richmond, Virginia

Screenland: May 11, 1921–June 7, 1927; published out of Seattle

Screenland: 1920–August 1952; became *Screenland plus TV-Land*, September 1952; ceased publication in June 1971, when it merged with *Silver Screen*; published initially out of Bethlehem, Pennsylvania; later published by Liberty Magazines, J. Fred Henry Publications, Popular Library, Inc., Affiliated Magazines, and Macfadden-Bartell Corp.; April 1926–July 1952 available on microfilm

Screenland from Hollywood: ceased publication between May and November 1923

Shadoplay [sic]: first published March 1933; extant as of December 1935; merged with *Movie Mirror*

Shadowland: 1919–1923; published by Brewster Publications out of Brooklyn, New York

Sheilah Graham's Family Album: number 9 is dated February–April 1954; number 12 is dated 1963; believed to be a quarterly publication at its beginning

Sheilah Graham's Hollywood Yearbook, see *Hollywood Yearbook*

Show: October 1961–May 1965; published until late 1964 by Huntington Hartford

Show: January 1970–December 1977; a resurrection by Huntington Hartford of the earlier magazine of the same name

Show Business Illustrated: September 5, 1961–November 1, 1961; renamed *SBI: Show Business Illustrated*, November 14, 1961–April 1962; combined with *Show*

Silver Screen: first published October 10, 1930; extant as of November 1976; merged with *Screenland plus TV-Land* under publisher Globe Communications Corp. in 1971

Silver Screen Album: 1957–1962; published by Popular Library, Inc.

Silver Screen Annual: 1950s and 1960s; published by Popular Library, Inc.

Silver Screen['s] Teen Album: 1959–1962; published by Popular Library, Inc.

So This Is Paris and Hollywood: first published March 1925 as *So This Is Paris*; became *So This Is Paris and Hollywood* October 1925; became *Paris and Hollywood* January 1927; became *Paris and Hollywood Screen Secrets* sometime in 1927; became *Screen Secrets* in April 1928 and *Screen Play Secrets* in April 1930; changed name to *Screen Play* circa late 1930/early 1931; merged with *Screen Book Magazine*; editors: Captain Roscoe Fawcett (first) and later Llewellyn Miller; published by Fawcett

Stage: 1910–1941; subtitled "The Magazine of After-Dark Entertainment" and includes much film coverage

Stage and Screen: December 1925–December 1926; published out of New York and also maintained Hollywood office

Stage and Screen Stories: published by Movie Digest, Inc., at least in 1936

Star: first published November 1957 (only issue seen); subtitled "The Magazine of Hollywood Brightest Stars," all of whom in the first issue are male; quarterly; published by Digest Publications, Inc., out of New York; not to confused with the Samuel Bronston Productions house organ of the same name

Star Album: first published September 1960; extant as of 1961; editor: Muriel Babcock; consists of nothing but full-page photographs of the stars; published by Ideal

Star Dust: circa 1928; subtitled "For Movie Fans by the Fans Themselves"; official organ of the Moving Picture Club of America, Inc., published out of Boston

Star Land: no information available

Stardom: February 1942–August 1944; editor: Carl A. Schroeder; published by Triangle Publications, Inc., out of Philadelphia

The October 1928 issue of *Star Dust*.

Stardom: volume 1, number 4 is dated September 1959; extant as of February 1961; bimonthly; editor: Bessie Little; published by Little Brand Publications, later the Forty Publishing Corp., out of New York

Starlog: first published 1976; devoted to the science fiction genre; published by Starlog Group and later Creative Group out of New York

Super Star Heroes: number 11 is dated January 1980; bimonthly; editor: Gene Wright; published by Ideal

Superstar Special: number 3 is dated 1976; published by Sterling/Macfadden Partnership

3D Movie Magazine: first published September 1953; editor: Abner J. Sundell; published by 3-D Magazines, Inc.; many other 3-D magazines were first published this same year, including *3-D Action*, *3-D Comics*, *3-D Tales of the West*, and *3-D Sheena, Jungle Queen*

Toni Holt's Movie Life, see *Movie Life*

Top Stars: first published September 1959

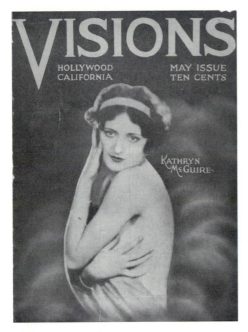

The May 1924 issue of *Visions*.

True Movie: volume 1, number 2 is dated November 1962; extant as of 1963; published by Sterling Group, Inc., out of New York

True Movie and Television: first published August 1950; possibly ceased publication March 1951; bimonthly; published by Toby Press, Inc., out of New York

TV and Movie Screen: 1953–1999; became *TVMS Tiger Beat*; bimonthly; editors include Richard Heller, Beryl Basher, Joan Goldstein, and Suzanne Munshower; published by Sterling Group, Inc., out of New York

TV and Screen Life: first published 1957; extant as of October 1960; bimonthly; published by Little Brand Publications, Inc., out of New York

TV and Screenworld: first published 1966; extant as of September 1971; published by Stanley Publications, Inc., out of New York

TV-Film Stars: first published 1960; bimonthly; editor: Bessie Little; published by Besscal Publications, Inc., out of New York

TV, Movie and Record Stars, see *Movies Illustrated*

TV Movie Parade: first published August 1969; extant in 1970; volume 10, number 12 is dated September 1970; published by the Woman Golfer Publishing Corp. and then Slim Publications out of New York

TV Movie Scene: first published October 1970; editor: Alice Simms; published by Barven Publications out of New York

TV Movie Scene: first published 1974; number 5 is dated 1976; semi-annual; editors: Fran Levine and later Ronnie Eisinger Blum; published by Ideal; connection to the earlier publication of the same name is unknown

TV Picture Life: first published 1956; extant as of March 1972; published by Publication House, Inc., and then Star Guidance, Inc.

TV Screen: November 1947–August 1951; formerly *Radio and TV Best*; published by Radio Best, Inc., out of New York

TV Screen Parade: first published April 1960; bimonthly; editor: Bessie Little; published by Arizill Realty and Publishing Co., out of New York

Visions: first published March 1924; "Published in the Interest of the Industry and Community and Its Policy is Constructive—Not Destructive"; published out of Hollywood

Weekly Film Review: A Magazine of Critical Comment: March 6, 1920–March 18, 1930; published out of Atlanta, Georgia

Weekly Movie Record: first published 1915; volume 1, number 3 is dated March 8, 1915

Who's Who in Hollywood: first published 1941; number 22 is dated 1967; consists of one-paragraph biographies broken down by category; published by Dell

Mabel Norman takes
time out to read the
British fan magazine
Picture Show.

SELECTED U.K. FAN MAGAZINES

Boys Cinema: 1919–1940; merged with *Screen Stories* in 1938
Cinema Chat: 1919–1920
Cinema World Illustrated: 1927–1929
Film Flashes: 1915–1916
Film Pictorial: 1932–1939
Film Star Weekly: 1932–1935; merged with *Picture Show*
Film Weekly: 1928–1939; merged with *The Picturegoer*
Girls Cinema: 1920–1932; merged with *Film Star Weekly*
Illustrated Films Monthly: 1913–1914, when name changed to *Picture Stories Monthly*
Photoplay: 1952–1981, when name changed to *Photoplay: Movies and Video*
The Picture News, Screen, Stage and Variety: 1915–1917; from 1915–1916 known as *The Picture Palace News*
Picture Parade: 1949–1952
Picture Show: 1919–1960; also incorporated *Film Periodical* and *T.V. Mirror*
Picture Stories Monthly: 1914–1915; previously known as *Illustrated Films Monthly*
The Picturegoer: 1911–1960; 1911–1920 known as *Pictures and the Picturegoer*; 1920–1921 as *Pictures for the Picturegoer*; 1921–1931 as *Picturegoer Monthly*
Screen Pictorial: 1935–1939; from 1931–1934 known as *The New Royal Magazine*
Screen Stories: 1930–1938; merged with *Boys Cinema*
Star Souvenir: first published 1946
Stars and Films: first published 1937

FAN CLUB JOURNALS

Because these publications are generally obscure and difficult to document, no effort has been made to provide years of publication for many of the journals.

All about Barbra (Barbra Streisand)
Bantha Tracks (Star Wars)
Barbra (Barbra Streisand), 1979–1983
Beulah Bondi Bulletin, 1940
The Call Board (Agnes Moorehead)
Chad's Quarterly (Chad Everett)
Deanna's Diary (Deanna Durbin)
Dove Tails (Billie Dove), 1931
E.T. Communicator
Elvis Monthly (Elvis Presley)
Elvisly Yours Magazine (Elvis Presley)
Enterprise (Star Trek)
Enterprise Incident (Star Trek)
Exclusively Elvis (Elvis Presley)
Film (John Stuart)
The Finishing Touch (Laurel and Hardy), first published 1977
The Freedonia Gazette (Marx Brothers), first published 1979
The Golden Comet (Jeanette MacDonald)
Graceland News (Elvis Presley), first published 1982
Hitchcock Annual, academic journal, first published in the U.K. in 1992
House of Hammer (Hammer Films); also known as *House of Horror* and *Halls of Horror*
Intimate Carolyn Jones, first published 1959
Jolie (Al Jolson)
The Jolson Journal (Al Jolson)
Life and Films of Michelle Pfeiffer (U.K. publication)
Limelight on Liza (Liza Minnelli), 1977–1980
Mac/Eddy Today (Jeanette MacDonald and Nelson Eddy)
The Max Steiner Journal, first published 1977
The Max Steiner Music Society Newsletter
Mel Gibson Fan Club Magazine, first published 1999
Monkees Monthly
Moorehead Memos (Agnes Moorehead)
Munsters: The Official Magazine, 1965

The Muppet Magazine, first published 1983
On the Mark (Mark Hamill), first published 1982
Our Club Journal (Esther Williams)
Pratfall (Laurel and Hardy), first published 1969
Rocky Horror Picture Show Official Magazine, 1979
The Shooting Star (Nelson Eddy)
Star Trek Communicator
Star Trek Official Poster Monthly
Star Trek: The Magazine
Star Wars Insider
Star Wars Official Poster Monthly
Steve Reeves International Society Newsletter
Sword (Errol Flynn), first published 1978
Taylor Topics (Elizabeth Taylor)
The Thespian (Cameron Mitchell), first published 1954
Trail Beyond (John Wayne), first published 1999
The Transylvanian (*The Rocky Horror Picture Show*)
2010: The Official Movie Magazine, 1984
Twilight Zone Magazine, first published 1980
Versatility (Agnes Moorehead)
The Westerner (Bill Elliott), first published 1949
Ye Club Dope Sheet (William Collier Jr.)

NOTES

INTRODUCTION

1. Carl F. Cotter, "The Forty Hacks of the Fan Mags," p. 18.
2. Murphy McHenry, "Dishing That Fan Mag Guff," p. 51.
3. Bob Thomas, Associated Press syndicated column, May 9, 1953.
4. Murphy McHenry, "Dishing That Fan Mag Guff," p. 51.
5. Gordon Kahn, "The Gospel According to Hollywood," p. 98.
6. Ibid., p. 99.
7. Alfred Cheney Johnson, who died on April 17, 1971, at the age of eighty-seven, was the official photographer for Florenz Ziegfeld from 1917 to 1931.
8. Harry Carr, "Marooned in London."
9. Ernest A. Dench, *Advertising by Motion Pictures*, pp. 153–154.
10. This delightful rhyme appeared in Cal York's column in October 1929, p. 46. Along with Joan Crawford, Clara Bow was a star whose entire career belonged to the fan magazines, from her discovery in a 1921 "Fame and Fortune" contest in *Motion Picture Magazine* to her autobiographical "My Life Story," as told to Adela Rogers St. Johns in *Photoplay*, February–April 1928, and beyond.
11. Examples from Carl F. Cotter, "The Forty Hacks of the Fan Mags," p. 21.
12. Ezra Goodman was a columnist with the *Los Angeles Daily News* from 1949 to 1952, a publicist at Warner Bros., and Hollywood bureau chief for *Time* magazine; he wrote at least one fan magazine article, on Jane Powell, in *Photoplay* (July 1950) as well as a biography of Humphrey Bogart, *Bogey: The Good-Bad Guy* (Lyle Stuart, 1965). Writing in *Motion Picture Herald* (February 25, 1961), Arthur L. Mayer praised Goodman's "rare talent for interpretation."
13. "Vultures of Hollywood," p. 345.

CHAPTER 1

1. "Musings of a Photoplay Philosopher," *The Motion Picture Story Magazine*, May 1911, p. 145.
2. From November 1925 through January 1927, Blackton returned to magazine publishing as editor of *The Motion Picture Director*, a mix of trade publication and fan magazine, published by the Motion Picture Directors Association, which began life in June 1924 as *The Director*.
3. Interview with Anthony Slide, Spring 1973.
4. *Motion Picture Magazine*, April 1919, p. 96.
5. The Corliss Palmer story has all the makings of a fan magazine piece. Born in a cabin on a Georgia plantation, she had become the wife of a powerful publishing executive. After his bankruptcy, she tried for a movie comeback in April 1931, signing with Universal for a series of short subjects to be directed by Harry Edwards. A month earlier, on March 19, Palmer and Brewster had undergone a second wedding ceremony in Los Angeles; presumably there was a question as to the legality of their original marriage in Ensenada. The couple became estranged in October 1931 and was divorced on December 6, 1933, with Palmer charging cruelty. In September 1932, Mrs. Estelle Cohen had filed a $100,000 suit against her, claiming alienation of the affections of her husband, tennis player Albert J. Cohen. Palmer became an alcoholic, and on January 31, 1933, she was taken

from the Bay City Hotel, San Francisco, where she had registered as Edith Mason of Pasadena, to the San Francisco Detention Hospital. She was able to sell her life story to the *Los Angeles Examiner*, which published it from October through December 1933, but by October 1935, Palmer was working as a five dollar a day model in a Tucson, Arizona, department store. Corliss Palmer died at the state mental institution in Camarillo, California, on August 27, 1952. Her profession was listed as "seamstress."

6. Interview with Anthony Slide, Spring 1973.

7. *The Motion Picture Story Magazine*, February 1911, p. 5.

8. Gordon Kahn, "The Gospel According to Hollywood," p. 98.

9. *The Motion Picture Story Magazine*, December 1919, p. 29.

10. All the winners with number of votes cast are reported in the November 1915 issue, pp. 123–125. How odd to categorize the great dramatic actress Norma Talmadge as a character woman!

11. *The Motion Picture Story Magazine*, October 1917, p. 112.

12. *The Motion Picture Story Magazine*, November 1917, p. 81.

13. It was actually the February issue that began volume 15.

14. W. R. Wilkerson, "TradeViews," p. 5.

CHAPTER 2

1. Carl F. Cotter, "The Forty Hacks of the Fan Mags," p. 20. I have documented at least thirty-one articles by Lee—in *Movie Classic* from 1932 to 1936, *Screen Book* from 1933 to 1938, *Movie Mirror* in 1934, *Modern Screen* from 1934 to 1939, *Motion Picture Magazine* in 1936, *Silver Screen* in 1941, and *Movieland* from 1944 to 1945.

2. Clifton Fadiman, "The Narcissi," p. 53.

3. Interview with Anthony Slide, Spring 1973.

4. Ibid. The competition was announced in the March 28, 1925, issue of *Movie Weekly*, pp. 5, 31. The result was published in the September 19, 1925, issue, pp. 16–17, 47. The winner was Mrs. Louis M. Antisdale of Rochester, New York, who received $1000. Suspiciously, she was unable, according to *Movie Weekly*, to provide a photograph of herself because she was "Not well enough to have one taken." In his autobiography, *Dancing in the Dark*, p. 176, publicist Howard Dietz recounted a different story in regard to Joan Crawford's name, but I believe Adele Whitely Fletcher's account to be correct.

5. It includes *Ainslee's*, *All Story Weekly*, *The American Weekly*, *Cosmopolitan*, *Fiction-Lovers Magazine*, *Filmplay*, *Ladies Home Journal*, *Metropolitan*, *Modern Marriage*, *The New Movie Magazine*, *Photoplay*, *Picture Play*, *Popular Photography*, *Romance*, *Saucy Stories*, *Screen Book*, *Screenland*, *Silver Screen*, *Smith's Magazine*, *Television Life*, *True Detective Magazine*, *True Experiences*, *True Romances*, *The Woman's Magazine*, *Young's Magazine*, and *Your Charm*.

6. "They Won Success with Unique Records," p. 28.

7. Carl F. Cotter, "The Forty Hacks of the Fan Mags," p. 21.

8. Although Louella Parsons claimed that it was she who broke the story.

9. Carol Taylor, "Stars in Her Eyes, Pen in Her Hand," p. 31.

10. Samuel Richard Mook, "Introducing an All-Star Cast," February 1930, p. 92.

11. Quoted in Wally [sic], "What's Hollywood without Myrtle," *Fanland*, July 1923.

12. Charles E. L. Wingate, Sunday editor, *The Boston Post*, undated letter in the Myrtle Gebhart Collection in the Margaret Herrick Library of the Academy of Motion Picture Arts and Sciences, Beverly Hills, California.

13. "The Chocolate Comedy," p. 17.

14. Gebhart and Hall were not the only fan magazine writers to use pseudonyms. Lillian May also wrote as Lillian Montanye; Roberta Courtlandt as Pearl Gaddis; and Edwin M. La Roche as Peter Wade. What is remarkable is that none of these writers did, or for that matter could, recycle articles under different names.

15. Letter to D. W. Griffith, dated December 1918, in the D. W. Griffith Collection at the Museum of Modern Art, New York.

16. Associated Press story dated February 12, 1958.

17. Telephone conversation with William Shallert, February 17, 2008.

18. Conversation with Kevin Thomas, December 2007.

19. *Photoplay* editorial, May 1925.

20. Anne Morey, "So Real as to Seem Like Life Itself," in Jennifer Bean and Diane Negra, *A Feminist Reader in Early Cinema*, p. 336.

21. John Paris Springer, *Hollywood Fictions: The Dream Factory in American Popular Culture*, p. 120.

22. Herbert Howe, "Our Adela," p. 124.

CHAPTER 3

1. Richard Griffith, *The Talkies: Articles and Illustrations from Photoplay Magazine, 1928–1940*, p. xv. This is a somewhat curious volume in that the majority of the introductory pages are devoted to the lauding of James R. Quirk and the denigration of *Photoplay* after his demise, yet the majority of the pieces in the anthology are taken from the post-Quirk era.

2. *Photoplay*, November 1925, p. 27.

3. Robert Grau, *The Theatre of Science*, p. 256.

4. *Photoplay*, April 1922, p. 53.

5. Quoted in Richard Griffith, *The Talkies*, p. vii.

6. An April 1919 editorial on p. 27 consists of the verse, "I Am the Universal Language," which has often been reprinted and appears to have been authored by Julian Johnson: "I am the Universal Language. / I call every man in the world Brother, and he calls me Friend. / I have unlocked the riddle of Babel after fifty centuries of misunderstanding. / I am the Voice of Home to Democracy's lonely sentinels on Liberty's frontier. / I am a chorus of Eagle and Lion and Cock, crying "Shame!" to the Bolshevik Bear. / I am the rising murmur of repentance on lips in the Kingdom of Sin. / I am California, springing a funny story on Constantinople. / I am a Chinese poet of a thousand years ago, singing gently in Chicago. / I am a salesman purveying harvesters, tractors, overalls, oil stoves and hog products to the Siberians. / I am a vertical and eternal Peace Table, and my Conference has five hundred million delegates. / I am a tenement doctor, telling mothers of twenty races how to wash their babies' milk-bottles. / I am the rusty tongue of Rameses, thrilling Broadway with the sunbright story of my lotus-columned temple on the Nile. / I am the voice of Christ in the country of Confucius. / I am the remembrance of Old Age. / I am the chatter of children with blue eyes or almond eyes. / I am the shy confession of Miss and Ma'amselle and Senorita. / I am a Caspian fisherman, visiting a coffee planter in Santos. / I am the Apostle of Kindness, the Orator of Tolerance, the Minstrel of Love. / I am the greatest Story-Teller of the Ages. / I am the Universal Language. / I am the Motion Picture."

7. Louise Brooks, *Lulu in Hollywood*, pp. 85–92.

8. *Photoplay*, March 1926, pp. 63, 129–130.

9. Quirk had written in October 1926 in an editorial on Valentino's death that the actor was "a great heart and a great friend." It was Quirk, supposedly, who organized Valentino's initial funeral at Campbell's Funeral Home in New York, deciding to substitute a wax dummy for the actor in order to avoid wear and tear on Valentino's body by his fans.

10. Lawrence J. Quirk, "Quirk of *Photoplay*," p. 105.

11. For more information, see *Photoplay*, December 1921, pp. 56, 113. Later winners were *Tol'able David* (1921), *Robin Hood* (1922), *The Covered Wagon* (1923), *Abraham Lincoln* (1924), *The Big Parade* (1925), *Beau Geste* (1926), *7th Heaven* (1927), *Four Sons* (1928), *Disraeli* (1929), *All Quiet on the Western Front* (1930), *Cimarron* (1931), *Smilin' Through* (1932), *Little Women* (1933), *The Barretts of Wimpole Street* (1934), *Naughty Marietta* (1935), *San Francisco* (1936), *Captains Courageous* (1937), and *Sweethearts* (1938).

12. In the January and April 1921 issues.

13. All quotes here and later from Ruth Waterbury are taken from an interview with Anthony Slide, April 13, 1972.

14. Lawrence J. Quirk, "Quirk of *Photoplay*," p. 106.

15. Kathryn Dougherty, "As I Knew Him," p. 27.

16. Ray Long began his career as a reporter on the *Indianapolis Star* and became police reporter on the *Cincinnati Post*, rising to managing editor. He left *Cosmopolitan* in 1931 and with Harrison Smith formed a book publishing concern that went bankrupt circa 1933. Long died of a self-inflicted gunshot wound in Beverly Hills, California, on July 9, 1935, at which time he was working for *Liberty*.

17. Interview with Adele Whitely Fletcher, Spring 1973.

18. *Shadoplay*, March 1934, p. 23.

19. I believe Ruth Waterbury to have been an honest and sincere individual, whose work for *Photoplay* was very much in the tradition of James R. Quirk. It is grossly unfair that Richard Griffith chose to denigrate her so in his introduction to *The Talkies*, pp. xxi–xxii. It is quite ridiculous to criticize her for the advertising that appears in the magazine during her period as editor, advertising that, quite frankly, is similar if not the same as that appearing in *Photoplay* during the Quirk era. Griffith also quoted Norbert Lusk from an unidentified source (actually *New Movies*), claiming that "The lady editors portrayed themselves as glamour-girl intimates and confidants of the stars, but this harmless deception was exposed by the photographs they published on the editorial page." In reality, Ruth Waterbury was relatively attractive in contemporary photographs, certainly far more so than Kathryn Dougherty.

20. Lori Landay, *Madcaps, Screwballs, and Con Women: The Female Trickster in American Culture*, pp. 118–119.

21. Interview with Adele Whitely Fletcher, Spring 1973.

22. For more information, see "Gallup Poll Reveals Fans of All Types Unanimous for 'Way,'" *The Hollywood Reporter*, February 17, 1945, p. 12.

23. Interview with Adele Whitely Fletcher, Spring 1973.

24. Quotes from Katherine Lowrie, "*Photoplay* Suspends Publication," p. 12.

25. Edward Wagenknecht published two annual reviews of films of the year in the December 1918 and November 1919 issues and a piece on "The Photoplay in American Life" in November 1918.

CHAPTER 4

1. Mary Carlisle in a telephone conversation with Anthony Slide, January 8, 2006; Marsha Hunt in a telephone conversation with Anthony Slide, April 30, 2008; Barbara Hale in a telephone conversation with Anthony Slide, April 2, 2008.

2. In a letter to Anthony Slide, January 6, 2006.

3. Theodore Peterson, *Magazines in the Twentieth Century*, p. 282.

4. A difficulty that one encounters in trying to determine if there is overemphasis by one fan magazine writer on the work of a specific player is that some of the writers were so prolific. Frederick James Smith may have contributed more than a usual number of pieces on Richard Barthelmess, but not as many as Gladys Hall, who wrote at least five between 1921 and 1934. Ms. Hall was unstoppable, writing, for example, four pieces on Nils Asther between 1930 and 1932, four pieces on Evelyn Brent between 1929 and 1931, and three each on Bebe Daniels between 1929 and 1930 and Dolores Del Rio between 1930 and 1932.

5. P. A. Parsons, "Doping It Out for the Papers," p. 327.

6. William J. Mann, *William Haines: The Life and Times of Hollywood's First Openly Gay Star*.

7. While Albert does not appear to have written articles specifically on Haines, she did reference him in the March 1932 episode of her series, as well as in other general pieces.

8. *Picture-Play*, January 1920, pp. 32–33.

9. André Soares, *Beyond Paradise: The Life of Ramon Novarro*, p. 57.

10. *Photoplay*, "Our Herb," p. 124.

11. Larry McMurtry, "Writers and the Hollywood of Romance," p. 6.

12. "The Opinion Leaders," p. 100.

13. Bob Thomas, *Joan Crawford*, p. 61.

14. Jane Ardmore was also a frequent contributor to fan magazines from the 1940s onward. She is, however, better known as coauthor of several show business autobiographies: Eddie Cantor's *Take My Life* (Doubleday, 1957), Edith Head's *The Dress Doctor* (Little, Brown, 1959), Mae Murray's *The Self-Enchanted* (McGraw-Hill, 1959), and the above-mentioned *Portrait of Joan* (Doubleday, 1962). She also wrote a 1956 biography of Rock Hudson, published by Star Stories, which is nothing more than a monograph posing as a fan magazine, and three novels: *Women, Inc.* (Henry Holt, 1946), *Julie* (McGraw-Hill, 1952), and *To Love Is to Listen* (Norton, 1967). Ardmore came to Los Angeles in the 1940s with her husband, Ted Morris (she also wrote as Ruth Morris), who was a studio advance exploitation man. He died in 1946, and five years later she married public relations executive Albert Ardmore. Her husband died in 1993, and Jane Ardmore died in Los Angeles on August 16, 2000, at the age of eighty-eight. Her papers are at the Margaret Herrick Library of the Academy of Motion Picture Arts and Sciences, Beverly Hills, California.

15. Norbert Lusk, "I Love Actresses," April–May 1947, p. 15.

16. Samuel Richard Mook, "Introducing an All-Star Cast," February 1930, p. 61.

17. Carl F. Cotter, "The Forty Hacks of the Fan Mags," p. 20.

18. Synopsis for proposed autobiography, *Once upon a Time in Hollywood*, Gladys Hall Collection in Margaret Herrick Library of Academy of Motion Picture Arts and Sciences, Beverly Hills, California.

19. Interview with Anthony Slide, April 20, 2006.

20. Carl F. Cotter, "The Forty Hacks of the Fan Mags," p. 18.

21. Information taken from the Constance Palmer Collection in the Cinema-TV Library of the University of Southern California, Los Angeles.

22. Carl F. Cotter, "The Forty Hacks of the Fan Mags," p. 18.

23. "The Opinion Leaders," p. 100.

24. Norbert Lusk, "I Love Actresses!," April–May 1947, pp. 19, 31.

25. Carl F. Cotter, "The Forty Hacks of the Fan Mags," p. 18.

26. Interview with Anthony Slide, February 29, 2008.

27. *Motion Picture Herald*, November 10, 1934, p. 15.

28. Carl F. Cotter, "The Forty Hacks of the Fan Mags," p. 20. The article appeared in the January 1939 issue of *Photoplay* and is discussed in chapter 8. There is no evidence that the piece damaged Kirtley Baskette's career.

29. Letter from John McGrail, June 29, 1937, unindexed microfilm, Production Code Administration files, Margaret Herrick Library of the Academy of Motion Picture Arts and Sciences, Beverly Hills, California.

30. Report dated March 23, 1938, unindexed microfilm, Production Code Administration files, Margaret Herrick Library of the Academy of Motion Picture Arts and Sciences, Beverly Hills, California.

31. Clifton Fadiman, "The Narcissi," p. 52.

32. *Photoplay*, February 1929, p. 27.

CHAPTER 5

1. This chapter is adapted in part from my book *They Also Wrote for the Fan Magazines: Film Articles by Literary Giants from e. e. cummings to Eleanor Roosevelt, 1920–1939*. That volume examines in considerable detail the relationship of the motion picture to the various individuals included therein. Such information is not repeated here because it is not particularly relevant to the subject at hand. Most

of the articles discussed are reprinted in their entirety in that volume. Full citations for the major articles discussed in this chapter are given below in the order in which they appear:

Katherine Anne Porter, "The Real Ray," *Motion Picture*, October 1920, pp. 36–37, 102.

Mary Roberts Rinehart, "The New Cinema Year," *Motion Picture*, February 1921, p. 21.

Mary Roberts Rinehart, "Faces and Brains," *Photoplay*, February 1922, pp. 47–48, 107.

Booth Tarkington, "What Tom's Pal Thinks of Him," *Photoplay*, August 1924, p. 47.

H. L. Mencken, "The Low-Down on Hollywood," *Photoplay*, April 1927, pp. 36–37, 118–120.

George Jean Nathan, "Celluloid Sirens," *The New Movie Magazine*, June 1932, pp. 20–21, 82.

Elinor Glynn, "In Filmdom's Boudoir," *Photoplay*, March 1921, pp. 28–30.

Elinor Glynn, "Sex and the Photoplay," *Motion Picture*, June 1921, p. 21.

Somerset Maugham, "The Author and the Cinema," *Motion Picture*, April 1921, p. 21.

Avery Hopwood, "The Future of Screen Comedy," *Motion Picture*, October 1921, p. 21.

Theodore Dreiser, "Hollywood: Its Morals and Manners," Part I, "The Struggle on the Threshold of Motion Pictures," *Shadowland*, November 1921, pp. 37, 62–63; Part II, "The Commonplace Tale with a Thousand Endings," ibid., December 1921, pp. 51, 61; Part III, "The Beginner's Thousand-to-One Chance," ibid., January 1922, pp. 43, 67.

Theodore Dreiser, "The Best Motion Picture Interview Ever Written," *Photoplay*, August 1928, pp. 32–33, 35, 124–125, 127, 129.

Louis Goulding, "The True Paul Muni," *Photoplay*, June 1936, pp. 29, 104–105.

Louis Goulding, "This Was My Hollywood," *Cinema Arts*, September 1937, pp. 27, 100.

Archibald MacLeish, "MacLeish on Spain," *Cinema Arts*, September 1937, pp. 59, 104.

e. e. cummings, "Miracles and Dreams," *Cinema*, June 1930, pp. 14, 55.

Vachel Lindsay, "To Mary Pickford (On Learning She Was Leaving the Moving-Pictures for the Stage)," *Photoplay*, December 1914, p. 102.

James M. Cain, "Lana," *Photoplay*, February 1946, pp. 52–54, 109.

CHAPTER 6

1. For more information on Grosset & Dunlap, see Emil Petaja, *Photoplay Edition* and Rick Miller, *Photoplay Editions: A Collector's Guide*.

2. The quotations from *Tide*, September 24, 1949, and January 28, 1949, are reprinted in Theodore Peterson, *Magazines in the Twentieth Century*, p. 39.

3. Charles Fulton Oursler, *Behold This Dreamer!*, p. 176.

4. Heather Addison, *Hollywood and the Rise of Physical Culture*, p. 160.

5. *Photoplay*, July 1926, p. 31.

6. Ruth Waterbury interview with Anthony Slide, April 13, 1972.

7. David Ragan to Anthony Slide, April 11, 2008.

8. Ruth Waterbury interview with Anthony Slide, April 13, 1972.

9. James L. C. Ford, *Magazines for Millions: The Story of Specialized Publications*, p. 252.

10. Gary Alan Fine, "Captain Billy's Whiz Bang," in David E. E. Stone, *American Humor Magazines and Comic Periodicals*, p. 40.

11. "Fawcett Publications," Wikipedia, the free encyclopedia, p. 7.

12. Carl F. Cotter, "The Forty Hacks of the Fan Mags," p. 19.

13. All recounted in Sheila Weller, *Dancing at Ciro's: A Family's Love, Loss, and Scandal on the Sunset Strip*.

14. John Tebbel, *A History of Book Publishing in the United States*, pp. 74–75.

15. James L. C. Ford, *Magazines for Millions: The Story of Specialized Publications*, p. 246.
16. Carl F. Cotter, "The Forty Hacks of the Fan Mags," pp. 19–20.
17. Ezra Goodman, *The Fifty-Year Decline and Fall of Hollywood*, pp. 73–74.
18. Sheila Weller, *Dancing at Ciro's*, p. 282.
19. Ruth Waterbury interview with Anthony Slide, April 13, 1972.
20. Carl F. Cotter, "The Forty Hacks of the Fan Mags," p. 19.
21. "Vultures of Hollywood," p. 345.

CHAPTER 7

1. "Fan Magazine Drop," p. 6.
2. Frank Pope, "TradeViews," p. 1.
3. Clifton Fadiman, "The Narcissi," p. 52.
4. For this information, I am indebted to the work of an incredible Shirley Temple fan, Genevieve C. Jones, who compiled *Shirley in the Magazines*, self-published in 1994.
5. "Thirty-Five Space Grabs in Fan Mags," p. 6.
6. Among such long-forgotten individuals were George Browning at the *Baltimore Post*, Dean Collins at the *Portland Telegram*, Waide Moore Condon at the *Salt Lake Tribune*, Harold Hefferman at the *Detroit News*, Landon Laird at the *Kansas City Star*, Clark Rodenbach at the *Chicago Daily News*, Vernon L. Smith at the *Palm Beach Times*, and Dorothy F. Whipple at the *Portland Evening News*.
7. P. A. Parsons, "Doping It Out for the Papers," p. 327.
8. *Moving Picture World*, March 26, 1927, pp. 309–310.
9. Margaret Farrand Thorp, *America at the Movies*, p. 89.
10. Ibid., p. 91.
11. Ibid., pp. 69–70.
12. Leo A. Handel, *Hollywood Looks at Its Audience: A Report of Film Audience Research*, p. 89.
13. "The Opinion Leaders," p. 100.
14. Lusk, Norbert, "I Love Actresses!," October 1947, pp. 17–18.
15. As reported in *The 1942 Film Daily Year Book*, p. 38.

16. Correspondence in the Myrtle Gebhart collection in the Hollywood Museum Collection, currently housed in the Margaret Herrick Library of the Academy of Motion Picture Arts and Sciences, Beverly Hills, California.
17. Humphrey Bogart, "Medal from Hitler: Here's How to Get One," pp. 28, 87.
18. *Directory of Newspapers and Periodicals*, N. W. Ayer and Sons, 1946, p. 1200.
19. Arthur Bell, "Oh, Those Movie Magazines!," p. 171.
20. Interview with Anthony Slide, April 13, 1972. For the record, Ruth Waterbury is exaggerating. In fact, there were feature articles on Victor Mature in *Modern Screen* (May 1942 and December 1947), *Movieland* (August 1946, February 1948, August 1948, and November 1953), *Screen Guide* (June 1948 and April 1947), and *Silver Screen* (March 1941, August 1942, November 1942, and May 1953). Also, Louella Parsons wrote a piece on Mature for the March 1946 issue of *Photoplay* (which published ten other articles on the actor from 1942 into the 1950s).

CHAPTER 8

1. Larry McMurtry, "Writers and the Hollywood of Romance," p. 6.
2. Louella Parsons, *The Gay Illiterate*, p. 40.
3. Ernest V. Heyn, *Photoplay*, January 1942, p. 21.
4. Hedda Hopper, "Resolutions the Stars Should Make," p. 20.
5. Katharine Lowrie, "Fan Magazine Reporters: Underrated as Journalists," p. 6.
6. Ibid.
7. Interview with Anthony Slide, April 13, 1972.
8. Robert Joseph, "Fidler, the Man Nobody Knows," p. 19.
9. As a result of a childhood accident, Harris had a wooden leg, which was the subject of much politically incorrect joking by the celebrities over whom she fawned. Noel Coward once announced that her favorite song was "Trees." She also hosted radio shows on Mutual and CBS and published

an autobiography, *Radie's World* (G. P. Putnam's Sons, 1975), in which she made no reference to her fan magazine career. She died on February 22, 2001, in Englewood, New Jersey, at the age of ninety-six.

10. Ezra Goodman, *The Fifty-Year Decline and Fall of Hollywood*, p. 95.

11. Ralph Daigh, editorial director of Fawcett Publications, Inc., to Hedda Hopper, June 29, 1961, Hedda Hopper Collection at Margaret Herrick Library of the Academy of Motion Picture Arts and Sciences, Beverly Hills, California, file folder no. 3875.

12. "Will Hays Tells *Movie Weekly* What He Is Doing and Will Do for the Movies," pp. 4–5.

13. "What's the Matter with the Movies?" p. 3.

14. "Moral House Cleaning in Hollywood," pp. 52–53.

15. The full citations for these articles are: Tom Ellis, "Just Let Me Work," *Photoplay*, March 1931, pp. 65, 127–128; Ruth Biery, "Plugging for Fatty," *Motion Picture*, March 1929, pp. 42, 90, 93; Jack Grant, "Doesn't Fatty Arbuckle Deserve a Break?," *Motion Picture*, September 1931, pp. 40–41, 90; "The Fans Want Fatty Arbuckle Back on the Screen," *Motion Picture*, November 1931, pp. 16, 95, 99, 102, 104–105; Edward J. Doherty, "Are You Going to Give Fatty a Break," *Modern Screen*, October 1932, pp. 28–29, 101–103; Edward R. Sammis, "The Tragic Comedian Passes," *Screen Book*, September 1933, pp. 27, 47, 55, 58.

16. The magazine is unpaginated.

17. "A Tribute from a Friend," p. 37.

18. J. Eugene Chrisman, "The Stars Vote on Prohibition," pp. 36–37, 55.

19. Lana Turner's autobiography, *Lana: The Lady, the Legend, the Truth* (E. P. Dutton, 1982), has a frontispiece showing the actress on the cover of twenty-five fan magazines.

20. "The Opinion Leaders," p. 100.

21. Hedda Hopper to Jack Podell, July 3, 1958, Hedda Hopper Collection at the Margaret Herrick Library of the Academy of Motion Picture Arts and Sciences, Beverly Hills, California, file folder no. 3875.

22. Ezra Goodman, *The Fifty-Year Decline and Fall of Hollywood*, p. 90.

23. "Vultures of Hollywood," p. 347.

24. Interview with Anthony Slide, March 21, 2008.

25. Ibid.

CHAPTER 9

1. Christopher Ogden, *Legacy: A Biography of Moses and Walter Annenberg*, p. 137.

2. On April 17, 1952, *The Hollywood Reporter* noted that "*Modern Screen* [was] the most powerful influence in behalf of the industry," and claimed its circulation to be 1,334,700.

3. Max Knepper, "Hollywood's Barkers," p. 359.

4. "The Film, Upward and Onward," pp. 34–35.

5. Leo A. Handel, *Hollywood Looks at Its Audience: A Report of Film Audience Research*, p. 86.

6. Carl Schroeder, "Dell News," p. 6.

7. "Big Increase in Film Fans Shown in Movie Mag Sales," pp. 1, 4.

8. Max Knepper, "Hollywood's Barkers," p. 362.

9. Arthur Bell, "Oh, Those Movie Magazines!," p. 171.

10. Ezra Goodman, *The Fifty-Year Decline and Fall of Hollywood*, p. 82.

11. Quoted in *Daily Variety*, December 1, 1960.

12. Jack Podell quoted in a letter from Helen Limke, west coast editor of *Motion Picture Magazine*, Hedda Hopper Collection, Margaret Herrick Library of the Academy of Motion Picture Arts and Sciences, Beverly Hills, California, file folder no. 3875.

13. A. Kent MacDougall, "More Fan Magazines Battle for Readers, Using Come-On Covers But Hollow Stories," p. 20.

14. David Ragan to Anthony Slide, April 11, 2008.

15. This and other quotes here from an interview with Anthony Slide, February 29, 2008.

16. "*Confidential*: Between You and Me and the Bedpost," p. 14.

17. Bob Thomas, *Winchell*, pp. 249–250.

18. Interview with Anthony Slide, April 16, 2008.

19. Quoted in Steve Govoni, "Now It Can Be Told," p. 43.

20. I am grateful to Leonard Maltin for this quote.

21. Margaret Hinxman, "Even a Fan Deserves an Honest Answer," p. 15.

CHAPTER 10

1. Clifton Fadiman, "The Narcissi," p. 53.

2. Dora Albert, "Pan-the-Fan Mag Types Oughta Say Which They Mean," p. 24.

3. Don Carle Gillette, "Hollywood-Image Wreckers," pp. 3–4.

4. This and other quotes from Patrick O'Connor interview with Anthony Slide, March 21, 2008.

5. Don Carle Gillette, "Hollywood-Image Wreckers," p. 6.

6. Quoted in Arthur Bell, "Oh, Those Movie Magazines!," p. 172.

7. Ibid., p. 201.

8. Dora Albert, "Pan-the-Fan-Mag Types Oughta Say Which They Mean," p. 24

9. "Macfadden-Bartell No Cheapie Fan Magazine," *The Film Daily*, January 11, 1967.

10. Undated press release from McFadden, Strauss, Eddy & Irwin, subsequently published almost intact in *Daily Variety*, January 8, 1969.

11. David Ragan to Anthony Slide, April 11, 2008.

12. All Patrick O'Connor quotes in this chapter from interview with Anthony Slide, March 21, 2008.

13. Lawrence B. Thomas to Anthony Slide, April 25, 2008.

14. David Ragan to Anthony Slide, July 3, 2008.

15. Interview with Anthony Slide, March 20, 2008.

16. David Ragan to Anthony Slide, April 11, 2008.

17. A. Kent MacDougall, "More Fan Magazines Battle for Readers," p. 20.

18. Hedda Hopper Collection at the Margaret Herrick Library of the Academy of Motion Picture Arts and Sciences, Beverly Hills, California, file folder no. 3860.

19. Samantha Eggar telephone conversation with Anthony Slide, May 2, 2008.

20. Hedda Hopper Collection at the Margaret Herrick Library of the Academy of Motion Picture Arts and Sciences, Beverly Hills, California, file folder no. 3875.

21. Tyler Cowen, *What Price Fame?*, p. 2.

22. David Ragan to Anthony Slide, April 11, 2008.

23. Patricia Bosworth, "That Old Star Magic," p. 196.

24. A. Kent MacDougall, "More Fan Magazines Battle for Readers," p. 20.

CHAPTER 11

1. Unless otherwise indicated, this and all other quotes from Rona Barrett interview with Anthony Slide, April 16, 2008.

2. David Ragan to Anthony Slide, April 11, 2008.

3. Aljean Harmetz, "Ms. Rona: Don't Call Her a Gossip," p. 290.

4. Rona Barrett, *Miss Rona: An Autobiography*, pp. 79–80.

5. Patricia Bosworth, "That Old Star Magic," p. 193.

6. Henry Edwards, "Sheilah Graham," p. 22.

7. Quoted in Ralph Benner, "Is This 30 for 'Scoop' Rona?," p. 254.

8. Quoted in Katharine Lowrie, "Inside Gossip on Rona vs. Laufer Feud," p. 6.

9. These and other quotes from Bill Royce interview with Anthony Slide, May 6, 2008.

10. Maureen Donaldson (b. 1946) became an international photographer, whose work has been published in the *New York Times*, *Cosmopolitan*, *TV Guide*, and elsewhere. She tells of her relationship with the actor in *An Affair to Remember: My Life with Cary Grant*, coauthored with William Royce, New York: G. P. Putnam's Sons, 1989.

11. Quoted in Jerry Stahl, "Chuck Laufer's Fan Mags Are Gonna Create Stars, Baby!," p. 165.

12. Katharine Lowrie, "Inside Gossip on Rona vs. Laufer Feud," p. 6.

CHAPTER 12

1. Ezra Goodman, *The Fifty-Year Decline and Fall of Hollywood*, pp. 91–93.

2. Lawrence B. Thomas to Anthony Slide, May 16, 2008.

3. Quoted in Ira Ellenthal, "*People*: A Good Reason to Advertise," p. 23.

4. Quotes in Martha Nolan, "Median Lines: New and of Note," p. 115.

5. Jill Goldsmith, "People Who Need People," p. 1.

6. "The People Perplex," p. 89.

7. Anna Quindlen, "Harsh Realities Killing Off Fan Magazines."

8. Ibid.

9. Information from David K. Henkel, *Collectible Magazines: Identification and Price Guide*.

10. Katharine Lowrie, "Somebody Is Reading Fan Magazines," p. 7.

11. Arthur Bell, "Oh, Those Movie Magazines!" p. 171.

12. Lawrence B. Thomas to Anthony Slide, May 16, 2008.

13. Micki Siegel to Anthony Slide, May 20, 2008.

14. Paul Denis, *Inside the Soaps*, acknowledgments page.

15. Dora Albert, "Soaper Fan Mags Replace Film Rags as Newsstand Favorites," p. 31.

16. Dade Hayes, "Tabloid Queen Ankling Star Gig," p. 2.

17. Anne Thompson, "Mags Drag as Biz Goes Online," p. 7.

18. Ruth Waterbury interview with Anthony Slide, April 13, 1972.

BIBLIOGRAPHY

Abrahamson, David. *Magazine-Made America: The Cultural Transformation of the Postwar Period*. Cresskill, N.J.: Hampton Press, 1996.

Addison, Heather. *Hollywood and the Rise of Physical Culture*. New York: Routledge, 2003.

Albert, Dora. "New Mag Slant: How Stars Cope with Booze, Bereavement, Babies; 'The Method' Dull Actor Theme." *Variety*, June 23, 1965, p. 18.

Albert, Dora. "Film Fan Mags on TV Kick." *Variety*, January 26, 1966, pp. 11, 23.

Albert, Dora. "Sister Fan Mags Bare Fangs in Fight to Scoop Each Other on Latest Tidbit." *Variety*, January 7, 1970, p. 5.

Albert, Dora. "Pan-the-Fan-Mag Types Oughta Say Which They Mean." *Variety*, January 6, 1971, p. 24.

Albert, Dora. "Soaper Fan Mags Replace Film Rags as Newsstand Favorites." *Daily Variety*, January 16, 1980, p. 31.

Alpert, Hollis. "Exciting New Magazines for Show Business." *Saturday Review*, September 9, 1961, pp. 48–49.

Austin, Thomas, and Martin Barker. *Contemporary Hollywood Stardom*. London: Arnold, 2003.

Baker, Peter. "When Private Lives Are Public Property." *Films and Filming*, March 1957, p. 12.

Barbas, Samantha. *Movie Crazy: Fans, Stars, and the Cult of Celebrity*. New York: Palgrave, 2001.

Barrett, Rona. *Miss Rona: An Autobiography*. Los Angeles: Nash Publishing, 1974.

Bean, Jennifer, and Diane Negra, eds. *A Feminist Reader in Early Cinema*. Durham, N.C.: Duke University Press, 2002.

Bego, Mark, ed. *The Best of Modern Screen*. New York: St. Martin's Press, 1986.

Bell, Arthur. "Oh, Those Movie Magazines!" *Cosmopolitan*, February 1975, pp. 169–172, 210.

Benner, Ralph. "Is This 30 for 'Scoop' Rona?" *Los Angeles*, December 1982, pp. 254–259, 381–382.

Bernstein, Samuel. *Mr. Confidential: The Man, His Magazine, and the Movieland Massacre That Changed Hollywood Forever*. New York: Walford Press, 2006.

"Big Increase in Film Fans Shown in Movie Mag Sales." *The Hollywood Reporter*, October 19, 1955, pp. 1, 4.

Bogart, Humphrey. "Medal from Hitler: Here's How to Get One," *Photoplay*, January 1945, pp. 28, 87.

Bosworth, Patricia. "That Old Star Magic." *Vanity Fair*, April 1998, pp. 189–190, 193–198.

"Boycott on Fan Mags." *Daily Variety*, March 6, 1935, pp. 1, 5.

Brady, Anna, Richard Wall, and Carolynn Newitt Weiner, eds. *Union List of Film Periodicals*. Westport, Conn.: Greenwood Press, 1984.

Brooks, Louise. *Lulu in Hollywood*. New York: Alfred A. Knopf, 1982.

Carr, David. "Gossip Goes Glossy and Loses Its Stigma." *New York Times*, Arts Section, August 4, 2003, pp. 1, 8.

Carr, Harry. "Marooned in London." *Photoplay*, April 1916, pp. 68–70, 175.

Carroll, Jon. "Hot Topix." *Village Voice*, April 27, 1982, p. 42.

Chen, Mei. "Gladys Hall Collection Inventory." Beverly Hills, Calif.: Academy of Motion Picture Arts and Sciences, 1992.

Chrisman, J. Eugene. "The Stars Vote on Prohibition." *Screen Play*, November 1932, pp. 36–37, 55.

Clear, Richard E. *Old Magazines: Identification and Value Guide*. Paducah, Ky.: Collector Books, 2003.

"*Confidential*: Between You and Me and the Bedpost." *Fortnight*, July 1955, pp. 24–26.

Conley, Walter. "Harriette Underhill." *The Silent Picture*, no. 14, spring 1972, pp. 24–30.

Cotter, Carl F. "The Forty Hacks of the Fan Mags." *The Coast*, February 1939, pp. 18–21.

Cowen, Tyler. *What Price Fame?* Cambridge, Mass.: Harvard University Press, 2000.

Curie, Dawn H. *Girl Talk: Adolescent Magazines and Their Readers*. Toronto: University of Toronto Press, 1999.

"The Curious Craze for 'Confidential' Magazine." *Newsweek*, July 11, 1955, pp. 50–52.

Daniel, Walter C. *Black Journals of the United States*. Westport, Conn.: Greenwood Press, 1982.

Davis, Kenneth C. *Two-Bit Culture: The Paperbacking of America*. Boston: Houghton Mifflin, 1984.

Dench, Ernest A. *Advertising by Motion Pictures*. Cincinnati: The Standard Publishing Co., 1916.

Denis, Paul. *Inside the Soaps*. Secaucus, N.J.: Citadel Press, 1985.

Dietz, Howard. *Dancing in the Dark*. New York: Quadrangle/New York Times Book Co., 1974.

Dougherty, Kathryn. "As I Knew Him." *Photoplay*, October 1932, p. 27.

Downs, Robert B., and Jane B. Downs. *Journalists of the United States: Biographical Sketches of Print and Broadcast News Shapers from the Late 17th Century to the Present*. Jefferson, N.C.: McFarland, 1991.

Edwards, Henry. "Sheilah Graham." *Andy Warhol's Interview*, August 1972, p. 22.

Eells, George. *Hedda and Louella*. New York: G. P. Putnam's Sons, 1972.

Ellenthal, Ira. "*People*: A Good Reason to Advertise." *Product Marketing*, November 23, 1981, p. 23.

Epstein, Jackie. "Gossip Is Still Music to Jimmy Fidler's Ears." *Los Angeles Times* Calendar, April 30, 1978, pp. 52, 55.

Fadiman, Clifton. "The Narcissi." *Stage*, July 1937, pp. 52–53.

"Fan Magazine Drop." *The Hollywood Reporter*, May 25, 1933, pp. 1, 6.

"Fan Mags May Raise Pix Attendance, But —." *The Film Daily*, January 4, 1967, pp. 1, 5.

"Film Fan Mags on TV Kick." *Variety*, January 26, 1966, pp. 11, 23.

"Film Studios Censor Fan Story Writers." *New York Times*, August 11, 1934. Reprinted in vol. 2 of *The New York Times Encyclopedia of Film*.

"The Film, Upward and Onward." *Flair*, March 1950, pp. 34–35.

Fishbein, Ed. "They Found It at the Movies." *Los Angeles Herald-Examiner*, December 21, 1980, Section E, pp. 1, 7.

Ford, James L. C. *Magazines for Millions: The Story of Specialized Publications*. Carbondale, Ill.: Southern Illinois University Press, 1969.

Fuller, Kathryn. *At the Picture Show: Small-Town Audiences and the Creation of Movie Fan Culture*. Washington, D.C.: Smithsonian Institution Press, 1996.

Gabler, Neal. *Winchell: Gossip, Power, and the Culture of Celebrity*. New York: Alfred A. Knopf, 1994.

Gebhart, Myrtle. "The Chocolate Comedy," *Extension*, November 1929, p. 17.

Gelman, Barbara, ed. *Photoplay Treasury*. New York: Crown, 1972.

Gillette, Don Carle. "Hollywood-Image Wreckers." *Journal of the Producers Guild of America*, June 1973, pp. 3–6, 17.

Goldsmith, Jill. "People Who Need People." *Variety*, July 10, 2006, pp. 1, 41.

"Good Things A-Coming for 1918 and the People Who Will Contribute Them."

Motion Picture Magazine, December 1917, pp. 120–122.

Goodman, Ezra. *The Fifty-Year Decline and Fall of Hollywood*. New York: Simon and Schuster, 1961.

"Gossipmania." *Newsweek*, May 24, 1976, pp. 56–64.

Govoni, Steve. "Now It Can Be Told." *American Film*, February 1990, pp. 28–33, 43.

Graham, Sheilah. *Confessions of a Hollywood Reporter*. New York: William Morrow, 1969.

"Graham, Sheilah." *Current Biography*, October 1969, pp. 23–26.

Grau, Robert. *The Theatre of Science*. New York: Broadway Publishing, 1914.

Griffith, Richard, ed. *The Talkies: Articles and Illustrations from Photoplay Magazine, 1928–1940*. New York: Dover Publications, 1971.

Haber, Joyce. "Confessions of a Nonfan." *Los Angeles Times* Calendar, October 2, 1966, p. 6.

Haining, Peter. *The Classic Era of American Pulp Magazines*. Chicago: Chicago Review Press, 2000.

Handel, Leo A. *Hollywood Looks at Its Audience: A Report of Film Audience Research*. Urbana: University of Illinois Press, 1950.

Hanson, Steve. "Fan Magazines." In *Encyclopedia of Popular Culture*, vol. 2, ed. Tom Pendergast and Sara Pendergast. Detroit: St. James Press, 2000, pp. 64–65.

Harmetz, Aljean. "Ms. Rona: Don't Call Her a Gossip." *Cosmopolitan*, May 1979, pp. 290–293, 346.

Hayes, Dade. "Tabloid Queen Ankling Star Gig." *Daily Variety*, May 14, 2008, p. 2.

Henkel, David K. *Collectible Magazines: Identification and Price Guide*. New York: Avon Books, 1993.

Hinxman, Margaret. "Even a Fan Deserves an Honest Answer." *Films and Filming*, July 1959, p. 15.

Hoffman, Irving. "Darling Fan Magazines." *The Hollywood Reporter*, January 29, 1951, pp. 3–4; January 30, 1951, pp. 3,

10; January 31, 1951, pp. 3–4; February 1, 1951, pp. 3, 8.

Hofler, Robert. *The Man Who Invented Rock Hudson: The Pretty Boys and Dirty Deals of Henry Willson*. New York: Carroll & Graf, 2005.

Holley, Val. *Mike Connolly and the Manly Art of Hollywood Gossip*. Jefferson, N.C.: McFarland, 2003.

Hopper, Hedda. "Resolutions the Stars Should Make." *Photoplay*, January 1942, p. 20.

Hopper, Hedda. *From under My Hat*. Garden City, N.Y.: Doubleday, 1952.

Hopper, Hedda, and James Brough. *The Whole Truth and Nothing But*. Garden City, N.Y.: Doubleday, 1963.

Howe, Herbert. "Our Adela." *Photoplay*, November 1923, pp. 54, 124.

Hunt, William R. *Body Love: The Amazing Career of Bernarr Macfadden*. Bowling Green, Ohio: Bowling Green University Popular Press, 1989.

"The Inside Skinny (psst!) on Gossip." *The Week*, May 12, 2006, p. 11.

Israel, Lee. "How Fan Magazines Can Make You a Real Woman." *Ms*, September 1972, pp. 38–43, 102–103.

"It's Been a Long and Wonderful Road for Fawcett Publications, Inc. and It All Started in Robbinsdale in 1919." Special edition of the *North Hennepin Post*, June 28, 1962.

Johnston, William A. "What Kind of a Fellow Is—Quirk?" *Motion Picture News*, May 11, 1918, pp. 2809–2810.

Joseph, Robert. "Fidler, the Man Nobody Knows." *The Coast*, October 1939, pp. 19–23.

Kahn, Gordon. "The Gospel According to Hollywood." *Atlantic Monthly*, May 1947, pp. 98–102.

Kear, Lynn, and John Rossman. *The Complete Kay Francis Career Record: All Film, Stage, Radio, and Television Appearances*. Jefferson, N.C.: McFarland, 2008.

Kessler, Judy. *Inside People: The Stories behind the Stories*. New York: Villard Books, 1994.

Knapp, Ed. "Hollywood's Razzle-Dazzle Magazines." *Remember*, December 1995, pp. 40–43.

Knepper, Max. "Hollywood's Barkers." *Sight and Sound*, January 1951, pp. 359–362.

Kreshel, Peggy J. "George T. Delacorte, Jr." In *Dictionary of Literary Biography*, vol. 91: *American Magazine Journalists, 1900–1960*, ed. Sam G. Riley. Detroit: Gale Research, 1990, pp. 89–94.

Kuczynski, Alex, and Geraldine Fabricant. "Lifelines Cut, Talk Magazine Goes Silent." *New York Times*, January 19, 2002, pp. A1, C3.

Landay, Lori. *Madcaps, Screwballs, and Con Women: The Female Trickster in American Culture*. Philadelphia: University of Pennsylvania Press, 1988.

Levin, Martin, ed. *Hollywood and the Great Fan Magazines*. New York: Wings Books, 1991.

Lewis, Lisa, ed. *The Adoring Audience: Fan Culture and Popular Media*. New York: Routledge, 1992.

Liberty Magazine Index, 1924–1950. Glen Rock, N.J.: Microfilming Corporation of America, 1973.

"*Liberty Magazine* 1924–1950: A Brief History with a Detailed Examination of Several 1935 Issues." www.magazines.things-and-other-stuff.com/liberty-magazine.html. Accessed March 2008.

Lipton, Edward. "Fan Mags Have Hurt Industry: Ferguson." *The Film Daily*, January 3, 1967, pp. 1, 2.

Lomazow, Steven. *American Periodicals: A Collector's Manual and Reference Guide*. West Orange, N.J.: the author, 1996.

Lowrie, Katharine. "Topsy-Turvy World of Fan Mags." *Los Angeles Times* Calendar, March 3, 1980, pp. 1, 5–7, 28.

Lowrie, Katharine. "*Photoplay* Suspends Publication." *Los Angeles Times*, Part II, March 29, 1980, p. 12.

Lowrie, Katharine. "From Froth to Scandal to TV Soaps." *Los Angeles Times* Calendar, March 30, 1980, p. 5.

Lowrie, Katharine. "Inside Gossip on Rona vs. Laufer Feud." *Los Angeles Times* Calendar, March 30, 1980, pp. 6–7.

Lowrie, Katharine. "Fan Mags: The Facts That Got Away." *Los Angeles Times* Calendar, May 11, 1980, pp. 4–5.

Lowrie, Katharine. "Fan Magazine Reporters: Underrated as Journalists." *Los Angeles Times* Calendar, July 6, 1980, pp. 6–7.

Lowrie, Katharine. "Somebody Is Reading Fan Magazines." *Los Angeles Times* Calendar, July 6, 1980, p. 7.

Lusk, Norbert. "I Love Actresses!" *New Movies*, March 1946, pp. 10–15, 30–32; April 1946, pp. 26–30; May 1946, pp. 12–17, 27–29; June–July 1946, pp. 20–27; August–September 1946, pp. 16–20, 28; October 1946, pp. 12–19, 28–29; November–December 1946, pp. 10–14, 17; January 1947, pp. 24–30; February–March 1947, pp. 14–20; April–May 1947, pp. 15–19, 31; October 1947, pp. 14–19; November 1947, pp. 15–19, 23; December 1947, pp. 18–25; January 1948, pp. 12–21, 29–30; February–March 1948, pp. 18–27, 32–33; April 1948, pp. 20–26.

Lyles, William H. *Putting Dell on the Map*. Westport, Conn.: Greenwood Press, 1983.

MacDougall, A. Kent. "More Fan Magazines Battle for Readers, Using Come-on Covers but Hollow Stories." *The Wall Street Journal*, May 31, 1967, pp. 20–21

MacDougall, A. Kent. "Some Teen Magazines Switch to Candor in Rapidly Growing Field Founded on Pap." *The Wall Street Journal*, December 14, 1967, p. 28.

Macfadden, Mary, and Emile Gauvreau. *Dumbbells and Carrot Strips: The Story of Bernarr Macfadden*. New York: Henry Holt, 1953.

Mann, William J. *William Haines: The Life and Times of Hollywood's First Openly Gay Star*. New York: Viking, 1998.

Mann, William J. *Behind the Scene: How Gays and Lesbians Shaped Hollywood, 1910–1969*. New York: Viking, 2001.

McHenry, Murphy. "Dishing That Fan Mag Guff." *Daily Variety*, September 24, 1936, p. 51.

McMurtry, Larry. "Writers and the Hollywood of Romance." *American Film*, April 1977, pp. 6–7.

Miller, Max. *For the Sake of Shadows*. New York: E. P. Dutton, 1936.

Miller, Rick. *Photoplay Editions: A Collector's Guide*. Jefferson, N.C.: McFarland, 2002.

Moffitt, Jack. "'Hearings' Stoop to Fidler." *The Hollywood Reporter*, September 16, 1941, pp. 1, 6–7.

Mook, Samuel Richard. "Introducing an All-star Cast." *Picture Play*, February 1930, pp. 60–62, 92; March 1930, pp. 52–55, 104, 108.

"Moral House Cleaning in Hollywood: What's It All About? An Open Letter to Mr. Will Hays." *Photoplay*, April 1922, pp. 52–53.

Mott, Frank Luther. *A History of American Magazines*. 5 vols. Cambridge, Mass.: Harvard University Press, 1930–1968.

Nadel, Lillian. "The 'Fans' Grow Older." *New York Times*, October 5, 1941. Reprinted in vol. 4 of *The New York Times Encyclopedia of Film*.

Nemcek, Paul L. *Screen Romances: The Golden Years (1929–1945); A Collector's Guide*. n.p.: the author, 1968.

Nolan, Martha. "Median Lines: New and of Note," *Madison Avenue*, May 1984, p. 115.

Nourie, Alan, and Barbara Nourie. *American Mass-Market Magazines*. Westport, Conn.: Greenwood Press, 1990.

Ogden, Christopher. *Legacy: A Biography of Moses and Walter Annenberg*. Boston: Little, Brown, 1999.

"The Opinion Leaders." *Time*, April 12, 1948, p. 100.

Orgeron, Marsha. "Making It in Hollywood: Clara Bow, Fandom, and Consumer Culture." *Cinema Journal*, Summer 2003, pp. 76–97.

Oursler, Charles Fulton. *Behold This Dreamer!* Boston: Little, Brown, 1964.

Parsons, Louella. *The Gay Illiterate*. Garden City, N.Y.: Doubleday, Doran, 1944.

Parsons, Louella. *Tell It to Louella*. New York: G. P. Putnam's Sons, 1961.

Parsons, P. A. "Doping It Out for the Papers." *The Moving Picture World*, July 20, 1918, pp. 327–328.

"The People Perplex." *Newsweek*, June 6, 1971, pp. 89–90.

Petaja, Emil. *Photoplay Edition*. San Francisco: Sisu Publishers, 1975.

Peterson, Theodore. *Magazines in the Twentieth Century*. Urbana: University of Illinois Press, 1964.

"'Photoplay' Winning Name in the Essanay New Name Contest." *Moving Picture World*, October 15, 1910, p. 858.

Pogrebin, Abigail. "*Us* and Them: Diary of a Launch." *Brill's Content*, May 2000, pp. 105–107, 132–133.

Pope, Frank. "TradeViews." *The Hollywood Reporter*, August 15, 1934, p. 1

Quindlen, Anna. "Harsh Realities Killing off Fan Magazines." *New York Times*, August 12, 1977. Reprinted in vol. 12 of *The New York Times Encyclopedia of Film*.

Quirk, Lawrence J. "Quirk of *Photoplay*." *Films in Review*, March 1955, pp. 97–107.

Quirk, Lawrence J. "May Allison and Jimmy Quirk." *Quirk's Reviews*, July 1989, pp. 3–5, 19.

Reed, George. "The Fan Mags." *Movie Advertising Collector*, April 1996, pp. 7–15; June 1996, pp. 6–16.

"Reviewing the Fan Mags." *The Hollywood Reporter*, June 2, 1933–June 6, 1934.

Rosenstein, Jaik. *Hollywood Leg Man*. Los Angeles: Madison, 1950.

Royce, Bill. *Cary Grant: The Wizard of Beverly Grove*. Beverly Hills, Calif.: Cool Titles, 2006.

Sanjek, David. "Fans' Notes: The Horror Film Fanzine." *Literature/Film Quarterly*, vol. 18, no. 3, 1990, pp. 150–157.

Scaramaza, Paul A., ed. *Ten Years in Paradise*. Arlington, Va.: The Pleasant Press, 1974.

Schickel, Richard. *Intimate Strangers: The Culture of Celebrity in America*. Chicago: Ivan R. Dee, 2000.

Schneirov, Matthew. *The Dream of a New Social Order: Popular Magazines in America, 1893–1914*. New York: Columbia University Press, 1994.

Schroeder, Carl. "Dell News." *The Holly-wood Reporter*, April 17, 1952, p. 6.

Schuster, Mel. *Motion Picture Performers: A Bibliography of Magazine and Periodical Articles, 1900–1969*. Metuchen, N.J.: Scarecrow Press, 1971.

Schuster, Mel. *Motion Picture Performers: A Bibliography of Magazine and Periodical Articles, Supplement No. 1, 1970–1974*. Metuchen, N.J.: Scarecrow Press, 1976.

Scott, Don E. "Can Rona and Toni Both Find Happiness Reporting on Hollywood?" *Hollywood Studio Magazine*, November 1970, pp. 4–6.

Sennett, Robert S. *Hollywood Hoopla: Creating Stars and Selling Movies in the Golden Age*. New York: Billboard Books, 1998.

Sewell, C. S. "Reviewing Pictures." *The Moving Picture World*, March 26, 1927, p. 324.

Slide, Anthony. "Ivy Crane Wilson." In *Film Review: 1978–1979*, ed. F. Maurice Speed. London: W. H. Allen, 1978, p. 131.

Slide, Anthony. "Early Film Magazines: An Overview." In *Aspects of American Film History prior to 1920*. Metuchen, N.J.: Scarecrow Press, 1978, pp. 98–104.

Slide, Anthony, ed. *International Film, Radio, and Television Journals*. Westport, Conn.: Greenwood Press, 1985.

Slide, Anthony. "Hedda Hopper's Hollywood." *LA Reader*, April 4, 1986, pp. 1, 8–9, 12.

Slide, Anthony. *The Big V: A History of the Vitagraph Company*. Metuchen, N.J.: Scarecrow Press, 1987.

Slide, Anthony. *They Also Wrote for the Fan Magazines: Film Articles by Literary Giants from e .e. cummings to Eleanor Roosevelt, 1920–1939*. Jefferson, N.C.: McFarland, 1992.

Soares, André. *Beyond Paradise: The Life of Ramon Novarro*. New York: St. Martin's Press, 2002.

Spiegel, Irwin O. "Public Celebrity v. Scandal Magazine: The Celebrity's Right to Privacy." *Southern California Law Review*, April 1957, pp. 280–312.

Springer, John Parris. *Hollywood Fictions: The Dream Factory in American Popular Culture*. Norman: University of Oklahoma Press, 2000.

Stahl, Jerry. "Chuck Laufer's Fan Mags Are Gonna Create Stars, Baby!" *Los Angeles*, May 1979, pp. 160–164, 304–307.

Starr, Jimmy. *Barefoot on Barbed Wire: The Autobiography of a Forty-Year Hollywood Balancing Act*. Lanham, Md.: Scarecrow Press, 2001.

Sterling, Anna Kate, ed. *The Best of Shadowland*. Metuchen, N.J.: Scarecrow Press, 1987.

Stingley, Jim. "Starmaker to the Bubble Gum Set." *Los Angeles Times*, Part IV, February 11, 1974, pp. 1, 4–5.

St. Johns, Adela Rogers. "Our Herb." *Photoplay*, November 1923, pp. 54, 124.

Stone, David E. E., ed. *American Humor Magazines and Comic Periodicals*. Westport, Conn.: Greenwood Press, 1987.

Studlar, Galyn. "The Perils of Pleasure? Fan Magazine Discourse as Women's Commodified Culture in the 1920s." *Wide Angle*, January 1991, pp. 6–33.

"Success in the Sewer." *Time*, July 11, 1955, pp. 90–91.

Swain, Bruce M. "Bernarr Macfadden." In *Dictionary of Literary Biography*, Vol. 91: *American Magazine Journalists, 1900–1960*, ed. Sam G. Riley. Detroit: Gale Research, 1990, pp. 205–215.

Taft, William H. *American Magazines for the 1980s*. New York: Hastings House, 1982.

Taylor, Carol. "Stars in Her Eyes, Pen in Her Hand." *New York World-Telegram*, December 4, 1947, p. 31.

Taylor, Robert Lewis. "Physical Culture: Profile of Bernarr Macfadden." *The New Yorker*, October 14, 1950, pp. 39–51; October 21, 1950, pp. 39–54; October 28, 1950, pp. 37–50.

Tebbel, John. *The American Magazine: A Compact History*. New York: Hawthorn Books, 1969.

Tebbel, John. *A History of Book Publishing in the United States*. New York: R. R. Bowker, 1981.

Tebbel, John, and Mary Ellen Zuckerman. *The Magazine in America, 1741–1990*. New York: Oxford University Press, 1991.

"They Won Success with Unique Records," *National Brain Power*, April 1923, p. 28.

"Thirty-five Space Grabs in Fan Mags." *Variety*, January 1, 1936, p. 6.

Thomas, Bob. *Winchell*. Garden City, N.Y.: Doubleday, 1971.

Thomas, Bob. *Joan Crawford*. New York: Simon and Schuster, 1978.

Thompson, Anne. "Mags Drag as Biz Goes Online." *Variety*, April 9, 2007, pp. 7, 39.

Thorp, Margaret Farrand. *America at the Movies*. New Haven, Conn.: Yale University Press, 1939.

Tinkerbelle [sic]. "All About Rona." *Andy Warhol's Interview*, September 1974, pp. 10–12.

"A Tribute from a Friend," *Photoplay*, March 1923, p. 37.

"2,000 in 20 Fan Clubs Join Forces to Stop False Stories on Stars." *Motion Picture Herald*, November 10, 1934, p. 15.

"Vultures of Hollywood." *The American Mercury*, March 1943, pp. 345–350.

Welkos, Robert W. "From 'It' Read to Has-Been." *Los Angeles Times*, March 10, 2007, pp. E1, E20.

Weller, Sheila. *Dancing at Ciro's: A Family's Love, Loss, and Scandal on the Sunset Strip*. New York: Macmillan, 2003.

"What's the Matter with the Movies?: Play Fair with the Public," *Movie Weekly*, October 28, 1922, p. 3.

Wikipedia. Entries on "Entertainment Weekly" and "Fawcett Publications." Accessed February 2008.

Wilde, Arthur. *Honestly! Confessions of a Hollywood Press Agent*. Danville, Ill.: Three Lions Publications, 1999.

Wilkerson, W. R. "TradeViews." *The Hollywood Reporter*, July 7, 1944, pp. 1, 5.

Wilkie, Jane. *Confessions of an Ex–Fan Magazine Writer*. New York: Doubleday, 1981.

"Will Hays Tells *Movie Weekly* What He Is Doing and Will Do for the Movies." *Movie Weekly*, October 21, 1922, pp. 4–5.

Wood, Clement. *Bernarr Macfadden: A Study in Success*. New York: Beekman, 1974.

INDEX

Academy of Motion Picture Arts and Sciences, 92
"Across the Silversheet: A Department of the Photodrama Review" column, 23
Actual Publishing Co., 236, 238, 239
Advertising Advisory Council, 90, 91
Affiliated Magazines, Inc., 221, 235, 243
African Americans, 38, 131, 198–200
Agnew, Frances, 40
AintItCoolNews.com, 230
Albert, Dora, 107, 114, 118, 190, 226
Albert, Jerry, 238
Albert, Katherine, 6, 33, 60, 77, 114, 165, 218
Albing Publications, 238, 239
Alexander of Russia, Grand Duke, 102
Alexandrov, G. V., 127
Allen, Elizabeth, 131
Allison, May, 6, 60–61, 63
Allyson, June, 143, 162
Ameche, Don, 84, 85, 140
American Film, 225
American Periodicals Corp., 234
American Photography, 240
American Weekly, The, 34
Ames, Adrienne, 128
Amsel, Robert, 223
Andre, Lona, 129
Andrews, Julie, 189–90
Andy Warhol's Interview, 220
Angel, Heather, 129
Annenberg, Moses, 170
Annenberg, Walter, 170
"Answer Man" column, 19
Anti-Semitism, 55–56, 115, 142
Arbuckle, Roscoe "Fatty," 7, 154–57, 257
Archerd, Army, 193
Ardmore, Jane, 121, 190, 254
Arizill Realty and Publishing Co., 245
Arlen, Richard, 137
Arliss, George, 99

Arnold, Maxine, 236
Arnold, Robert, 238
Arthur, Bea, 215
Arthur, Jean, 127
Asher, Jerry, 83–84, 199
Ashley, Peter, 138
Associated Mimeo Publications, 236
Associated Professional Service, Inc., 242
Astaire, Fred, 83, 131, 134
Astor, Mary, 15
Astro Distributing Co., 238
Atlas Magazines, 240
Ayres, Lew, 134, 139

Babcock, Muriel, 111, 176, 177, 240, 244
Baby Peggy, 74–75
Baer, Ruth L., 236
Baker, Carroll, 242
Baldwin, Faith, 114, 126
Ball, Gladys, 34
Ball, Lucille, 185
Ball, Russell Earp, 37
Balling, Fredda Dudley, 119–20
Banton, Biddy, 69
Bara, Theda, 91
Barclay, McClelland, 124
Baronet Publishing Co., 234
Barrett, Rona, 207–17, 218
Barrett, Wilton A., 127
Barrett Report, The, 217
Barry, Frank G., 25
Bartell Broadcasting Corporation, 108
Barthelmess, Richard, 76, 79
Bartholomew House, Inc., 241
Bartlett, Randolph, 6, 52
Barven Publications, 242, 245
Basher, Beryl, 245
Baskette, Kirtley, 65, 89, 132, 162, 163
Baumgarten, Elza. *See* Schallert, Elza
Beach, Barbara, 25
Beach, Rex, 21

Beardsley, A. H., 240
Beban, George, 145
Beck, Lars, 241
Beery, Wallace, 151
Bell, Arthur, 185
Bell, Caroline, 38
Bell-McClure-Nana syndicated, 211
Benner, Ralph, 212
Bennett, Constance, 128, 163
Bennett, Joan, 131, 141
Benny, Jack, 214
Benson, Rachel, 87
Benson, Sally, 40, 95
Bergman, Ingrid, 76, 158–59, 161, 162
Besscal Publications, Inc., 237, 245
Best Screen Stories, 234
Better Books, Inc., 234
Biery, Ruth, 65, 87, 114, 124, 135
Bijou, 234
Bilbara Publishing Co., 237, 238, 239
Binney, Constance, 5
Blacklisting, 159–61
Blackton, J. Stuart, 6, 14, 16, 18, 21, 25, 75, 250
Blake Publishing Corp., 234
Blondell, Joan, 90
Bloom, Victor, 234
Blum, Ronnie Eisinger, 245
Blyth, Ann, 115
Blythe, Betty, 5
Bogart, Humphrey, 140, 142, 161
Bogdanovich, Peter, 215
Boles, John, 131
Bond, Lillian, 128
Bondage, 91
Boone, Pat, 176
Borie, Marcia, 190
Bosworth, Patricia, 210
Bow, Clara, 6, 15, 128, 162, 250
Boy with Green Hair, The, 159–60
Boyd, Leonard, 236
Boyer, Charles, 85
Boyle, Mary, 39
Boys Cinema, 247
Bradley, J. E. H., 50
Branden, Elsa, 159
Brando, Marlon, 172, 176
Brennan, Lillian W., 39
Brennan, Terry, 235
Brewster, Eugene V., 6, 14–16, 24, 31, 34, 103

Brewster Publications, Inc., 17–18, 22, 35, 40, 42, 79, 237, 239, 243
British fan magazines, 247
Bromfield, Louis, 31
Broun, Heywood, 31, 101
Brown, Joe E., 131, 135
Brown, Kevin, 239
Brown, Tina, 229
Brown, Tom, 167
Bruce, Virginia, 131
Buck Jones Western Stories, 234
Burton, Richard, 68, 175, 196, 197, 219
Busby, Marquis, 42, 168
Buse Publications, Inc., 238
Bushman, Francis X., 28

Cain, James M., 102, 160
"Cal York," 8, 50, 62, 71, 144, 159
Calhoun, Dorothy Donnell, 36, 43, 157
Calhoun, Jean, 25
Calhoun, Rory, 180
Callahan, Mary, 235
Callahan, Peter J., 71, 176, 221
"Calling All Girls," 166–67
Campbell, Gwen, 234
Campbell, Pat, 240
Campbell, Virginia, 227
Candid photographs, 90
Cannon, Regina, 90, 114, 124
Captain Billy's Whiz Bang, 9, 109–10
Captain Publications, 243
Carol, Sue, 4
Carlisle, Mary, 73, 131
Carr, Harry, 5, 41, 91, 112
Carter, Aline, 25
Cary, Augusta, 50
Castle of Frankenstein, 234
Caward, N. [Neil] G. [Gladstone], 48
Celebrity, 234
Celebrity Hairdos, 227, 234
Censorship, 54–55
Central Press Co., 241
Challenge, Inc., 240
Chaplin, Charlie, 20, 75–76, 158
Character actors, and fan magazines, 4
Charles, Ray, 199
Charm, 29, 235, 241
Cheatham, Maude, 25, 107, 163
Chrisman, J. Eugene, 88, 158
Christie, George, 150–51
Churchill, Reba and Bonnie, 88, 177–79

Cinema, 101, 127, 234
Cinema Arts, 100–1, 127, 234
Cinema Chat, 247
Cinema Magazine, Inc., 234
Cinema Magazine Publishing Co., 234
Cinema Review, 234
Cinema World Illustrated, 247
Classic. See *Motion Picture Classic*
Cline, Doris, 239
Clive, Henry, 69, 111
"Close-Ups and Long Shots" column, 54, 65, 69
Cloud, Kenneth G., 49
Cloud Publishing Company, 50
Cohn, Alfred A., 52
Colbert, Claudette, 4, 69, 70, 85, 90, 115, 128, 131, 160
Colby, Richard, 71
Colvin, Edwin M., 49, 51
Comic books, 103, 116
Communism, 159–61
Condé Nast, 235
Condon, Mabel, 49, 50
Confidential, 179–82, 198, 231
Conlon, Lillian, 22, 25
Connolly, Mike, 2, 27, 144, 151, 180, 197
Cooper, Gary, 131, 134, 165
Corpening, Sara, 237
Cortez, Ricardo, 62
Cotter, Carl F., 3, 9, 33, 85, 88, 114
Cotton, William M., 104, 239, 240
Courtlandt, Roberta, 22, 25, 39
Cowboy Movie Thrillers, 234
Crawford, Joan, 4, 35, 69, 77, 81–83, 90, 115, 126, 128, 131, 133, 141, 151, 161, 180, 201, 218, 251
Creative Group, 234, 244
Crestwood Publishing Co., 238
Crosby, Bing, 131, 137, 140
Crosby, Dixie Lee, 131
Crowther, Bosley, 115
Croy, Homer, 124
Cummings, Constance, 129, 131
cummings, e. e., 101
Cummings, Robert, 163
Cuneo, John, 103
Curtis, Joan, 177, 236, 237, 238, 242, 243

D. S. Publishing Co., Inc., 240
Daily Variety, 54, 128, 138, 193, 231
Daly, Marsha, 238

Daniels, Bebe, 34
Dantine, Helmut, 142
Davenport, Delbert Essex, 71
Davies, Marion, 128, 131
Davis, Bette, 120, 129, 131, 140–41, 201–2
Davis, Sammy, Jr., 198
Davis, William H., 220
Day, Doris, 171
Daytime TV, 226
de Jager, Patricia, 103, 223
Dean, James, 235, 242
Dee, Frances, 128
Del Rio, Dolores, 64, 129, 131, 133
Delacorte, Albert P., 116
Delacorte, George T. (Thomas), Jr., 112–16
Dell Publishing, 113–16, 172, 202, 234, 235, 236, 240, 242, 243, 245
Delvigne, Doris, 25
Denis, Paul, 226
Dennis Publishing, 229
Denton, Frances, 52
Detroit Free Press Weekly, 242
"Diary of a Professional Movie Fan" series, 37
Dickinson, Angie, 205
Dietrich, Marlene, 128, 131, 133, 137
Digest Publications, Inc., 244
Disney, Walt, 101, 131, 172
Dobie, Duncan A., Jr., 22
Dodsmith Publishing Co., 239
Doherty, Edward J., 156
Donahue, Troy, 210
Donaldson, Maureen, 214, 258
Donnell, Dorothy, 24, 37, 88
Doty, Douglas Z., 235
Dougherty, Kathryn, 63–66, 90, 122
Douglas, Melvyn, 134
Dove, Billie, 132
Downs Publishing Co., 234
Dreiser, Theodore, 98–99
Dunne, Irene, 115, 131, 134
Dunne, James, 129
Durbin, Deanna, 4, 137–38, 141

E. W. A. Publications, Inc., 239
Eastman, Robert M., 49, 51
Ebony, 199–200
Eckels, Eddy, 235
Eddy, Nelson, 131, 133, 134
Edison, Thomas A., 19, 21
Eggar, Samantha, 197–98

EGO Enterprises, 242
Eilers, Sally, 128, 129
Eisenstein, Sergei, 127
Eller, Madeline, 238
Elliott, John Addison, 39
Ellis, Patricia, 129, 199
Ellis, Tom, 156
Elmo Movie Club, 238
Elsa Maxwell's Café Society, 234
End of St. Petersburg, The, 56
Entertainment Weekly, 228
Epstein, Florence, 236
Ergenbright, Eric, 43, 135
Ericson, Ruth, 239
Essanay Company, 75
Etter, Betty, 238, 241
Evans, Dale, 177
Evans, Delight, 39, 84, 117–18, 158
Evans, Joan, 77, 115
Evans, Madge, 129, 131
Everett, David, 234

Fabry, Jaro, 127
Fadiman, Clifton, 9, 91, 123, 184
Fairbanks, Douglas, Jr., 134, 150, 218
Fairbanks, Douglas, Sr., 30, 37, 133
Fairchild, Monica, 240
Fame and fortune contests, 15
Famous Monsters of Filmland, 234
Famous Monsters of Filmland Yearbook, 234
Fan Club Federation, 89, 235
Fan Club Journals, 248–49
Fan Club League, 235–36
Fan magazines: advertising in, 4, 18, 25, 33–34,
    133; British, 247; circulation, 3, 20, 49, 71,
    122, 132, 142, 171, 172, 182, 204, 225; cov-
    er art, 68, 69, 111, 124, 126, 127, 128–29,
    141–42, 198; divorce coverage, 135; female
    readership, 4, 9, 18–19, 134, 137, 172, 177,
    222, 226; first film star featured, 18; first
    star interview, 18; literary contributions,
    93–102; male readership, 5, 19, 169; male
    stars in, 4; monies paid to writers, 38, 85,
    117, 151, 192; origin of term, 13; origins,
    11–12, 21; politics and, 19–20, 22, 105,
    145, 158, 159–61, 185; prices of, 18, 123–
    24, 127–28, 224; reviews in, 22, 23, 38, 41,
    52–53, 56, 57, 66, 107, 115, 124, 127, 128,
    132, 148, 159–60, 172; social change docu-
    mented in, 5; studio relationship, 7, 8, 13,
    75–80, 86–89, 133, 135–37
Fan-Fare, 234

Fangora, 234
Fantastic Films, 234
Farrell, Glenda, 15, 128
Farrow, Mia, 195, 197, 199, 219, 222
Fawcett, Gordon, 112
Fawcett, Roger, 112
Fawcett, Roscoe, 110, 112, 242, 244
Fawcett, Wilford H., 9, 109–12
Fawcett Publications, Inc., 27, 42, 88, 104,
    105, 110–12, 192, 234, 235, 237, 238, 239,
    242, 243, 244
Fawcett-Dearing Printing Co., 110
Fawcett's Women's Group, 112
Faye, Alice, 131
Feature Movie Magazine, 234
Features Publishing Co., 234
Female writers, 25, 39
Feminine hygiene products, 4–5
Fetchit, Stepin, 38, 199
Fiddler, James (Jimmy), 65, 88, 111, 147–49
Fielding, Romaine, 20
Fighting Stars, 227, 234
Fillion, Loretta G., 239
Film Album, 234
Film and TV Careers, 234
Film Arts Monthly, 234
Film buff periodicals, 11
Film Flashes, 13, 247
Film Fun, 91, 112, 120, 121, 122, 234
Film Humor, 234
Film Humor, Inc., 234
Film in Focus, 231
Film Kiddies Herald, 234–35
Film Periodical, 247
Film Pictorial, 247
Film Players Herald, 235, 238
Film Star Weekly, 247
Film Stories, 235
Film Truth, 56, 235
Film Weekly, 247
FilmFare, 195
Filmplay Journal, 199, 235
Filmways, Inc., 92
Fink, Hyman, 68
Finkelstein, Carol, 193, 237, 239
Fisher, Eddie, 209
Fitzgerald, F. Scott, 146
Flagg, James Montgomery, 69, 95
Flanner, Janet, 5, 31, 98
Fletcher, Adele Whitely, 15, 17–18, 23, 25,
    31, 34, 35, 39, 64, 69, 70–71, 106, 107,
    114, 132, 139, 206

Flight Plan, Inc., 239
Flynn, Errol, 140, 232
Flynn, Hazel E., 50
Foley, John D., 238
Fonda, Jane, 185
Foolish Wives, 56
Ford, Henry, 55–56
Forty Publishing Corp., 244
Fountain, Ruth, 191
Francis, Kay, 114, 128, 131, 134
Frank, Anne, 4
Friedman, Bruce Jay, 210
Fuller, Frances, 150

Gable, Clark, 129, 131, 141, 147, 151, 161, 162
Garbo, Greta, 4, 128, 129, 130, 131, 132, 133, 147, 242
Gardener, Frederick H., 112, 238, 241
Gardner, Ava, 171
Garland, Judy, 115, 141
Gatchell, Charles, 38
Gaynor, Janet, 128, 131, 135, 147, 163
Gebhart, Myrtle, 6, 25, 38–39, 121, 140
Getwood Publications, 241
Gibson, Stanley V., 42
Gilbert, John, 58, 129, 147
Gilmore, Helen, 69
Girls Cinema, 247
Gish, Lillian, 58
Glamour of Hollywood, 235
Glaum, Louise, 79
Globe Communications Corp., 244
Glynn, Elinor, 60, 97
"Going Hollywood," 64
Goldbeck, Elizabeth, 199
Goldbeck, Willis, 74
Golden Apple Awards, 68
Golden Screen, 235
Goldstein, Joan, 238, 245
Goodman, Ezra, 9, 117, 151, 169, 174, 218, 250
Goodman, Martin, 210, 240
Goona-Goona: An Authentic Melodrama of the Isle of Bali, 91
Gordon, James Craig, 152–53
Gossip. See *Rona Barrett's Gossip*
Gossip columnists, 8, 23, 27, 42, 50, 82, 104, 107, 111, 112, 114, 115, 120, 124, 125, 127, 144–52, 180, 211, 217
Gothic Castle Publishing Co., 234
Goulding, Louis, 99–100

Grable, Betty, 141–42, 162
Grady, Lester C., 121, 178, 234, 239
Graham, Sheilah, 145–47, 173, 193
Granger, Farley, 163, 165, 168
Granger, Stewart, 178
Grant, Cary, 140, 163–64, 201, 214, 217
Graphic Arts Corp., 242
Gray, Tony, 241
Grayson, Kathryn, 141
Great McGinty, The, 27
Greed, 56
Gregory, James, 240
Gregory, Nina Dorothy, 22, 39
Griffin, C. W., 49
Griffith, D. W., 21
Griffith, Merv, 168, 213
Grosset & Dunlap, 104
Grubbs, Patricia, 243
Guerin, Bruce, 38
Gunst, A. M., 243
Gwynn, Edith, 144

Haines, William, 6, 77, 165, 168
Hairdo Ideas, 227, 235
Hale, Barbara, 74
Hall, Gladys, 5, 22, 24, 25, 35–38, 74, 84, 85, 87, 106, 107, 114, 121, 253
Hall, Leonard, 62
Hamilton, James Shelley, 127
Hamilton, Neil, 232
Hamilton, Sara, 65, 69, 84
Handel, Leo A., 134, 172
Handy, Truman B., 154
Hanford, Roy S., 238
Hanro Corp., 236
Harding, Ann, 129, 131
Harlequin, Inc., 216
Harlow, Jean, 30, 85, 87, 128, 129, 131, 133, 135, 147
Harmetz, Aljean, 193
Harrington, Guy L., 25
Harris, Frank, 31
Harris, Radie, 149–50, 256–57
Harrison, Louis Reeves, 21
Harrison, Robert, 180
Hart, Moss, 115
Hartford, Huntington, 243
Hartley, William, 242, 243
Hartwell Publishing Corporation, 112
Harvey, Lillian, 128, 131, 147
Hatfield, Hurd, 165
Haver, June, 162

Hawkins, Tim, 215
Hayes, Helen, 128
Hays, Will, 54, 152, 153
Hays Card, 88–89
Hays Office. *See* Motion Picture Producers and Distributors of America
Hayworth, Rita, 162, 171, 178
Hear, Inc., 235
Hear Hollywood, 173, 235
Heinemann, Elizabeth M., 19, 22, 25
Heiskill, Marian, 219
Heller, Richard, 224, 236, 245
Henie, Sonia, 134
Henry, J. Fred, 177, 178
Hepburn, Katharine, 128, 131, 136
Herald House, Inc., 235
Herzog, Dorothy, 25
Heyn, Ernest V., 69, 107, 114, 120–21, 223, 234, 242
Hickman, Dwayne, 210
Higginbotham, Ann, 241
Hi-Hat, 235
Hillman, Alex L., 103
Hillman Periodicals, Inc., 103, 242
Hilton, James, 141
Hinxman, Margaret, 183
Hinz, Roland, 215
Hodiak, John, 142
Holcomb, Wynn, 31
Holly Leaves, 235
Hollywood, 3, 91, 112, 122, 131, 135, 164, 235
"Hollywood Beauty Shop" column, 65
Hollywood Family Album, 172, 196
Hollywood Guys and Gals, 235
"Hollywood High Lights" column, 43
Hollywood Hi-Hat. See Hi-Hat
Hollywood Hot-Line, 92, 235
Hollywood Life, 135, 228, 235
Hollywood Life Stories, 235
Hollywood Love and Tragedy, 235
Hollywood Love Life, 235
Hollywood Low-Down, 235
Hollywood Men, 236
Hollywood Mirror, 236
Hollywood Movie Fan, 236
Hollywood Movie Nights, 236
Hollywood Movie Novels, 129, 130, 135, 235, 236
Hollywood News, 147
Hollywood Nights, 91

Hollywood Parade, 238
Hollywood Picture Life, 236
Hollywood Playtime, 236
Hollywood Rebels, 236
Hollywood Reporter, The, 27, 66, 87, 88, 122, 128, 135, 138, 146, 149, 151
Hollywood Romances, 173, 236
Hollywood Screen Life, 235
Hollywood Screen Parade, 71, 201, 236, 238
Hollywood Screenland, 236
Hollywood Secrets Annual, 236
Hollywood Secrets Yearbook, 236
Hollywood Sex Queens, 236
Hollywood Star News, 236
Hollywood Stars, 177, 236, 238, 242
Hollywood Studio Magazine, 77
Hollywood Talent Parade, 236
Hollywood Teen Agers, 236
Hollywood Teen Album, 236
Hollywood Women's Press Club, 68
Hollywood Yearbook, 236
"Hollywood's Unmarried Husbands and Wives" article, 89, 162
Holmes, A. Laurance, 241
Holt, Toni, 217, 238
Homosexuality, 77–80, 83, 163–69
Hope, Bob, 140
Hopkins, Miriam, 128, 131
Hopper, Hedda, 8, 42, 69, 145, 151, 168, 175, 197, 200, 209, 211, 223
Hopwood, Avery, 98
Hornblow, Arthur, Jr., 52
Hosking, Dorothy, 239
"Hot Chocolates and Reminiscences at Nine of the Morning" series, 50
House Organs, 13
House Un-American Activities Committee, 159–61
Hover, Helen. *See* Weller, Helen
Howe, Anne, 111
Howe, Herbert, 6, 60, 77–80, 93, 115, 124, 125, 135, 157
Hudson, Rock, 119, 164, 165, 166, 168
Hughes, Rupert, 94
Humor Magazines, 91
Hunt, Marsha, 73–74
Hunter, Tab, 166–67
Hunter Publications, 239
Hurrell, George, 69, 114, 126
Hurst, Fannie, 101, 203
Husserl, Paul F., 234

"I Am the Universal Language," 252
Ideal Publishing Company, 42, 104–5, 176, 177, 235, 236, 238, 239, 240, 243, 244, 245
Illustrated Films Monthly, 247
In Cinema, 92
In Touch, 229
Ince, Thomas H., 21
Independent Publishing Co., 241
Ingenue: New Hollywood at Work and Play, 236
Ingram, Rex, 56
Inside Hollywood, 224, 236
Inside Movies, 196, 223, 236
Inside TV, 109
International Movie Data Base, 230
Internet, 230–32
Interstate Publishing Corp., 243
Irving, Doris, 39

J. Fred Henry Publications, 243
Jackson, Michael, 212
Jacobsen Publishing Co., 236
Jamison, Jack, 87
Jannings, Emil, 96
Jensen, Marta, 174
Johnson, Alfred Cheney, 5, 250
Johnson, Elmer Edmond, 101
Johnson, John H., 199
Johnson, Julian, 6, 51–52
Johnson, Van, 142, 143, 159, 171, 172, 173
Jolie, Angelina, 220
Jolson, Al, 185
Jones, Charles Reed, 239
Jones, Lloyd Kenyon, 235
Jordan, Dorothy, 128
Joyce, Alice, 20

Kahn, Gordon, 4, 5, 19
Kane, Christopher, 115, 234, 236
Kaplan, Richard, 221
Katterjohn, Monte M., 50
Keeler, Ruby, 128, 131
Kelley, Mary C., 240
Kelly, Kitty, 52
Kelly, May C., 127
Kennedy, Bobby, 199
Kennedy, Jacqueline, 193, 202–6, 213, 218, 219
Kerr, Martha, 163
Kerrigan, J. Warren, 49, 165

Kerry, Norman, 137, 139
Kerwin, Grace, 235
Kilgallen, Dorothy, 115
King, Martin Luther, 199
Kingsley, Grace, 114
Klaw, Irving, 91
Klein, Frederick, 189, 192
Knowles, Harry, 230
Kodachrome photographs, 68–69

La Roche, Edwin M., 22, 24
La Verne Publishing Co., 241
Ladd, Alan, 162
Lake, Veronica, 142
LaMarr, Barbara, 157
Landon, Michael, 210
Lang, Harry, 107
Larkin, Mark, 76
Lasky, Jesse L., 22, 123
Latest Hollywood and TV Hairdos, 227, 236
Latham, Maude, 65, 114
Laufer, Chuck, 6, 212, 214, 215, 216, 218
Laufer, Ira, 212, 214
Laughton, Charles, 180
Lawford, Peter, 5, 147
Lawrence, Florence, 18, 50
Lear, Frank A., 48
Lee, Sonia, 33, 251
"Leg Art," 90, 141–42
Lennon Sisters, 188
Lenoir, Celeste, 166
Leopold of Austria, Archduke, 102
Leslie-Judge Co., 234
Levine, Fran, 245
Lewis, Sinclair, 101
Liberty, 40, 41, 132
Liberty Publishing Company, 178, 243
Life, 132–33, 219
Lindsay, Margaret, 163
Lindsay, Vachel, 13, 101
Lippincott, Franklyn, 241
Literary Enterprises, Inc., 236
Little, Barbara, 39
Little, Bessie, 209–10, 213, 221, 236, 237, 240, 244, 245
Little Brand Publications, 244, 245
Liz and Mike, 174, 236
Lombard, Carole, 4, 128, 162
Long, Ray, 45, 64, 65, 253
Look, 133, 229
Lopez, Jennifer, 220

Lorentz, Pare, 127
Love, Virginia T., 163
Loy, Myrna, 128, 131
Lucas, Bob, 236
Lurvey, Diana, 235, 236, 239
Lusk, Norbert, 22, 82, 85–86, 134–35, 168
Lyne, Susan, 227

MacDonald, Jeanette, 131, 134
MacDonald, Katherine, 4
Macfadden, Bernarr, 6, 34, 105–9, 113, 132, 152
Macfadden Holdings, 221
Macfadden Publications, 66, 71, 103, 105–9, 172, 241
Macfadden-Bartell Corporation, 108, 189, 190, 191, 192, 197, 203, 243
MacLeish, Archibald, 100
Maco Magazine Corp., 236
Maddox, Ben, 164, 168
Magazine Management Company, 190, 210, 237, 243
Magazine Productions, Inc., 238
Magus Publishing Company, 62
Majors, Lee, 215
Manheimer, Irving S., 172
Mann, May, 141, 151
Mann, William J., 77, 168
Manners, Dorothy, 42, 81–82, 114, 143, 166
Mantle, Burns, 6, 53, 57
Margolies, Albert, 243
Margood Publishing Corp., 243
Marion, Frank, 21
Martin, Dean, 191
Martin, Robert, 234
Martin, Tony, 138
Marx, Harpo, 133
Masden, Martha, 39
Mastin, Mildred, 65
Matetsky, Harry, 237
Mature, Victor, 143, 256
Maugham, Somerset, 79, 97–98
Maurice, Mary, 20
Maxim, 229
Maxwell, Elsa, 34, 234
May, Lillian, 25
McClure's magazine, 11, 62
McCord, David Frederick, 131
McCoy, Gertrude, 30
McCrea, Joel, 232
McDaniel, Hattie, 199

McDowall, Roddy, 166–67, 168
McEvoy, Dorothy Lee, 240
McGeehan, Bernice, 187
McIlvane, Ellen, 237
McKee, Mrs. John [Marie], 234
McLaughlin, A. H., 49
McNelis, Catherine, 124
Meade, Esther, 163
"Medals and Birds" column, 80
Mediascene. See Prevue
Meighan, Thomas, 38, 95
Mencken, H. L., 6, 96–97
Metacritic.com, 230
Meteor Publications, Inc., 239
Meyer, Helen, 116
Mickey Mouse, 131
Miller, Llewellyn, 243, 244
Minneapolis, 9
Minter, Mary Miles, 152, 154
Mitchell, Curtis, 234
Mitchell, George, 234
Mitchell, John, 88
Mitchum, Robert, 179, 180
Modern Guide Publications, 236
Modern Movies (1930s), 85, 90, 103, 104, 117, 127, 150, 236–37, 240
Modern Movies (1960s/1970s), 193–94, 237
Modern Movies Hollywood Exposed, 237
Modern Romances, 178
Modern Screen, 10, 34, 44, 82, 83, 87, 88, 90, 97, 114–16, 118, 120, 122, 129, 131, 135, 137, 141, 142, 147, 148, 150, 151, 156, 161, 163, 166, 168, 171, 172, 174, 176, 177, 178, 182, 187, 188, 194, 196, 199, 201, 203, 218, 220, 221, 222, 223, 224, 225, 227, 237, 257
Modern Screen's Country Music, 224
Modern Screen's Hollywood Yearbook, 237
Modern Stars, 237, 239
Monroe, Marilyn, 115, 171, 175, 179, 185
Monsters to Laugh With, 237
Monsters Unlimited, 237
Montanye, Lillian, 24
Montgomery, Elizabeth, 151
Montgomery, Robert, 8
Monthly Magazine Productions, Inc., 238
Mook, Samuel Richard, 80, 82, 168
Moore, Colleen, 4
Moore, Grace, 131
Moore, Isabel, 241
Moreno, Antonio, 6, 78

Morris, Betty, 39

Morris, Gouverneur, 8, 156–57

Motion Picture, 5, 6, 12, 14–25, 34, 36, 37, 38, 39, 40, 41, 43, 48, 49, 50, 51, 75, 79, 82, 88, 91, 93, 94, 97, 109, 112, 118, 122, 131, 135, 143, 147, 151, 153, 154, 156, 168, 171, 174, 175, 177, 182, 188, 189, 190, 191, 192, 193, 210, 219, 221, 235, 237, 239, 242

Motion Picture and Television Magazine, 237

Motion Picture Classic, 15, 16, 31, 40, 41, 74, 131, 237

Motion Picture Producers and Distributors of America, 8, 54, 86, 88, 90

Motion Picture Publications, Inc., 237, 243

Motion Picture Story Magazine. See Motion Picture Magazine

Motion Picture Supplement, 30, 237

Movie Action Magazine, 237

Movie Adventures, 237

Movie Album (1940s), 237

Movie Album (1950s/1960s), 210, 237

Movie and Radio Guide, 170, 237

Movie and TV Album, 177

Movie and TV Fan-Fare. See Fan-Fare

Movie and TV Gossip, 237

Movie and TV Gossip Album, 237

Movie and TV Tattler. See Movie and TV Gossip

Movie Classic, 26, 30, 37, 42–43, 88, 118, 122, 131, 135, 168, 177, 237, 243

Movie Digest (1920s), 238

Movie Digest (1970s), 238

Movie Digest, Inc., 242, 244

Movie Fan (1920s), 238

Movie Fan (1950s), 177, 238, 243

Movie Fan, The (1930s), 238

Movie Fun, 238

Movie Glamor Guys, 238

Movie Guide, 92

Movie Humor, 91, 238

Movie Lies, 223

Movie Life, 92, 103, 104, 105, 141, 163, 177, 182, 238

Movie Life Yearbook, 238

Movie Love Stories, 238

Movie Magazine (1915), 238

Movie Magazine (1920s), 238

Movie Melody Magazine, 238

Movie Merry-Go-Round, 91, 238

Movie Mirror (1930s), 68, 69, 80, 88, 92, 106–7, 108, 118, 120, 131, 135, 136, 151, 163, 168, 177, 238, 243

Movie Mirror (1950s–1990s), 172, 174, 182, 225, 238

"Movie Mirror Junior" column, 107

Movie Mirror Yearbook, 238

Movie Monthly, 238

Movie Parade, 236, 238

Movie Pictorial, 153, 235, 238

Movie Pin-Ups, 238

Movie Pix, 177, 236, 238, 242

Movie Play, 236, 238

Movie Show Magazine, 121, 239

Movie Songs Magazine, 239

Movie Spotlight, 239

Movie Stars. See Movie Stars Parade

Movie Stars Album, 177

Movie Stars Parade, 104, 105, 138, 142, 168, 174, 177, 239

Movie Stars Parade Album, 239

Movie Stars-TV Close-Ups, 174, 182, 239

Movie Story, 26, 112, 239

Movie Story Year Book, 27, 239

Movie Tattler, 239

Movie Teen, 239

Movie Teen Illustrated, 239

Movie Thrillers, 239

Movie Thrills, 239

Movie Time, 239

Movie Today, 239

Movie Topics, Inc., 240

Movie TV and Record Time, 237, 239

Movie TV Confidential, 239

Movie TV Secrets, 174, 239

Movie TV Tattler, 239

Movie Weekly (1920s), 10, 34, 38, 42, 106, 152–54, 239

Movie Weekly (1950s), 239

Movie Weekly (1980s), 239

Movie Western, 239

Movie World, 174, 210, 226

Movie World Annual, 239

Movieland, 83, 103, 118, 119, 142, 143, 176, 239–40

Movieland and TV Time, 210

Movieline, 227, 232

Movieline's Hollywood Life, 228

Moviepix, 240

Movie-Radio Guide, 137, 139, 238–39

Movies (1930s), 135, 240

Movies (1930s/1940s), 104, 237, 240
Movies (1950s), 167–68, 240
"Movies Eavesdropping" column, 149
Movies Illustrated, 223, 240
Movies in Review, 240
Movies International, 240
Movies Now, 92, 240
Moving Picture Club of America, Inc., 244
Moving Picture Monthly, 240
Moving Picture Stories, 13, 26, 240
Moving Picture Weekly, The, 13
Mumsey's magazine, 11
Muni, Paul, 99
Munshower, Suzanne, 245
Murah, Amanda, 243
Murnau, F. W., 57
Murphy, Pat, 239
Muto, Frank, 90

Nabors, Jim, 166
Nanook of the North, 57
Nanovic, John L., 237
Nansen, Betty, 5
Nash, Johnny, 199
Nathan, George Jean, 96, 101
National Association of Theatre Owners, 92
Naylor, Hazel Simpson, 22, 23, 25, 39, 41
Nazimova, Alla, 25
Needham, Col, 230
Negri, Pola, 5, 132
New Movie Album: A Who's Who of the Screen, 240
New Movie Magazine, The, 9, 10, 73, 79, 88, 95, 99, 101, 102, 119, 123, 124–26, 128, 131, 135, 167, 168, 240
New Movies, 82
New Royal Magazine, The, 247
New Stars, 240
New Stars over Hollywood, 240
Newman, Paul, 215
Nichols, Wade, 223
Ninomíya, May, 26, 243
Non-Pareil Publishing Corp., 236, 237
Normand, Mabel, 82, 152, 246
Normandy Associates, 238
North, Betty, 62
North, Jean, 52
Novarro, Ramon, 6, 77, 79, 80, 165
Nudity, 5, 24, 31, 91, 167, 168
Nugent, John Peter, 214

Oakie, Jack, 87
Oberon, Merle, 131
O'Brien, Eugene, 165
O'Connor, Patrick, 169, 185, 191, 194, 198
Odza, H. G., 239
Official Magazine Corp., 243
Ogden, Helen, 39
Old Hollywood, 221, 240
Olmsted, Victor C., 240
Onassis, Jacqueline Kennedy. *See* Kennedy, Jacqueline
One Woman, 240
OnMovies, 92
Ormandy, Ella, 203
Orowitz, E. M., 238
Osborne, F. M., 31

Palmer, Constance, 84
Palmer, Corliss, 15–17, 25, 250–51
Pantomime, 240
Pardec, M. Clifford, 240
Paris and Hollywood Screen Secrets. See *Screen Secrets*
Parker, Jean, 128
Parsons, Harriet, 107, 114, 135, 145
Parsons, Louella, 8, 6, 82, 114–15, 143, 144–45, 151, 158, 180, 207, 209, 211, 223
Paul, Frederick F., 235
Peck, Gregory, 142
Peck, Ira, 191, 221, 235, 236
Peet, Creighton, 127
People magazine, 215, 219–22, 224, 228
Perelman, S. J., 223
PerezHilton.com, 231
Periodical House, Inc., 238, 242
Perkins, Tony, 235
Petrova, Olga, 24, 31, 72
Phillips, Henry Albert, 22
Photo Drama Magazine, 72
Photo Dramatist, 240
Photo Play Topics. See *Photoplay Vogue*
Photo Playwright, The, 72
Photo Story Book, 241
Photo-Era, 240
Photoplay, 3, 4, 5, 6, 9, 10, 27, 34, 38, 39, 40, 41, 44, 45, 46, 47–71, 75, 79, 81, 85, 88, 89, 90, 94, 95, 96, 97, 98, 99, 101, 102, 107, 108, 109, 114, 118, 120, 122, 124, 128, 131, 135, 137, 138, 140, 141, 142, 143, 144, 145, 147, 150, 151, 154, 156, 157, 159, 160, 161, 162, 163, 164, 165,

168, 171, 175, 176, 177, 182, 188, 191, 197, 198, 199, 200, 201, 202, 203, 210, 217, 221, 222, 223, 224, 227, 238, 241
Photoplay (British), 247
Photoplay Annual, 241
Photoplay Associates, 235
Photoplay Author, The, 241
Photo-Play Journal, 71–72, 79, 241
Photoplay Medal of Honor/Gold Medal, 60, 69–70, 115, 252
Photoplay Mirror Publishing Corp., 241
Photoplay Pinups, 241
Photo-Play Review, 72, 241
Photoplay Tribute to Elvis Presley, A, 176
Photoplay Vogue, 72, 241
Photoplay Weekly Mirror, 72, 241
Photo-Play World, 72, 241
Photoplayers Weekly, 72, 241
Photoplay's Directory of Stars, 241
Photoplaywrights' Association of America, 235
Photostar, 241
Pic: Hollywood-Sport-Broadway, 241
Pickford, Mary, 22, 30, 37, 41, 52, 76, 101, 128
Pictorial Movie Fun, 241
Picture Life, 222
Picture News, Screen, Stage and Variety, The, 247
Picture Palace News, The, 247
Picture Parade, 129, 135, 241
Picture Play, 10, 27–29, 38, 40, 43, 44, 75, 82, 88, 91, 122, 131, 134, 149, 165, 177, 241
Picture Show, 246, 247
Picture Stories Monthly, 247
Picturegoer, The, 183, 247
Picturegoer Monthly, 247
Picture-Play Weekly. See *Picture Play*
Pictures. See *Movie Magazine*
Pictures and the Picturegoer, 247
Pictures for the Picturegoer, 247
Picture-Wise, 241
Pitt, Brad, 220
Podell, Jack J., 168, 175, 191–92, 197, 202, 203, 210, 234
Poetry, 19, 101
Poitier, Sidney, 198
Popular Library, Inc., 235, 243, 244
Popular Movie, 195, 241
Popular Screen, 151, 241
Popularity Contests, 15, 20

Porter, Katherine Anne, 94
Potamkin, Harry Alan, 127
Powell, David, 98
Powell, Dick, 131
Powell, Jane, 171
Powell, William, 131
Power, Tyrone, 218
Premiere, 227, 228, 229, 232
Presley, Elvis, 175–76, 203, 215, 224
Preview, 215, 241
Prevue (1970s), 241
Prevue (1981), 241
Price, Vincent, 163
Producers Guild of America, 184
Prohibition, 158
Provine, Dorothy, 210
Pseudonyms, 35, 39, 251
"Public Opinions of Popular Plays and Players" column, 22
"Public Pulse" column, 28
Publication House, Inc., 245
Puzo, Mario, 210

Questar, 241
Quirk, James R., 6, 44, 46, 47–64, 98, 103, 122, 124, 144, 154, 155, 165, 207
Quirk, Lawrence J., 71, 201–2, 210
Quirk's Reviews, 71

Radar, 229
Radio Album, 170
Radio and Television Best, 170
Radio and Television Mirror, 170
Radio Art, 170
Radio Best, 170
Radio Best, Inc., 245
Radio Broadcast, 170
Radio Digest, 170
Radio Fan Magazines, 170
Radio Guide, 170, 237
Radio Mirror, 170
Radio Romances, 170
Radio Stars, 114, 170
Raft, George, 134, 137, 162
Ragan, David, 176, 190–91, 192, 193, 202, 238
Rainbow Publications, Inc., 234
Ramer, Jean, 235, 236
Ramsay, Walter, 88
Ramsaye, Terry, 58–60, 127
Ray, Charles, 94, 95

Real Screen Fun, 91, 241
Red Star News Co., 234
Redford, Robert, 216
"Reduceomania," 107
Reed, Rex, 221
Reel Humor, 91, 241
Reese, M. R., 238
Regal Press, Inc., 242
Reid, James E., 43
Reid, Janet, 35
Reid, Laurence, 30, 41–42, 237
Reid, Sally, 160
Reid, Wallace, 7, 22, 39, 152, 157
Religion, 161
Remont, Fritzi, 7, 23, 25
Rettig, Tommy, 210
Reynolds, Debbie, 174, 193, 203
Reynolds, Vera, 4
Rhea, Marian, 107
Rinehart, Mary Roberts, 25, 94
Robbens, Diane, 237
Roberts, Sue, 25
Robeson, Paul, 131
Robinson, Edward G., 160
Rogers, Bonnie, 213
Rogers, Ginger, 129, 131, 132, 134
Rogers, Roy, 177
Rogers, Will, 131
Roland, Gilbert, 163
Rollins, David, 166
Romance Publishing Co., 235
Romances of Hollywood, 242
Romances of Hollywood Movies, 242
"Romantic History of the Motion Picture"
    series, 58
Romantic Movie Stories, 242
Romero, Cesar, 163
Rona Barrett's Daytimers, 6, 216
Rona Barrett's Gossip, 6, 213, 214, 216, 242
Rona Barrett's Hollywood, 6, 212–13, 214,
    242
Rona Barrett's Preview, 241
Rona January's Gossip World, 217, 242
Roosevelt, Eleanor, 102
Rosemon, Ethel, 240
RottenTomatoes.com, 230
Rowling, J. K., 228
Royce, Bill, 213–14, 215, 216, 217
Rubens, Alma, 62–63
Ruggles, Charlie, 131
Ryan, Edwin J., 49

Salome, 57
Salvation Hunters, The, 56
Sammis, Fred Rutledge, 241
Sands, Tommy, 210
Sangster, Margaret E., 132
Sargent, Epes Winthrop, 21
Sari Publishing Co., 236
Saucy Movie Tales, 242
Saxon, George, 234
SBI: Show Business Illustrated. See *Show
    Business Illustrated*
Schallert, Edwin, 43–44
Schallert, Elza, 43–44, 65, 88
Scheuer, Philip K., 44, 114
Schoninger, Alice, 189
Schroeder, Carl A., 239, 244
Schulberg, B. P., 49
Schwarzenegger, Arnold, 214
Scott, Randolph, 163–64
Screen (1920s), 242
Screen (1950s), 242
Screen Actors Guild, 88
Screen Album, 143, 242
Screen and Radio Weekly, 242
Screen and TV Album, 198, 242
Screen Annual, 177, 242
Screen Book, 112, 122, 130, 131, 135, 149,
    150, 177, 242
Screen Comedy, 242
Screen Fan, 177, 242
Screen Greats, 242
Screen Guide, 117, 120, 143, 170, 242
Screen Hits Annual, 242
Screen Humor, 91, 242
Screen Legends, 242
Screen Life, 177, 242
Screen Mirror (1930s), 243
Screen Mirror (1970s), 243
Screen Pictorial, 247
Screen Play, 111, 112, 122, 130, 131, 135,
    158, 242, 243
Screen Romances, 26–27, 74, 114, 122, 127,
    135, 243
Screen Romances Album, 243
Screen Secrets, 9, 10, 110–11, 243
Screen Snapshots, 243
Screen Star Stories, 26, 210, 243
Screen Stars, 71, 120, 174, 226, 243
Screen Stars Yearbook, 243
Screen Stories, 26, 27, 114, 151, 173, 182,
    197, 201, 214, 215, 221, 243

Screen Stories (British), 247
Screen Stories Annual, 243
Screen Teen Co., 177, 239, 242
Screen Weekly, 243
Screenland, 6, 7, 38, 39, 40, 80, 83, 88, 103, 105, 109, 117, 118, 121, 122, 131, 135, 136, 143, 147, 151, 156–57, 158, 163, 165, 171, 177, 178, 185, 191, 192, 199, 223, 243
Screenland from Hollywood, 243
Screenland plus TV-Land, 171, 182, 198
Sears, Elizabeth, 234
Seldes, Gilbert, 126
Select Publications, Inc., 234, 237
Sellers, Patricia, 221
Sennett, Mack, 98
Sennett, Ted, 234
Service, Faith, 35
Seventeen, 134, 170, 172
Shadoplay, 66, 88, 108, 135, 163, 243
"Shadow Stage," 6, 40, 41, 47, 52, 57
Shadowland, 31, 37, 40, 91, 98, 165, 243
Shallenberg, William, 51
Sharpe, Howard, 84
Shearer, Norma, 8, 128
Sheilah Graham's Family Album, 243
Sheilah Graham's Hollywood Family Album, 235
Sheilah Graham's Hollywood Romances, 173, 236
Sheilah Graham's Hollywood Yearbook, 173, 236
Sheridan, Ann, 108, 142
Show (1960s), 243
Show (1970s), 243
Show Business Illustrated, 243
Shute, George, 241
Sidney, Sylvia, 128, 137
Sidney Skolsky's This Was Hollywood, 221
Siegel, Micki, 103, 223, 236, 240
Sielke, Leo, Jr., 23, 25
Sign of the Cross, The, 90
Silke, James R., 240
Silver Screen, 3, 65, 66, 67, 68, 83, 88, 103, 105, 109, 117, 118, 121, 122, 131, 135, 143, 147, 164, 165, 168, 169, 171, 175, 177, 178, 182, 185, 188, 191, 192, 194, 203, 205, 223, 244
Silver Screen Album, 244
Silver Screen Annual, 244
Silver Screen['s] Teen Album, 244

Simms, Alice, 245
Simon, Simone, 135
Sinatra, Frank, 142, 176, 215
Skolsky, Sidney, 125–26, 144, 221
Skye Publishing Co., 177, 238, 242, 243
Slander, 181
Slim Publications, 245
Smalley, Jack, 117
Smith, Agnes, 40
Smith, Frederick James, 18, 25, 40–41, 52, 57, 66, 76, 93, 97, 124, 132
Smith, Laurie Halpern, 227
Smith, Lillian, 240
Smith, Liz, 151
Smith, Lorraine Zenka, 216
Smith, Milburn, 236
Smokehouse Monthly, 9
So This Is Paris!. See *Screen Secrets*
So This Is Paris and Hollywood. See *Screen Secrets*
Soap opera fan magazines, 226–27
Soap Opera Special, 226
Soares, André, 80
Sothern, Ann, 131, 141
Spanking, 91
Spotlight Publishing Co., Inc., 239
Springer, John, 221
Spurr, A. Sharpe, 39
St. Johns, Adela Rogers, 5, 44–46, 60, 78, 80, 84, 124, 132, 139, 230
St. Johns, Ivan, 46, 60, 66, 88
Stage, 244
Stage and Screen, 244
Stanlaws, Penrhyn, 69, 124
Stanley Publications, Inc., 239, 245
Stanwyck, Barbara, 132, 135, 136, 163
Star, 244
Star, The, 229
Star Album, 177, 244
Star Comics, 103
Star Dust, 244
Star Guidance, Inc., 237, 245
Star Land, 244
Star Souvenir, 247
Stardom (1940s), 170, 244
Stardom (1950s/1960s), 195, 244
Starlog, 244
Starlog Group, 234, 244
Starr, Jimmy, 149
Stars and Films, 247
Steele, Joseph Henry, 76, 159

Stein, Herb, 144
Steirman, Hy, 180
Sten, Anna, 129, 131
Steranko, James, 241
Sterling and Company, 177
Sterling Group, Inc., 238, 245
Sterling Women's Group, 92
Sterling-Macfadden, 216, 244
Sternberg, Josef von, 56
Stevens, Dodie, 210
Stewart, James, 140
Stewart-Gordon, James, 238, 239
Stoley, Richard B., 219, 228
Storm, Gale, 185
Story adaptations, 18, 21, 23, 25–27, 48, 49, 50, 76, 197
Stowitts, Hubert, 31
Strakosch, Edgar, 47
Street & Street, 27, 235, 237, 241
Streets of Sorrow, 56
Streisand, Barbra, 215
Strickling, Howard, 8
Stroheim, Erich von, 56
Stuart, Gloria, 128, 131
Sullavan, Margaret, 128, 131
Sullivan, Ed, 140
Sullivan, Kay, 239
Sundell, Abby, 238, 239
Sundell, Abner J., 244
Sunrise, 57
Super Star Heroes, 244
Superstar Special, 244
Swanson, Gloria, 37, 60, 97, 147, 199
Syndicate Publishing Company, 114

"Tales Their Houses Tell" series, 34
Talk Magazine, 229
Talley, Alma, 106
Talmadge, Norma, 22, 23, 60
Tapley, Rose, 22
Tarkington, Booth, 94–95
Tashman, Lilyan, 151
Tate, Sharon, 161–62
Taylor, Don, 194
Taylor, Elizabeth, 68, 151, 171, 173–75, 194, 195–98, 213, 214, 216, 217, 219, 234
Taylor, Robert, 135, 163
Taylor, Ruth, 239
Taylor, William Desmond, 7, 152, 153, 154
Teen Beat, 172
Teen magazine, 212

Tele-Views, 191
Television Life Magazine, 191
Temple, Mildred, 62
Temple, Shirley, 69, 85, 108, 130, 131, 160, 162
Ten Eyck, John, 165, 168
Thanhouser Company, 49, 59
This Was Show Business, 221
Thomas, A. W., 49
Thomas, Bob, 43, 192–93
Thomas, Lawrence B. "Larry," 192, 210, 213, 219, 223
Thomas, Lowell, 126
Thomas, Olive, 152, 157
Thompson, Alice, 235
Thorp, Margaret Farrand, 134
3D Movie Magazine, 244
Thursh, Joan, 220, 222
Tidyman, Ernest, 210
Tiger Beat, 6, 172, 212, 213, 216
Tilsam Publishing Co., 241
Time-Life Corp., 219
Timpone, Anthony, 234
Toby Press, Inc., 245
Todd, Mike, 174
Tomlin, Lily, 223
Tone, Franchot, 131
Toni Holt's Movie Life, 217, 238
Top Stars, 244
Torney, Carol, 217, 238
Tousey, Frank, 240
Tower magazines, 114, 123–24, 126
Tracy, Spencer, 80
Trade Papers, 13
Triangle Publications, Inc., 170, 239, 244
True Confessions, 109, 110, 112, 132, 182, 192
True Movie, 245
True Movie and Television, 171, 245
True Story, 105, 109, 120, 182, 192
Tufts, Sonny, 142
Turner, Lana, 102, 115, 141, 158–59, 162, 257
TV and Movie Screen, 171, 177, 187, 190, 224, 225, 245
TV and Record Stars, 243
TV and Screen Life, 171, 245
TV and Screenworld, 171, 245
TV Mirror, 247
TV Movie and Record Stars, 240
TV Movie Parade, 171, 245

TV Movie Scene, 198, 245
TV People, 171
TV Picture Life, 177, 245
TV Radio Mirror, 109, 170, 190, 191, 192
TV Screen, 245
TV Screen Parade, 245
TV Star Parade, 171
TV World, 171
TV-Film Stars, 171, 174, 245
TVMS Tiger Beat, 244, 245

U.K. fan magazines, 247
Ultem Publications, 103, 104, 238
Underhill, Harriette, 25, 40, 60, 106, 132
Universal Weekly, The, 13, 49
Us magazine, 71, 220, 221, 222, 224

Valentine, Jimmy, 235
Valentino, Rudolph, 96, 97, 132, 157, 232, 252
Van de Water, Frederic F., 124–25
Van Dine, S. S. *See* Wright, Willard H.
Van Horne, Evelyn, 26, 74, 234, 242, 243
Van Loan, H. H., 25
Van Wyck, Carolyn, 60, 65
Vargas, Albert, 30, 31
Velez, Lupe, 129
Visions, 245
Vitagraph Company of America, 14, 20, 21, 23, 35, 75, 79
von Aspe, G. T., 236
Votsis, Dorothy, 234

W. F. Hall Printing Company, 49–50
W. G. Wilson/MW Communications, 241
Wagenknecht, Edward, 53, 72, 93, 154, 253
Wagner, Robert, 176, 193
Wald, Jerry, 114
Wallace, Edgar, 101
Walsh, Wiliam T., 66, 127, 236
WAMPAS, 86
Warren, Mary Jane, 39
Warren Publishing Co., 234
Warwick Publications, Inc., 240
Waterbury, Ruth, 57, 58, 62, 64–65, 66–68, 88, 99, 107, 108, 121, 124, 132, 143, 145, 164, 182, 190, 206, 232
Wayne, John, 185, 232
"We Interview" series, 25
Weekly Film Review, 245
Weekly Movie Record, 245

Weir, Hugh, 124
Welk, Lawrence, 186–88, 213, 224
Weller, Helen, 115, 187, 201
Welles, Orson, 140, 151
West, Mae, 87, 128, 129, 130, 131, 214
Western Associated Motion Picture Advertisers, 86
Western Publishing Co., Inc., 241
What Price Hollywood?, 84
Wheeler-Reid Publications, Inc., 235
White, Alice, 34, 129
Whitney, Diane, 66
Who's Who in Daytime TV, 226
Who's Who in Hollywood, 172, 245
Wilkerson, W. R. "Billy," 27, 54, 146
Wilkie, Jane, 194
Willard, Clark, 239
Williams, Clara, 18
Williams, Earle, 20
Williams, Esther, 143, 162, 171, 173
Willis, Richard, 50, 153, 168
Willson, Henry, 125, 167, 168
Wilson, Elizabeth, 88, 101, 132
Wilson, Ivy Crane, 118–19
Winchell, Walter, 8, 140, 180
Winters, Shelley, 172
Woman Golfer Publishing Corp., 245
Women's Association of Screen Publicists, 39
Wood, Natalie, 176
World Publishing Corp., 236
World War I, 5, 22, 144
World War II, 137–43, 145
Wright, Gene, 244
Wright, Willard H., 31, 95–96

Young, Clara Kimball, 20
Young, Loretta, 80, 129, 131

Zanuck, Darryl F., 138
Zeitlin, Ida, 114, 118
Zenith Publishing Corp., 237